COVID-19 and Pandemics in Austrian History

Marc Landry, Dirk Rupnow (Editors)

CONTEMPORARY AUSTRIAN STUDIES | VOLUME 32

UNO PRESS

innsbruck **university press**

University of New Orleans Press
2000 Lakeshore Drive, Earl K. Long Library, Room 221
New Orleans, LA, 70148, USA
www.unopress.org

Printed in the United States of America on acid-free paper

Published in the United States by
University of New Orleans Press
ISBN: 978-1-60801-252-7

UNIVERSITY OF NEW ORLEANS PRESS

Published and distributed in Europe
by *Innsbruck* University Press
ISBN: 978-3-99106-115-1

iup

Publication of this volume has been made possible through a generous grant by the Austrian Federal Ministry of Education, Science and Research through Austria's Agency for Education and Internationalization (OeAD). The Austrian Marshall Plan Anniversary Foundation in Vienna has been very generous in supporting Center Austria: The Austrian Marshall Plan Center for European Studies at the University of New Orleans and its publications series. The College of Liberal Arts at the University of New Orleans, as well as the Vice Rectorate for Research and the International Relations Office of the University of Innsbruck provided additional financial support.

THE UNIVERSITY *of* NEW ORLEANS
CENTER AUSTRIA

universität innsbruck

The Dietrich W. Botstiber FOUNDATION

Federal Ministry
Republic of Austria
Education, Science
and Research

Marshallplan-Jubiläumsstiftung
Austrian Marshall Plan Foundation

Contemporary Austrian Studies

Sponsored by the University of New Orleans and University of Innsbruck

Table of Contents

NON-TOPICAL ARTICLE

REVIEW ESSAY

BOOK REVIEWS

COVID-19 and Pandemics in Austrian History

Introduction

Marc Landry and Dirk Rupnow

On February 26, 2020, the headlines of the *Salzburger Nachrichten* contained worrisome news: "First Corona Cases in Austria: Hotel in Innsbruck under Quarantine." This was one of the first newspaper articles to appear declaring that the novel coronavirus, which was in the process of unleashing the Covid-19 pandemic, had now arrived in Austria. Apparently, an infected couple originally from the Italian region of Bergamo—one of the early global coronavirus epicenters—had carried the virus with them as they returned to Innsbruck from a weekend at home. Authorities placed the couple in quarantine and closed the hotel where one of them worked. The next day more infections became public. An elderly patient in the Innsbruck hospital had tested positive for the virus. An additional pair in the provincial capital had also become infected, and their children were beginning to exhibit symptoms. In a short time, the virus would spread throughout the country.[1]

In Austria as in the rest of the world, Covid-19 would continue to dominate the headlines for nearly two years after these initial cases. At times, Austria would even find itself at the center of global media attention. In late February 2020, the Austrian ski resort Ischgl (also in Tyrol) became one of the first "superspreader" events in Europe. Over a dozen skiers returning to Iceland after a weekend in the "Ibiza of the Alps" tested positive at the airport. The government of Iceland placed Tyrol on par with Wuhan in terms of coronavirus risk. The country of Norway would claim that half of its initial infections could be traced back to Ischgl; Denmark said one third. The preeminent German weekly *Der Spiegel* declared Ischgl "*Die Brutstätte*"—the breeding grounds. Particularly in Europe, partying skiers in the Austrian Alps seemed to symbolize official incompetence and public indifference.[2] In the United States, Austria and the rest of German-speaking Europe would later stand out for other reasons during the Covid-19 epidemic. These regions possessed the largest shares of unvaccinated populations in all of Western Europe. This was chalked up to a history of decentralized politics and a "cultural inclination among the population toward homeopathy and natural cures." At the same time, Austria's government went the furthest of any in imposing restrictions on the unvaccinated in Europe. When, in the spring of 2021, Austria became one of the only European Union states to mandate Covid-19 vaccination, it was apparent that Austria was, in some ways, following a unique course through the pandemic.[3]

The long history of Austria as a political entity in one form or another means there has been ample opportunity to formulate experience with infectious disease. Historians have done much work on bubonic plague in Austria, particularly the initial "Black Death" outbreak of the fourteenth century. Two Habsburg innovations, the *Pestsäule* and the *cordon sanitaire* at the Military Border with the Ottoman Empire, have even made their way into general histories of disease.[4] Tuberculosis, the "Viennese disease," is another topic that has received a great deal attention from Austrian historians.[5] Still, there are very few overview works on the topic of epidemics in Austria more broadly, particularly for the contemporary period.[6] There also exists very little in English.

Addressing these gaps, providing historical context to help make sense of the last few years, and contributing research on one country's path through the recent crisis, were among the main motivations for dedicating this volume of *Contemporary Austrian Studies* to Covid and health emergencies past. The focus here is on pandemic or epidemic infectious diseases in contemporary Austrian history, and on selected aspects of the Covid-19 experience as well. This requires some explanation. Certainly, chronic and occupational diseases—think heart disease or the black lung affliction of coal miners—have had important impacts on societies. But in light of the fact that Covid-19 is caused by an infectious virus, we thought it best to focus on this group of conditions.

There are other good reasons for this choice. In many respects, the impacts of infectious diseases are historically distinct. Up until the twentieth century, they were far more lethal than other illnesses, and they remain leading causes of mortality. The experience of being infected with polio (and the social ramifications), moreover, are qualitatively different than suffering from emphysema. Finally, infectious diseases will continue to emerge and likely with continued devastating effects.[7] As many scholars have persuasively argued, tracing the fallout from an epidemic can be a particularly insightful lens through which to view a society. As with so-called "natural disasters," how disease outbreaks play out is not only—or even primarily—a matter of Mother Nature, but of the contours of the societies they effect.[8] Pandemic prevention is a public good, like clean water or air. It can only be fairly and efficiently provided by public authorities. It is also a global public good, like a stable climate. As with the latter case, it depends on international cooperation.[9]

Epidemics and Pandemics in Contemporary Austria

At the outset of this volume, it is perhaps helpful to fashion an overview of contemporary Austria's relationship with infectious illnesses. If we take the contemporary Austrian period to be the time since the collapse of the

Habsburg Monarchy, Austria's experience of epidemic disease has been in many ways typical of other Western, industrialized countries. An attempt to establish an overview of the major epidemics that have impacted Austria would include Spanish flu, tuberculosis, polio, HIV/AIDS, and the raft of emerging diseases that have occupied global health authorities since around the turn of the millennium. Hoof and mouth disease probably deserves to be on this list as well. Even though this virus is usually not too dangerous for humans, its annihilation of livestock lends it outsize importance for the Austrian agricultural economy.

Austria being the integral component of a long-standing, multi-national empire is surely one of the most salient factors in the existence of a comparatively robust public health system. One result of this reality is the existence of legal frameworks to deal with disease that go back centuries. The first documented *Infektionsordnung* in current Austrian territory, what might be considered the forerunner to present-day public health policies, stems from the year 1521. It pertained to the inner-Austrian lands of Styria, Carinthia, and Carniola. Over the following centuries, different Austrian municipalities and lands passed additional measures to deal with various disease outbreaks, plague in particular. The results of such actions ranged from attempts to improve hygienic conditions to the creation of proto-public health authorities. In Vienna, an imperial commission called on the medical school to develop strategies to combat the plague. At least in the sixteenth century, however, the academics preferred to take a mostly hands-off approach. They worried about official decrees causing panic in the population and preferred to let things take their course.[10]

It is worth noting that much of contemporary Austrian history has fallen in a brief, unprecedented window of insulation from the most ravaging effects of epidemic disease. Through a combination of improvements in public health and the availability of vaccines and antibiotics, certain developed societies have been able to break out of a world historical trend and experience significant population growth.[11] In some ways, trying to understand the history of disease in contemporary Austria means engaging with the country's environmental history. From a global perspective, the Austrian republics emerged during a century when energy was cheap as never before, allowing for unprecedented consumption and environmental change. Austria was typical in that it participated in these global processes as well. Nevertheless, while environmental history in the twentieth century requires attention to the global, the nation-state remained the dominant form of governance, and this reality ensures that the country possessed some peculiarities within this broader trend. Austria was a latecomer to industrialization. It also was a pioneer in some ways in terms of environmental politics in the early 1990s before joining the EU.[12] This, it seems to us, is a sensible way to conceive of Austria's experience with disease and epidemics as well. Austria seems to have followed global patterns for the most part, with some specifically Austrian wrinkles. Below, we will consider some of these peculiarities of contemporary Austrian history as relates to the emergence of disease, epidemics, and pandemics.

Does Austria's geographic position in the center of Europe (and bestriding one of the most important Alpine passes) continue to play a role in Austria's experience with disease? It is interesting to note that the *Bundesland* of Tyrol seems to have played a key role in the two pandemics that bookend contemporary Austria. As noted at the beginning of this introduction, the first Austrian Covid cases came to Tyrol from its southern neighbor. The Spanish flu first came to Austria in spring 1918 via similar circumstances as well. Geography (or geopolitics), in another respect, seems to have influenced Austria's trajectory. As the chapter by Maria Hilber details, Austria was the first western country to implement the oral polio vaccine in its campaign against polio. This pioneer role stemmed in part from Austria's willingness to adopt a Cold War pose of "striking a balance" between East and West.[13] Former Austrian Chancellor Kurz's negotiations with Vladimir Putin to obtain the *Sputnik V* Covid-19 vaccine would suggest that Austria continues to play this role today. On the other hand, jet travel has in many ways negated these spatial and geographical considerations.

A further question concerns whether contemporary Austria also possesses peculiar considerations of health and justice. As part of the Greater German Reich, Austria shares in the legacy of National Socialism and its entanglements with the medical community. As several contributions below highlight, Nazi medicine was often characterized by coercive, degrading, and dehumanizing measures. By contrast, to the extent that the *Sozialpartnerschaft* and the Austrian welfare and health systems of the Second Republic have reduced inequality in the country, they may have led to what some would now call environmentally just health outcomes in contemporary Austria. Determining the impact of Austria's welfare system during the Covid-19 crisis will require further research. The role that it plays in future crises remains to be seen.

As a participant in the global capitalist economy, Austria is at once deeply embedded in intensifying transport networks and a contributor to the dynamics prompting infectious disease evolution.[14] In this regard, the country is nothing special. But there is at least one major aspect of the Austrian economy that could potentially set the country apart going forward. Austria's economic reliance upon tourism means that it requires a regular influx of people, and thus potential carriers (see the chapter by Peters and Steiger). The importance of winter tourism in the Austrian Alps also necessitates bringing people together in the dry air of heated common spaces—ideal circumstances for the proliferation of airborne pathogens. The emergence of Iscghl, then, as an early hotspot was not exactly a random event. Tourism, it would seem, exposes Austria to additional risk of the spread of infectious disease and additional hardship if travel and public gatherings are restricted.

In the spring of 2020, the president of the American Historical Association, Mary Lindemann, warned historians against immediately trying to write about Covid as *history*. She also cautioned against drawing rash or simplistic comparisons. But Lindemann also argued that the humanities and social sciences had a crucial role to play in public discourse on Covid-19.[15] History, in particular, might help combat one remarkable aspect of the history of epidemic disease, at least for the Spanish flu. This is the reality that the 1918–1919 pandemic itself—and along with it many of the potential lessons for the future—faded rather rapidly from collective memory.[16] As noted above, epidemics are not really "natural" disasters, but heavily shaped by the societies in which they unfold. We hope that this volume, with its multidisciplinary approach to historical episodes and the Covid-19 emergency, can contribute to the important effort of comprehending the human and social aspects of this crucial topic.

In November 2020, the University of Innsbruck was one of the first universities to hold a large (virtual) conference, titled "Understanding Corona: The Corona Pandemic from the Perspective of the Humanities and Cultural Studies, Take 1." Organized by Elisabeth Dietrich-Daum, Marina Hilber, Wolfgang Meixner, and Dirk Rupnow, and supported by the university's Research Center Medical Humanities, the Center Interdisciplinary Gender Studies Innsbruck (CGI), and the Research Area Cultural Encounters—Cultural Conflicts, this initial conference was followed by two further iterations in yearly intervals. A fourth conference will take place in November 2023. These conferences were both the inspiration for and formed the basis of the present volume.[17]

As vaccination has been such a central component of the Covid-19 pandemic, this volume begins with a study of the world's first vaccination campaign, that against smallpox. Using detailed vaccination records, physicians' reports, court records, and testimonials from clergy and parents, Elena Taddei investigates the case of smallpox vaccination in the historical state of Tyrol starting in the nineteenth century. The author shows that Tyrol mostly resisted mandating vaccinations for its population. Compulsory vaccination was implemented while the state was under Bavarian rule until 1815, only to be given up upon reunion with the Habsburgs. Only in 1939, as part of the National Socialist state, did vaccination finally become compulsory. The peculiarity of the Tyrolean case seems to lie in the connection of the vaccine to "foreign"—external—rule and to the insufficient modernization of the Habsburg state to implement compulsory vaccination.

Of all historical disease corollaries, the current pandemic has most often been compared to the so-called "Spanish flu," which caused over fifty million deaths from 1918–1919. As Eva Pfanzelter argues in her study, examining newspapers from the time can give us a detailed understanding of the prevailing societal discourses. Using digital tools, Pfanzelter is able to analyze a large corpus of newspaper articles to determine how the media discussed the Spanish flu, first at the twilight of the Habsburg Monarchy and thereafter during the infancy of the first Austrian republic. Despite the vast differences between societies and media landscapes, Pfanzelter notes some striking similarities to the present. From the outset, the Spanish flu's supposed foreign origins received great attention; eventually, societal scapegoating ran rampant. Governments, doctors, and compatriots also came in for criticism for the privations caused by the influenza. As Pfanzelter notes, Covid-19 is hardly an unprecedented situation.

In the next chapter, Eva Hallama demonstrates the close connections between disease prevention measures against typhus and political ideology during the National Socialist period. She does so through the lens of a delousing facility in Linz, one of a handful established in National Socialist Austria to process civilian forced laborers being sent to the Reich from all corners of occupied Europe to labor for the war economy. Hallama adds to existing research by utilizing court documents concerning the operator of the facility, Anton Slupetzky, particularly witness statements about the delousing process. The harrowing details of this ordeal show how the repeated rituals of violence and humiliation prepared laborers for their inferior status, and highlight the convergence of hygiene, health, and the Holocaust in Nazi ideology.

The rollout of the worldwide vaccination campaign against polio in the 1950s is recent enough to still loom large in the memory of postwar youth. In her article, Marina Hilber traces the difficulties and regional peculiarities involved in the implementation of the breakthrough vaccine in Austria. Based on source material from the Austrian state archives, Hilber reconstructs prevailing medical, political, and public discourses. The initial euphoria surrounding the introduction of a vaccine in the United States in 1955 gave way to fear stemming from the "Cutter Incident"—the circulation of insufficiently inactivated batches that led to paralysis and even the deaths of several Americans. Hilber concludes that the overall number of vaccines provided in Austria was disappointing. This was the result of a weak Austrian federal state, whose delegation of responsibility for distribution and financing to the provinces signaled its lack of commitment to Austrians. Nevertheless, vaccine acceptance was high enough to prevent serious illness in thousands of cases. Over the course of the 1960s, polio ceased to be a social scourge and became instead an individual tragedy.

Though large swaths of the global north often fail to remember it as such, the AIDS pandemic of the 1980s is probably the most proximate analogue to our present experience. Andreas Brunner's chapter provides an early history of the AIDS pandemic in Austria, where much less research has been done than in places like the United States and Germany. The first cases of AIDS deaths in Austria were announced in March 1983. Brunner focuses primarily on the interaction between politics, the just-forming Austrian gay and lesbian community, and the media. He finds that the social confrontation with AIDS and same-sex lifestyles on an unprecedented scale led to a strengthening of the political self-confidence of the gay and lesbian emancipation movement. This occurred despite considerable fearmongering in the German-language press. Brunner also concludes that, even though the collaboration between stakeholders and policymakers was not without conflict, in the case of AIDS it must be viewed as a relative success—especially when compared to the record during Covid.

As the Covid-19 pandemic unfolded, Austria stood out for being one of the few European states to pass a compulsory vaccination law for certain adults over the age of eighteen. In their contribution, Maria Bertel and Andreas Th. Müller provide a valuable analysis of the constitutional and legislative context in Austria regarding the Covid-19 emergency. They address the role of the federal state, the division of labor between legislative and administrative authorities, and the state of civil rights during a crisis that challenged civil liberties like no other since 1945. While the compulsory vaccination law was never really executed, its passage showed that the Austrian Constitutional Court believed in the compatibility of civil liberties and coercive health measures—with allowance for certain exceptions and monitoring of the results and the epidemiological situation. They conclude by noting that the entire episode has raised important questions about the federal structure of the country, and Austria's Covid-related legislative positions could prove influential for future epidemics.

Zooming in from the federal level, in the next chapter Silke Meyer investigates everyday life during the pandemic in Austria. Based on individual stories collected during the first lockdown of March 2020 and Austrian social science surveys on the impacts of distance learning on pupils, Meyer shows how narratives of "community" and "retrotopia" helped Austrians make sense of the crisis. The concept of community could be seen in both individual and official pronouncements, including a song commissioned by the Tyrolean government declaring that the state would stand "together" ("*zsamm*"). The idea of retrotopia—that hard times of the past are in actuality the good old days—colored many a Covid remembrance. Nevertheless, these notions did not last. In 2021, even as deaths exceeded those during the initial lockdown, the tune of solidarity did not return. Meyers's anthropological analysis then seems to confirm a phenomenon of previous pandemics like the Spanish flu. Namely, that they quickly fade from public memory.

Another empirical reality of past epidemics is the emergence of conspiracy theories. Austria during Covid-19 was no exception in this regard, and Claus Oberhauser's contribution examines the presence of conspiracy theories in Austria and the role of the media in their spread. His analysis demonstrates that, while Austrians did not create unique conspiracy theories, they had their own peculiar reactions to the similar speculations that prevailed in comparable Western countries. Among these was perhaps the most controversial of all Covid conspiracies, that the disease was purposefully created as a bioweapon. According to quantitative studies, the idea received broad approval in Austria. Oberhauser concludes that the pandemic should be a lesson on how to avoid alarmism and sensationalism, to which the antidotes are a strengthening of quality media and the promotion of media literacy. The connection between populism, societal discontentedness, and incidence of conspiracy theories also requires further research.

The role of Austrian populism is also at the center of the chapter by Reinhard Heinisch and Amélie-Jacqueline Apke. This quantitative analysis is based on an original survey conducted in 2020. The idea being tested is whether voters' subjective political dispositions have effects on their perception of health and economic wellbeing. Using various regression models, the study shows that radical political attitudes such as authoritarianism and populism increased Austrian perceptions of relative health and economic security, particularly when coupled with a lack of trust in the government.

Tourism is one of the most important pillars of the Austrian economy, and one of the reasons that the country witnessed some of the earliest and most intense outbreaks of Covid-19 in Europe. Mike Peters and Robert Steiger observe that the emergency had devastating consequences for the branch. Up until the spring of 2020, tourism in the country had been characterized by steady growth. But the restrictions on travel abruptly halted this trajectory. Even if visitor numbers return to pre-Covid levels, the authors note that the financial pressures created by the emergency will have lasting impacts on Austria's tourist branch, which is dominated by small- and medium-sized enterprises. As is often the case, however, the crisis has presented Austria with an opportunity to potentially shift its tourism industry to a more sustainable model.

In the volume's only non-topical article, Katja Maierhofer explores the construction of an Austrian national identity after the Second World War. She does so through the lens of a patriotic organization, the *Österreichische Gemeinschaft*, in the immediate postwar period. This organization, started in the interwar years by Catholic students in Austria, has not yet received much scholarly attention. But Maierhofer shows that their actions after 1945 are symptomatic of an early, uncertain phase of Austrian identity construction.

Finally, this volume of CAS also features a review essay by Günter Bischof on Nazism in Austria. Surveying several recent works, Bischof determines that, far from being victims, Austrians at every level of society were perpetrators who were deeply implicated in the Nazi terror regime as well.

We would like to thank a number of people for their help in making the completion of this volume possible. First, we are sincerely grateful to all the contributing authors. Katja Maierhofer, the 2022–2023 Austrian Ministry of Education, Science, and Research Dissertation Fellow at UNO and PhD student in the Department of German Studies at the University of Vienna, has done a fine job in tracking every manuscript through both the copyediting and proofreading processes and toward final publication. She also has been relentless in correcting and aligning footnotes with our style sheet and humoring authors toward the completion of their manuscripts. Special appreciation goes to the artist Hubert Schmalix, who graciously allowed us to use a portion of his 1985 wall mosaic, located in the University of Innsbruck Humanities Building, that bears a striking resemblance to the virus responsible for Covid-19. We would also like to thank our anonymous peer reviewer for their thorough and timely assessments.

Katie Pfalzgraff at UNO Press put her enthusiasm into the final round of copyediting the individual manuscripts, and Alex Dimeff prepared the cover image. Kevin Stone swiftly designed the final volume.. G.K. Darby and Abram Himelstein, the leadership team at UNO Press, have been hugely supportive in spiriting this volume through to final publication. At Center Austria: The Austrian Marshall Plan Center for European Studies, Director Günter Bischof has as always been helpful with sage advice.

Gertraud Griessner conducted the Center's daily business with superb efficiency to allow the co-editor to work on managing the completion of this volume. Without the dedicated teams at Center Austria and the UNO Press, there would be no CAS series. At *innsbruck* university press, Birgit Holzner was helpful with the final round of proofreading, and the production of the volume for the European market. Cooperating with her has become a big bonus in the production of these volumes.

As always, we are happy in acknowledging our sponsors and supporters for making the publication of the *Contemporary Austrian Studies* series possible at all—not a small matter in the age of diminishing budgets for higher education in general and the social sciences and humanities in particular. At the University of Innsbruck, our thanks go to the Vice *Rektorat* for Research and the International Relations Office for grants towards the printing of this volume. The support of Barbara Tasser, Matthias Schennach, and Gerhard Rampl in International Relations, and Center New Orleans, respectively, is always a pillar of the partnership and for it we are appreciative. At UNO, thanks to new Dean of the College of Liberal Arts, Education, and Human Development Samuel Gladden and new chair of the History Department, Kathryn Dungy. We are also grateful to the outgoing leaders President John Nicklow and *Rektor* Tilmann Märk for their support of the entire UNO-University of Innsbruck partnership agenda, including its publication series. We look forward to working with *Rektorin* Veronika Sexl in the future. In the Federal Ministry of Education, Science, and Research and its agency for education and internationalization OeAD, we are grateful to Barbara Weitgruber, Christoph Ramoser, Felix Wilcek, Josef Leidenfrost, Lydia Skarits, and Florian Gerhardus. Markus Schweiger, the executive secretary, Ambassador Wolfgang Petritsch, the chairman of the board, as well as the board members of the Austrian Marshall Plan Foundation have been our strongest supporters for two decades now. It is a great pleasure and privilege to work with them all and acknowledge their unwavering support of Center Austria: The Austrian Marshall Plan Center for European Studies at UNO and its activities and publications.

St. Leonhard in Passeier/Innsbruck, July 2023

Endnotes

1. Daniela Angetter-Pfeiffer, *Pandemie sei Dank! Was Seuchen in Österreich bewegten* (Vienna: Almathea, 2021), 205.

2. Sam Jones, "Return to the Superspreader Ski Resort," *Financial Times*, February 9, 2022.

3. Katrin Bennhold, "Vaccinated vs. Unvaccinated: Europe's Covid Culture War," *New York Times*, November 17, 2021. Another expose in the New York Times focused on the resistance to vaccination in the former Austrian province of South Tyrol: Emma Bubola, "In Italy's Alps, Traditional Medicine Flourishes, As Does Covid," *New York Times*, December 16, 2021.

4. Frank Snowden, *Epidemics and Society: From the Black Death to the Present* (New Haven: Yale University Press, 2019), 32; 72–3.

5. Elisabeth Dietrich-Daum, *Die "Wiener Krankheit". Eine Sozialgeschichte der Tuberkulose in Österreich* (Vienna: Verlag für Geschichte und Politik, 2007).

6. A search of the comprehensive bibliography on Austrian environmental history (as of November 2020) returned eighty-five titles that considered "disease" as a subject term. This from a corpus of 3,751 entries: Zentrum für Umweltgeschichte, *Materialien zur Umweltgeschichte Österreichs* (Vienna, 2020). A recent exception, prompted by the pandemic, is Daniela Angetter-Pfeiffer, *Pandemie sei Dank!*, though this work too focuses primarily on the Habsburg era.

7. Here we borrow the justification in Frank M. Snowden, *Epidemics and Society: From the Black Death to the Present* (New Haven: Yale University Press, 2019), 2–3.

8. Christian Pfister, "Learning from Nature-induced Disasters. Theoretical Considerations and Case Studies from Western Europe," in *Natural disasters, Cultural Responses: Case Studies toward a Global Environmental History*, ed. Christof Mauch and Christian Pfister (Lanham, MD: Publications of the German Historical Institute, 2009), 17–40.

9. J.R. McNeill, "Bats, Battiness, and the Covid-19 Pandemic," *Environmental History* 25 (October 2020): 635–9.

10. Daniela Angetter-Pfeiffer, *Pandemie sei Dank! Was Seuchen in Österreich bewegten* (Vienna: Almathea, 2021), 30–34.

11. McNeill and Engelke, *Great Acceleration*, 44–5.

12. Schmid and Veichtlbauer, *Umweltgeschichte Österreichs*, 14–5.

13. As in Günter Bischof and Peter Ruggenthaler, *Österreich und der Kalte Krieg: Ein Balanceakt zwischen Ost und West* (Vienna: Leykam, 2022).

14. Mike Davis, *The Monster Enters: Covid-19, the Avian Flu, and the Plagues of Capitalism* (London: Verso, 2020), 17–8.

15. Mary Lindemann, "The Historian and the Virus: A Time Capsule from Mid-March," April 22, 2020. https://www.historians.org/publications-and-directories/perspectives-on-history/may-2020/the-historian-and-the-virus-a-time-capsule-from-mid-march

16. Alfred Crosby, *America's Forgotten Pandemic: The Influenza of 1918*, 2nd ed. (Cambridge: Cambridge University Press, 2003); Heiner Fangerau, "Zu Paläopathologie und Geschichte der Medizin: Das Beispiel der Influenzapandemie," Der Urologe 49, no. 11 (2010): 1406–10.

17. For information on the series see https://www.uibk.ac.at/congress/corona-verstehen/.

Smallpox in Nineteenth Century Tyrol and the Struggle of Prevention by Vaccination

Elena Taddei

Introduction

Infectious diseases, their prevention and control, and public health responses are topics that were polarized in former societies as much as they are in today's private life and social media communities, as can be seen currently regarding Covid-19. Debates about the containment or eradication of infectious diseases such as the Black Death, smallpox, measles, malaria, influenza, and recently Covid-19 using incentives for voluntary vaccination, constraint, and direct or indirect compulsion[1] have kept media, governments, and institutions of health occupied.[2] Concomitant is the highly topical question of why some areas of Central Europe, especially the Alpine regions, seem to be—from a historical point of view as well as nowadays—more renitent toward measures of prevention than other regions. The frequency of demonstrations and riots against the governmental Covid-19 policies suggests that vaccination in today's Austria, and especially in Tyrol, is still seen as a state requirement rather than a measure of health protection/prevention. Therefore, we may ask if there really is a historically proven Tyrolean way of handling epidemics.

Measures against epidemics and pandemics were tightly connected to state-building processes in the past. While social rights and values, such as personal freedom, a sense of responsibility for one's own health, and collective responsibility, were consolidated in the time of the Enlightenment, governments in the nineteenth century elaborated a growing system of rules and controls. Order, control, and paternalism concerned the social sphere in general and especially the field of health and safety in the growing states. A prosperous state was one with healthy subjects fit for work and military service; the state, namely, the ruler and the regional and local governments as his executors, carried out its duty to take care of the preservation and augmentation of health, strength, and prosperity, in an economic and reproductive sense, of the proper population. This phenomenon of state-related health policies is known as the process of medicalization—the term used in the territories of the Holy Roman Empire and, after its dissolving, for the Austrian Empire's "medicalization process" (*Medikalisierungsprozess*).[3]

The present paper concerns the first opportunity to eradicate an infectious disease by the use of vaccination: smallpox.[4] With the help of educational advertising, incentives, constraint, and compulsion since the nineteenth century, smallpox was indeed eradicated in the second half of the twentieth century and the vaccination against this highly infectious disease is no longer in the catalogue of recommended immunizations.[5] The World Health Organization could announce in its magazine in May 1980: "Smallpox is dead."[6]

Even if this disease is no longer a danger for the moment, the vaccination against smallpox was the first and longest developed method of immunization in a time of state-building processes and is, therefore, still interesting concerning the medical and social perception, acceptance, and refusal of a measure of prevention in contemporary time. The vaccination against smallpox is a benchmark and, to date, a guideline for the handling of the prevention of and fight against infectious diseases with the help of promotion, education, constraint, and compulsion.

The topic of this paper is embedded in the wider context of the history of medicine and the specific research field of voluntary and compulsory measures against infectious diseases. It also deals with the considerations about the building of the state and its apparatus in the eighteenth and nineteenth century. The tight connection between industrialization and rationalization of lifestyle ("*Rationalisierung der Lebensführung*")[7] has been studied by Ute Frevert in her breakthrough analysis of the Prussian state and Erna Lesky regarding the Austrian monarchy.[8] The response to social issues and riots required an improvement in work and life conditions, especially for the working class, and for a governmental health policy. The administration of health care and welfare consequently became a matter of the state as well as the professionalization of the operators.[9] Naturally, the fight against infectious diseases was also an aspect of this process of medicalization. The state tried to reach as many people as possible, including the educationally deprived social classes, with the help of ordinances, sanctions, reports, and control, as well as with popular publications for health education and the commitment of the clergy. This was not a completely new approach and had already been adopted in the context of inoculation, but the understanding of health and disease as a value of individual conduct *and* state policies was new. Measures to increase the health and growth of the population became part of the state-building process. While governmental authorities made an argument for gentle measures of control in health care policy—also because of the high cost and the lack of personnel accompanying them—physicians and the local authorities claimed more rigor and—if needed—force. The state displayed the majority of its activity in health policy in the field of epidemics prevention and especially in the fight against smallpox with the help of firstly inoculation and secondly vaccination.[10]

The focus of this paper concentrates on the vaccination against smallpox in the regional area of the Princely County of Tyrol, a *Kronland* of

Austria-Hungary from 1867, and today the state of Tyrol in the western part of the Republic of Austria and part of the present-day Euregio (together with South Tyrol and Trentino in Italy). Tyrol is the third largest state in today's Austria with a land area of 12,683.85 km^2. It was even larger in the nineteenth century, going from the city of Kufstein on the border with Bavaria to the city of Ala on the border with the Kingdom of Lombardy-Venetia, another territory of the Austrian Empire created by resolution of the Congress of Vienna in 1815. The crownland of Tyrol covered today's area of Tyrol, South Tyrol, and the Trentino (a total of 26,683 km^2 in 1880).[11]

The Austrian Monarchy was forced to cede Tyrol to the Kingdom of Bavaria in the Peace of Pressburg following defeat in the Third War of Coalition in 1805. The Tyroleans rebelled three times under their national hero, Andreas Hofer, defeating Bavarian and French troops trying to retake the country in vain. The northern part of Tyrol remained under Bavaria and the southern part went to the Napoleonic Kingdom of Italy for another four years. Tyrol returned to the Austrian Empire in 1814, by decision of the Congress of Vienna, and became a *Kronland* of Cisleithania in 1867 until the end of the monarchy in 1918. According to the London Pact of 1915 and following the Treaty of Saint Germain of 1919, South Tyrol and the Trentino had come to the Kingdom of Italy, created in 1861, by the end of World War I.[12] Due to this tumultuous past, the most important archival records of the former crown land of Tyrol are, therefore, in the provincial archive of Innsbruck (*Tiroler Landesarchiv*) in today's Austria, in the provincial archive in Bozen (*Südtiroler Landesarchiv*), and in the state archive of Bozen and Trento (*Staatsarchiv Bozen, Archivio di Stato di Trento*) in today's Italy. The archival sources consist of vaccination tables of the individual districts and parishes of Tyrol, reports of physicians and local juridical authorities[13] (e.g., district judges and district commissioners), and the voices of the clergy and parents. Of course, most of the archival records report failures in vaccination, the lack of trust in this measure of prevention, and complaints about the difficulties in the vaccination management. The point of view is primarily that of the local, regional, and state authorities, and the vaccinators rather than the children to be vaccinated or the parents as deciders.

Starting with the difficult period during the Napoleonic Wars, the territory of Tyrol was, at that time, under the Bavarian regency from 1805 to 1814. Within this framework, the region moved on to a compulsory vaccination against smallpox in 1808; before then, and after 1814 under the Austrian regency, we find a highly recommended but ultimately voluntary vaccination against smallpox during the nineteenth and at the beginning of the twentieth century. Even though compulsory vaccination was discussed, and we see an increasing enforcement of restraint and several endorsements coming not only from Austrian physicians but also from local authorities, the introduction of a compulsory vaccination did not occur until 1939, when the twenty-year-old Austrian Republic became part of the *Third Reich*.[14]

The Fight against Smallpox in Tyrol and Austria

When asking for the reason for not introducing compulsory vaccination in the Austrian monarchy, we cannot assume a lower rate of infections there. Smallpox epidemics came frequently in the nineteenth century, in five- or seven-year waves, often accompanied by secondary damage and death, especially for babies and children.[15] As we can see in the tables of death statistics, the peaks in the 1830s, 1860s, and 1870s were around 1,000 deaths per year in Tyrol (until 1864 with Vorarlberg).[16] According to estimates, around one-third of the children younger than five years old died from smallpox in the Austrian territories before the introduction of vaccination.[17]

There was thus a clear need for action in Tyrol and, on a larger scale, in Austria.[18] The method of prevention since 1767 had been inoculation,[19] the less controllable immunization through infectious human smallpox,[20] which was endorsed by Empress Maria Theresa[21] (1717–1780), who had herself suffered from smallpox and lost children and daughters-in-law to the disease. When Edward Jenner's (1749–1823) method of vaccination (immunization with the help of harmless cowpox) arose,[22] the Viennese court was again one of the first in 1799 to put forward this measure of prevention, testing it on orphans as it did with the inoculation.[23] Since 1802, children could have been vaccinated in the Viennese orphanage in *Alserstraße/Lange Gasse*, where the city had set up a vaccination institute free of charge, which opened daily, the so-called *Schutzpockenimpfungs-Hauptinstitut*.[24]

However, the turn of the century was problematic. Under the pressure and threat of Napoleon Bonaparte, who had been Emperor of the French since 1804, the last Emperor of the Holy Roman Empire, Franz II (1768-1835), founded the Austrian Empire in 1804 and became Franz I of Austria before his abdication as Roman Emperor in 1806. After Napoleon's victory at Austerlitz and the Peace of Pressburg in 1805,[25] Franz II/I [26] was more concerned about his monarchy falling apart, and losing portions of it to the French and Bavarians, rather than enforcing the vaccination against smallpox. Therefore, he endorsed this new method of health prevention but did not impose it by compulsion. Subjects were summoned to vaccinate their children by an imperial ordinance of June 30, 1804, written in the different languages of the monarchy, and, within a child's baptism, the clergy should persuade the reluctant parents by handing out a copy of the imperial ordinance or—if the parents and the godparents were illiterate—by reading it out.[27]

Even with the imperial endorsement, vaccination did not take off in the early years of the Austrian monarchy. Only individual physicians vaccinated their loved ones first and, subsequently, selected patients in their sphere of action and the population solicited with the help of popular science publications to vaccinate their children.[28] The motivation for this engagement came, of course, from not only the first possibility of immunization against an omnipresent and perilous infectious disease, but also the concomitant opportunity for physicians to increase their income, prestige, and influence in the public health domain. Vaccination was seen as an opportunity to promote medical professionalization and expertise[29] as the correspondence between some physicians and the regional authority shows. We can read this in a few examples from the early period of vaccination. District medical officer von Ceschi asked the regional government to invest the town and mine doctor Anton Canestrini to "*k. k. Rath*" (imperial and royal counselor) for his outstanding dedication in introducing smallpox vaccination.[30] Physicians volunteered for vaccinations with the prospect of reward and asked for the assignation of a certain vaccinations district.[31] The town physician of Rovereto, Giovanni Battista Vincenzi, asked for the nomination to "*Medico Vaccinatore d'Officio*" (official vaccinator) for the district of Rovereto, reminding the authorities of his capacity ("*abilità*") and his eagerness ("*incessante zelo*").[32]

The diffusion of this measure of prevention remained in the competence of individual Austrian medical practitioners, graduated physicians and surgeons (*Wundärzte*). In the meantime, governmental compulsory vaccination against smallpox was introduced in neighbouring Bavaria in August 1807 after two years of voluntary vaccination.[33] Consequently, the compulsion was extended to the territory of Tyrol after the latter's transition to the Bavarian regency during the Napoleonic wars in 1808.[34] The Austrian Empire matched this course of action by an ordinance in 1808 concerning the smallpox vaccination: the so-called *Schutzpocken-Impfungsordnung für die österreichischen Erblande* (Smallpox Vaccination Regulations for the Austrian Hereditary Lands).[35] The order regulated the management of smallpox vaccination and the documentation of success and failure. The clergy—obviously Catholic in Austria—was instructed to compile annually (later half-yearly) a list of children between three months and three years of age who were not vaccinated or had survived the disease. Children up to the age of three (deadline July 1) could be vaccinated; children of the age of three by the same deadline had to be vaccinated. The clergy had to announce the vaccination appointment during mass and accompany and support the vaccinator during the process of immunization and certification (*Impfschein/Impfungsausweis*). The majority of the churchmen did this—often with great zeal—out of conviction or in order to satisfy their new obligation as an organ of the state since the Josephinism.[36] The vaccination and the two following appointments for a check-up on the pustule that developed took place not only in schools and parish halls but also in roadhouses and inns. An usher going from house to house also informed the parents of three-year-old children about the vaccination appointment.[37] Physicians and surgeons authorized to vaccinate had to report that they had done so in vaccination tables and explain in a separate column if and why the vaccination was or was not successful. The regulation and endorsement of the business of immunization increased during the nineteenth century, but the Austrian government did not insist on compulsory vaccination.[38]

Why the multi-ethnic Austrian state wanted but hesitated to introduce a compulsory vaccination both as a measure of prevention and as an opportunity to enforce the governmental centralization has many reasons.[39] Similar to other German-speaking territories, the scepticism about the vaccine, its safety and efficiency, was generally large.[40] Arm-to-arm transmission was the primary mode of maintaining a supply of vaccine for most of the first half of the nineteenth century. Therefore, the most important reason for not bringing children to the vaccination appointment was the concern about the transmission of other diseases and of so-called bad habits, for example, alcoholism. Furthermore, there was the worry about the inculcation of Lutheranism through the vaccine, the interference in God's will, and the opinion that vaccinated children would not live longer than twenty years, or would suffer from incontinence.[41] Another reason for rejection was the mixing of human and animal humoral fluids.[42] At the beginning, the animal fluid was taken from the pustules of cows and inserted freshly via a superficial cut with a vaccination lancet on the child's arm. If there was no fresh cowpox *materia* available, the vaccinator could use dried lymph conserved between two glass plates or on a woollen yarn. However, the vaccination with dried lymph was often ineffective. The vaccinator withdrew the fluid for the next vaccination from the pustules of the first vaccinated child (there were mostly two to four pustules on the arm); thus, the method was called an arm-to-arm vaccination. The risks of the transmission of other diseases, such as measles, scarlet fever, syphilis, or the very common scabies, were high here.[43] The frequent shortage and ineffectiveness of the vaccine, even in the late nineteenth century, due to the lack of a proper institute for its production and, consequently, the death by smallpox of vaccinated children, aggravated the breakthrough of vaccination as an effective measure against the infectious disease.[44] However, the records for Tyrol bring up another reason concerning the poor acceptance of this health measure: the reminiscence of the Bavarian imposition. The reports of physicians and local authorities in the year after the return of Tyrol to the Austrian Empire show the break-up through the diminishing numbers of children voluntarily taken to vaccination. The Tyrolean authorities pointed out to the regional government that a compulsory vaccination would remind the people of the foreign Bavarian regency in a bad way and would be rejected because of this. Parents did not want to be seen to be devotees of the late Bavarian rule.[45] While the government and some of the physicians worried about the reluctance of the population to accept the (re)introduction of a former Bavarian ordinance, other protagonists of the local and regional administrative authorities still bemoaned the past Bavarian compulsion forty years later and the fact that no ruler had had the heart to make vaccination compulsory since the building of the Austrian monarchy. The mayor of the city of Meran in today's South Tyrol (Italy) advised the regional administrative authority in 1853 that only 21 of the 180 children listed in the parish registers were brought to the vaccination appointment.[46] The lack of trust in the immunization is documented in the numbers: in 1853, the district of Brixen in today's South Tyrol (Italy) had 11,552 children to vaccinate; 3,624 were vaccinated successfully, 122 were vaccinated without success, and 262 with no proof of success. A total of 7,544 children did not even attend the vaccination appointment.[47] Of course, the parents of this many children were not all anti-vaccinationists as we know them today. Many of them could not attend the arranged vaccination appointment in the late wintertime because of snow and ice blocking the way. Others did not bring their children because of other ongoing infections or weakness. The rest did not see the necessity to go to the vaccination appointment without obligation.

Vaccinators and priests noted all those reasons and "excuses"; the regional and local authorities saw the cause of the decrease of voluntary vaccination in the loss of compulsion and not in the lack of trust in the vaccination or the lack of flexibility of the vaccination business. When the government decided in 1815 that vaccinations had to be operated in February within fourteen days, many physicians and local authorities objected. It was all but impossible to find enough vaccine or produce enough for all the children and undertake the vaccinations in the middle of the wintertime in a mountainous region.[48] The excited letters of different district court physicians in the archival records show how government policy failed to consider the logistic difficulties of vaccination.

The end of the Bavarian government automatically meant the end of the compulsion to vaccinate their children for the Tyrolean people. The benefits of the first opportunity to erase an infectious disease had not yet become accepted not only because of the risks connected to the vaccination but also because of the failure of the state during the Napoleonic conflict and the general distrust, as the recorded invective against vaccinators showed.[49] Therefore, the suggestion to reintroduce compulsory vaccination or at least to use forms of indirect compulsion was repeatedly put forward on the lower political level to avoid the increase of the smallpox infection and the death rate among babies and children and, consequently, the weakening of the state. In fact, beginning in 1808 (and since 1814 for the returned Tyrol), the Austrian monarchy used different forms of indirect compulsion within the framework of vaccination against smallpox in all parts of the Austrian Empire.

Examples of Indirect Compulsion within the Framework of Smallpox Vaccination

The Austrian government—similar to other states without direct compulsion—tied the access to different social benefits to the certificate of vaccination because the humble improvement of the vaccine and the hard words of most of the clergy who tried to convince parents to attend vaccination appointments did not work out. While the Bavarian regency forced their own subjects and the newly acquired Tyrolean people to be vaccinated under the threat of legal punishment (monetary penalty, arrest), the Austrian Empire used financial incentives and social discrimination to increase the voluntary vaccination in the returned crown land of Tyrol and the rest of the Austrian Empire. During the Bavarian regency, school access, apprenticeship, and marriage presupposed a certificate of vaccination or of immunization after the smallpox disease had been endured.[50] In the Austrian Empire, the certificate of vaccination (or recovery from smallpox) became a precondition to several forms of welfare, poor relief (so-called *Armenfonds*), education, and daily life without the *ultima ratio* of a fine (except for the costs of quarantine in the case of causing an outbreak of smallpox). In both cases, with direct or indirect compulsion, the aim was to increase the number of vaccinations to prevent, control, or at best eradicate the disease; most of the Tyrolean parents followed the orders of the Bavarians because of the threat of penalty, and under the Austrian *Kaiser*, because of the economic advantages connected to the certificate of vaccination. If those benefits, such as poor relief, were not certain or needed, the interest in vaccination diminished. The district judge of Kastelruth (today South Tyrol, Italy) complained of the lack of facilities for poor relief, which would support the vaccination as a measure to increase children's health. He reported that some parents did not bring their children to vaccination because it would be a blessing if the disease could halve the number of children who had to share a loaf of bread.[51] This proves once again that vaccination against smallpox throughout the nineteenth century was, to a great degree, not seen as a blessing but as an imposed, legal, direct, or indirect obligation coming from the top of the state or merely from its executors on the ground. A great number of parents brought up the certification that their children had been vaccinated against smallpox not for the possible safety of all of their offspring but for the financial and medical support in precarious conditions and for the survival of the family through the eldest and/or strongest children. This precondition was severe, especially in the time after the Tyrolean uprising in 1809 and the devaluation of the currency (by about 50 percent) due to the Bavarian monetary and tax reform.[52]

The financial situation should be considered even more because, at the very end, both voluntary and compulsory vaccination were not generally free of charge. The two medical check-up appointments after vaccination had to be paid for as well as the revenue stamp for the certificate. Vaccinators in the time of the Bavarian government had to buy the dry lymph and the preprinted Bavarian certificates by themselves and deferred the cost at least to those patients who could afford it.[53] The vaccination against smallpox was, despite all popular education and instruction, an economic issue, and to prevent as many children as possible from death was primarily on behalf of the state and often not on the behalf of poor families with many children to feed.

A more sensitive issue was the interference with popular and religious traditions when punishing parents who did not vaccinate their children. The Austrian Empire kept the Bavarian ordinance to deny a proper funeral within a religious service to families who lost a non-vaccinated child.[54] Therefore, the difference between a vaccinated child who died from smallpox because of the ineffectiveness of the vaccine and a non-vaccinated child who died from smallpox was that the former could be buried in the family/community circle accompanied by a priest and the latter would be buried in the silence of the night consecrated only by a priest. Since this poor and plain farewell ceremony fulfilled the religious requirements, there is not—at the current state of research—any evidence of clerical objections to this policy. However, another source shows the futility of the law. Franz von Ottenthal (1818–1899), a practitioner, community doctor, and forensic physician in the rural area of the Tauferer valley (today South Tyrol, Italy), exculpates himself for having allowed a conventional burial for a smallpox victim in 1884 by explaining to the district commissioner that, following the latest research, microbes could not survive a few days in a well-closed coffin and infect someone outside.[55] Therefore, from the medical side, the long-lasting burial restriction was obsolete and mainly a social disciplinary action.

How tight the connection between immunization and state care/control was can be shown by another example in the field of university education. The certificate of vaccination (or immunization after smallpox infection) was a required field on the preprinted form of application for a grant at the University of Innsbruck in Tyrol but not for matriculation. The University of Innsbruck, founded in 1669 by Emperor Leopold I, reduced to a secondary school during the Bavarian time and then reopened in 1826, was not completed and still without the faculty of theology (transferred to the diocesan town of Brixen) and without a proper faculty of medicine until 1869.[56] Despite this, students of all social classes attended the university in the second half of the nineteenth century for better employment opportunities, especially in the new fields of study (pharmacy, veterinary medicine, and teacher education). Many of them could not afford the university taxes and living in the capital and applied for financial support. There were many private, institutional, and religious grants for students of different ranges (from 50 to 300 fl.) and there was a great demand for this form of support. While students could attend university without a certification of vaccination against smallpox, they would only get a grant for the study if they had been vaccinated or had endured the disease. The proof of vaccination or recovery through certification had to be filled in the preprinted form under the only column *geimpft* (vaccinated) and was of the same importance as the good study grades and the certification of good behaviour.[57] Therefore, vaccination was not seen as a method of disease's prevention in the academic setting but as a further instrument of social control and an act of obedience to the state power outright compulsion, as Malte Thießen has also demonstrated for Germany after the introduction of compulsory vaccination (*Reichsimpfgesetz*) in 1874.[58]

Not only university education but also preschool attendance depended partially on immunization. With the increase of industrialization and female employment, children's day care for boys and girls between three and six years old became progressively more important in the growing urban centres in Tyrolean cities such as Innsbruck or Bozen. Wilhelmine Kofler (born Grätzel) founded the first institution called the *Kleinkinderbewahranstalt der Stadt Bozen*, similar to today's kindergarten, in the city of Bozen, in today's South Tyrol, in 1847. Wilhelmine Grätzl (1802–1866), the daughter of a businessman, married the physician Josef Kofler. She bequeathed all her possessions in her last will and testament to the poor and orphans. A conspicuous part of this legacy came to the *Kleinkinderbewahranstalt*, which would later become the *Koflerkindergarten* and a juvenile home for girls and women.[59] Wilhelmine Kofler and fifteen other noble and middle-class women cared for almost 300 children in the *Kleinkinderbewahranstalt* in the 1880s, giving them food, religious instruction, and health care support.[60] The mayor and the city council of Bozen repeatedly put pressure on the well-organized women and instructed them (because of their obstinacy) to allow admission only to children with the certificate of vaccination or immunization and to remove those children whose parents refused the vaccination out of conviction or tardiness.[61] The legal authority to do so came from the ordinance of 1836,[62] which forbade accepting non-vaccinated or recovered children in publicly granted educational institutes (especially orphanages). The institute was, to a certain extent, under the city's control, even though it was sponsored by legacies and private donations. The local authorities patronized the female board of the Kindergarten and called on them to put at least a legally indirect coercion on recalcitrant parents concerning the immunization of those children who lived generally in poor and unhealthy conditions.[63] We also miss the care of the children in the reading of archival records. The focus is placed on the control and paternalism of poor, unknowing, and careless working-class parents.[64]

Conclusion

Smallpox vaccination was fostered in the regional state of Tyrol through a mixture of voluntariness, persuasion, and indirect or direct compulsion, similar to what was experienced in the fight against Covid-19. While voluntary vaccinations remained constant but modest through the nineteenth century, the need for an enforcement after the revocation of the compulsory vaccination of the Bavarian regency in Tyrol called for new persuasive measures. Without introducing a proper coercion in the Austrian monarchy and in Tyrol as part of it, the state helped itself with different forms of indirect compulsion, incentives, persuasion, but also public shaming of parents who did not bring their children for vaccination. To mix education and incentives with direct and/or indirect compulsion in the context of health prevention measures was not unique in the area of Tyrol, Austria, or in other German-speaking territories. While Hessen, Bavaria, Baden, Württemberg, and Hannover, for example, introduced compulsion in vaccination early in the century (between 1807 and 1821), other German states, such as Prussia, worked with persuasion, education, and indirect compulsion.[65] The same can be said for the Austrian monarchy, which established an administrative structure based on the issues of the *Medizinische Policey* to introduce and enforce vaccination without legal compulsion. The legally established approach of indirect compulsion outlined concerned different aspects of state welfare and daily life in the Austrian Empire of the nineteenth century. This chosen way of increasing state health prevention was, on the one hand, an invasion of the personal freedom and freedom of decision to the same degree as a compulsory vaccination and, on the other hand, less effective and not always practicable. In the end, it avoided the introduction of a compulsory vaccination against smallpox, as the Bavarians had done in their territories and, respectively, in Tyrol between 1808 and 1814, or the government of Württemberg in 1818. The means of indirect compulsion in order to increase the number of children vaccinated did not succeed and became the subject for new debates. When, in 1891, the Austrian government department for education determined that children should provide the certificate of vaccination at school entry, access to instruction was not to be denied to those who refused the vaccination. Basic education had also become a compulsory form of state care, and a possible refusal of vaccination could not compromise this. This situation from 130 years ago reminds one of today's Italy where compulsory vaccination (in this case, against the classical childhood diseases, such as measles, rubella, and diphtheria) since 2017 has conflicted with compulsory school attendance. While vaccinations are an unavoidable precondition for preschool attendance, for school attendance, the refusal of vaccination leads to an extensive fine but cannot bar children from basic education.

The difference in the level of pressure placed on the prevention through immunization could come from the opinion that more could be achieved by voluntariness than by compulsion, as was stated by Peter Baldwin.[66] This cannot be assumed for Tyrol and the Austrian monarchy, given the very rude tone in the records concerning the vaccination's management. Since the caring incitement of the imperial ordinance from 1804, the words describing parents who did not vaccinate their children had changed into "murderers of their own offspring."[67]

The particularity of the Tyrolean example lays, therefore, in the incapacity of the multiethnic Austrian monarchy to use an already introduced measure of medical prevention as an instrument of state control and power despite the connection of the compulsory vaccination to foreign rule.[68] Even in the second half of the nineteenth century, when the Bavarian coercion was merely a memory, and the local and regional political authorities, the clergy, and physicians called for a reintroduction of compulsion in the prevention of smallpox, the state hesitated to comply with this request for a strong policy. However, expectations came from both sides: the local and regional administrative and medical authorities asked for a political parameter to put a medical control on the population[69] and prosecute disobedience in the framework of child vaccination. The government, interested in increasing the population and, along with this, military and financial power,[70] called for engagement and perseverance in the persuading of hesitant or renitent parents through the intermediate authorities avoiding coercion. In Tyrol, this was the fact not only because of the "Bavarian aftertaste," but also because of the challenge of the vaccination management (disposability and effectiveness of the vaccine) and possibly because of the opinion that compulsory vaccination was not necessary or not the only measure of prevention, as Hennock had shown for England.[71] Another reason might be the opinion that the state could not or should not "intervene so directly in the familial sphere or in the parent's right to decide about their children's well-being" as Huerkamp has assumed.[72] Regarding the Tyrolean and Austrian example, the act of not introducing a compulsory vaccination against smallpox, contrasting with other European and German-speaking territories, did not mean that the former states cared more about the self-determination of the recipients of the vaccination or, in this case, of the caregivers and deciders. On the contrary, the reasons for the refusal of vaccination put forward by parents were not taken seriously and were debased as ignorant, prejudiced, and uncaring. The distrust of the people in the local, regional, and—after the failure in the framework of the Napoleonic wars—in the state authorities seems to have contributed merely to the refusal of this measure of health prevention. The failure of Austrian vaccination policy is, therefore, one indicator among others of the insufficient modernization of the state apparatus during the nineteenth century. Together with the experience of a foreign rule, this failure and distrust shaped a Tyrolean way of facing measures of epidemics prevention, although it does not put out a sufficient statement for today's situation, where Tyrol ranks low in the hit list of the vaccination development of Austrian regional states.[73] The difficult relationship between the individual and the state characterized to what extent measures were accepted. This reminds us of today's pandemic situation and the varying acceptance of vaccination programs in the individual countries.

Endnotes

1. While voluntariness in the context of vaccination is defined as choice being made of free will to vaccinate a child or not, compulsion means the obligation by pressure and constraint to bring children to vaccination under the threat of punishment. Indirect compulsion means that access to important financial support, and educational and care institutions, is tied to the certification of vaccination or recovery.

2. Exemplarily: Kurt Widhalm, "Impfen oder Nichtimpfen, das ist hier die Frage," *Pädiatrie & Pädologie* 54, (2019): 118–21, https://doi.org/10.1007/s00608-019-0689-3.

3. The term *medicalization* refers to a longer development process in the course of which, from the second half of the eighteenth century onwards, doctors, with the help of the state, made their medical services available to a broader section of the population. This expansion of the medical market was accompanied by the emergence of medical experts through their professionalization. In the age of medical enlightenment, i.e. from 1770 onwards, these experts brought about a change in the understanding of health-damaging and disease-promoting behaviour and in traditional medical knowledge. Wolfgang Uwe Eckart and Robert Jütte, "Medikalisierung," in *Enzyklopädie der Neuzeit Online*, accessed June 6, 2023, http://dx.doi.org/10.1163/2352-0248_edn_COM_309074; Ute Frevert, *Krankheit als politisches Problem 1770–1880: Soziale Unterschichten in Preußen zwischen medizinischer Polizei und staatlicher Sozialversicherung* (Kritische Studien zur Geschichtswissenschaft 62, Göttingen: Vandenhoeck & Ruprecht, 1984); Francisca Loetz, *Vom Kranken zum Patienten: 'Medikalisierung' und medizinische Vergesellschaftung am Beispiel Badens 1750–1850* (Medizin, Gesellschaft und Geschichte, Supplement 2, Stuttgart: Franz Steiner Verlag, 1993).

4. For an overview of the history of smallpox and vaccination, see Gareth Williams, *Angel of Death: The Story of Smallpox* (New York: Palgrave Macmillan, 2010).

5. Impfplan Österreich, accessed Nov. 22, 2022, https://www.sozialministerium.at/Themen/Gesundheit/Impfen/Impfplan-%C3%96sterreich.html.

6. D.A. Henderson, "A Victory for All Mankind," *World Health*, May 1980, 2–5, accessed Nov. 22, 2022, https://apps.who.int/iris/handle/10665/202490.

7. Frevert, *Krankheit als politisches Problem*, 14. The term rationalization derives from the Latin word "ratio," which means reason. According to

this, a methodical, reasonable approach shapes the human way of life. In work and economics, rationalization combines measures that can make work easier and reduce costs but allow the same results to be achieved. See "Radikalisierung," in *BWL-Lexikon*, accessed June 6, 2023, https://www.bwl-lexikon.de/wiki/rationalisierung/#der-begriff-der-rationalisierung.

8. Erna Lesky, Österreichisches Gesundheitswesen im Zeitalter des aufgeklärten Absolutismus (Archiv für österreichische Geschichte 12 2/1, Vienna: Verlag der Österreichischen Akademie der Wissenschaften, 1959).

9. Lesky, Österreichisches Gesundheitswesen im Zeitalter des aufgeklärten Absolutismus, 69.

10. Frevert, *Krankheit als politisches Problem*, 16, 21, 62, 69. Frevert defines it as process of "politicization" of health and disease.

11. Birgit Bolognese-Leuchtenmüller, *Bevölkerungsentwicklung und Berufsstruktur, Gesundheits- und Fürsorgewesen in Österreich 1750–1918* (Wirtschafts- und Sozialstatistik Österreich-Ungarns 1, Vienna: Verlag für Geschichte und Politik, 1978), 6–7.

12. Josef Riedmann, *Geschichte Tyrols* 3rd Edition (Vienna: Verlag für Geschichte und Politik, 2001), 180–282; Hans Heiss and Thomas Götz, *Am Rande der Revolution: Tyrol 1848/49* (Vienna: Folio-Verlag, 1998).

13. For an overview on the local administration and especially of the health care system in Tyrol see: Otto Stolz, *Geschichte der Verwaltung Tyrols* (Geschichte des Landes Tyrol 2/2, Innsbruck: Universitätsverlag Wagner, 1998), 71–84.

14. Deutsches Reichsgesetzblatt bzw. Gesetzblatt für das Land Österreich (1938–1940), Impfgesetz, Geltung in der Ostmark, 1939, 936, accessed Nov. 22, 2022, https://alex.onb.ac.at/tab_dra.htm.

15. Eberhard Wolff, "Die Schlacht auf dem Zahlenberge. Impfgegnerschaft im späten 19. Jahrhundert – Das Beispiel Sachsen," in *Pocken zwischen Alltag, Medizin und Politik. Begleitbuch zur Ausstellung,* ed. Ragnhild Münch (Berlin: BibSpider, 1994), 113–28.

16. Eberhard Wolff, *Einschneidende Maßnahmen: Pockenschutzimpfung und traditionale Gesellschaft im Württemberg des frühen 19. Jahrhunderts* (Medizin, Gesellschaft und Geschichte, Supplement 10, Stuttgart: Franz Steiner Verlag, 1998), 22–6.

17. Michael Pammer, "Pocken I. Gesundheitspolitik unter Franz II./I," *Historicum: Zeitschrift für Geschichte. Medizin* I (spring 2003), 17–21 (here 17); Lesky, Österreichisches Gesundheitswesen im Zeitalter des

aufgeklärten Absolutismus, 146.

18. Alois Unterkircher, "'Tiroler! Lasset eure Kinder impfen:' Sterblichkeitsverhältnisse und frühe Seuchenprophylaxe in Tirol am Beispiel der Pocken im 19. Jahrhundert," in *Medikalisierung auf dem Lande/Medicalizzazione in area alpina,* ed. Elisabeth Dietrich-Daum and Rodolfo Taiani (Geschichte und Region/Storia e regione 14/1) (Innsbruck: Studienverlag, 2005), 42–68.

19. Arnold C. Klebs, *Die Variolation im achtzehnten Jahrhundert: Ein historischer Beitrag zur Immunitätsforschung* (Gießen: Verlag Arnold Töpelmann, 1914), also available online, accessed Nov. 22, 2022, https://wellcomecollection.org/works/wwgbyy2y.

20. Besides the risk of a serious course of disease and an outbreak through this method, there was also the moral dilemma because a healthy child could die from inoculation. Jennifer D. Penshaw, *Battling Smallpox before Vaccination: Inoculation in Eighteenth-century Germany* (Clio Medica 105, Leiden: Brill, 2022), 5.

21. Barbara Stollberg-Rilinger, *Maria Theresia: Die Kaiserin in ihrer Zeit. Eine Biographie* (Munich: H. C. Beck, 2017), 504–15.

22. Eduard Jenner, *An Inquiry into the Causes and Effects of the Variolae Vaccinae: A Disease Discovered in Some of the Western Counties of England, Particularly Gloucestershire, and Known by the Name of the Cow Pox* (London: Sampson Low, 1798); Otto Nowotny, "Über die Entdeckung der Schutzpockenimpfung im Jahre 1796," Österreichische Apothekerzeitung 50 (1996): 504–7.

23. Friedrich Katscher, "Vor 200 Jahren: Die ersten Pockenschutzimpfungen in Wien," *Wiener Klinische Wochenschrift* 111 (1999), 299–306.

24. Heinz Flamm and Christian Vutuc, "Geschichte der Pocken-Bekämpfung in Österreich," *Wiener klinische Wochenschrift. The Middle European Journal of Medicine* 122 (2010): 265–75, 267–8.

25. Martin P. Schennach, *Revolte in der Region: Zur Tiroler Erhebung von 1809* (Innsbruck: Universitätsverlag Wagner, 2009), 106–10. For more details: Scott Bowden, *Napoleon and Austerlitz: An Unprecedentedly Detailed Combat Study of Napoleonic's Ulm-Austerlitz Campaigns of 1805 (The Glory Years of 1805–1807)* (Chicago: Emperor's Press, 1997).

26. Hugo Hantsch, "Franz II," in *Neue Deutsche Biographie* (NDB) vol. 5 (Berlin: Duncker & Humblot, 1961), 358–61.

27. Tiroler Landesarchiv, Jüngeres Gubernium, Sanität 2416, November 7,

1804.

28. Anton Canestrini, *Nachricht an das Tirolische Publikum über den Fortgang der Schutzblattern-Impfung in und um Schwatz: nebst einer zweyten Aufmunterung und Widerlegung einiger noch hie und da herrschenden Vorurtheile* [News to the Tyrolean public on the progress of the vaccination against smallpox in and around Schwaz: Together with a second exhortation and refutation of some preconceptions still prevalent here and there] (Innsbruck: Schiffner, 1803).

29. Claudia Huerkamp, "The History of Smallpox Vaccination in Germany: A First Step in the Medicalization of the General Public," *Journal of Contemporary History* 20/4 (1985): 617–35 (here 622).

30. Tiroler Landesarchiv, Jüngeres Gubernium, Sanität 2414, 1802 district medical officer von Ceschi to the regional government, Sept. 6, 1802.

31. Troler Landesarchiv, Jüngeres Gubernium, Sanität 2421, 1808.

32. He ended his letter by asking to forward his request to the Bavarian king if the position as vaccinator was given to another, "undeserving" candidate. Tiroler Landesarchiv, Jüngeres Gubernium, Sanität 2423, 1808 physician Vincenzi to the regional government, Dec. 31, 1807.

33. Bayerische Staatsbibliothek, Königlich-Baierisches Regierungsblatt, München 1807, columns 1426–37, accessed Nov. 22, 2022, http://opacplus.bsb-muenchen.de/title/3341234/ft/bsb10345219?page=771.

34. Bayerische Staatsbibliothek, Königlich-Baierisches Regierungsblatt, München 1808, columns 441–5, accessed Nov. 22, 2022, http://opacplus.bsb-muenchen.de/title/3341235/ft/bsb10345220?page=233.

35. Franz von Zimmeter Treuherz, *Die Fonde, Anstalten und Geschäfte der Tyroler Landschaft geschichtlich und sachgemäß dargestellt* [The funds, institutions and businesses of the Tyrolean diet presented historically and factually] (Innsbruck: Verlag der Tyroler Landschaft, 1894), 162–3.

36. For the Austrian Monarchy, the clergy used for the promotion of the smallpox vaccination was Catholic also in the areas with a considerable Protestant presence, i.e., Styria and Carinthia. However, Lutheran pastors encouraged inoculation and vaccination in Protestant parts of the Holy Roman Empire, such as Prussia. See Penshow, *Battling smallpox*, 6. Elke Hammer-Luza, "'Lässt nicht impfen:' Widerstände gegen die Vakzination in der Steiermark in der ersten Hälfte des 19. Jahrhunderts," in *Virus: Beiträge zur Sozialgeschichte der Medizin, Schwerpunkt: Kulturgeschichte(n) der Impfung* 20 (2021): 101–30.

37. As an example of this way of communication, see the complaint of the physicians in the archival records: Tiroler Landesarchiv, Jüngeres Gubernium, Sanität 1814/15, k. k. prov. Landgericht Mühlbach an das k. k. prov. Generalkommissariat Innsbruck [The imperial district court of Mühlbach in today's South Tyrol to the General Commissariat of Innsbruck], No. 144/11, Aug. 23, 1814.

38. Pammer, "Pocken I: Gesundheitspolitik unter Franz II./I," 17–21; Michael Pammer, "Pocken II: Die Impfung im 19. Jahrhundert," *Historicum: Zeitschrift für Geschichte. Medizin II* (Summer 2003): 15–9.

39. Frevert, *Krankheit als politisches Problem*, 12–20.

40. Wolff, *Einschneidende Maßnahmen*; Sabine Falk and Alfred Stefan Weiss, "'Hier sind die Blattern': Der Kampf von Staat und Kirche für die Durchsetzung der (Kinder)Schutzimpfung in Stadt und Land Salzburg (Ende des 18. Jahrhunderts bis ca. 1820)," *Mitteilungen der Gesellschaft für Salzburger Landeskunde* 131 (1991): 163–86; Michael Memmer, "Die Geschichte der Schutzimpfungen in Österreich. Eine rechtshistorische Analyse," in *Schutzimpfungen – Rechtliche, ethische und medizinische Aspekte (= Schriftenreihe Ethik und Recht in der Medizin 11 2016)* ed. Gerhard Aigner et al., 9–36, accessed Nov. 22, 2022, https://elibrary.verlagoesterreich.at/book/99.105005/9783704674791.

41. See the "excuses" for not attending the vaccination appointment in the archival records: Tiroler Landesarchiv, Jüngeres Gubernium, Sanität 1814/15, Vernehmungsprotokolle der Eltern durch den Landrichter Candidus von Samern [Records of the interrogation of parents by the district judge Candidus von Samern], Dec. 17, 1814.

42. Eberhard Wolff, "'Volksmedizin' als historisches Konstrukt. Laienvorstellungen über die Ursachen der Pockenkrankheit im frühen 19. Jahrhundert und deren Verhältnis zu Erklärungsweisen in der akademischen Medizin," Österreichische Zeitschrift für Geschichtswissenschaften 7, no. 3 (1996): 405–30.

43. To the concept of risk in this framework, see: Malte Thießen, "Risk as Resource: On the Interplay between Risks, Vaccinations and Welfare States in Nineteenth- and Twentieth-Century Germany," in *Historical Social Research / Historische Sozialforschung* 41, 1 (2016): 70–90.

44. See the complaint and the excuse for the mingy vaccination table of the district of Rattenberg with only three vaccinated children: Innsbruck, Tiroler Landesarchiv, Jüngeres Gubernium, Sanität, Anmerkung des Pflegers Sebastian Eisenthaler zu einer Impftabelle im Patrimonialgericht

Rattenberg [Notes on the vaccination tables from the period fall 1806/ spring 1807 of the district of Rattenberg in today's Tyrol (Austria) from the district judge Sebastian Eisenthaler], Apr. 6, 1807.

45. "Wenn die Impfung blos der Willkür der Aeltern unterlassen wird, so unterliegt es keinem Zweifel, daß dieselbe ganz in Verfall komme; Denn da die Impfung unter der vorigen Regierung gesetzlich eingeführt wurde, und das Volk von seiner vorgefaßten Meynung, daß alles das was Baiern eingeführt hat, etwas Schlechtes sey, nicht abgebracht werden kann; so glauben die Aeltern, die Impfung schon aus dem Grunde unterlassen zu müßen, um ja nicht für Anhänger der bairischen Regierung gehalten zu werden." [If the vaccination remains in the arbitrariness of the parents, there will be without doubt a break-up. The vaccination was introduced by the previous government by law and the people have the unchangeable prejudice that all that the Bavarians had introduced was bad; therefore, parents think they have to avoid the vaccination because they do not want to be seen as followers of the Bavarian government.] Tiroler Landesarchiv, Jüngeres Gubernium, Sanität 1815, Nr. 1568 Bericht des prov. k. k. Landgerichtes Klausen [Report of the imperial district court of Klausen in today's South Tyrol (Italy)], July 12, 1814.

46. Staatsarchiv Bozen, Verwaltungsakten der politischen Unter- und Mittelbehörden, Sanität Nr. 210, Fasz. 338, der Bürgermeister von Meran und der Stadtrat an die Bezirkshauptmannschaft Meran [The mayor and the city council of Meran to the administrative district authority], June 14, 1853.

47. Staatsarchiv Bozen, Verwaltungsakten der politischen Unter- und Mittelbehörden, Sanität Nr. 210, Fasz. 338, Kreispräsident von Brixen an Bezirkshauptmann in Meran [The county chief of Brixen to the chief district commander], June 20, 1853.

48. Tiroler Landesarchiv, Jüngeres Gubernium, Sanität 1815, Nr. 1763 das Landgericht Rattenberg an das k. k. prov. Generalkommissariat in Innsbruck [The district court of Rattenberg in today's Tyrol (Austria) to the General Commissariat of Innsbruck], Feb. 10, 1815.

49. Tiroler Landesarchiv, Jüngeres Gubernium, Sanität 1814/15, Nr. 520, das Landgericht Sterzing an das Generalkommissariat Innsbruck [The district court of Sterzing in today's South Tyrol (Italy) to the General Commissariat of Innsbruck], Oct. 25, 1814.

50. Reinhard Heydenreuter, *Tyrol unter dem bayerischen Löwen* (Regenburg: Pustet 2008), 124–6.

51. Tiroler Landesarchiv, Jüngeres Gubernium, Sanität 1814/1815, Bericht des Landrichters von Kastelruth [Report of the district judge of Kastelruth

in today's South Tyrol (Italy)], Oct. 30, 1814: "daß blos diejenigen Eltern die Schutzblattern-Impfung unterlassen zu wissen wünschten, deren Vermögens-Umstände ein weit größerer Gefallen geschehen würden, wenn der reichliche Seegen ihrer Kinder durch die Blattern eine Reduktion wenigstens um die Hälfte erleiden würde, um das ohnehin so schmale Stück Brod nicht in so viele kurze Theile mit denselben dividieren und somit den Lebensgenuß sich manchmal sehr verbittern zu müssen wofür geeignete Versorgungsanstalten an denen es aber hier zu Lande ganz gebricht, das einzige Mittel seyn werden This argument has already been pointed out by Eberhard Wolff for Württemberg: Eberhard Wolff, "Der 'willkommene Würgeengel:' Verstehende Innenperspektive und 'genaue' Quelleninterpretation – am Beispiel des erwünschten Kindertods in den Anfängen der Pockenschutzimpfung," in *Neue Wege in der Seuchengeschichte*, ed. Martin Dinges and Thomas Schlich (Medizin, Gesellschaft und Geschichte. Vol. 6, Stuttgart: Steiner, 1995), 105–41.

52. Heydenreuter, *Tyrol unter dem bayerischen Löwen*, 122–3.

53. See the complaint of the vaccinator in Kufstein: Tiroler Landesarchiv, Jüngeres Gubernium 1808, Impfarzt Wisend in Kufstein [Vaccinator Wisend in Kufstein today's Tyrol (Austria)], Mar. 26, 1807.

54. Bayerische Staatsbibliothek, Königlich-Baierisches Regierungsblatt München 1808, Apr. 23, 1808, columns 934–5, accessed Nov. 22, 2022, https://www.digitale-sammlungen.de/de/view/bsb10345220?page=522,523.

55. Elena Taddei, *Franz von Ottenthal: Arzt und Tyroler Landtagsabgeordneter (1818–1899)* (Vienna: Böhlau 2010), 159–60.

56. Christof Aichner, "Die Verbindung von Lehre und Forschung: Auf dem Weg zur modernen Universität im 19. Jahrhundert," in *Geschichte der Universität Innsbruck 1669–2019, vol. 1: Phasen der Universitätsgeschichte, part 1: Von der Gründung bis zum Ende des Ersten Weltkrieges*, ed. Margret Friedrich and Dirk Rupnow (Innsbruck: university press iup, 2019), 295–470 (here 295–300).

57. Universitätsarchiv Innsbruck, Competententabelle der Bewerber um ein landesfürstliches Stipendium, Medizinische Fakultät, WS 1898/99 [Competence table of applicants for a national prince's scholarship, faculty of medicine, winter term 1898/99]. Also see the examples of university grants and the 'preconditions' in: Elena Taddei, "'Paupertatis gratia:' Das Stipendienwesen an der Universität Innsbruck in der zweiten Hälfte des 19. Jahrhunderts," in *Geschichte der Universität Innsbruck 1669–2019, vol. 2: Aspekte der Universitätsgeschichte*, ed. Margret Friedrich and Dirk Rupnow

(Innsbruck: university press iup, 2019), 249–79.

58. Malte Thießen, *Immunisierte Gesellschaft. Impfen in Deutschland im 19. und 20. Jahrhundert.* (Kritische Studien zur Geschichtswissenschaft 225, Göttingen: Vandenhoeck & Ruprecht, 2017), 107.

59. Herrmann Vigl, "Kofler Wilhelmine," Österreichisches Biographisches Lexikon 1815–1950 4 (1969), 57; Florian Huber, *Aus dem Verzeichnis des Archivs des Koflerschen Kindergartens Bozen (Koflerstiftung)* [From the index of the archives of the Kofler Kindergarten in Bolzano (Kofler Foundation)], unpublished manuscript available in the Südtiroler Landesarchiv 2007; Giuseppe Pantozzi, *Il governo della beneficenza in Tyrolo secoli XVIII-XX* (Pubblicazioni del Museo storico in Trento. Grenzen/Confini 3, Trento: Museo storico in Trento, 2006), 145–66.

60. Südtiroler Landesarchiv, Archiv des Koflerschen Kindergartens, No. 195.

61. Südtiroler Landesarchiv, Archiv des Koflerschen Kindergartens No. 195, Bürgermeister Kappeller an die Vorstehung der Kleinkinderbewahranstalt [Mayor Kappeller to the board of the Kindergarten], 17 April 1857 and No. 176, May 17, 1886.

62. Josef Daimer, *Handbuch der österreichischen Sanitäts-Gesetze und Verordnungen für Behörden und Gemeinden, amtliche Sanitäts- und Veterinär-Organe, Districts- und Gemeindeärzte, Aerzte, Thierärzte, Apotheker, Verwaltungen von Heil- und Humananstalten etc. etc., Zweiter Theil*, (Leipzig: F. Deuticke, 1898), 246–7; "Vorschrift über die Kuhpocken-Impfung in den Kaiserl.-Königl. Staaten," July 9, 1836 Zl 13192.

63. "um dadurch wenigstens einen nach den bestehenden Gesetzen zuläßigen indirekten Zwang auf die Impfrenitenten auszuüben" [to have at least a legally approved indirect compulsion on the recalcitrant people], Südtiroler Landesarchiv, Archiv des Koflerschen Kindergartens No. 134, Der Bürgermeister von Bozen an die Vorstehung der Kleinkinderbewahranstalt [The mayor of Bozen to the board of the Kindergarten], June 10, 1876.

64. Elena Taddei, "Aspekte von indirektem Impfzwang im Rahmen der Pockenschutzimpfung im Tyrol des 19. Jahrhunderts," in *Virus: Beiträge zur Sozialgeschichte der Medizin, Schwerpunkt: Kulturgeschichte(n) der Impfung* 20 (2021): 131–146, in print.

65. Huerkamp, "The History of Smallpox Vaccination in Germany," 623.

66. Peter Baldwin, *Contagion and the State in Europe 1830–1930.* (Cambridge: University Press, 1999), 531.

67. "Gewiß, ihr würdet in diesem Falle nichts geringeres als die Mörder euerer eigenen Kinder seyn!" [Surely in this case you would be nothing less than the murderers of your own children], Südtiroler Landesarchiv, Nachlass Rasmo I. Nr. 3 Aufruf zur Pockenimpfung / call to vaccination against smallpox, July 1824.

68. Wolff, *Einschneidende Maßnahmen,* 16.

69. Huerkamp, "The History of Smallpox Vaccination in Germany," 621.

70. Huerkamp, "The History of Smallpox Vaccination in Germany," 620, 623.

71. In this case for vaccination and revaccination. E. P. Hennock, "Vaccination Policy Against Smallpox, 1835–1914: A Comparison of England with Prussia and Imperial Germany," *The Society for the Social History of Medicine* (1998): 49–71, (here 67ss). See also Naomi Williams, "The Implementation of Compulsory Health Legislation: Infant Smallpox Vaccination in England and Wales, 1840–1890," *Journal of Historical Geography* 20, 4 (1994): 396–412.

72. Huerkamp, "The History of Smallpox Vaccination in Germany," 623.

73. https://orf.at/corona/daten/impfung, accessed Nov. 22, 2022.

The Spanish Flu 1918-19 in the Austrian Press

Eva Pfanzelter

Introduction

Ever since early 2020, the Covid-19 pandemic has kept the world on its toes. Its outbreak reminds us of other pandemics that occurred over past centuries, among which the great influenza epidemic of 1918–1919, wrongly named the Spanish flu,[1] has often been used as a precedent for the present health crisis. The H1N1 Spanish flu virus was identified as the origin of a series of respiratory viral pandemics in the twentieth and twenty-first centuries and was therefore aptly named as the "Mother of Pandemics"[2] by some scholars. The first case of the flu was registered in March 1918 in Kansas, USA, and the last was identified two years later, in March 1920. The virus raged across the globe in mainly three waves. The first wave in spring and summer 1918 and the third wave, which scattered in isolated outbreaks on all continents in 1919 and 1920, were mild, with many infected people but comparatively few deaths. The second wave, however, which started building up in August 1918, was lethal, killing especially young people aged fifteen to forty by the millions all over the world until November 1918. Ultimately, the disease infected about one third of the population worldwide and caused between fifty and one hundred million deaths. This means that it caused more than two and a half times as many casualties as World War I, which claimed roughly twenty million human lives excluding the estimated thirty million Russian military and civilian victims. It probably was the most lethal epidemic since the Plague, the Black Death, in the Middle Ages.[3]

The many cautious wordings and estimates indicate, as Laura Spinney has phrased it, "our collective forgetting of the greatest massacre of the twentieth century."[4] The reason for the omission has to do with the limited medical insights and communication capabilities of the time but also with the time period in which the Spanish flu took place. It came up during the last months of World War I and peaked in the fall of 1918, right when "the great seminal catastrophe of this century"[5] ended. After the deadly second wave of the epidemic, the cemeteries all over Europe were filled with the remains of the casualties of war and, from September through December, they were also clustered with the victims of the flu.

Although the virus severely decimated the fighting forces, especially in the US and French army, it also had a decisive impact on the Central Powers. In Germany and the Habsburg Empire, the Spanish flu aggravated the disastrous situation on the warfronts and added to the grievances on the home front. For the societies in the two empires, the illness struck at a time when public health was a disaster due to the shortages brought about by the war. Equally, morale was low because, despite the huge war effort, defeat in World War I became tangible. While elaborating somewhat on the history of the Spanish flu at the end of the war in the regions that were to become the Austrian Republic, the following pages will therefore have a closer look at Austrian newspaper reporting. Despite war censorship and political control on the content of the news, even at the time newspapers were the vehicle for discussion of the intricate relationship between society, politics, and media—or, in other words, they were the social media of the time. In this essay, I will show that newspaper research on pandemics of the past, such as the Spanish flu, can give us a detailed insight into discourses prevailing in society during times of crisis. As we will see, there are many similarities and some differences in topics, themes, and frustration to media coverage today.

The essay begins with an overview of the historiography of the Spanish flu, goes on to the history of the Spanish flu at the end of World War I in the western regions of the Habsburg Empire. These chapters are followed by a short introduction into the newspaper research and several topics talked about in Austrian newspapers of the time. The essay concludes with a short summary of the discourses found in Austrian newspaper reporting of the time.

Historiographical Overview

Despite its worldwide impact, the Spanish flu has not become a place of remembrance—neither in the world's societies nor in historiography. In fact, the latter has been slow to address the topic up until the 1970s. English historian and journalist Richard Collier was one of the first to dedicate a monography to the pandemic. His *The Plague of the Spanish Lady: The Influenza Pandemic of 1918-1919*,[6] published in 1974, received a lot of attention and was even reviewed in the TimeMagazine.[7]

Ever since then, the Spanish flu has been written about once and again both in popular culture and in historical research, where books, essay, and news titles recurrently labeled it as the neglected pandemic or talked about the silence surrounding it. For example, Alfred Crosby's account of 2003 was headlined *America's Forgotten Pandemic*.[8] In 2020, Maria Luisa Lima and José Manuel Sobral wrote "Threat and Oblivion: Interpreting the Silence over the Spanish Flu."[9] Even in 2021 Herwig Czech talked about "Die Spanische Grippe von 1918. Blick auf eine lange vergessene Pandemie" ("The Spanish Flu of 1918: a look at a long-forgotten pandemic")[10] and in the Sunday Telegraph Simon Heffe reported on "Never Forgotten? Why the Spanish Flu has No Memorials"[11] that same year. To summarize the discussions, Guy Beiner in 2022 analyzed these trends in the publication *Pandemic Re-Awakenings: the Forgotten and Unforgotten 'Spanish flu' of 1918-1919.*[12]

As Czech pointed out, this forgetting of the most disastrous pandemic of the twentieth century had to do with, first, its co-occurrence with the end of World War I, where everyday news from the front and day-to-day politics superseded all other topics. Second, censorship prevented reporting on a large scale, which ultimately also led to the unjust naming of the pandemic, since it was in free Spain where newspapers started to write about the new flu in the spring of 1918. Third, there was also the turmoil of the war's end, with new borders being drawn, old regimes disintegrating, and new nation states emerging over the next years contributing to the lack of remembrance.[13]

At the same time, the history of the Spanish flu was sometimes analyzed with a focus on advancements in medicine, as Wilfried Witte showed in his essay about "Die Grippe-Pandemie 1918-1920 in der medizinischen Debatte" ("The flu pandemic 1918-1920 in medical debate").[14] John Barry's "The Great Influenza: The Epic Story of the Deadliest Plague in History" from 2004 also focuses on the history of medicine.[15] The edited volume of Walter Haas *Influenza: Prävention, Diagnostik, Therapie und öffentliche Gesundheit* ("Influenza: prevention, diagnostics, therapy, and public health")[16] of 2009 is based on a thorough historiographical account of the Spanish flu. Heiner Fangerau elaborated on the "forgotten pandemic" from a perspective of public health systems and medical as well as scientific debates.[17] Robert G. Webster's edited volume, *Flu Hunter: Unlocking the Secrets of a Virus,*[18] from 2019 traces the history of the H1N1 virus throughout the twentieth and twenty-first centuries. Also, the bibliography of epidemics in the German language by Heiner Fangerau, Ulrich Koppitz, and Alfons Labisch,[19] as well as its English counterpart composed by Mark Honigsbaum,[20] show that the economic impact of natural disasters and pandemics has been visited and revisited many times in the context of the Spanish flu. To name one example of the studies that are aggregated here: Marco Percoco investigated the impact of the Spanish flu on human capital accumulation in Italian regions in "Health Shocks and Human Capital"[21] in 2015.

In the early 2000s, a certain rediscovery of the topic from a historical perspective can be noted. Publications like Howard Philips and David Killingray's *The Spanish Influenza Pandemic of 1918-19: New Perspectives*[22] and Gina Kolata's *Influenza. Die Jagd nach dem Virus* ("Influenza: the hunt for the virus")[23] were both published in 2001. Kirsty E. Duncan's *Hunting the 1918 Flu*[24] and Marc Hieronimus' *Krankheit und Tod 1918: Zum Umgang mit der Spanischen Grippe in Frankreich, England und dem Deutschen Reich* ("Sickness and death 1918: on the handling of the Spanish flu in France, England, and the German Reich")[25] came out in 2006. Wilfried Witte's *Tollkirschen und die Quarantäne* ("Belladonna and quarantine")[26] from the year 2008 as well as the volume edited by M. Isabel Porras Gallo and Ryan A. Davis, *The Spanish Influenza Pandemic of 1918-1919*,[27] from 2014 are among the publications that show a revisiting of the episode. This increased interest was also discussed by one of the pioneering medical historians, Howard Philips, in his essay "The Recent Wave of 'Spanish' Flu Historiography"[28] in 2014. In the wake of the one hundredth anniversary of the pandemic in 2018, Laura Spinney published her well researched *Pale Rider: The Spanish Flu of 1918 and How it Changed the World*,[29] which justly received high praise in several reviews. Catharina Arnold published *Pandemic 1918: Eyewitness Accounts from the Greatest Medical Holocaust in Modern History*,[30] which gained special attention in 2020 due to its focus on the voices from the past during the newly evolving worldwide health crisis.

Just as the history of medicine and public health experienced an upswing ever since the early 2000s, so did publications on the history of epidemics and consequently those also covering the Spanish flu, as Fangerau's and Honigbaum's bibliographies show.[31] Manfred Vasold reprinted his overview of the epidemics in Europe *Grippe, Pest und Cholera* ("Flu, plague, and cholera")[32] in 2009. 2014 saw several important publications: Malte Thiessen analyzed epidemics in Europe during the "long twentieth century" in his book *Infiziertes Europa* ("Infected Europe"),[33] Howard Philips published an account of epidemics in Africa in *Epidemics: The Story of South Africa's Five Most Lethal Human Diseases*,[34] and Mark Jerome Walters wrote about "Seven Modern Plagues: And How We Are Causing Them."[35] Finally, Judy Dodge Cummings' book, *Epidemics and Pandemics: Real Tales of Deadly Diseases*,[36] came out in 2018.

Another important context for the historiography of the Spanish flu is World War I. Peter Wilton's short essay, "Spanish Flu Outdid WWI in Number of Lives Claimed," from 1993 increased awareness of the influence the flu might have had on the outcomes of the peace negotiations in Versailles, since American president Woodrow Wilson became sick in Paris. As Wilton summarized, "[t]he flu left Wilson in a weakened physical and mental state that had a direct bearing on the final form that the flawed peace treaty took."[37] The 1990s were also the years where autopsies and the gathering of forensic evidence in the graveyards of World War I became popular. While by 1990 research had not been able to answer the question of why the pandemic in the

Fall of 1918 was so devastating, in 1995 a research team was able to identify the original H1N1 virus in graveyards all over the world.[38] Since then, the intertwining of the history of the Spanish flu and World War I has been constant.

Research in this context gained traction in the wake of the centenary of the outbreak of World War I. In 2009, Manfred Vasold published *Die Spanische Grippe: Die Seuche und der Erste Weltkrieg* ("The Spanish flu: the epidemic and World War I").[39] In the essay "'Das Sterben will nicht enden.' Die 'Spanische Grippe-Epidemie' 1918/19 in der Schweizer Armee," ("'Dying that doesn't end': The Spanish flu epidemic 1918/19 in the Swiss army")[40] Armin Rusterholz in 2010 wrote about the difficulties of the army in Switzerland, and in 2013 Frieder Bauer and Jörg Vögele published their article "Die 'Spanische Grippe' in der Deutschen Armee" ("The 'Spanish flu' in the German army")[41] about the same issue in the German army. Mark Osborn Humphries traced the beginning of the flu in 2014 in "Paths of Infection: The First World War and the Origins of the 1918 Influenza Pandemic."[42] In 2018's "Concurrent Conflicts: The Great War and the 1918 Influenza Pandemic,"[43] Terence Chorba and Byron Breedlove discussed the overlapping of the two crises at the war's end. A year later, Craig Molgaard analyzed military records for his study, "Military Vital Statistics: The Spanish Flu and the First World War."[44]

To narrow down the historiographic output to what was to become Austria after World War I, it must be stated that an overall study on the Spanish flu in the Habsburg Empire is still outstanding. One fact, however, is well known and is being cited in many studies of the time. With Egon Schiele, world famous artist, the Spanish flu here claimed a prominent victim.[45] Only in the wake of Covid-19, in 2022, an overall study entitled *Pandemie sei Dank! Was Seuchen in Österreich bewegten* ("Thanks to the pandemic! What epidemics brought about in Austria")[46] on epidemics in Austria that included the Spanish flu was submitted by Daniela Angetter-Pfeiffer. Apart from this, most historical analysis in Austria were regional studies, for example Thomas Hörzer's and Ursula Kunze's analysis of Styria,[47] Margit Craß of the Burgenland,[48] Wolfgang Scheffknecht's[49] and Michael Kasper's[50] of Vorarlberg, and Michael Forcher's chapter on the Spanish flu in Tyrol.[51] Some, like Kasper's and the special edition of the *Tiroler Chronist* no. 154 of 2020 dedicated to "*COV-19, Pandemien & Epidemien in Tirol*" ("COV-19, pandemics & epidemics in Tyrol"), which contained an essay by Sarah Oberbichler, Stefan Hechl, and Eva Pfanzelter on the press reporting on the Spanish flu in Austria,[52] were written during the Covid-19 pandemic.

Indeed, the Covid-19 pandemic was the reason for a renewed interest in the Spanish flu (and other epidemics) from a historical point of view in Austria. This can be seen in university theses and dissertations that came into being over the past years. For example, in 2022 in Vienna, Florian Seidl finished a master-thesis with a study on "Pandemie in Wien. Die Spanische Grippe in Sterbematriken des 23. Bezirks" ("Pandemic in Vienna: the Spanish flu in death records of the twenty-third district).[53] In Innsbruck, Kathrin Weger wrote her diploma-thesis on "Die Spanische Grippe im Ersten Weltkrieg in Innsbruck" ("The Spanish flu in World War I in Innsbruck")[54] and Martina Maria Sonderegger focussed her master-thesis on "Pandemieberichterstattung im Wandel der Zeit" ("Pandemic reporting over time").[55]

Increased attention can also be noted in a peak in academic publications. Harald Salfellner *Die Spanische Grippe: Eine Geschichte der Pandemie von 1918* ("The Spanish flu: a history of the pandemic of 1918")[56] was re-published in 2021. That year indeed saw a striking number of publications. In addition to those already mentioned, the following can be named: Mark Honigbaum *Das Jahrhundert der Pandemien* ("The century of pandemics")[57], Patric Vogel and Günter Schaub *Seuchen, alte und neue Gefahren* ("Epidemics: old and new dangers")[58] and the essay of Michael Kaspar "Die Spanische Grippe 1918/19 im Montafon" ("The Spanish flu 1918/19 in the Montafon").[59]

To summarize, the academic production on the Spanish flu is remarkable, and it is therefore somewhat inconsistent to term the Spanish flu as the forgotten pandemic. Still, it certainly true that this specific pandemic has not entered graveyards or memorial culture as a singularly outstanding event. The reason for this is certainly World War I, which had been going on for four years and had dominated—and continued to dominate—world news despite the emergence of the Spanish flu.

The Spanish Flu in Media Coverage

Historical accounts of earlier pandemics can give important insights into various aspects of disease transmission and development, public health measures, or vulnerabilities of societies. But oftentimes, adequate source material is difficult to obtain, especially if information beyond official administrative documentation is sought. This, however, is needed when investigating public perception of events, and this is why historians turn to newspapers when trying to grasp public opinion. With every new epidemic or pandemic since the middle of the nineteenth century, media coverage lies at the heart of the flow of information from administrative units to the public. Media outlets report on (official) numbers, ordinances, measures to contain the disease, lockdowns, rumors, remedies, and many other challenges that come up with exceptional public health situations. During the 1918/19 pandemic, newspapers were the only media available to a large public. Still, in Europe and especially in

Germany and the Habsburg Empire, newspapers were censored and media coverage hampered because of the ongoing war. Hence, as Laura Spinney argued, in Europe the flu remains to be seen as a "footnote of World War I,"[60] and this can also be noted in newspaper reporting.

Gaining an overall view of the content of newspaper reporting on the Spanish flu is not easy. This is because, next to censorship, news coverage can spread over articles, statistics, images, obituaries, and the advertising pages. To find out what is being reported on, newspaper research has to deal with methodological challenges. In the past, evaluation of news was usually done manually, originating in qualitative analysis of smaller samples of newspapers. For example, James Derek Shidler chose such an approach in his paper on "A Tale of Two Cities: The 1918 Influenza,"[61] where he compared the news coverage of the Spanish flu in the two local newspapers of the towns Mattoon and Charleston in Illinois, USA. Although lying only ten miles apart, the cities' papers, the *Charleston Courier* and the *Mattoon Journal-Gazette*, reported quite differently on the disease and sometimes came to opposing recommendations on how to behave. Similarly, Ivona Jelčić and Matthias Breit collected news, comments, and advertisements from the *Allgemeinen Tiroler Anzeiger*[62] from November 1918 showing the wide variety of news articles on soldiers, the Spanish flu, and the new Austrian republic. Also, Martina Maria Sonderegger in 2022 analyzed the Swiss *Neue Züricher Zeitung* focusing on a smaller sample of news data.[63] Equally, in the absence of an overall study of the Spanish flu in the Habsburg Empire, Herwig Czech's re-visiting of the period focused on a qualitative analysis of news of the time.[64]

One of the first studies using digital quantitative methods in newspaper reporting about the Spanish flu was written about by E. Thomas Ewing, Samah Gad, and Naren Ramakrishnan in "Gaining Insight into Epidemics by Mining Historical Newspapers" in 2013.[65] Using data mining and network analysis methods, they studied the *New York Herald Tribune* and some smaller newspapers and gazettes to investigate how "extensive newspaper reporting paved the way for public acceptance of stringent, and only partially effective, countermeasures."[66] Using automated computer analysis they were able to show that authorities reacted to increasing media coverage with restrictive measures like banning gatherings and closing down schools.[67]

In 2020, Sarah Oberbichler, Stefan Hechl, and Eva Pfanzelter[68] used similar automated methods analyzing the digital historical newspaper collection available through ANNO, the digital newspaper portal of the Austrian National Library, ÖNB.[69] We worked with a subset of the ANNO collection and applied a more novel tools and methods set that was being developed within the Horizon-2020 project "NewsEye."[70] Using both qualitative and quantitative approaches, the study brought to light interesting, curious, and well known facts and made us reconsider the seemingly new challenges of the Covid-19 pandemic.[71]

The following pages will elaborate on some of the findings of that study but will also include additional research into news reporting of the time in Austrian newspapers.

Methodology: Research in the Digital Newspaper Collection ANNO

It should be stressed once more that news coverage on the Spanish flu in the Habsburg Empire (or Austria) coincided with the last, devastating months of World War I. Media reporting was therefore mainly focused on military and political events and newspapers were strictly censored by the authorities. This went so far as to result in white columns in the papers, where last minute interventions of the government forced the editors to eliminate paragraphs or entire articles by leaving spaces blank, as the example from the *Allgemeine Tiroler Anzeiger* in Figure 1 shows.[72]

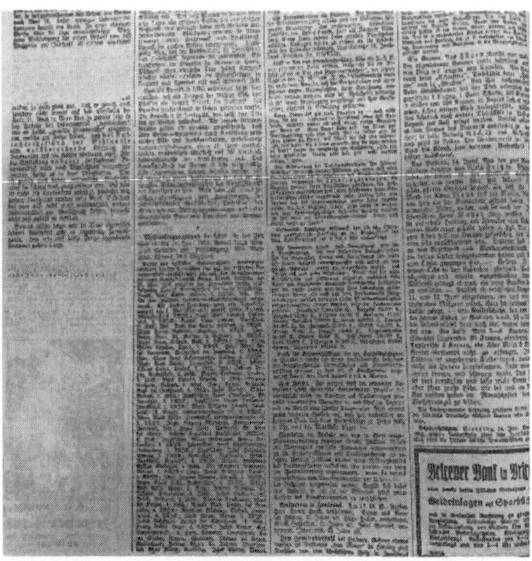

FIGURE 1: Allgemeiner Tiroler Anzeiger, June 15, 1918, 4.
On the right column, this particular newspaper reported on the "Spanish disease" in Tirol for the first time.

In the historical newspaper collection, ANNO media coverage of the Spanish flu is observable especially for the first two waves of the disease. For this period, the Spanish flu is rather easy to research. The keyword combinations "Spanish" with "disease" or "flu" (the German words "*spanisch,*" "*krankheit,*" and "*grippe*" and very rarely "*kripp,*" which is an old German variant of the term "*grippe*"/"flu") yield over 1,000 results for the period between 1917 and 1920. To extend the findings and eliminate unknown variants, the team also checked the respective Wikipedia article[73] and the "NewsEye" keyword suggestion tool, which extracts similar word usages in the corpus of newspapers uploaded to its platform, as well as the newspaper coverage in the "impresso" platform, which mainly consists of German and Swiss newspapers.[74] The contemporary word usage brought about additional findings, e.g., "Spanish influenza" and, as mentioned before, "*Spanische Kripp.*" All in all, 1,352 news articles on the Spanish flu were found.

As Figure 2 shows, a diachronic quantitative analysis of the terms between 1918 and 1919 indicates that newspapers started reporting on the flu in the third quarter of 1918, during the first wave, and peaked during the second, deadly wave in the fourth quarter of that year. During the first quarter of 1919 with the third, milder wave ongoing, only few newspaper articles could be found.

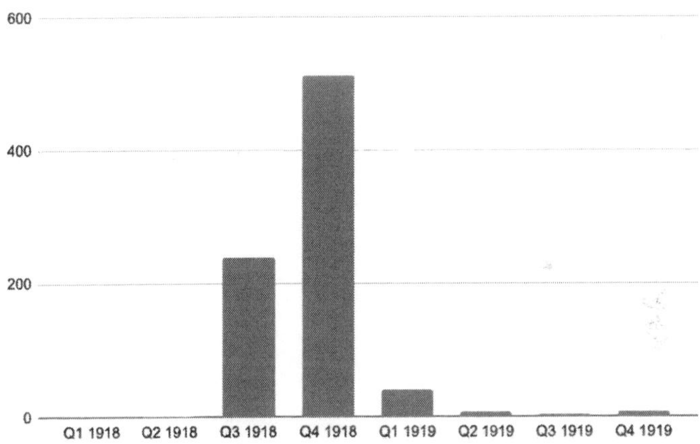

FIGURE 2: Chronological distribution of search results for "Spanish flu" in 1918 and 1919 (absolute frequencies, i.e., it is not taken into account whether after the war's end in the fourth quarter of 1918 more newspapers may have simply been published).

A search in the "NewsEye" platform, in which only four German-language newspapers were available, albeit with better text and formatting quality and an advanced tool repertoire, mirrors this result for the same period (see Figure 3). Since here the analysis is more granular, it can be observed that, in October 1918, the newspapers wrote about the disease on a daily basis and sometimes more than once per day.

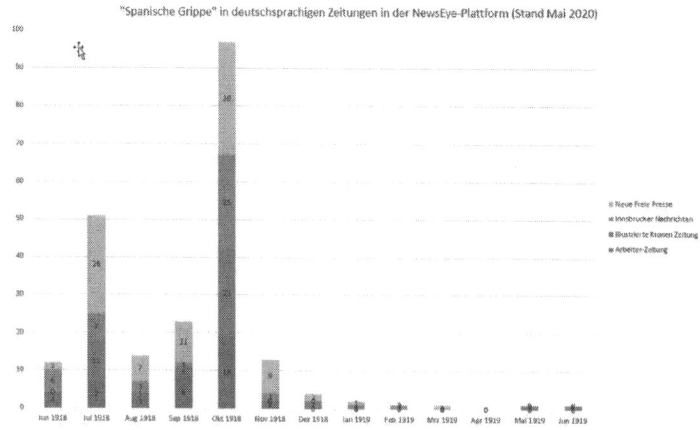

FIGURE 3: Chronological distribution of search results for "Spanish flu" from June 1918 to June 1919 in the dailies covered by "NewsEye" (absolute frequencies).

This automated evaluation was confirmed by a manual analysis of the *Allgemeine Tiroler Anzeiger* of October 1918, which reported on the pandemic in every issue (although it was not published every day) usually in the section "*Aus Stadt und Land*" ("From town and country") on page two or page four. Here the disease was also reflected in the obituaries that tell us of many deaths at a young age within a very short period, with the subjects having been sick or suffering from a fatal illness.[75]

One of the questions that historians are often interested in when investigating topics in media is the search for the first mention of a term. Stephane Dufoix called this the "religion of first appearance" in 2011 (translated 2017).[76] In the Austrian press, we find the first mention of the pandemic on May 29, 1918, in the *Deutsches Volksblatt*,[77] where the headline "Spanish disease" reported on a "mysterious intestinal inflammation" spreading in Spain, affecting the Spanish royal family and political representatives, and preventing theater performances and even church attendance. That same day the *Neues Wiener Tagblatt*[78] also brought a short article speculating about an influenza epidemic that had infected the Spanish family and which most likely was a variant of a well-known spring cold of previous years. Interestingly, such attempts to compare the outbreak with medical incidents in the past were soon frequent, as an article in the *Innsbrucker Nachrichten*[79] of June 14, 1918, shows. Here it was speculated that this "Spanish disease" had already occurred fifty years earlier in Tyrol.

To get a rough overview of a specific theme or topic, tracking the occurrence of keywords in a digital collection is usually sufficient. It allows users to select articles on the results page and read them or analyze them qualitatively. For more detailed analysis, however, there are additional ways to narrow down the search results. It is possible to focus on a time period or a specific newspaper and to limit the search geographically. The so-called distance search allows to search for a combined occurrence of several terms close to each other. For example, the combination of words in the phrase "flu school"~10 ("*grippe schule*"~10) induces the system to search for text passages in which the words "flu" and "school" occur within 10 words. In this way, one can approach certain aspects of the pandemic thematically—provided, of course, that the search terms are well chosen.

For more complex analyses, however, the application of automated analysis and deep learning or artificial intelligence is needed to help researchers, but also interested laypersons, to cope with sometimes incredibly large amounts of data. Projects like "NewsEye" or "impresso" address the gap between close reading of smaller amounts of articles by individual readers and a quantitative textual analysis of "big data" that need expert knowledge to handle the data. Beyond these projects, there exist tools and methods in the realm of so-called data mining that help researchers from non-computational fields to use digital research methods to some extent. To get an insight into what users can get out of analyzing their data with such platforms and tools, the following pages will include analysis conducted with Voyant Tools[80] and the Orange Data Mining[81] Suite.

The distance search conducted on the ANNO corpus as mentioned above brought eighty-eight relevant articles combining the "flu" with "school" to light. A closer look at these roughly ninety articles reveals the proximity of schools being hit by the pandemic and the closing of them.[82] For example, already in July 1918, the *Innsbrucker Nachrichten*[83] reported on an increasing occurrence of the "epidemic Spanish flu" in the Swiss army that had authorities consider the closing down of schools. An article in the Austrian *Neue Freie Presse* dated September 20 indicated that it was especially in Hungarian schools where a rapid rise of the flu was reported. Some classes had to be closed because so many pupils were ill.[84] At the same time, in Vienna, the closure of entire schools was a daily occurrence in September and October of that year, and there is a substantial number of articles reporting on this.

It is interesting to note that the tone of the news articles changes between July and the end of November 1918. While at first the newspapers downplayed the fatality of the flu, communicating that there was nothing to worry about, by the second week of October, the tone was panicky, with recurring articles about children and very young adults dying from the disease. Overall, a clear shift from a prevalent fearful emotion in July to a predominant feeling of sadness can be noted in this small collection of articles.[85]

Moving away from the distant look at the reporting on the Spanish flu in the ANNO collection, the following sections will address some of the more important discourses that can be found in the pre-selected roughly 300 newspaper articles that we found and processed in the "NewsEye" platform.

An Old, Mild, Infectious Cold or Toxic Chemical Weapons Abroad

We can learn from history that events never play out identically. It is therefore interesting to note that in newspapers reactions, linguistic patterns, discussions, and argumentations seem to repeat themselves when events are resembling each other. When digging into the reporting on the Spanish flu, for example, some similarities with the discourses during the Covid-19 pandemic came to light.

FIGURE 4: A simple visualization of the most common words in daily newspapers in "NewsEye" with Voyant Tools (Cirrus word cloud). In comparison: left June/August, right September/November 1918.

A quantitative analysis of the articles located in the "NewsEye" platform reveals that different things were talked about during the first wave and the second wave (see Figure 4). In the (early) summer of 1918, the disease originally prevalent in Spain is depicted as something "foreign": Berlin, Spain, Germany, Paris, and other foreign cities appear most frequently in the articles. Also, the spreading of the disease in Paris increased daily. On July 1, 1918, the *Neue Freie Presse* spoke of the influenza epidemic that had been imported from the western front where it had infected soldiers from both fighting powers from Dunkirk to the Vosges.[86] Under the headline "See that you move on, you don't have a passport" a caricature of "Señora Influenza" highlights this "foreign character" of the flu. It even made it to the front page of the *Illustrierte Kronen Zeitung*[87] on July 3 (Figure 5).

FIGURE 5: "Illustrierte Kronen Zeitung," July 3, 1918, page 1.

There is talk of increasing numbers of sick people, and some reference is made to the first Austrian cases. However, according to the rather uniform tenor of the domestic press, the disease has a rather benign course and recovery is rapid. Local newspapers underline that "[t]here is not the slightest cause for concern."[88] In Germany, however, there were larger numbers of cases, specifically in factories and other workplaces with crowds of people. In Munich, the disease, while nothing more than an influenza, can be called an epidemic, the *Illustrierte Kronen Zeitung* reported. Workers in industrial facilities and tramways were especially infected in high numbers. In the telephone exchange, the number of sick employees was so high that the continuation of its services was threatened.[89]

By July the epidemic had, however, also reached Austria, and the uncertainty had increased enough for newspapers to try to get exact information. The *Illustrierte Kronen Zeitung*[90] made an inquiry at the Vienna city physics and was thereafter able to calm the public: it was not impossible that the Spanish flu had reached the capital, since an increasing number of notifications about an influenza illness had been registered. It could, however, not be excluded that the rise in cases had to do with the weather and was therefore nothing out of the ordinary. In any case, the notified flu cases did not give "the slightest cause for concern." Still, it was worth a note that the Empress had recovered from the influenza although she seemed fragile even after several days.[91]

As far as the origin of the epidemic is concerned, there was a lot of speculation, especially at the beginning. On June 28, 1918, the *Innsbrucker Nachrichten*[92] quoted an article in the French newspaper *L'Œuvre* in which the question had been raised whether the epidemic in Paris was in fact the flu imported from Spain or in truth the effects of German poison gas attacks on the Western Front. Equally, it was a common theme in the newspaper articles to downplay the newness of the Spanish flu. Some journalists found evidence of previous outbreaks of this specific infection, e.g., in influenza epidemics in Asia in 1889.[93] Others saw similarities both in the name and the symptoms in the influenza that had come from Russia, which spread over most of the European mainland and showed itself especially persistent in East and West Prussia in 1775. Here it had induced famous writers of the time, such as G. Chr. Lichtenberg and Immanuel Kant, to address it in their writings.[94] These speculations continued throughout the year and proved persistent even during the second, more deadly wave in the fall. The *Innsbrucker Nachrichten*[95] identified the new illness to be the same as the "*Katharrfieber*" ("Cathartic fever") of 1729 and the "*russiche Krankheit*" ("Russian disease") of 1782. It had resurged in May 1833 and a fourth time in 1857. The last time it had been endemic was at the end of 1889, beginning of 1890, when it had been named Influenza for the first time. Overall, the article summarized, it was always a mild cold that was much less fatal than the recurring cholera epidemics of the past.

In any case, despite the newspaper's predictions, the Spanish flu did not vanish over the summer. On the contrary, at the end of August, numerous cases were reported from regions south of the Brenner Pass[96] and gradually similar accounts came from Vorarlberg,[97] Carinthia,[98] and other parts of the country.

At this point, the mood also changed in the press and the seriousness of the situation was dramatically conveyed. By September 1918, the situation had clearly shifted. The epidemic had arrived in Austria; schools, theaters, cinemas, and sporting facilities were closed; people fell ill by the hundreds, and many deaths were recorded.

Old Enemies and New Remedies

With almost every pandemic in historical retrospect, we can observe some continuities: accusations and the search for those responsible are a constant part of media discourses in crisis situations. Uncertainty, powerlessness, and traditional stereotyping, as well as shaky social fabric, led to a search for supposedly "easy" solutions or culprits for social inequality that becomes evident. These discourses have long been accompanied by banal antisemitism. A look at historical newspaper holdings shows that crude antisemitic rhetoric has been present in "traditional" press reporting, and it was extremely popular especially during the first decades of the twentieth century. For example, the *Wiener*

Sonn- und Montags-Zeitung[99] somewhat ironically reported on the many "faults" of the Jews, among which the Spanish flu competes with the war and food shortages for which they are made responsible. Political debates to blame Jews for the flu led to sometimes heated discussions, as the news reports.[100]

In any case, in the fall of 1918, although the final phase of the World War and the conditions of peace remained on the front pages of Austrian newspapers, now reports on the epidemic became a daily occurrence. It becomes evident, that people, despite continuous reassurances by the governments and the press, no longer believed the calming and soothing narratives.[101] Articles about taking the disease seriously and not to dismiss it as a rumor became more frequent. The tone of the reporting can be seen in an article from October 7, 1918, where the Viennese morning paper *Der Morgen*[102] reported in detail about school closures, quarantine measures, and the isolation of patients:

> This week, Vienna has for the first time come closer to the Spanish flu with scientific and prophylactic honors. Following the example of Budapest, it is beginning to develop from a harmless epidemic of headaches and colds into an epidemic requiring sacrifices and leading to heart and lung infections. Questions of isolation of the sick, temporary closure of schools, quarantine for travelers were discussed at the city physics. Doctors and professors took part in this public discussion. Newspapers cease to treat the flu as a malicious domestic political or strategic enemy rumor, intended to harm public moral, that is best nipped in the bud of appeasing small print.[103]

Likewise, frequent reports of casualty figures at home and abroad, as well as of measures taken to stop or slow down the spread of the epidemic, can now be found. In Vienna, the Ministry of Health estimated that up to 100,000 people had fallen ill with influenza, reported the *Innsbrucker Nachrichten*[104] on October 20, 1918. At this point, news of the epidemic made it to the front pages of the Austrian press.

Measures to contain the spread of the disease were now a daily topic. There was talk of isolating the sick, curfew, and confinement to barracks and homes; bans on public gatherings, disinfection measures, and overall social restrictions were announced. These measures were unknown to the public even during past deadly cholera epidemics, as the *Innsbrucker Nachrichten*[105] phrased it at the beginning of October.[106] Another important measure mentioned was the closure of cultural institutions, theatres, cinemas, and places of sport and entertainment.[107]

The *Neue Freie Presse*[108] of October 2, 1918, took up yet other restraints that seemed necessary. For example, the question of border closures to contain the spread of the disease was raised mockingly:

> Now, however, it gradually became apparent that the Spanish influenza, with a most unlawful indifference towards border regulations and entry bans, was vaulting over all barriers and passport constraints, claiming a freedom of movement for itself, as it probably had commonly existed in mythically pondered peace times, but has completely disappeared from our weapon-clashing present . . . . But there are still skeptics who doubt its originality and, despite its foreign garment, simply declare it as a persistent cold . . . . At most, it is announced as a pesky influenza, only more alarming and annoying, because, due to our current nutritional conditions, we are all not equipped to receive guests, least of all that suspicious and dangerous guest from Spain.[109]

Soon, newspapers also started reporting and speculating about remedies, as well as appropriate behavior to best treat the symptoms and prevent the deterioration of health. Already during the first wave in the spring and summer of 1918, doctors prescribed bed rest as the only necessary and effective treatment, and quinine, which had been used for feverish diseases for some time, in severe cases.[110] By October, the recommendations sounded quite different. Now severe pneumonias were feared because they led to many deaths. Patients should be separated from the rest of the household, kept on strict bed rest, and receive sweat inducing remedies such as elderflower or "Russian tea" (black tea) in combination with cross-packs (warm, wet compresses).[111] Feverish people should furthermore receive immediate medical assistance, and military authorities announced hospital confinement for sick soldiers.[112]

In addition, of course, there were recommendations to take various medications, most of which contained dubious ingredients and were expensive. Along with the advice to sing arias, expensive drugs without active ingredients were sold and novel serums were offered.[113] A Viennese clinician recommended for his patients a daily disinfection of the nasopharynx and oral cavity with "small quantities of finely powdered boric acid…, possible rinsing of the nasal cavity with a solution of boric acid or salicylic acid or introduction of small quantities of a menthol salicylic ointment into the nose, rinsing of the oral cavity and gargling with boric acid water and weak hypermanganese solutions."[114] "*Mundwasser* 555" ("mouthwash 555") was the "most effective and best remedy"[115] against the Spanish flu and whoever took "*Anacotpastillen*,"[116] throat tablets made from formaldehyde, menthol, and citric acid, could protect themselves from infection.

Despite these effective and imaginative recommendations, the spread of Spanish flu in Austria could not be prevented. Soon the hospitals were overcrowded and the cemeteries full of the newly deceased. Despite the scale of the outbreak, the Ministry of Health could not bring itself to impose mandatory notifications, which would have facilitated the isolation of sick people. Authorities argued that the Spanish flu was difficult to distinguish from other common colds and that targeted isolation of those with the new disease therefore seemed impossible.[117] The lack of mandatory reporting, however, ultimately also made it impossible to provide precise figures on the number of infections and deaths.[118]

Overwhelmed Health Care Systems and Social Reactions

Measures against the spread of diseases often lead to major interventions in public life or even in personal freedoms. As shown above, during the Spanish flu several actions were taken to prevent the spread of the virus, like isolation, confinement, curfew, prohibition of public gatherings, disinfection, and other social constraints. Despite these attempts to contain the spread of the illness, the health care systems were soon overwhelmed. Already in July,[119] newspapers reported on the strain on health insurance companies caused by the war and now also by the Spanish disease. The combined challenges raised fears of an increase in expenditure on sick payments, doctors' fees, and the cost of drugs.

By October, such worries seemed trivial. Health authorities in Vienna, for example, were able to arrange additional 700 hospital beds by closely collaborating with the military hospitals. Although a lot more beds were needed, care institutions and doctors warned against them because there were not enough personnel to care for the sick. Doctors and nurses were still tied up in military hospitals, or they became sick or died themselves.[120] Other worries were phrased by overwhelmed pharmacies. Apothecaries had worked for four years understaffed and with limited supplies, but, as the director of the Board of Pharmacists complained, the flu had quadrupled the working hours and multiplied the difficulties. Often it was impossible to dispatch the prescriptions in a reasonable amount of time, and clients had to wait many hours.[121]

This dramatic situation was also a result of the hoarding of chemical substances.[122] Aspirin was an especially desirable ingredient and had it not been for a generous delivery from Germany, by the second half of October the situation would have been dire indeed. As a report in the *Neue Freie Presse*[123] explained:

At first, aspirin hoarders ran up and down the street. Aspirin and

> aspirin substitutes gradually disappeared from pharmacies. In the meantime, however, the contrabandists were not idle and today we have happily made it so far that a tablet of aspirin is offered and also paid for on the black market with only a crown. Councilor Doctor Löwenstein will draw the mayor's attention to this regrettable mischief at the municipal council meeting to be held on Friday.[124]

Social reactions to the crisis, such as the hoarding of food, medicines, or hygiene articles, were therefore not only the result of the shortages due to the war but also because of the increased need for these articles during the epidemic.

Conclusion

As the paragraphs above show, many discourses prevalent in the Austrian press re-emerged a hundred years later during the recent health crisis. Other reactions to the pandemic were also not new: critique of governments, measures, doctors, and compatriots was a common outlet for the frustrations caused by the damages of war and disease. For example, one letter to the editor writer pronounced: "I want to emphasize at the outset that science is pretty powerless against an influenza epidemic"; and another opined, "I consider the closure of schools and even theaters to be completely unnecessary. The whole social life would have to be reduced if we wanted to prevent the epidemic from spreading."[125]

Yet another one condescended to write a long letter:

> Now you have to become a hypochondriac, whether you want to or not. Wherever one goes, one hears only variations of the one vexed topic, the flu, which has become a food substitute, so to speak, because it has completely supplanted the four-year lasting conversation about eating. However, in addition to the thousands of unfortunates who are afflicted with flu, there are many more fellow human beings who suffer from flu fear. You can recognize them by the fearful, shy posture with which they appear, by the mistrust with which they regard anyone who blows his nose or clears his throat in their vicinity. Their main occupation and purpose in life now is prophylaxis, and all day they long they speculate about the question: How do I behave and what do I do to prevent the flu? ... But that is by no means all. To be on the safe side, you have to counteract the threat of illness in advance with aspirin. It is now

> time to have aspirin-connections. Until now, you only had to curry for butter, cheese, cigarettes, now we are lucky enough to have to procure medications by trickery and backhanded favoritism.[126]

On the other hand, the doubt arises, if "this closure-idea does not in the end also represent one of those excellent ideas for which our old Austria, of course before it was still a federal state, was always too late."[127]

Ultimately, one of the reasons why the Spanish flu was so deadly all over the world was that the pathogen that caused the illness was unknown at the time—and this is also one of the major differences from epidemics of later times. At the beginning of the twentieth century, viruses were yet unknown and therefore inoculation was not even an option. Until the fall of 1918, more or less well known physicians repeatedly claimed to have found the bacterium or bacillus that caused the Spanish flu. One doctor claimed to have identified the "*Genickstarrebazillus*" ("stiff-neck bazillus," which would be meningitis)[128] "with one hundred percent certainty" as the cause of the disease. Another made the same "indubitable" claim about the "*Bazillus der Beulenpest*" (the bazillus of the "bubonic plague")[129]; yet another recognized the "*Influenza-Bazillus,*"[130] and also the "*Pneubazillus Friedländer,*"[131] which did ultimately not make it into the medical books, was found.

It is therefore all the more astonishing that on October 15, 1918,[132] the news of two French doctors, Nicolle and Lebuilly, having identified a virus as the originator of the Spanish flu circulated widely. In fact, up until today the first isolation of human influenza viruses after experimental transmission is attributed to Charle-Jules-Henri Nicolle, a French physician, philosopher and historian,[133] and his colleague C. Lebailly, who had announced their findings to medical societies in France on September 1, 1918. Despite equivocal results and semi-successful inoculation test throughout the fall 1918 and winter 1919, a cautious hope began to spread among doctors. With the influenza becoming a manageable winter disease after that, research stopped, and it took another decade before the virus could finally be identified unequivocally.[134]

There are thus many similarities between historical and current reporting, although there are of course many differences. These lie in the completely different social, economic, and, above all, medical conditions, which make the situation in 1918 and 2020 hardly comparable. The media coverage, however, is strikingly similar—regardless of whether we are talking about the censored state press of the Austro-Hungarian monarchy or unbridled speculation on the (social) media of the twenty-first century. In a way, reading these reports about an epidemic that is over a hundred years old gives us a familiar feeling and shows us that we are not in an "unprecedented situation" after all.

Endnotes

1. The term Spanish flu comes from its contemporary use. While the spread of the H1N1-virus that caused severe respiratory symptoms was downplayed for several months, it became then well know because in 1918 it affected several members of the Spanish royal family severely. By then the flu had already spread worldwide, and we know now that its most likely origin was in Kansas, USA (although also other convincing theories abouts its provenance exist). However, due to its usage at the time, the "Spanish flu" or "Spanish disease" became the most used synonyms for this disease.

2. Jeffrey K. Taubenberger and David M. Morens, "1918 Influenza: The Mother of all Pandemics," *Emerging Infectious Diseases* 12, no. 1 (2006): 15–22, https://doi.org/10.3201/eid1201.050979.

3. Laura Spinney, *Pale Rider: The Spanish Flu of 1918 and How It Changed the World* (New York: Public Affairs, 2017), 2.

4. Ibid.

5. George F. Kennan, *The Decline of Bismarck's European Order: Franco-Russian Relations, 1875–1890* (Princeton: Princeton University Press, 1979), 3.

6. Richard Collier, *The Plague of the Spanish Lady: The Influenza Pandemic of 1918–1919* (London: Collier, 1974).

7. R. Z. Sheppard, "Books: Pale Horse, Pale Rider: The Plague of the Spanish Lady by Richard Collier," *TIME Magazine*, Jan. 20, 1975, 72.

8. Alfred W. Crosby, *America's Forgotten Pandemic: The Influenza of 1918*, 2nd ed. (Cambridge, UK: Cambridge University Press, 2003).

9. Maria L. Lima and José M. Sobral, "Threat and Oblivion: Interpreting the Silence Over the Spanish Flu (1918–19)," in *Societies Under Threat: A Pluri-Disciplinary Approach*, Frontiers in Sociology and Social Research 3, ed. Denise Jodelet et al. (Cham: Springer, 2020), 187–199.

10. Herwig Czech, "Die Spanische Grippe von 1918: Blick auf eine lange vergessene Pandemie," in: *Corona und die Welt von Gestern*, ed. Manfried Rauchensteiner and Michael Gehler (Vienna: Böhlau Verlag, 2021), S. 23–46.

11. Simon Heffe, "Never Forgotten? Why the Spanish Flu Has No Memorials," *Sunday Telegraph*, Jan. 31, 2021.

12. Guy Beiner, *Pandemic Re-Awakenings: The Forgotten and Unforgotten 'Spanish' Flu of 1918–1919* (Oxford: Oxford University Press, 2022),

https://ebookcentral.proquest.com/lib/kxp/detail.action?docID=6811556.

13. Czech, "Die Spanische Grippe von 1918," 23–4.

14. Wilfried Witte, "Die Grippe-Pandemie 1918–20 in der medizinischen Debatte," *Berichte zur Wissenschaftsgeschichte* 29, no. 1 (2006): 5–20, https://doi.org/10.1002/bewi.200501184.

15. John M. Barry, *The Great Influenza: The Epic Story of the Deadliest Plague in History* (New York: Viking, 2004).

16. Walter Haas, ed., *Influenza: Prävention, Diagnostik, Therapie und öffentliche Gesundheit* (Munich: Elsevier, Urban & Fischer, 2009).

17. Heiner Fangerau, "Zu Paläopathologie und Geschichte der Medizin: Das Beispiel der Influenzapandemie," *Der Urologe* 49, no. 11 (2010): 1406–10, https://doi.org/10.1007/s00120-010-2435-0.

18. Robert G. Webster, *Flu Hunter: Unlocking the Secrets of a Virus* (Chicago: Otago University Press, 2019), https://ebookcentral.proquest.com/lib/kxp/detail.action?docID=5651791.

19. Heiner Fangerau et al., *Seuchengeschichte in deutscher Sprache: eine Bibliographie (ca. 1866–2021)* (CERN, Genf, 2022), https://doi.org/10.5281/zenodo.7078506.

20. Mark Honigsbaum, "Influenza: Bibliographic Review," *IsisCB Special Issue* (2021), accessed Jan. 10, 2023, https://drive.google.com/file/d/1tCvh8W86CM0pxt1C6p4Limqo5Uaxv8BK/view?usp=sharing.

21. Marco Percoco, "Health Shocks and Human Capital Accumulation: The Case of Spanish Flu in Italian Regions," *Regional Studies* 50, no. 9 (2016): 1496–1508, https://doi.org/10.1080/00343404.2015.1039975.

22. Howard Phillips and David Killingray, *The Spanish Flu Pandemic of 1918: New Perspectives* (London: Routledge, 2001).

23. Gina B. Kolata, *Influenza: Die Jagd nach dem Virus* (Frankfurt: S. Fischer Verlag, 2001).

24. Kirsty E. Duncan, *Hunting the 1918 Flu* (Toronto: University of Toronto Press, 2006).

25. Marc Hieronimus, *Krankheit und Tod 1918: Zum Umgang mit der Spanischen Grippe in Frankreich, England und in dem Deutschen Reich* (Berlin: Lit Verlag, 2006).

26. Wilfried Witte, *Tollkirschen und Quarantäne: Die Geschichte der Spanischen Grippe* (Berlin: Verlag Klaus Wagenbach, 2008).

27. M. I. Porras Gallo and Ryan A. Davis, eds., *The Spanish Influenza Pandemic of 1918–1919: Perspectives from the Iberian Peninsula and the Americas*, Rochester studies in medical history 30 (Rochester: University of Rochester Press, 2014).

28. Howard Phillips, "The Recent Wave of 'Spanish' Flu Historiography," *Social History of Medicine* 27, no. 4 (2014): 789–808, https://doi.org/10.1093/shm/hku066.

29. Spinney, *Pale Rider*.

30. Catharine Arnold, *Pandemic 1918: Eyewitness Accounts from the Greatest Medical Holocaust in Modern History* (New York: St. Martin's Griffin, 2020).

31. Fangerau et al., *Seuchengeschichte in deutscher Sprache*; Honigsbaum, "Influenza".

32. Manfred Vasold, *Grippe, Pest und Cholera: Eine Geschichte der Seuchen in Europa*, 2nd ed. (Stuttgart: Franz Steiner Verlag, 2010).

33. Malte Thiessen, ed., *Infiziertes Europa: Seuchen im langen 20. Jahrhundert*, Historische Zeitschrift/Beihefte 64 (Munich: De Gruyter Oldenbourg, 2014).

34. Howard Phillips, *Epidemics: The Story of South Africas Five Most Lethal Human Deseases*, Ohio Short Histories of Africa (Athens: Ohio University Press, 2012), https://ebookcentral.proquest.com/lib/kxp/detail.action?docID=1762841.

35. Mark J. Walters, *Seven Modern Plagues: And How We Are Causing Them* (Washington, D.C.: Island Press, 2014).

36. Judy D. Cummings, *Epidemics and Pandemics, Real Tales of Deadly Diseases*, Mystery & Mayhem (North Mankato: Nomad Press, 2018).

37. Peter Wilton, "Spanish Flu Outdid WWI in Number of Lives Claimed," *Canadian Medical Association Journal* 148, no. 11 (1993): 2036–7 (here 2036).

38. Taubenberger and Morens, "1918 Influenza," 16.

39. Manfred Vasold, *Die Spanische Grippe: Die Seuche und der Erste Weltkrieg*, Geschichte erzählt 21 (Darmstadt: Primus Verlag, 2009).

40. Armin Rusterholz, *"Das Sterben will nicht enden!": Die "Spanische Grippe-Epidemie" 1918/19 in der Schweizer Armee mit besonderer Berücksichtigung der Glarner Militäropfer*, Jahrbuch des Historischen Vereins des Kantons Glarus 90 (Glarus: Küng Druck AG, 2010).

41. Frieder Bauer and Jörg Vögele, "Die 'Spanische Grippe' in der deutschen Armee 1918: Perspektive der Ärzte und Generäle / The 'Spanish Flu' in the German Army 1918: The Perspectives of Physicians and Generals," *Medizinhistorisches Journal* 48, no. 2 (2013): 117–152, accessed Jan. 10, 2023, https://www.jstor.org/stable/24573346.

42. Mark O. Humphries, "Paths of Infection: The First World War and the Origins of the 1918 Influenza Pandemic," *War in History* 21, no. 1 (2014): 55–81, https://doi.org/10.1177/0968344513504525.

43. Terence Chorba and Byron Breedlove, "Concurrent Conflicts: The Great War and the 1918 Influenza Pandemic," *Emerging Infectious Diseases* 24, no. 10 (2018), https://doi.org/10.3201/eid2410.AC2410.

44. Craig A. Molgaard, "Military Vital Statistics the Spanish Flu and the First World War," *Significance* 16, no. 4 (2019): 32–7, https://doi.org/10.1111/j.1740-9713.2019.01301.x.

45. Cait Caffrey, "Egon Schiele 2020," *Salem Press Biographical Encyclopedia* (2020), accessed Jan. 10, 2023, https://search-ebscohost-com.ezproxy.uno.edu/login.aspx?direct=true&db=ers&AN=129815225&site=eds-live&scope=site.

46 Daniela Angetter-Pfeiffer, *Pandemie sei Dank! Was Seuchen in Österreich bewegten*, 2nd ed. (Vienna: Amalthea Verlag, 2022).

47. Thomas Hörzer and Ursula Kunze, "'Kaum ein Haus in dem nicht Kranke lagen:' Die Spanische Grippe in der Steiermark," *Wiener Medizinische Wochenschrift* 162, no. 7–8 (2012): 148–57, https://doi.org/10.1007/s10354-012-0069-0.

48. Margit Craß, "Die Spanische Grippe," in *Land im Krieg: Zwischen Schützengraben und Heimatfront, Burgenland 1914–1918: Begleitband zur Ausstellung*, Wissenschaftliche Arbeiten aus dem Burgenland 149, ed. Pia Bayer (Eisenstadt: Amt der Burgenländischen Landesregierung, Abteilung 7 – Landesmuseum Burgenland, 2014), 120–122.

49. Wolfgang Scheffknecht, "Die Spanische Grippe," in *Lustenau 1914–1918: Eine Gemeinde im Ersten Weltkrieg: Katalog zur Ausstellung des Historischen Archivs der Marktgemeinde Lustenau in der Galerie Stephanie Hollenstein 14. Juni bis 11. Oktober 2014*, ed. Vanessa Hämmerle et al. (Lustenau: Marktgemeinde Lustenau, 2014), 31–33.

50. Michael Kasper, "Nachrichten über die Spanische Grippe 1918/19 im Montafon," in *Krank – heil – gesund: Medizingeschichte(n) aus dem Montafon*, Sonderband zur Montafoner Schriftenreihe 31, ed. Michael

Kasper and Marina Hilber (Innsbruck: Universitätsverlag Wagner, 2022) 179–188.

51. Michael Forcher, *Tirol und der Erste Weltkrieg: Ereignisse, Hintergründe, Schicksale*, Haymon Taschenbuch 164, 4th ed. (Innsbruck, Vienna: Haymon Verlag, 2017), 332–55.

52. Sarah Oberbichler et al., "Als eine andere Epidemie die Welt in Atem hielt: Die Spanische Grippe 1918/19 in der österreichischen Presse," *Tiroler Chronist – Fachblatt von und für Chronisten in Nord-, Süd- und Osttirol* 154 (2020): 15–22. The parts on press-reporting in this essay here are in fact translations from this essay.

53. Florian Seidl, "Pandemie in Wien" (Master's thesis, University of Vienna, 2022).

54. Kathrin Weger, "Die Spanische Grippe im Ersten Weltkrieg in Innsbruck: Mit methodischer-didaktischer Aufarbeitung für den Geschichtsunterricht" (Master's thesis, University of Innsbruck, 2022).

55. Martina M. Sonderegger, "Pandemieberichterstattung im Wandel der Zeit: Untersuchung der Evolution der Zeitungsberichterstattung von Pandemien im Verlauf des 20. und 21. Jahrhunderts am Beispiel der Neuen Zürcher Zeitung" (Master's thesis, University of Innsbruck, 2022).

56. Harald Salfellner, *Die Spanische Grippe, Eine Geschichte der Pandemie von 1918* (Haselbach: Vitalis, 2020).

57. Mark Honigsbaum, *Das Jahrhundert der Pandemien: Eine Geschichte der Ansteckung von der Spanischen Grippe bis Covid-19* (Munich: Piper Verlag, 2021).

58. Patric U. Vogel and Günter A. Schaub, *Seuchen, alte und neue Gefahren: Von der Pest bis Covid-19* (Wiesbaden: Springer, 2021).

59. Michael Kasper, "Die Spanische Grippe 1918/19 im Montafon," in *Jahresbericht 2021*, ed. Montafoner Museen, Heimatschutzverein Montafon, and Montafon Archiv (Montafon: Montafoner Museen, 2021).

60. Spinney, *Pale Rider*, 8.

61. James D. Shidler, "A Tale of Two Cities: The 1918 Influenza," *Journal of the Illinois State Historical Society* 103, no. 2 (2010): 165–79, https://doi.org/10.2307/25701282.

62. Ivona Jelčić and Matthias Breit, *14 Tage 1918: Die Anfänge der Republik in Tirol in 53 Zeitungsausschnitten* (Innsbruck: Tyrolia Verlag, 2018).

63. Sonderegger, "Pandemieberichterstattung im Wandel der Zeit."

64. Czech, "Die Spanische Grippe von 1918."

65. E. T. Ewing et al., "Gaining Insights into Epidemics by Mining Historical Newspapers," *Computer* 46, no. 6 (2013): 68–72, https://doi.org/10.1109/MC.2013.205.

66. Ibid., 68.

67. Ibid., 72.

68. Oberbichler et al., "Als eine andere Epidemie die Welt in Atem hielt."

69. Österreichische Nationalbibliothek, "ANNO – AustriaN Newspapers Online," accessed Jan. 8, 2023, http://anno.onb.ac.at/.

70. NewsEye Project, "NewsEye Platform (Beta)," accessed Jan. 8, 2023, https://platform.newseye.eu/.

71. Diese Arbeit wurde durch das Forschungs- und Innovationsprogramm Horizon 2020 der Europäischen Union unter der Förderung 770299 ("NewsEye") unterstützt.

72. Barbara Klaus, "Can Umlauts Ruin Your Research in Digitized Newspaper Collections? A NewsEye Case Study on 'The Dark Sides of War' (1914–1918)," *Proceedings of the Digital Humanities in the Nordic Countries 5th Conference*, no. 2612 (2020): 267–74, https://doi.org/10.5281/ZENODO.4686731.

73. Wikipedia. Die freie Enzyklopädie, "Spanische Grippe," accessed Jan. 8, 2023, https://de.wikipedia.org/w/index.php?title=Spanische_Grippe&oldid=228665150; Wikipedia. The Free Encyclopedia, "Spanish Flu," accessed Jan. 8, 2023, https://en.wikipedia.org/w/index.php?title=Spanish_flu&oldid=1132125865.

74. NewsEye Project, "NewsEye Platform (Beta);" impresso Project, "Impresso: Media Monitoring of the Past," accessed Jan. 8, 2023, https://impresso-project.ch/.

75. *Allgemeiner Tiroler Anzeiger*, October 1–31, 1918.

76. Stéphane Dufoix, *The Dispersion: A History of the Word Diaspora*, Brill's specials in modern history 1 (Leiden, Boston: Brill, 2017).

77. "Eine Spanische Krankheit," *Deutsches Volksblatt*, May 29, 1918.

78. "Mitteilungen eines Arztes," *Neues Wiener Tagblatt*, May 29, 1918.

79. "Die 'Spanische Krankheit' Vor Fünfzig Jahren in Tirol," *Innsbrucker Nachrichten*, June 14, 1918.

80. Voyant Tools, "Voyant: See Through Your Text," accessed Feb. 2, 2023, https://voyant-tools.org/.

81. Janez Demšar et al., "Orange: Data Mining Toolbox in Python," *Journal of Machine Learning Research* 14 (2013): 2349–53, http://jmlr.org/papers/v14/demsar13a.html.

82. Eva Pfanzelter, "Analysis: Corpus Spanish Flu, German Newspapers," *Voyant Tools*, accessed Jan. 22, 2023, https://voyant-tools.org/?stopList=keywords-48efc865afbb94ba77bc0f4acd83d558&panels=cirrus%2Creader%2Ctrends%2Ctopics%2Ccontexts&corpus=ce73f606248d25696f126243d05a3e21.

83. "Schwere Grippe-Epidemie in der Schweizerischen Armee," *Innsbrucker Nachrichten*, July 16, 1918.

84. "Stärkere Ausbreitung der Spanischen Grippe in Budapest," *Neue Freie Presse*, Sept. 20, 1918.

85. Sentiment analysis conducted with the Orange Data Mining Suite using SentiArt analysis for German: https://orangedatamining.com/blog/2020/2020-07-27-story-arcs/ (accessed Jan. 26, 2023).

86. "Die Spanische Grippe in Paris," *Neue Freie Presse*, June 1, 1918.

87. "Cover Image," *Illustrierte Kronen Zeitung*, June 3, 1918.

88. "Die Spanische Krankheit in Wien," *Illustrierte Kronen Zeitung*, July 3, 1918.

89. Ibid.

90. "Erkrankungen in Wien?," *Illustrierte Kronen Zeitung*, July 2, 1918.

91. "Die Kaiserin wieder hergestellt," *Neue Freie Presse*, July 6, 1918.

92. "Spanische Grippe oder deutsche Giftgase," *Innsbrucker Nachrichten. Abendausgabe*, June 28, 1918.

93. "Auftreten der Spanischen Grippe in Deutschland," *Neue Freie Presse*, July 1, 1918.

94. "Zum ersten Auftreten der Influenza in Europa," *Neue Freie Presse*, July 7, 1918.

95. "Die Seuchenplage in Tirols Vergangenheit," *Innsbrucker Nachrichten*, Oct. 17, 1918.

96. "Ein unheimlicher Gast," *Innsbrucker Nachrichten*, Aug. 29, 1918.

97. "Die Grippe," *Innsbrucker Nachrichten*, Sept. 13, 1918, 3.

98. "Gradenegg (Allerlei)," *Kärntner Zeitung*, Sept. 28, 1918.

99. "Wohnungsnot und Flüchtlingsfrage," *Wiener Sonn- und Montags-Zeitung*, Aug. 26, 1918.

100. "Zweierlei Wien," *Illustrierte Kronen Zeitung*, July 17, 1918; "Ein antisemitischer 'Diskurs,'" *Arbeiter Zeitung*, July 17, 1918.

101. "Epidemien in Italien," *Innsbrucker Nachrichten*, Oct. 3, 1918.

102. "Die Spanische Grippe Und Die Chinesische Zensur," *Der Morgen*, Oct. 7, 1918.

103. "Wien ist in dieser Woche der spanischen Grippe, die sich nach Budapester Beispiel aus einer harmlosen Kopfweh- und Schnupfenepidemie zu einer opferfordernden, Herz- und Lungenaffektionen im Gefolge führenden Seuche zu entwickeln beginnt, zum erstenmal mit wissenschaftlich-prophylaktischen Ehren nähergerückt. Im Stadtphysikat wurden die Fragen nach Krankenisolierung, zeitweiligem Schulschluß, Quarantäne der Reisenden erörtert, Ärzte und Professoren beteiligten sich an einer öffentlichen Diskussion, die Zeitungen hören auf, die Grippe als böswilliges innenpolitisches oder strategisches, vom Feind als Schädigung zugedachtes Gerücht zu behandeln, das man am besten im Keim beschwichtigenden Kleindrucks erstickt;" Ibid.

104. "Tagesneuigkeiten," *Innsbrucker Nachrichten*, Oct. 20, 1918.

105. "Epidemien in Italien," *Innsbrucker Nachrichten*, Oct. 3, 1918, 1.

106. Some examples: "Über die spanische Krankheit in Wien," *Innsbrucker Nachrichten*, Oct. 3, 1918; "Weitere Vorkehrungen des Militärs," *Arbeiter Zeitung*, Oct. 24, 1918; "Der Böswillige Charakter der Grippe," *Innsbrucker Nachrichten*, Oct. 20, 1918; "Die spanische Grippe in Wien," *Neue Freie Presse*, Oct. 6, 1918; "Die spanische Grippe in Wien," *Neue Freie Presse*, Oct. 18, 1918; "Eine amtliche Verlautbarung über die Grippe," *Neue Freie Presse*, Oct. 6, 1918; "Die 'spanische Grippe:' Schließung der Wiener Schulen bis 20. Oktober," *Illustrierte Kronen Zeitung*, Oct. 10, 1918.

107. "Vorübergehende Schließung der Kinos, Theater und Vergnügungslokale," *Illustrierte Kronen Zeitung*, Oct. 20, 1918; "Schließung sämtlicher Vergnügungslokale in Budapest," *Neue Freie Presse*, Oct. 19, 1918.

108. "Die 'Spanische Grippe' in Wien," *Neue Freie Presse*, Oct. 2, 1918.

109. "Nun stellte sich aber allmählich heraus, daß die spanische Grippe mit höchst polizeiwidriger Gleichgültigkeit über alle Grenzvorschriften und Einreiseverbote, über Sperre und Paßzwang hinwegvoltigiere, daß sie

für sich eine Freizügigkeit in Anspruch nehme, wie sie wohl in mythisch gewogener Friedenszeit ziemlich allgemein bestand, aber aus unserer waffenklirrenden Gegenwart zur Gänze und restlos verschwunden ist. […] Noch gibt es aber Skeptiker, die ihre Originalität bezweifeln und sie trotz ihres fremdländischen Gewandes einfach als einen hartnäckigen Schnupfen erklären […]. Höchstens sei sie eine verneverte Influenza, nur bedenklicher und ärgerlicher, weil wir alle bei unseren heutigen Ernährungsverhältnissen auf den Empfang von Gästen nicht eingerichtet sind, am allerwenigsten auf jenen verdächtigen und gefährlichen Gast aus Spanien;" Ibid.

110. "Die spanische Grippe," *Innsbrucker Nachrichten*, July 2, 1918.

111. "Bekämpfung im Anfangsstadium der Krankheit," *Arbeiter Zeitung*, Oct. 12, 1918; "Die Verbreitung der spanischen Grippe in Wien," *Neue Freie Presse*, Oct. 5, 1918.

112. "Eine Verlautbarung der Militärbehörde," *Neue Freie Presse*, Oct. 8, 1918.

113. "Die Grippe," *Innsbrucker Nachrichten*, July 19, 1918; "Ein Serum gegen die Grippe," *Illustrierte Kronen Zeitung*, Oct. 12, 1918.

114. "Wie schützt man sich gegen Grippe?," *Neue Freie Presse*, Oct. 15, 1918.

115. "Werbeanzeige: Gegen spanische Grippe," *Neue Freie Presse*, Oct. 29, 1918.

116. "Gegen spanische Krankheit," *Neue Freie Presse*, Oct. 1, 1918.

117. "Die spanische Grippe in Wien," *Neue Freie Presse*, Oct. 6, 1918; "Die spanische Grippe in Wien," *Neue Freie Presse*, Oct. 18, 1918.

118. "Die Verbreitung der spanischen Grippe in Wien," *Neue Freie Presse*, Oct. 5, 1918.

119. "Neuerliche Belastung der Krankenkassen durch den Krieg," *Innsbrucker Nachrichten*, July 16, 1918.

120. "Die spanische Grippe," *Neue Freie Presse*, Oct. 12, 1918.

121. "Die Apotheker und die Grippe," *Neue Freie Presse*, Oct. 19, 1918.

122. "Interpellationsbeantwortung," *Wiener Zeitung*, Oct. 10, 1918.

123. "Die spanische Grippe in Wien," *Neue Freie Presse*, Oct. 24, 1918.

124. "Zuerst liefen die Aspirinhamster straßauf, straßab. Aspirin und Aspirinersatz verschwand allmählich aus den Apotheken. Unterdessen waren aber auch die Schleichhändler nicht müßig und heute haben wir

es glücklich so weit gebracht, daß die Tablette Aspirin im Winkelverkehr mit einer Krone angeboten und auch bezahlt wird. Gemeinderat Doktor Löwenstein wird in der am Freitag stattfindenden Gemeinderatssitzung die Aufmerksamkeit des Bürgermeisters auf diesen bedauerlichen Unfug lenken;" Ibid.

125. "Vorschläge Zur Bekämpfung Der Influenza," *Neues Wiener Journal*, Oct. 14, 1918.

126. "Prophylaxe," *Neue Freie Presse*, Oct. 24, 1918.

127. "Ohne Theater, ohne Konzert und ohne Kino," *Neue Freie Presse*, Oct. 20, 1918.

128. "Die spanische Krankheit," *Innsbrucker Nachrichten*, Aug. 8, 1918.

129. "Der Bazillus der spanischen Grippe," *Innsbrucker Nachrichten*, Nov. 8, 1918.

130. "Der Bazillus der spanischen Krankheit," *Innsbrucker Nachrichten*, July 12, 1918; "Die spanische Grippe – Influenza," *Illustrierte Kronen Zeitung*, July 15, 1918.

131. "Die spanische Grippe," *Neue Freie Presse*, Oct. 12, 1918.

132. "Der Urheber der Spanischen Grippe," *Neue Freie Presse*, Oct. 15, 1918.

133. Myron G. Schultz and David M. Morens, "Charles-Jules-Henri Nicolle," *Emerging Infectious Diseases* 15, no. 9 (2009): 1519–22, https://doi.org/10.3201/eid1509.090891.

134. Jeffery K. Taubenberger et al., "Discovery and Characterization of the 1918 Pandemic Influenza Virus in Historical Context," *Antiviral Therapy* 12, no. 4 pt. B (2007): 581–91 (here 586–7).

Typhus Prevention in the Context of Nazi Forced Labor: The Delousing Facility Linz[1]

Eva Hallama

Epidemic-Related Monitoring of Civilian Forced Laborers

From the invasion of Poland by Nazi Germany in 1939, civilians of the defeated countries were recruited and forcefully deported to work in the "German Reich." Right from the start, the state of health of the "civilian workers"—as the forced laborers were called by the Nazi regime to distinguish them from prisoners-of-war—was of great importance to the Nazi apparatus. On the one hand, their state of health referred to their ability to carry out work and was therefore to be determined by means of medical examinations; on the other hand, the Nazi health authorities saw the German-speaking population threatened by the infiltration of infectious and venereal diseases from Eastern Europe. Among them, spotted fever or typhus,[2] which is transmitted through the feces of the body louse, was a particular foe. Endemic in Eastern and Southeastern Europe, it was associated with ideas of dirt due to its transmission through lice excrement. Thus, it was seen as an epidemic whose origin could be attributed to the "lice-ridden" population in Eastern Europe, who were considered to lack basic hygiene standards.[3] Forced laborers from Eastern Europe were thought to be carriers of diseases that could be dangerous to the German nation. Alongside the selection, preservation, and restoration of labor power, epidemic hygiene monitoring of the foreign laborers was therefore one of the most important medical tasks for the Nazi health authorities in connection with the use of forced laborers. In order to reduce the infection routes of typhus as much as possible, a screening and selection system was developed that provided for the forced laborers to be deloused several times before their work assignment in the German Reich. It also prescribed an obligatory three-part medical examination: once before entering a deportation train, once before crossing the border to Germany, and once in Germany before starting to work.[4] From 1941 onwards, the "*Landesarbeitsämter*" (regional labor offices) were also to set up a central transit camp for civilian forced laborers, where they were to be deloused and examined by doctors but also registered by the police before being distributed to the individual workplaces.[5] Such transit camps existed for example in Straßhof (Wien-Niederdonau), Spallerhof/Linz "*Durchgangslager* 39" (Oberdonau), Woergl (Alpenland), and Graz (Steiermark-Kärnten).[6]

In the following, I will describe such delousing measures in detail, using the municipal delousing facility of Linz as an example. Since court cases were brought against the operator of the facility, Anton Slupetzky, detailed statements exist from several witnesses about the delousing process.[7] This provides a more comprehensive insight into delousing practices than the records of most camps would allow. The example shows particularly well the extent of violence inherent in the delousing procedures carried out on forced laborers. At the same time, the fact that the statements are court testimonies means that careful historical critique of sources is required, especially in regard to the motivations of the witnesses concerned. I will therefore begin this article with an overview of the investigations against Slupetzky in order to be able better to classify the statements about the delousing of civilian forced laborers at the delousing facility in Linz. Moreover, the example of Slupetzky and the investigations against him illustrate well the overlap between pest control, delousing as an epidemic prevention measure, and the murder of people in the context of Nazi mass murder. Although this article focuses on the process of delousing and the louse, it is important to remain aware of the oft-made association, in the perpetrators' minds, between the concept of the animal carrier and the human carrier of disease and dirt.[8]

State of Research

Epidemic prevention measures to which forced laborers were subjected are mentioned within the topic of forced labor and the health system[9] and were described in several histories of transit camps that were located within the German Reich.[10] The present author has recently presented an overview of the ramified system of "*Sammellager*," (collecting camps), "*Grenzentlausungslager*," (border delousing camps), and "*Durchgangslager*," (transit camps), for delousing and the medical examination of civilian forced laborers also in the territory of occupied Eastern Europe.[11] Wieland Mittmannsgruber has supplied concrete details about the delousing facility in Linz, which was located outside the transit camp and was operated by the "*Reinigungs- und Entwesungsanstalt Anton Slupetzky*." Mittmannsgruber, however, leaves Slupetzky's role as a Nazi perpetrator unmentioned and also does not place the disease prevention measures in a National Socialist context.[12]

Investigations against Slupetzky for Mistreatment of Forced Laborers[13]

In 1925, Anton Slupetzky founded a company that, in addition to cleaning services, also specialized in epidemic control using highly toxic substances. During the National Socialist era, his *Reinigungs- und Entwesungsanstalt* (cleaning and disinfestation company[14]) operated the delousing facility of the city of Linz, where it carried out delousing of forced laborers and disinfestation of their clothing by means of hydrocyanic acid fumigation as National Socialist epidemic prevention.

As a delousing specialist, Slupetzky carried out large-scale disinfestations in prisoner-of-war camps, forced labor camps, and concentration camps, in the course of which he was involved in the murder of about 150 concentration camp inmates by means of the pesticide Zyklon B at the Gusen concentration camp in March 1942.[15] For this involvement, he was sentenced to five years in prison by the Dachau Military Court in 1948.[16] After his early release in 1949, the *Volksgericht* Linz continued investigations against him, including (among others) charges under §3 of the *War Crimes Act* (KVG),[17] which concerned mistreatment of forced laborers in the course of delousing at the delousing facility in Linz.[18]

In the course of the Dachau trials, the former forced laborer Pawel Chapiorsky, who had worked for Anton Slupetzky as a hairdresser and unskilled laborer in the delousing station, was questioned as a witness. He described the delousing procedure, which he had first undergone himself and then witnessed on thousands of other forced laborers after being recruited as a laborer for the delousing facility. Chapiorsky stated:

> These delousing procedures took place very often and 2,000 people were driven through the buildings of the fumigation. Sometimes they had to stand from five to ten hours on the cold floors completely naked, Slupetzky standing by with a club in his hand which he used fairly frequently. Slupetzky often put on a white robe and played the role of a doctor. […] Many times there would be people coming into the delousing institution with carbuncles or ulcers on their bodies of one kind or another and Slupetzky, by means of a set or forceps or a lancet, would cut cruelly into the wounds of these people, causing them terrible pains and acting in other sadistic and unhygienic manners. The groans and cries of the people who went through these miseries and tortures were something I will never forget.[19]

Chapiorsky also said that he had heard of people who had died as a result of the methods used in the delousing facility because their resistance was so weakened after transport that they would not withstand the cold showers and standing naked on cold floors for up to ten hours. In addition to the mistreatment by Slupetzky, he also told of an employee of Slupetzky's named Anzinger, who, like his supervisor, regularly beat the forced laborers. And he spoke of another employee, Anna Haiböck, who stole jewelry and watches from the forced laborers in the course of disinfecting their clothes.[20] Josef Prix, a manager of the Red Cross in Linz and head of the medical service at the labor office in Linz also made incriminating statements about Slupetzky when he was questioned by the criminal investigation department of Linz in July 1946.[21] He mentioned scalds of the skin caused by too-strong Lysol and cresol solutions, which were then treated by the doctor present at the time. He also agreed with Chapiorsky's statement that Slupetzky had held a "rubber truncheon" in his hand during delousing, although Slupetzky had not used it in his presence. However, he told of Slupetzky saying that "these people should all be exterminated"[22] and confirmed that "Slupetzky grabbed the women by the breasts and hair and snatched them up if they did not come in time and fast enough for the examination."[23] He described Anton Slupetzky as brutal and sadistic, a man who "shouted at and insulted the foreigners constantly and often without reason," "put the persons entrusted to him in a tormenting condition," and "insulted and offended their human dignity."[24] Regarding the thefts, he stated that "the foreigners stole from each other."[25] Seven years later, Josef Prix denied ever having made the statement in these words.[26] At that time, however, Slupetzky as well as other witnesses had already been confronted with the accusations mentioned here, which is why their statements are to be seen as corresponding reactions to them. To bring up arguments against his former statement in 1952, Josef Prix had to describe certain situations in particular detail because he was under pressure to justify himself. His 1952 version of the delousing process is therefore no less significant. Slupetzky's request for evidence (*Beweisantrag*),[27] in which he reports on the delousing procedure, responds in many places to these early incriminating statements.

Already in a report by the Linz public prosecutor dated April 7, 1951, the mistreatment of forced laborers was described as groundless and unfounded.[28] On the one hand, reference is made to a report on the discontinued investigations against Johann Anzinger, who was an employee of Slupetzky's and had likewise been accused of mistreating forced laborers during delousing procedures. However, since the main witness Pawel Chapiorsky was deemed untrustworthy,[29] the case of Anzinger was dropped.[30] On the other hand, the letter reports on a request for a new hearing of the witness Josef Prix.[31] Josef Prix, the former head of the medical service of the Labor Office, had incriminated Anton Slupetzky in a police statement dated July 6, 1945. However, during his examination as a witness by the Linz *Volksgericht* that took place on November 3, 1952, he denied ever having made the first statement. Since this statement was considered decisive for the complete clarification of this case, it can be assumed that the accusations with regard to §3 of the *War*

Crimes Act were considered sufficiently invalidated. No further steps were taken in the investigation with regard to the mistreatment of forced laborers. On December 10, 1955, the proceedings against Anton Slupetzky on suspicion of mistreatment of forced laborers were terminated.[32] Most of the witnesses interrogated had been proposed by Anton Slupetzky himself. They were representatives of the former National Socialist health and labor offices, who themselves were responsible for the proper conduct of the delousing procedure. Quite independently of their close relationship to Slupetzky, they had their own interest in presenting the procedures in accordance with the rules. Not even the majority of the witnesses named by Slupetzky were examined by the *Volksgericht* Linz. Completely neglected, moreover, was the questioning of former forced laborers who had themselves been gone through the delousing facility or had worked there. Once Pawel Chapiorsky had been deemed by the court an untruthful witness, the perspective of the forced laborers was no longer represented. Yet there were few practical obstacles to doing so: the search for testimonies at the time when many of them were still in Austria should not have been too difficult.[33]

The Delousing Facility in Linz

The increased fear of infection anticipated from foreign workers led the city of Linz to plan the construction of a disinfection facility as early as 1940.[34] In 1941, the city started with the construction of a municipal delousing facility, the planning of which involved the city councilor for health Ernst Wainke; the head of the health department in Linz, Dr. Demelbauer; and Anton Slupetzky as a specialist in disinfestation.[35] Already in 1939, Slupetzky had become "*Gaufachschaftswalter*" for pest and disease control.[36] His company also expanded: both Anna Haiböck and Leopold Fischer began working for Slupetzky in 1939.[37] Furthermore, in 1940, Slupetzky received the highly competitive license for the use of Zyklon B for pest control,[38] whereas before that he had only been able to proceed with the product under the license of a Viennese company. As his wife Hedwig Slupetzky reports, Anton Slupetzky's cleaning and disinfestation facility was ranked as the fourth largest enterprise in this field in Germany in 1942, according to the head of the *Deutsche Gesellschaft für Schädlingsbekämpfung und des Arbeitsausschusses für Seuchenabwehr* (German Society for Pest Control and the Working Committee for Disease Control).[39] This illustrates the increased importance that the Nazi regime had attached to the company and its work in the service of epidemic control since the beginning of the war. This was expressed not least by the fact that Slupetzky's company was classified by the *Oberkommando der Wehrmacht* (German army high command) as a key company crucial to the war.[40] Thus, Anton Slupetzky and other disinfectors at the facility were declared "u.k.,"[41] meaning indispensable, and were not drafted into the military service. Instead, the war against vermin was given militaristic wording, as illustrated by the slogan of the fight against the louse—also, significantly, the title of an Antisemitic propaganda film, *Krieg dem Fleckfieber* ("War against Typhus"), in which Jews are portrayed as lice-bearing carriers of typhus.[42] In a similarly military style, Slupetzky was described as a "war general" who now also belonged "to the front-line soldiers" because he was "fighting against the armies of vermin" and "delivering extraordinarily successful battles."[43]

This helps in understanding why the mayor of the city of Linz ordered that the delousing facility be leased to the *Reinigungs- und Entwesungsanstalt Anton Slupetzky* (Anton Slupetzky cleaning and disinfestation facility) immediately after its construction, while responsibility remained with the health department.[44]

On February 1, 1942, when the mass deportations of forced laborers from the occupied Soviet Union began, the large delousing facility was opened near the supply house (*Versorgungshaus*).[45] According to Josef Kammesberger, a medical officer of Linz, Slupetzky ran the facility by himself while there were frequent controls by the health administration. Doctors from Linz hospitals were also present for examination during most of the transports.[46] The delousing facility was primarily used by the *Landesarbeitsamt* Linz and the *Reichsarbeitsministerium*, while Josef Prix, the administrator of the medical service at the *Arbeitsamt*, functioned as controlling body:

> So that the foreigners could not carry any epidemics into the Reich, they had to be deloused. It is true that Josef Prix was the administrator of the medical service at the *Arbeitsamt* Linz from around 1941 onward, and in this capacity he was frequently present at the delousing sessions at the delousing facility. He had to supervise that only deloused foreigners were released for placement.[47]

Information about the buildings, equipment and capacity of the delousing facility in Linz is given by Wieland Mittmannsgruber:

> The institution [...] consisted of a main building, six gas chambers in which the clothes were cleaned by means of hydrocyanic gas procedures, as well as various adjoining rooms, such as bathing, doctor's, changing, and sanitary rooms. Per day, the clothes of approximately 700–900 people could be cleaned. There were 40 showers available for body cleaning, and 20 minutes of bathing time were calculated per person.[48]

According to Mittmannsgruber, the people to be deloused were sent primarily by the *Reichswerke* Hermann Göring, the *Stickstoffwerke*, the *Wehrmacht*, and the *Landesarbeitsamt* (regional labor office).[49] In the first year, 57,000 foreigners passed through the facility, whereby in addition to a "heavy infestation of lice," many cases of tuberculosis, venereal diseases, typhoid, scabies, and even typhus fever were found.[50]

Anton Slupetzky mentioned in a report to the *Landesgericht* Linz that the modern delousing facility of Linz was so exemplary that experts came from various cities of the German Reich to inspect and then copy it.[51] It had offered not only the possibility "to disinfest the clothes and luggage of 1,500 to 2,000 people per day in six disinfestation chambers, but also to physically delouse the aforementioned crowd."[52] The practice thus exceeded the calculated capacity by more than double. Josef Kammesberger states even higher capacities. According to him, the "capacity of the institution [...] was assumed to be 1,200 persons in a twenty-four-hour work cycle."[53] Even with this figure, however, he states that "[d]ue to the frequent arrival of mass transports [...] the number of delousings was often exceeded contrary to the regulations."[54] Even the twenty minutes of bathing time originally calculated per person mentioned by Mittmannsgruber could not have been adhered to with 2,000 people, since in this case showering alone would have taken over sixteen hours with forty showers.

Delousing as Forced Labor

The delousing facility was not only responsible for delousing the forced laborers, it also became the workplace of the same. Slupetzky named an employee at his disposal who was trained in scabies treatment, as well as one male and one female worker who had yet to be trained. The *Arbeitsamt* would "also assign three hairdressers, four cleaning women, the above-mentioned staff for scabies treatment, four German-speaking Czechs or Poles to help in the delousing facility."[55] In Dachau, Anton Slupetzky testified that he had had up to forty-six employees since 1941, the majority of whom had been foreigners. One of them had been Pawel Chapiorsky. In his testimony before the US military court, Chapiorsky speaks of his deportation to Linz as a forced laborer.[56] He had been taken to Kovel in Poland on July 16, 1943, together with other youths from Volodymyr.[57] From there, he was transported via Białystok, Warsaw, and Vienna to Linz, where he arrived on July 23, 1943. His transport, consisting of 1,000 people, was taken to the delousing facility, where they were "deloused" from morning to night. All the hairdressers among them were supposed to step forward, which Pawel Chapiorsky did.

They had to shave the head of all persons, including the women, as well as the armpit hair and in most cases the pubic hair. Slupetzky beat some people during this haircutting procedure, including a woman who resisted the cutting of her head hair.[58] Afterwards, they went through the shower rooms, where they were first given hot and then cold showers. At the same time, they were sprayed with a disinfectant solution. After that, they were given back their clothes, which had been deloused in the course of the same day. After delousing, they were taken to the transit camp in Linz. The next morning, farmers from the surrounding area, railroad officials, and representatives of other companies came to select forced laborers. Chapiorsky, however, had been told by Slupetzky the day before, during delousing, that he would work for him. After a few days, he indeed began to work for Slupetzky as a hairdresser and assistant for different tasks.[59]

Delousing Procedure

General information about procedures to follow in a delousing station and the delousing process can be found in the unpublished dissertation by Therese Schranner. According to her, the "clean" and "unclean parts" of the facility had to be strictly separated. The delousing process of body and clothing is described as follows:

> In the unclean part of the plant, the foreign workers hand in their clothes. From there, they are taken to the delousing chambers. In the meantime, the workers undergo a medical examination and are then cleaned. The examination takes place before the people are deloused, so that any infectious people can be eliminated immediately. The doctors and their assistants wear protective clothing against lice. [...] During the cleansing of the people, the greatest emphasis is again placed on the elimination of lice. All hairy parts of the body are most reliably treated with Cuprex. The main hair of men and women is also subjected to the same treatment, mechanically removing lice and nits for up to half an hour per person.[60]

After that comes "the cleansing bath,"[61] following which the workers are taken to the clean part of the facility and given back their disinfected clothes and luggage.[62]

This procedure is also reflected in Anton Slupetzky's description. According to him, those to be deloused first entered a large waiting room on the unclean side and had to hand over their belongings, which were immediately taken to the disinfestation chambers. The people were then taken to the treatment room, where the physical delousing took place, and then took a shower. In the waiting room on the clean side, the just deloused people had to wait for the medical examination as to their work ability and to the presence of contagious diseases. Only after that were they given back their belongings.[63] However, unlike the ideal-typical procedure described by Schranner, the medical examination took place only after delousing. In other words, delousing and purification preceded the identifying of infected persons and had priority over medical diagnosis.[64]

Delousing of Bodies

To present the norm of body delousing, I would like to take as an example the "Spotted Fever Circular" of the Reich Minister of the Interior of February 13, 1942.[65] In it, delousing was regulated to the last detail. The circular differentiated between body lice, head lice, and crab lice, whereby only the body louse could carry typhus, although—according to the circular—it can also be found in the hair of the head and face.[66] For the physical cleansing, which in the case of women was to be carried out by female workers, the persons were to be completely undressed, the case of "severe lice [...] all hairy parts of the body (beard, eyebrows, eyelashes, auditory canal, head hair, anal hair, pubic hair, armpit hair) [were] to be checked."[67] This should be followed by "a thorough wash (in a tub or shower bath) using warm water and soft soap."[68] Thereupon it is recommended:

> [T]he parts of the body mainly visited by the body lice (neck, the areas between the shoulder blades and above the sacrum, furthermore the pubic region up to the cleft of the buttocks, as well as the armpits) [...] rub vigorously with petroleum for two minutes, rub in with soft soap, leave to act for ten minutes, and then bathe.[69]

Shaving and removal of body hair will—the circular continues—"only be necessary in exceptional cases." However, the circular does not prescribe the shaving of head hair as a preventive measure against spotted fever. It is only suggested in the case that the persons (in addition to the dangerous body louse) also have (medically speaking harmless) head lice or crabs on them. At the same time, these persons should be "cleansed of these vermin" by "preferably removing the hair on the head with clippers" and "then cleaning the shaved areas vigorously with warm soapy water." However:

> [I]f cutting off the hair meets with insurmountable opposition, as is often the case, especially with females, the hair should be

> soaked generously with a lice-killing agent [...], but none of the liquid should get into the eyes, and the head should be covered for twelve to twenty-four hours with a bathing cap, a woolen cap or a tight-fitting cloth.[70]

In the circular of the Reich Minister of the Interior, less importance is attached to the shaving of body hair, but rather special reference is made to the removal of all clothing and textiles (such as bandages, etc.) that could be considered lice-ridden, as well as to physical cleansing, the rubbing with solutions or washing with water and soap. The physical cleansing of females was also to be carried out by female workers, as cited above.

Although the delousing procedure was to be carried out in accordance with the spotted-fever circular described above,[71] the actual practice in the delousing facility in Linz nevertheless deviate from it, as I will show in the following.

Shaving of Hair

After the forced laborers had given all their clothes, the first thing that was done was to treat their head and body hair. In a report that refers to an agreement that the *Arbeitsamt Linz* had made with Anton Slupetzky only a few months after the delousing facility was opened, the shaving of the head is described as a standard procedure for men who are recognized as "having lice."[72] Women could be exempted from this if the doctor does not explicitly deem it necessary. There is no mention here of the alternative of twelve to twenty-four hours of hair treatment proposed in the Circular Decree, presumably due to the long duration of the exposure time. The order concerning Nisska combs, however, points to the practice of treating the hair with a lice or nit-killing agent. In the agreement between the *Arbeitsamt* Linz and Anton Slupetzky, however, no differentiation is made between body, head, and crab lice, since men, "as soon as they have lice, have their head hair cut," regardless of which lice were found on them.[73] In 1952, Slupetzky stated that "the hair on the heads of the men coming from the Eastern territories was shorn obligatorily"[74] (whether they had lice or not). The women's hair, on the other hand, was moistened with Cuprex and put under a louse cap. After one and a half hours of exposure, the women had to comb out the dead lice and nits with nit combs. Only in cases of very severe lice infestation, "where the measures shown did not show any success," was the head shaved. However, this had happened—so said Slupetzky—with at most 10 to 12 persons per 1,000 deloused women.[75]

The shaving of women's heads was not described by everyone as an exceptional situation. The former head of the *Arbeitsamt* Linz, Wilhelm

Büttner, recalled in 1952 that he "opposed the shaving of the heads of certain female "*Ostarbeiterinnen*" because he "considered that it was an insult even to the most primitive woman to be shaved."[76] Büttner, who claimed of himself that his "treatment of the foreigners was anything but 'inhumane,'" had, however, been told by the doctors "that in certain cases there was no other way to deal with the vermin and that all preventive measures would be illusory if one capitulated to such cases."[77] His given order "that such interventions must be limited to truly exceptional cases,"[78] makes it clear that the practice did not correspond to an exemption for women.[79]

With this assertion, Büttner not only linked to the racist and National Socialist notion of the "primitiveness" of forced laborers, on which the legitimization of their exploitation was based, but he also implicitly referred to a colonial, anthropological discourse according to which the distinctness of gender identity depended on the degree of civilization of a "race."[80] On the other hand, Büttner recognized that for women shaving their head hair was linked to particular humiliation and shame. Women thus lost not only their individuality, but also part of their gender identity.[81] From another perspective, however, the delousing process was also one of gendering because the delousing procedure was so closely associated with nakedness and shame.

It is therefore no coincidence that Slupetzky describes scenes of violence in connection with the shaving of hair. According to him, some women met the "radical shaving of the hair" with "resistance," which is why "it [...] was sometimes necessary to hold the woman by her hands and feet to be able to comply with the official doctor's order."[82] Slupetzky justifies the violence with the official medical directive, which had to be followed at all costs. The report cited above, however, presents this practice as the result of an agreement between Slupetzky and the *Arbeitsamt* Linz and not as an instruction from the Health Office.[83] The circular of the Reich Minister of the Interior had also recommended a different treatment of the scalp precisely for such cases.

But the delousing procedure also included shaving the pubic hair—or at least thinking about it. The employee of *Arbeitsamt* Linz had opposed shaving the other body hair "because suitable persons, especially among women, are not available, because incidentally—especially in women—shaving the genitals is practically impossible."[84] He justifies the non-shaving with reference to women, although even in the circular the shaving of the other body hair (without distinction of sex) was only ordered for exceptional cases. No justification would have been necessary here. Genitals—especially the female ones—became reference points within the argumentation about the delousing process. The emphasis on the lack of suitable persons "especially for the women" also suggests that the delousing of the naked women by exclusively female personnel—as stipulated in the circular—was not implemented in practice. Later reports by Anton Slupetzky in court also show that he treated and examined naked women, although he was not a doctor, as discussed below.

Agents on the Skin

According to the circular, physical cleansing consisted of undressing and removing the lice, rubbing the "lice-ridden" parts of the body with special agents, and then showering or bathing. According to Slupetzky's report, the further process of the cleaning procedure affected women and men equally. First the "armpit and pubic hair [...] were cleaned with petroleum," and then "the bodies were moistened with a 3 to 5% solution of cresol soap."[85] The agreement between the *Arbeitsamt* Linz and Anton Slupetzky describes this process somewhat more clearly as "spraying with cresol,"[86] which, however, "is omitted as soon as soft soap is available."[87] "Spraying with cresol" is a practice that does not appear in the Ministry of the Interior circular. It is associated with a greater distance between the person performing the act and the person being deloused, because direct physical contact does not take place—in contrast with the act of rubbing certain areas of the body with soft soap, which also evokes associations with sexual acts. With the increased distance, however, comes a hierarchy according to the Nazis' racist dehumanization. This becomes particularly obvious in a series of photos in which Slupetzky can be seen hosing down prisoners of war with a garden sprayer, which is usually used to combat vermin infestations on plants.[88] In addition, the risk of cauterization by cresol was not insignificant. Josef Prix mentioned that scalding of the skin by too strong Lysol and cresol solutions had occurred, which were then treated by the attending physician.[89] Josef Kammesberger stated that

> [In] one case [...] a burn of a lighter degree was observed on the chest of a woman and she [was] admitted to the hospital. The investigation revealed that the burn resulted from the woman bypassing the shower bath after body delousing with the disinfectant liquid and dressing immediately.[90]

According to Kammesberger's report, the undisciplined behavior of the woman in question was the cause of the chemical burn, since she had not gone through the delousing procedure according to order. The responsibility for the cauterization lay, of course, with the Linz Health Department as well as with Anton Slupetzky himself, insofar as he had directed the delousing.

Josef Prix also commented on the process of the body cleaning procedure, intending to play down his statement that "Slupetzky pulled or tugged at the hair and breasts of the women":

> When delousing, Slupetzky of course had to take apart the hair of the women to be deloused and search them for lice and nits. In the early days, when many people were not yet informed about the delousing process, it happened that Slupetzky lifted up the women's breasts when spraying them with a soap preparation so that the parts underneath were also covered by the preparation. Later, the people already knew the procedure and lifted the breasts of their own accord, also lifting their arms so that the armpits were free.[91]

The description reveals how close the delousing operated to the sexual body and what a violation it meant when delousing was performed on women by non-medical male personnel. When Slupetzky was confronted with Prix's early accusations in an interrogation, he countered:

> If he now claims that women were touched by the hair, this may perhaps be true, but not from the circumstance of mistreatment, but because these people forcefully resisted the prescribed delousing. I must call it a bottomless meanness when the witness subsequently makes the claim that I tore women's breasts. I am surprised that the witness does not claim that I touched the women by the genitals.[92]

Here, Slupetzky admitted his acting on women's bodies, but legitimized it with the resistance of women to be deloused along the instructions. Slupetzky's statement illustrates how close the mistreatment of naked bodies is to sexual mistreatment and how powerful the sexual gaze is during the delousing procedure in general.

Cold Showers

After the disinfectants had taken effect for ten minutes, those to be deloused—according to Anton Slupetzky's report again—went under the shower, where the water temperature was thirty-eight to forty degrees Celsius. After the warm bath, the forced laborers had to take extensive cold showers "to avoid colds."[93] Slupetzky emphasized that the health authorities had issued strict instructions to do so. In the Reich Minister of the Interior's circular from February 13, 1942, such an instruction is not to be found; on the contrary, it speaks of washing "using warm water and soft soap."[94] The former head of the *Arbeitsamt* Linz, Wilhelm Büttner, also referred to the cold shower:

> I further remember that I was against cold showers before delousing because I had heard that the foreigners (especially the female "*Ostarbeiterinnen*") did so only with reluctance, and often could only be persuaded to do so with "gentle coercion." Here, too, I had to bow to medical arguments to the effect that cold showers were in the interest of the foreigners because they closed the pores and prevented colds.[95]

It is important that Büttner tells a different version of the cold showers, namely that they had taken place before delousing and not after delousing and warm baths, as Slupetzky had described it. This order (to shower before delousing and not after) would have meant that the forced laborers did not have the opportunity to shower off the disinfectants after they had been sprayed with them. This supports the thesis that the forced laborers were only made unclean in the delousing facility. The cold shower and the cleaning as a chicane, but also the caustic disinfectant, could then painfully make true precisely the racist prejudice of impurity and inferiority. But beyond that, Büttner also describes a reluctance that the cold showers had caused and which—according to Büttner—could only be dealt with by coercion. Here also the resistance against the procedure underlined the prejudice of their impurity, as they resisted the cleaning and purification measures. In his description, it was again the female workers who caused the use of violence, thus justifying the act of violence on an intersectional exclusion.

Gazes

In connection with the delousing and medical examinations described here, Gabriella Hauch has pointed out the violation in terms of shame that these measures often represented for the forced laborers, for example, when men were present at the showers and saw the women naked, even though they were not doctors.[96] Annette Schäfer also mentions that "in particular the delousing procedure [...] was experienced as very degrading by those affected."[97]

The male gaze on the undressed female bodies manifested itself also in a photo camera. Anton Slupetzky took photos of the delousing process. He showed the *Volksgericht* a photograph taken at the delousing facility, "which shows that the examination of the women was carried out in a completely proper manner."[98] Elsewhere, a colleague thanked Slupetzky for "the very impressive photographs sent to him," with which the other man had "given him great pleasure":[99]

> One cannot have enough material available of such things, which have not been captured in pictures so far. The lack of understanding

> of the lice-ridden prisoners is great, and here only good visual material can be convincing.[100]

Waiting for Clothes

After the showers, per Slupetzky, each person was given a clean towel to dry off. In the waiting room on the clean side, the deloused persons had to wait for the medical examination.[101] Only after the examination of their bodies for ability to work and absence of contagious diseases[102] did they receive their belongings back.[103] The fact that these were not always returned to their owners after the delousing procedure is testified to by the justifications used to counter the accusation of theft against Anna Haiböck. It was not disputed in court that there had been theft. The question was who had stolen, the "German employees or the foreigners among themselves."[104] In any case, delousing facilities were places of loss not only of personal identity but also of personal belongings.

After delousing, the forced laborers were then taken to work in various districts in Upper Austria under the guidance of the labor offices.[105] However, it could also happen that the delousing procedure was repeated several times. On March 20, 1944, a representative of the municipal health office wrote that because of the frequent cases of typhus, and "because of the recently arriving transports of workers from the East [...] every transport from the East that passes through the transit camp in Linz has now been ordered to undergo delousing three times at intervals of five days each."[106] Slupetzky had also been "admonished to observe the regulations very carefully and to supervise the delousing."[107] Tightening of the delousing measures (here the threefold repetition) was also ordered in other documents when cases of spotted fever or lice infestation were found despite delousing. The occurrence of lice despite delousing was particularly problematic, as it threatened to disprove the assumption that lice and typhus came from outside.

Race and Gender

A defense strategy of Anton Slupetzky was the humiliation of the forced laborers according to Nazi ideology that could still be argued after 1945. When he spoke about violence, Slupetzky not seldom added "that they were sometimes extremely primitive people who had no idea at all about hygienic facilities."[108] Slupetzky supported this statement with the following account:

> It repeatedly happened that people who were to be deloused used the water from the toilet shells for drinking purposes, although there was a hygienic drinking fountain on both the clean and the

> unclean side, while they often defecated near the radiators. We had to delouse 500 to 800 women and girls daily. Among them was a certain percentage who were unwell at the time. The pulp pads issued were almost never used as they were unaware of its use.[109]

Violent acts on the part of Slupetzky or—as he calls it—"incidents" were also legitimized by the former chief physician (Chefarzt) of the Hermann Göring *Werke*, Ernst Kortschak, on account of the "primitiveness [...] especially of the Eastern workers" and excused with the necessity of calling them to order.[110]

Both the resistance to the cleaning measures and the supposed lack of knowledge of hygiene articles were addressed in particular using the example of women and "*Ostarbeiterinnen*." The degradation and thus the relativization of violence was most evident where the categories of gender and "race" were intertwined. While Slupetzky speaks of the supposed primitiveness of the forced laborers, their needs also become obvious between the lines. These passages rather testify that the forced laborers, when they arrived at the delousing facility, were undersupplied in terms of drinking water and opportunities to relieve themselves.[111] Moreover, these descriptions confirm once again how forced laborers were not only turned into "others" by Nazi propaganda, but were also forced to act like "others" by the very conditions created by the Nazis.[112]

In the responses to the allegations of mistreatment of forced laborers, the reports of those involved in the delousing process include not only the degradation of the forced laborers whose behavior had supposedly made coercion necessary, but also the argument that the controlling authorities of the health and labor offices would have reported such incidents. This never happened, however.[113] It is also pointed out in several accounts—as Wilhelm Büttner does here—that "whatever one may feel about Mr Slupetzky [...] the fact that no epidemics of typhus arose in the population of far more than 100,000 foreigners in Upper Austria at that time is due not least to the expert and careful delousing of the foreigners by Mr Slupetzky."[114] The necessity of this kind of disease control and prevention was neither questioned nor placed in a racist, Nazi context by the courts after 1945. This circumstance probably also contributed to the fact that the investigations against Anton Slupetzky for the mistreatment of forced laborers were ultimately discontinued.

Conclusion

The example of the delousing facility in Linz illustrates the extent to which delousing procedures were interwoven with racist and National Socialist ideology and, not least, made the latter a reality through the repeated rituals of the violent, shameful, and humiliating delousing procedure. Delousing practices in the various transit camps and delousing stations helped to assign forced laborers their subordinate new status in terms of the Nazi hierarchy. Moreover, the example of the delousing station in Linz, through the person of Anton Slupetzky and the technology of fumigation of pests in gas chambers, highlights the proximity between pest control, epidemic prevention, and the Holocaust.

Endnotes

1. The article is based on the author's diploma thesis, which was submitted in 2013 to the University of Vienna. Eva Hallama, "'Bis dann der Krieg kam…' Selbstdarstellung und Unternehmensgeschichte des Allgemeinen Reinigungs- und Entwesungsdienstes Anton Slupetzky im Kontext von Reinigung, Seuchenbekämpfung und nationalsozialistischem Massenmord." (Master's thesis, University of Vienna, 2013). Some parts are already published in German in: Eva Hallama, "Praktiken nationalsozialistischer Seuchenprävention und ihre Legitimierung vor Gericht. Die Entlausungsanlage Linz in Gerichtsverfahren gegen Anton Slupetzky," *zeitgeschichte* 42, no. 2 (2015): 100–115.

2. Typhus in English means spotted fever, which is "*Fleckfieber*" in German and is not to be confused with the German term "Typhus," which means typhoid fever.

3. Therese Schranner, "Ärztliche Erfahrungen beim Einsatz fremdländischer Arbeitskräfte" (PhD diss., University of Vienna, 1943).

4. Eva Hallama, "Between the projection of danger, objectification, and exploitation. Medical examination of polish civilian forced laborers before their deportation into the German Reich," *Acta Universitatis Lodziensis: Folia Philosophica Ethica – Aesthetica – Practica* 38 (2020): 35–50.

5. Annette Schäfer, "Durchgangs- und Krankensammellager im Zweiten Weltkrieg. Schnittstellen zwischen 'Arbeit' und 'Vernichtung' beim Zwangsarbeitereinsatz," in *Medizin und Zwangsarbeit im Nationalsozialismus: Einsatz und Behandlung von "Ausländern" im Gesundheitswesen*, ed. Andreas Frewer and Günther Siedbürger (Frankfurt/Main: Campus-Verlag, 2004), 203–230 (here 206f).

6. Ibid., 207.

7. Dachau Trials: Mauthausen Trials, US vs. Karl Glas et al. 000-50-5-31/RG 549/410–412, National Archives and Records Administration (NARA), Washington. I refer to copies of the trial at the institute of contemporary history at the University of Vienna; proceedings of Volksgericht and Landesgericht Linz against Anton Slupetzky, LG Linz Sondergerichte VgVr 1950 Zl. 115/540, Oberösterreichisches Landesarchiv (OÖLA), Linz. I refer also to copies of the proceedings at the Dokumentationsarchiv des Österreichischen Widerstands (DÖW), Vienna: 19968/1–10.

8. Sarah Jansen, *Schädlinge: Geschichte eines wissenschaftlichen und politischen*

Konstrukts, 1840–1920 (Frankfurt/Main: Campus Verlag 2003).

9. Andreas Frewer and Günther Siedbürger, eds., *Medizin und Zwangsarbeit im Nationalsozialismus: Einsatz und Behandlung von 'Ausländern' im Gesundheitswesen* (Frankfurt/Main: Campus Verlag 2004).

10. Leonore Scholze-Irrlitz, "Das Durchgangslager für Zwangs- und Fremdarbeiter des Landesarbeitsamtsbezirks Brandenburg in Berlin-Wilhelmshagen: Realität und ihr Widerschein im kollektiven Gedächtnis der Betroffenen und Anwohner," in *Zwangsarbeit während der NS-Zeit in Berlin und Brandenburg: Formen, Funktion und Rezeption*, ed. Winfried Meyer and Klaus Neitmann (Potsdam: Verlag für Berlin-Brandenburg, 2009), 211–222; Christine Sämann, *Das Durchgangslager in Bietigheim: Zwangsarbeit im Nationalsozialismus – Bedeutung und Funktionen des Durchgangslagers für ‚ausländische Arbeitskräfte' in Bietigheim mit seinen Krankensammellagern in Pleidelsheim und Großsachsenheim* (Bietigheim-Bissingen: Archiv der Stadt Bietigheim-Bissingen, 2018). An overview of further publications is provided by Schäfer, "Durchgangs- und Krankensammellager," 203–230, (here 207).

11. Eva Hallama, "Sammellager, Grenzentlausungslager, and Durchgangslager," in *Encyclopedia of Camps and Ghettos, 1933-1945*, vol. VII: *Camps for Foreign Forced Laborers*, ed. United States Holocaust Memorial Museum (Bloomington: Indiana University Press), (forthcoming, manuscript accepted).

12. Wieland Mittmannsgruber, "Die Linzer Stadtverwaltung während der NS-Zeit 1938–1945: Organisation – Führungskräfte – Aktivitäten," *Historisches Jahrbuch der Stadt Linz 1992* (1993): 19–150, (here 122f).

13. While this article focuses on the court cases regarding the delousing facility, see for a detailed overview of all court proceedings against Anton Slupetzky, Hallama, "'Bis dann der Krieg kam…,'" 35–45.

14. The term disinfestation contained in the company's name refers to the killing of animal pests and differs from disinfection, which destroys disease germs. See Heinrich Kliewe, *Leitfaden der Entseuchung und Entwesung*, 3rd ed. (Stuttgart: Enke, 1951).

15. Slupetzky's involvement in the murder of more than 150 people in Gusen concentration camp in the course of delousing and disinfection procedures is described in detail here: Eva Hallama, "Von der Seuchenbekämpfung zum NS-Massenmord: Die Tätigkeitsbereiche der Reinigungs- und Entwesungsanstalt Anton Slupetzky in Mauthausen und Gusen," *Jahrbuch der KZ-Gedenkstätte Mauthausen* 7 (2013): 2014, 45–57; It is mentioned also in Pierre Serge Choumoff, *Les chambres à gaz de Mauthausen: La vérité historique. A la demande de l'amicale de Mauthausen*

(Paris: Amicale des Déportés et Familles de Disparus du Camp de Concentration de Mauthausen 1972), 19; Hans Maršálek, *Die Geschichte des Konzentrationslagers Mauthausen*, 3rd ed. (Vienna: Österr. Lagergemeinschaft Mauthausen, 1995), 212; Pierre Serge Choumoff, *Nationalsozialistische Massentötungen durch Giftgas auf österreichischem Gebiet 1940–1945* (Vienna: Bundesministerium für Inneres, 2000); Bertrand Perz and Florian Freund, "Tötungen durch Giftgas im Konzentrationslager Mauthausen," in *Neue Studien zu nationalsozialistischen Massentötungen durch Giftgas: Historische Bedeutung, technische Entwicklung, revisionistische Leugnung*, ed. Günter Morsch and Bertrand Perz (Berlin: Metropol, 2011), 244–259.

16. Internal Route Slip, Mar. 12, 1948, 000-50-5-31/RG549/411, NARA, Washington.

17. §3 of the *War Crimes Act* of June 26, 1945, provides for severe prison sentences of ten to twenty years for torture and maltreatment. See StGBl Nr.32/45, 56, accessed Jan. 30, 2023, https://www.ris.bka.gv.at/Dokumente/BgblPdf/1945_32_0/1945_32_0.pdf.

18. Staatsanwaltschaft Linz to Oberstaatsanwaltschaft Linz, Jul. 5, 1950. 41 LG Linz – Sondergerichte Vg11Vr15 1950/Sch.1185/Slupetzky, OÖLA, Linz.

19. Testimony of Pawel Chapiorsky, Feb. 11, 1947, 000-50-5-31/RG549/410, NARA, Washington.

20. Ibid.

21. Testimony of Josef Prix at the criminal investigation department of Linz, Jul. 6, 1946, 19968/3, 115, DÖW, Vienna.

22. Ibid.

23. Ibid.

24. Ibid.

25. Ibid.

26. Testimony of Josef Prix, Nov. 3, 1952, 19968/9, DÖW, Vienna.

27. Anton Slupetzky to Landesgericht Linz als Volksgericht, Sep. 18, 1952, 19968/9, DÖW, Vienna.

28. Staatsanwaltschaft Linz to Oberstaatsanwaltschaft Linz, Apr. 7, 1951, 41 LG Linz – Sondergerichte Vg11Vr15 1950/Sch.1185/Slupetzky, OÖLA, Linz.

29. Brunner, Jul. 11, 1946, 19968/3, 122, DÖW, Vienna. For example,

Chapiorsky was accused of having testified in Dachau that Slupetzky produced Zyklon B in his company, which could not be true. A defamation of prosecution witnesses as liars and a literal victim-perpetrator reversal was carried out by: Hedwig Slupetzky: "Memorandum," Feb. 26, 1948, 19968/2–3, DÖW, Vienna.

30. Johann Anzinger was investigated for §§1,3 and 4 of the *War Crimes Act*. Polizeidirektion Linz to Staatsanwaltschaft Linz, Jul, 8, 1946, 19968/2, 117, DÖW, Vienna.

31. Staatsanwaltschaft Linz to Oberstaatsanwaltschaft Linz, Apr. 7, 1951, 41 LG Linz – Sondergerichte Vg11Vr15 1950/Sch.1185/Slupetzky, OÖLA, Linz.

32. Tagebuch Staatsanwaltschaft Linz, Dec. 4, 1975, 41 LG Linz – Sondergerichte Vg11Vr15 1950/Sch.1185/Slupetzky, OÖLA, Linz.

33. Pawel Chapiorsky named at least one witness together with her current whereabouts, a nurse who also worked as a forced laborer in the delousing facility and was at that time in a DP Camp near Salzburg. Testimony of Pawel Chapiorsky, Feb. 11, 1947, 000-50-5-31/RG549/410, NARA, Washington.

34. Hermann Rafetseder, "Der 'Ausländereinsatz' zur Zeit des NS-Regimes am Beispiel der Stadt Linz," in *Nationalsozialismus in Linz*, vol. II, ed. Fritz Mayrhofer and Walter Schuster (Linz: Archiv der Stadt Linz, 2002), 1107–1270 (here 1244).

35. Interrogation of Anton Slupetzky by Landesgericht Linz, Dec. 5, 1946–Jan 18, 1947, 19968/2, 137, DÖW, Vienna.

36. Minutes of the Dachau Military Tribunal against Anton Slupetzky, 19968/5, 366, DÖW, Vienna.

37. Testimony of Anna Haiböck at the criminal investigation department of Linz, Jul. 8, 1946, 19968/2, 118, DÖW, Vienna; Testimony of Leopold Fischer before the Dachau Military Tribunal, Aug. 11–12, 1947, 19968/5, 353, DÖW, Vienna.

38. Interrogation of Anton Slupetzky by Landesgericht Linz, Dec. 5, 1946–Jan 18, 1947, 19968/2, 141, DÖW, Vienna; In another source, Slupetzky states that he had already received the concession in 1939: Slupetzky to Heeressanitätsinspektion, Jul. 23, 1941, 19968/1, 33, DÖW, Vienna.

39. Hedwig Slupetzky: "Memorandum," Feb. 26, 1948, 19968/2, 121 DÖW, Vienna.

40. Testimony of Josef Kammesberger before the Dachau Military Tribunal, Aug. 8, 1947, 19968/5, 351, DÖW, Vienna.

41. Oberkommando des Heeres to companies Tesch & Stabenow, Dr. A. Jencic & Co, Zentral-Desinfektionsanstalt Diebl & Söhne, Slupetzky, Degesch, Dr. Breymesser & Co, Dr. Rudolf Grunert and Heerdt-Lingler, Jul. 28, 1942, 19968/1, 42, DÖW, Vienna.

42. Paul Weindling, *Epidemics and Genocide in Eastern Europe, 1890–1945* (Oxford: Oxford Univ. Press, 2000), 274.

43. Association "*Frohsinn*" to its association members, Nov 1943, 19968/3, 84, DÖW, Vienna.

44. Mittmannsgruber, "Stadtverwaltung," 122.

45. Ibid.; Rafetseder, "'Ausländereinsatz' zur Zeit des NS-Regimes," 1243.

46. Kammesberger to Kriminalpolizeistelle Linz, Jul. 9, 1946, 19968/2, 119, DÖW, Vienna.

47. "Damit die Ausländer keine Seuchen ins Reich schleppen konnten, mussten sie entlaust werden. Es ist richtig, dass Josef Prix von etwa 1941 an der Sachbearbeiter des ärztl. Dienstes beim Arbeitsamt Linz war und in dieser Eigenschaft bei den Entlausungen in der Entlausungsanstalt häufig dabei war. Er hatte zu überwachen, dass nur entlauste Ausländer zur Vermittlung freigegeben wurden." Testimony of Wilhelm Büttner at Amtsgericht Lindau, Sep. 22, 1952, 19968/9, DÖW, Vienna.

48. "Die Anstalt lag zehn Meter tief und bestand aus einem Hauptbau, sechs Gaskammern, in denen die Kleider mittels Blausäureverfahren gereinigt wurden sowie aus verschiedenen Nebenräumen, wie Bade-, Arzt-, Umkleide- und Sanitärräume. Pro Tag konnte die Kleidung von zirka 700–900 Personen gereinigt werden. Für die Körperreinigung standen 40 Brausen zur Verfügung, pro Person rechnete man mit 20 Minuten Badezeit." Mittmannsgruber, "Stadtverwaltung," 122.

49. Ibid.

50. Ibid.

51. Anton Slupetzky to Landesgericht Linz als Volksgericht, Sep. 18, 1952, 19968/9, DÖW, Vienna.

52. Ibid.

53. Josef Kammesberger to Kriminalpolizeistelle Linz, Jul. 9, 1946, 19968/2, DÖW, Vienna.

54. Ibid.

55. Arbeitsamt Linz to Landesarbeitsamt Oberdonau, Apr. 14, 1942, 19968/1, 39, DÖW, Vienna.

56. Testimony of Pawel Chapiorsky, Feb. 11, 1947, 000-50-5-31/RG549/410, NARA, Washington.

57. Till 2021 Volodymyr-Volynskyi in today's Ukraine, on the border with Poland, which in Polish is called Włodzimierz.

58. "This Slupetzky, whom I was also later on to discover, was the chief of the firm of Slupetzky, walked amongst the transport personnel and in many cases, I personally having seen this, administered blows across the face. For example, a woman would get on her knees and in a weeping tone, beg not to have her hair cut off. Slupetzky would answer her by striking her across the face. This was done fairly indiscriminately." Testimony of Pawel Chapiorsky, Feb. 11, 1947, 000-50-5-31/RG549/410, NARA, Washington.

59. Ibid.

60. "Im unreinen Teil der Anlage geben die ausländischen Arbeiter ihre Kleidungsstücke ab. Von dort kommen diese in die Entlausungskammern. In der Zwischenzeit werden die Arbeitskräfte einer ärztlichen Untersuchung unterzogen und dann gereinigt. Die Untersuchung findet vor der Entlausung der Menschen statt, damit etwaige infektiös Erkrankte sofort ausgeschieden werden können. Die Ärzte und ihr Hilfspersonal tragen Schutzkleidung gegen Läuse. [...] Bei der Reinigung der Menschen wird wiederum der grösste Wert auf die Beseitigung der Läuse gelegt. Alle behaarten Stellen des Körpers werden am zuverlässigsten mit Cuprex behandelt. Die Haupthaare der Männer und Frauen werden ebenfalls der gleichen Behandlung unterzogen und mechanisch bis zu einer halben Stunde pro Person Läuse und Nissen entfernt." Schranner, "Erfahrungen," 33–34; Gabriella Hauch, "Zwangsarbeiterinnen und ihre Kinder: Zum Geschlecht der Zwangsarbeit," in *NS-Zwangsarbeit: Der Standort Linz der Reichswerke Hermann Göring AG Berlin 1938-1945,* vol. I, ed. Oliver Rathkolb (Vienna: Böhlau, 2001), 355–448, (here 370).

61. Schranner, "Erfahrungen," 34.

62. Ibid.; For this procedure see also Ludwig Decker, "Der ärztliche Dienst beim Arbeitseinsatz ausländischer Arbeitskräfte," in *Arbeitseinsatz und Arbeitslosenhilfe* 8/21 (1941): 237–240.

63. Anton Slupetzky to Landesgericht Linz als Volksgericht, Sep. 18, 1952, 19968/9, DÖW, Vienna.

64. Schranner did state that in some places the medical examination takes

place after the delousing of the people on the grounds that the laborers should recover after transport so that their work ability can be better assessed. According to her, however, the immediate elimination of infectious patients was of greater value. Schranner, "*Erfahrungen*," 33–34.

65. Circular of the Reich Minister of the Interior, Feb. 13, 1942, in *Ministerialblatt des Reichs- und Preußischen Ministerium des Innern*, ed. Reichsministerium des Innern (Berlin 1942/no.7), 382.

66. Ibid., 378.

67. Ibid., 382. [Wobei bei "starker Verlausung [. . .] auch alle behaarten Körperstellen (Bart, Augenbrauen, Wimpern, Gehörgang, Kopfhaare, Afterhaare, Schamhaare, Achselhaare) zu kontrollieren [sind]."]

68. Ibid.

69. "[...] die von den Kleiderläusen vorwiegend aufgesuchten Körperstellen (Nacken, die Gegenden zwischen den Schulterblättern und über dem Kreuzbein, ferner die Schamgegend bis in die Gesäßspalte, sowie die Achselhöhlen) [...] noch mit Petroleum kräftig 2 Minuten einreiben, mit Schmierseife nachreiben, 10 Minuten einwirken und dann baden zu lassen [sic]." Ibid.

70. "das Abschneiden der Haare auf nicht überwindbaren Widerspruch stößt, wie dies namentlich bei weiblichen Personen öfter der Fall ist, tränkt man die Haare reichlich mit einem läusetötenden Mittel [. . .], wobei aber von der Flüssigkeit nichts in die Augen gelangen darf, und umhüllt den Kopf 12 bis 24 Stunden lang mit einer Badehaube, einer wollenen Haube oder einem festsitzenden Tuche." Ibid. It was added that two hours were sufficient if the lice-killing agents "Cuprex, Lauto" or "Antiparasit-W" were used.

71. Arbeitsamt Linz to Landesarbeitsamt Oberdonau, Apr. 14, 1942, 19968/1, 39, DÖW, Vienna.

72. Ibid.

73. Ibid.

74. Anton Slupetzky to Landesgericht Linz als Volksgericht, Sep. 18, 1952, 19968/9, DÖW, Vienna.

75. Ibid.

76. Wilhelm Büttner to Landesgericht Linz, Jun. 8, 1952, 19968/10, DÖW, Vienna.

77. Ibid.

78. Ibid.

79 Pawel Chapiorsky also reports that men and women had their head hair shaved without distinction of sex. Testimony of Pawel Chapiorsky, Feb. 11, 1947, 000-50-5-31/RG549/410, NARA, Washington.

80. Brigitte Fuchs, "'Rasse,' 'Volk,' Geschlecht und Sexualität. Anthropologische Diskurse und deren politische Funktionalisierung in Österreich 1860–1945," in *Gebrochene Kontinuitäten? Zur Rolle und Bedeutung des Geschlechterverhältnisses in der Entwicklung des Nationalsozialismus*, ed. Ilse Korotin and Barbara Serloth (Innsbruck: Studien-Verlag 2000), 151–179.

81. Gisela Bock, eds., *Genozid und Geschlecht. Jüdische Frauen im nationalsozialistischen Lagersystem*, (Frankfurt/Main: Campus 2005), 17; Helga Amesberger, et al., *Sexualisierte Gewalt. Weibliche Erfahrungen in Konzentrationslagern*, 2nd ed. (Vienna: Mandelbaum, 2004), 79–88.

82. Anton Slupetzky to Landesgericht Linz als Volksgericht, Sep. 18, 1952, 19968/9, DÖW, Vienna.

83. Arbeitsamt Linz to Landesarbeitsamt Oberdonau, Apr. 14, 1942, 19968/1, 39, DÖW, Vienna.

84. "[W]eil geeignete Personen, besonders bei den Frauen, nicht zur Verfügung stehen, weil übrigens – gerade bei Frauen – das Rasieren der Geschlechtsteile praktisch unmöglich ist." Ibid.

85. Anton Slupetzky to Landesgericht Linz als Volksgericht, Sep. 18, 1952, 19968/9, DÖW, Vienna.

86. Cresols are used in disinfectants for their bactericidal, insecticidal, and fungicidal effects. They are highly corrosive and are considered carcinogenic. At high skin exposures, they can be life-threatening. *Toxikologie,* vol. II, *Toxikologie der Stoffe*, ed. Hans-Werner Vohr (Weinheim: WILEY-VCH 2010), 111–112.

87. Arbeitsamt Linz to Landesarbeitsamt Oberdonau, Apr. 14, 1942, 19968/1, 39, DÖW, Vienna.

88. Pictures of the disinfection of prisoners of war by Slupetzky are illustrated by several authors: Helmut Lackner and Gerhard A. Stadler, *Fabriken in der Stadt. Eine Industriegeschichte der Stadt Linz* (Linz: Archiv der Stadt Linz, 1990), 411; Hermann Rafetseder, "Der 'Ausländereinsatz,'" in *Bilder des Nationalsozialismus in Linz,* ed. Fritz Mayrhofer and Walter Schuster (Linz: Archiv der Stadt Linz, 1997), 129–135, (here 135); Mittmannsgruber, "Die Linzer Stadtverwaltung," 123

.89. Testimony of Josef Prix at the criminal investigation department of Linz, Jul. 6, 1946, 19968/3, 115, DÖW, Vienna.

90. "[in] einem Falle [...] eine Verätzung leichteren Grades bei einer Frau auf der Brust beobachtet und diese in das Spital eingewiesen [wurde]. Die Untersuchung ergab, daß die Verätzung dadurch zu Stande kam, daß die Frau nach der Körperentlausung mit der Desinfektionsflüssigkeit das Brausebad umging und sich sofort ankleidete." Kammesberger to Kriminalpolizeistelle Linz, Jul. 9, 1946, 19968/2, 119, DÖW, Vienna.

91. "Slupetzky musste bei den Entlausungen natürlich die Haare der zu entlausenden Frauen auseinander nehmen und sie nach Läusen und Nissen durchsuchen. Es ist auch in der ersten Zeit, als die Leute noch vielfach nicht über den Vorgang der Entlausung informiert waren, vorgekommen, dass Slupetzky anlässlich der Besprühung mit einem Seifenpräparat den Frauen die Brüste hochgehoben hat, damit auch die Stellen unter denselben von dem Präparat erfasst wurden. Später haben die Leute den Vorgang schon gekannt und haben die Brüste von selbst hochgehoben, auch die Arme hochgehoben, damit die Achselhöhlen frei waren [...]." Testimony of Josef Prix, Nov. 3, 1952, 19968/9, DÖW, Vienna.

92. "Wenn er nun behauptet, dass Frauen bei den Haaren angefasst wurden, so mag dies vielleicht stimmen, doch nicht aus dem Umstande einer Misshandlung, sondern, weil diese Leute sich mit aller Gewalt der vorgeschriebenen Entlausung widersetzten. Ich muss es als eine bodenlose Gemeinheit bezeichnen, wenn der Zeuge in weiterer Folge noch die Behauptung aufstellt, ich hätte Frauen an den Brüsten gerissen. Mich wundert es, dass der Zeuge nicht behauptet, ich hätte die Frauen an dem Geschlechtsteil berührt." Interrogation of Anton Slupetzky by Landesgericht Linz, Dec. 5, 1946 to Jan 18, 1947, 19968/2, 137, DÖW, Vienna.

93. Anton Slupetzky to Landesgericht Linz als Volksgericht, Sep. 18, 1952, 19968/9, DÖW, Vienna.

94 Circular of the Reich Minister of the Interior, Feb. 13, 1942, in *Ministerialblatt des Reichs- und Preußischen Ministerium des Innern*, ed. Reichsministerium des Innern (Berlin 1942/no.7), 382.

95. "Ich erinnere mich ferner, dass ich gegen das kalte Duschen vor der Entlausung war, weil ich gehört hatte, dass die Ausländer (insbesondere die Ostarbeiterinnen) das nur mit Widerstreben taten, und oft nur mit 'sanftem Zwang' dazu bewogen werden konnten. Auch hier musste ich mich ärztlichen Argumenten beugen, die dahin gingen, dass gerade die kalte Dusche

im Interesse der Ausländer vorgenommen werde, weil sich dadurch die Poren schlössen und Erkältungskrankheiten vermieden würden." Wilhelm Büttner to Landesgericht Linz, Jun. 8, 1952, 19968/10, DÖW, Vienna.

96. "Die Person, die uns im Duschraum Seife und Handtuch reichte, war ein Mann und keine Frau … kein Mann hatte mich bisher nackt gesehen, abgesehen von Ärzten … und neben dem Gefühl der Scham empfand ich ein Gefühl der Wut, daß man Menschen so grundlos verletzen mußte. Hätte man nicht eine Frau mit dieser Aufgabe betrauen können?"; "[T]he person who handed us soap and towel in the shower room was a man and not a woman ... no man had seen me naked before, except for doctors ... and besides the feeling of shame, I felt a sense of anger that people had to be hurt so needlessly. Couldn't a woman have been entrusted with this task?" Levin Meyer, *Die Geschichte der Eva Korngold. Nach Aufzeichnungen von Ida Löw* (Frankfurt am Main: Fischer Taschenbuch Verlag, 1995), 36. Cited after: Hauch, "Zwangsarbeiterinnen," 370.

97. Schäfer, "Durchgangs- und Krankensammellager," 209.

98. Interrogation of Anton Slupetzky by Landesgericht Linz, Dec. 5, 1946–Jan 18, 1947, 19968/2, 137, DÖW, Vienna. The photo that also shows a female official of the Arbeitsamt Linz is not attached to the copy of the court file at DÖW.

99. Reichmuth to Slupetzky, Jan. 5, 194[.] (Year not readable), 19968/3, DÖW, Vienna.

100. "Man kann ja von derartigen Sachen, die im Bild bisher so gut wie gar nicht festgehalten worden sind, nicht genug Material zur Verfügung haben. Das Unverständnis den verlausten Gefangenen gegenüber ist gross, und hier kann nur gutes Anschauungsmaterial überzeugen." Ibid.

101. Anton Slupetzky to Landesgericht Linz als Volksgericht, Sep. 18, 1952, 19968/9, DÖW, Vienna.

102. Kammesberger to Kriminalpolizeistelle Linz, Jul. 9, 1946, 19968/2, 119, DÖW, Vienna; Instructions for and implementation of the medical examinations for forced laborers from Eastern Europe were described in detail here: Hallama, "Between the projection of danger."

103. According to the circular issued by the Reich Minister of the Interior, after treatment with hydrocyanic gas, the clothes were to be aired in the open air for at least one hour before they could be taken for use again. Circular of the Reich Minister of the Interior, Feb. 13, 1942,

in *Ministerialblatt des Reichs- und Preußischen Ministerium des Innern*, ed. Reichsministerium des Innern (Berlin 1942/no.7), 383.

104. Testimony of Josef Prix at the criminal investigation department of Linz, Jul. 6, 1946, 19968/3, 115, DÖW, Vienna; Testimony of Hedwig Slupetzky, Jun. 5, 1946, 19968/3, 102, DÖW, Vienna; Testimony of Anna Haiböck (daughter) at the criminal investigation department of Linz, Jul. 8, 1946, 19968/2, 118, DÖW, Vienna.

105. Anton Slupetzky to Landesgericht Linz als Volksgericht, Sep. 18, 1952, 19968/9, DÖW, Vienna.

106. Oberbürgermeister Linz to Gesundheitsamt Oberdonau, Mar. 20, 1944, Sanitätsverwaltung der Reichsstatthalterei 1940–45, IIIaM/1944/180Fleckfieber/MF 502, OÖLA, Linz.

107. Ibid.

108. Anton Slupetzky to Landesgericht Linz als Volksgericht, Sep. 18, 1952, 19968/9, DÖW, Vienna.

109. "Es kam wiederholt vor, daß zu Entlausende das Wasser aus den Klomuscheln zu Trinkzwecken benützten, obwohl sowohl auf der reinen als auch auf der unreinen Seite je 1 hygienischer Trinkbrunnen vorhanden war, während oftmals die Notdurft bei den Heizkörpern verrichtet wurde. Wir hatten täglich 500 bis 800 Frauen und Mädchen zu entlausen. Darunter befand sich ein gewisser Prozentsatz, der zu diesem Zeitpunkt unwohl war. Die ausgegebenen Zellstoffvorlagen wurden fast nie benützt, da ihnen der Gebrauch unbekannt war." Ibid.

110. Ernst Kortschak cites exactly the same examples as Anton Slupetzky to illustrate "primitiveness." Testimony of Ernst Kortschak at Bezirksgericht Judenburg, Oct. 20, 1952, 19968/9, DÖW, Vienna.

111. Anton Slupetzky to Landesgericht Linz als Volksgericht, Sep. 18, 1952, 19968/9, DÖW, Vienna.

112. Hauch, "Zwangsarbeiterinnen," 369.

113. Anton Slupetzky to Landesgericht Linz als Volksgericht, Sep. 18, 1952, 19968/9, DÖW, Vienna; Kammesberger to Kriminalpolizeistelle Linz, Jul. 9, 1946, 19968/2, 119, DÖW, Vienna; Wilhelm Büttner to Landesgericht Linz, Jun. 8, 1952, 19968/10, DÖW, Vienna.

114. Wilhelm Büttner to Landesgericht Linz, Jun. 8, 1952, 19968/10, DÖW, Vienna. Similar remarks by Josef Kammesberger, Ernst Kortschak and Anton Slupetzky can be found here: "Die Gefahr der Weiterverbreitung dieser gefährlichen Krankheit [Fleckfieber], welche

durch die Kleiderlaus übertragen wird, konnte nur durch eine sorgfältige Entlausung verhindert werden. Daher muß diese Einrichtung als segensreich für die Bevölkerung betrachtet werden." Kammesberger to Kriminalpolizeistelle Linz, Jul. 9, 1946, 19968/2, 119, DÖW, Vienna; "Meiner Ansicht nach war vielmehr die Entlausungsstation, damit auch der Leiter dieser Einrichtung der Besch[uldigte], dasjenige Institut, das die Stadt Linz und wahrscheinlich ganz O[ber]ö[sterreich] vor der grossen Gefahr von Epidemien bewahrt hat." Testimony of Ernst Kortschak at Bezirksgericht Judenburg, Oct. 20, 1952, 19968/9, DÖW, Vienna; "Nur bei rigorosester Durchführung der erteilten Maßnahmen war die Gewähr geboten, daß durch das Einströmen von Hunderttausend Ausländern für die Bevölkerung Österreichs das Seuchenmoment auf ein Minimum reduziert werden konnte." Anton Slupetzky to Landesgericht Linz als Volksgericht, Sep. 18, 1952, 19968/9, DÖW, Vienna.

Preventing Paralysis: The Use of Inactivated Poliomyelitis Vaccine in Austria, 1955–1960

Marina Hilber

Introduction

"Considering that Austria records numerous cases of poliomyelitis every year, it is an urgent necessity to use all means available to prevent the disease."[1] With this striking announcement, the Austrian Federal Ministry of Social Administration (*Bundesministerium für soziale Verwaltung*, hereafter BMfsV) addressed the nine provincial governments in April 1955, only days after the licensing of Jonas Salk's inactivated poliovirus vaccine (IPV) in the United States was celebrated worldwide. Because of its unpredictability, the lack of effective medical prevention strategies, and the severe aftereffects, such as permanent paralysis and disfigurement, poliomyelitis was one of the most feared diseases at the time. Alison Day attributes the public horror to the visibility of the disease.[2] In the words of Alfons Labisch, polio is a "scandalized disease."[3] An opinion poll conducted in the United States in the 1950s even concluded that polio was the second most feared catastrophe; only the threat of an atomic bomb was considered worse.[4]

After the introduction of a nationwide obligation to report polio cases in 1927, the Austrian medical authorities recorded regional epidemics every year.[5] Polio incidence steadily increased, especially after the end of the Second World War. Although an absolute peak was reached as early as 1947, with over 3,500 cases and 315 deaths, the disease did not subside in the 1950s but instead became more virulent.[6] Therefore, medical professionals initially assumed that vaccination against poliomyelitis would inevitably be a popular success.[7] However, the occurrence of the so-called Cutter Incident, which resulted in over 200 cases of vaccine-derived polio,[8] caused the Austrian health authorities to fall into a long phase of disillusionment and hesitation. It was not until 1958 that the first general vaccination campaigns with IPV were implemented. This article traces the difficulties involved and the regional peculiarities in the implementation of these vaccination campaigns. Based on source material from the Austrian State Archives, particularly the holdings of the BMfsV's Public Health Department, which include not only official correspondence but also the minutes of the Supreme Medical Council (*Oberster Sanitätsrat*, hereinafter OSR), the prevailing medical, political, and public discourses are reconstructed. Supplementary sources from federal state archives provide further insights into the regional implementation of polio vaccination campaigns. The article assumes that the Cutter Incident severely damaged confidence in vaccination with inactivated virus, which was initially touted as a magic wand. The analyzed sources show how the initial euphoria was replaced by an overriding need for security in the decision-making bodies. A lack of financial resources and supply chain constraints also hampered early attempts at introduction. It was not until provincial governments took action that the first vaccination campaigns could finally begin in 1958. How the population reacted to the hesitant attitude of the authorities and the general level of acceptance of IPV in Austria are discussed for the period from 1955 to 1960. In 1961, IPV was replaced by the oral polio vaccine (OPV), which was deemed more effective from a public health perspective.

The history of poliomyelitis was long considered a genuinely American story. In fact, the United States was severely affected right from the first devastating epidemic in New York City in 1916.[9] This is probably why historical awareness was high and the reappraisal of polio history began comparatively early.[10] In Europe, polio has only become the subject of more intensive debate since the millennium. The focus has been on the history of polio prevention in the form of public hygiene as well as passive and active immunization strategies. In the German-speaking world, thorough research is available from Ulrike Lindner, Malte Thießen, and Annette Hinz-Wessels.[11] The topic has also been addressed in Sweden,[12] Great Britain,[13] the Netherlands,[14] Italy,[15] Spain,[16] Hungary,[17] and most recently in Poland.[18] In Austria, however, the history of poliomyelitis still constitutes a striking research desideratum in contemporary and medical history.[19]

The Cutter Incident and Austrian Polio Policy

In the early 1950s, efforts to develop a vaccine against poliomyelitis were in full swing. In 1953, Jonas Salk (1914–1995) was the first to succeed in inactivating the virus with formalin. The injection of the inactivated virus caused an immune response in healthy individuals, who did not develop any apparent symptoms of the disease. The following year, the vaccine was tested in large-scale field trials in the United States, Canada, and Finland. A total of more than 1.8 million children were successfully immunized without any significant side effects. On April 12, 1955, Thomas Francis, chair of the Department of Epidemiology at the School of Public Health at the University of Michigan, who had observed the trials, announced that the vaccine was an effective and safe means of combating poliomyelitis.[20]

Only four days after Salk's vaccine received approval,[21] a group of experts met at the City Medical Office (*Stadtphysikat*) in Vienna to discuss this significant advance in polio prevention and its immediate relevance to Austria. Salk's vaccine was considered "scientifically well-founded, reliable, and effective."[22] The experts believed that the population should not be deprived of such a promising preventive measure and wanted to immediately import the vaccine from the United States or from the Behring Werke in Marburg, Germany, which produced a vaccine based on similar principles. Although a mass campaign could not be implemented immediately due to the lack of sufficient quantities of importable vaccine, the experts urged the Vienna City Medical Officer to ensure that at least the vulnerable group, comprising two- and three-year-old children, was offered a shot. This meant that the approximately 24,000 children belonging to the 1952 and 1953 birth cohorts needed to receive an injection not only once but at least two or even three times to develop full protection. The cost of the endeavor was estimated at six million schillings. This recommendation came from three high-ranking members of the OSR, namely Richard Bieling (1888–1967), head of the Hygiene Institute of the University of Vienna; Hanns Hoff (1897–1969), head of the Neurological-Psychiatric University Hospital of Vienna; and Karl Kundratitz (1889–1975), head of the Vienna University Children's Hospital. The latter even offered to make the personnel and premises of his clinic available for vaccination purposes.[23] The medical experts opined that Austria should follow the general European trend of the rapid introduction of immunization campaigns and take its place as a pioneer in the field of immunization together with Sweden, Denmark, Finland, West Germany, Great Britain, France, and Switzerland.[24]

However, the federal government was not willing to bear the cost of vaccination. For this reason, the provinces were contacted as early as April 21, 1955, to explore possible cost-sharing arrangements. The cost of full immunization was estimated at 150 schillings per person. However, the provincial governments (*Länder*) objected strongly to covering the costs. The Vienna City Council played a leading role in the debate surrounding the financial management of possible vaccination campaigns. It argued that health care—including the prevention and control of infectious diseases—was a federal responsibility. Additionally, it stated that the health insurance funds should also contribute, as they would benefit significantly from minimizing the risk of infection. The majority of the provincial governments agreed with this interpretation, with only Burgenland and Upper Austria declaring their willingness to bear a share of the costs.[25]

However, very shortly thereafter, the initial euphoria in Austria was curbed by the shocking news arriving from the United States that several cases of paralysis and even death had occurred as a result of polio vaccination. This medical disaster, later referred to as the Cutter Incident, was caused by the circulation of incompletely inactivated batches of vaccine from the Cutter plant in Berkeley, California, and shaped public and medical opinions.[26] By the time the OSR convened for a plenary session on May 7, 1955, to debate the future of polio vaccination in Austria, the situation had changed dramatically. Considering that forecasts for the summer of 1955 predicted a major polio epidemic in Austria, the head of the Public Health Department in the BMfsV, Dr. Alfred Khaum, spoke of the "embarrassing situation" the political decision-makers found themselves in, "for the simple reason that the public is inflamed by the newspaper reports from America, on the one hand, that poliomyelitis can be successfully controlled, on the other, that the vaccine is unreliable and cases of the disease have occurred."[27]

In the OSR, opinions differed: while Professor Bieling still maintained the view that vaccination was harmless and that the incidents were merely due to the failure of a single pharmaceutical company, Karl Fellinger (1904–2000), internist and chair of Vienna's Second Medical University Clinic, expressed his skepticism about a large-scale campaign. Professors Hoff and Kundratitz echoed this skepticism and recommended waiting until the incidents in the United States had been clarified. Karl Kundratitz summarized the situation by simply stating, "I believe that if we were to say 'Let's vaccinate,' no one would show up."[28] The experts agreed that the vaccination issue in Austria was a highly emotional one, and that it was necessary to proceed with tact and sensitivity to achieve widespread acceptance among the population.[29]

Another factor that hindered the introduction of vaccination against poliomyelitis to the general public in 1955 was the availability of vaccines. Neither the Behring Werke in Marburg nor Parke Davis in the United States could supply sufficient quantities of vaccine in the foreseeable future. However, both companies guaranteed the delivery of 100,000 individual doses within six weeks. Since this amount would only suffice to immunize 50,000 children and a selection of suitable individuals, this would probably have led to public suspicion and rumors regarding a search for "guinea pigs," and the import of such small quantities of the vaccine was rejected by the Austrian federal government. In early May 1955, the OSR thus voted against the immediate introduction of general, state-organized, and state-financed polio vaccination but gave general practitioners as well as pediatricians the freedom to vaccinate their patients privately.[30] However, since the US Surgeon General had ordered a ban on the export of American vaccines at the end of May 1955,[31] and the German Behring Werke did not export its vaccine either,[32] private vaccination in Austria remained only a theoretical possibility.

To adequately assess further developments in the field of polio research, a sub-commission of the OSR was established. Unsurprisingly, this board included the physicians Richard Bieling, Hanns Hoff, and Karl Kundratitz. The four-person commission was completed by the orthopedist Karl Chiari (1912–1982).[33] As of December 1955, this commission continued to warn against general public mass vaccination in Austria, with safety concerns and the insufficient availability of the vaccine continuing to dominate the discourse.[34]

Although it was simply not possible to procure vaccines for mass vaccination campaigns, the BMfsV now assumed that smaller quantities could be imported. According to Austrian law, there was no ban on importing foreign vaccines. Thus, the commission once again reminded physicians in private practices of their right to vaccinate. However, only vaccines that had been tested abroad as per the standard minimum requirements were to be used.[35] María-Isabel Porras-Gallo and María-Victoria Caballero see the dependence on foreign pharmaceutical companies as a major reason for the delayed introduction of national vaccination campaigns.[36] Attempts to produce the vaccine at the Federal Serotherapeutic Institute in Vienna had been discontinued due to a lack of profitability. However, the Vienna-based pharmaceutical company Austrian Institute for Hemoderivatives (*Österreichisches Institut für Haemoderivate*) had also immediately started trials, and in mid-1956, reported that the first batches of its IPV would be ready for testing by the end of the year.[37] The availability of foreign polio vaccines also improved throughout 1956. Several companies, including the well-known US companies Eli Lilly and Parke Davis, offered to provide the ministry with vaccines for state-directed mass vaccination.[38] However, the decision-making bodies were still uncertain even though representatives of the Austrian medical profession[39] and the media were increasingly calling for a political commitment to protect the population. In 1957, a polemical article in the Styrian communist newspaper *Volksstimme* pointed out that large-scale vaccination campaigns had been launched in several countries around the world and only Austria wanted to wait a little longer. A source within the medical administration was quoted as saying, "In the near future, a government-led vaccination campaign is out of the question. Let's wait a few more years ..."[40]

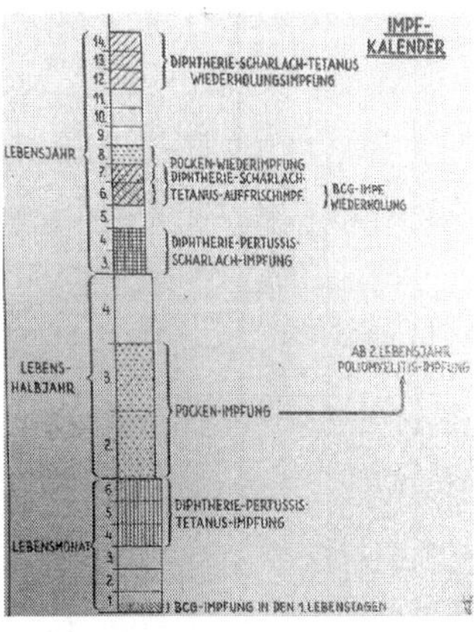

FIGURE 1: Austrian Immunization Schedule 1957, Source:

Österreichische Ärztezeitung, December 25, 1957, 1040.

It is unclear whether increasing public pressure, medical reasoning, or the release of a comprehensive special report by the US Surgeon General confirming the safety and efficacy of the Salk vaccine prompted the OSR's polio commission to issue a statement in late 1957. Regardless, the Austrian polio commission's recommendation of general vaccination was now unequivocal: "Active immunization now seems to have progressed to the point where we are justified in proposing vaccination to the general public or to certain high-risk cohorts."[41] The official Austrian immunization schedule, a visual guide for physicians and parents, also included IPV at the end of 1957.[42] However, by the end of 1957, Austria had long lost its opportunity to play a pioneering role in Europe as intended. Denmark began a state-organized vaccination program in 1955; Great Britain and France followed in 1956; and the Federal Republic of Germany,[43] the Netherlands,[44] and Italy[45] introduced IPV in 1957. IPV campaigns also commenced in the communist countries of the Eastern Bloc, namely Hungary, Czechoslovakia, and Poland, in 1957.[46] Although the BMfsV informed the provincial governments in late February 1958 that the state administration no longer held any reservations against public immunization if the minimum requirements for the vaccine were fulfilled, a state-funded vaccination campaign was still rejected. IPV protected the individual from disease, especially from severe paralysis; however, virus transmission was not prevented, and therefore, no immediate epidemiological benefit was reached. As IPV was only insufficiently promoting public health, the Austrian government deliberately refrained from state-organized and state-financed mass vaccination.[47] At this point, however, intensive preparations were already underway in some of the nine provinces. The *Länder* took matters into their own hands and paved the way for general, voluntary vaccination against poliomyelitis in Austria.

Nine Vaccination Schemes

The turning point in the hitherto ambivalent attitude of Austrian politics was reached at the beginning of 1958. On January 22, 1958, Lois Weinberger, Vienna's deputy mayor and city councilor for public health, announced the introduction of general polio vaccination in Vienna.[48] The city of Vienna had forged ahead in this matter, significantly without consulting the other provincial governments. Vienna decided to vaccinate all children born in 1950 and 1951 and those born between 1952 and 1955 attending a public kindergarten free of charge. Those born between 1947 and 1949 were also invited, although they were to contribute fifteen schillings per shot.[49] The capital city's government thus brought about a trend-setting policy shift that forced the other federal states into action, leading to a patchwork of different regulations in Austria.[50] Tyrol and Styria, the latter having just experienced a severe epidemic in 1957,[51] also considered general vaccination campaigns in spring 1958. However, the cohorts targeted varied according to the assessment of the individual medical councils. Tyrol called upon the 1951–1956 birth cohorts to be vaccinated. In addition, Tyroleans had to contribute ten schillings per injection.[52] In Styria, too, the population was to contribute to the cost of vaccination. For the first two shots, twenty-five schillings were charged; only families with more than two children saw their financial contribution reduced to twenty schillings. Styria extended the campaign to a large group of recipients: everyone aged one to forty years could voluntarily register for a public vaccination appointment. Only schoolchildren were enrolled collectively through the school board.[53]

While the aforementioned provinces had the foresight to allocate the necessary funds in their budgets, the remaining provinces made no or hardly any provisions for protecting the population. The Salzburg provincial medical officer requested 50,000 schillings from his government, but a vaccination campaign was not to begin until the fall of 1958 at the earliest. The responsible medical officials of Burgenland also made a similar request, but unfortunately, the province was unable to finance a vaccination campaign with its own resources. Upper Austria also reported that it could not bear the high costs. Carinthia likewise refused to bear the costs for 1958 but planned to introduce vaccination in 1959. The province of Lower Austria was also initially hesitant, and in January 1958, *Landesrat* Wenger reiterated that physicians in private practice were authorized to administer vaccines on a private basis. Lower Austria would consider subsidizing the costs of vaccination, but only if the federal government made vaccination a legal requirement. The government itself did not plan a vaccination campaign.[54] Finally, in March 1958, the westernmost province of Vorarlberg simply stated, "Vorarlberg is currently not preparing general public poliomyelitis vaccination."[55]

The vaccine for the first large-scale campaigns in Austria was mainly imported. The vaccine developed by the French Institute Pasteur and produced by the laboratories of *Recherche et Industrie Therapeutique Gerval* (RIT) in Belgium was used, as were US products from Parke Davis. Only the German vaccine from the Behring Werke, much preferred by members of the OSR, could not be acquired. In 1958, a conflict arose regarding the vaccine from the only Austrian supplier, the Institute for Hemoderivatives. In its February 1958 dispatch, the BMfsV had indirectly recommended the vaccines of American and German provenance. The domestically produced Austrian vaccine was decidedly not included in the list, although the necessary tests had all been carried out by a Swiss laboratory and the vaccine was already being exported in large quantities. The Institute for Hemoderivatives considered this oversight to be damaging to its reputation. The BMfsV's recommendation was probably based on information from the Federal Serotherapeutic Institute, which had also tried its hand at producing vaccines in 1955/56 but had to discontinue the experiments due to a lack of funding. At the beginning of 1958, this former competitor decided that "the polio vaccine produced in Austria must not only be regarded as insufficiently tested on humans, but moreover, cannot be tested by the state in a way that is self-evident and generally prescribed by law."[56] Thus, the institute criticized the absence of an Austrian test laboratory while simultaneously discrediting the privately developed vaccine of the Institute for Hemoderivatives. In fact, the Serotherapeutic Institute tried to position itself as an importer and distributor of foreign vaccines by applying for an import permit for the vaccine of the Canadian Connaught Laboratories, which had already been administered millions of times.[57] However, the deal did not materialize because Connaught had already established a branch in Austria and did not consider business relationships with the Serotherapeutic Institute. The Institute for Hemoderivatives, on the other hand, supplied its vaccine—albeit in smaller batches than other companies—especially to Vienna, Lower Austria, and Burgenland.[58] By September 1958, the vaccine had been used "without a complaint" for about 200,000 vaccinations in Austria. Karl Kundratitz concluded: "I think we should be proud to have such an institute in Vienna."[59]

Vaccine Acceptance throughout Austria

Vaccination in Austria was always accompanied by widespread advertising campaigns. Posters and flyers were used to raise public awareness, while doctors provided information about the vaccination process and emphasized its safety in radio interviews and newspaper articles. Vaccination enrollment lists were available in businesses and schools. To allay mothers' fears regarding the performance of a potentially painful procedure on their children, the Graz city physicist Dr. Studeny compared vaccination to a "flea bite"; however, the after-effects would cause only a tenth of the pain and discomfort. It was always emphasized that vaccination with inactivated poliovirus was one of the least problematic vaccinations, showing hardly any bodily reactions, let alone side effects.[60]

The acceptance of IPV varied in the nine provinces of Austria. The

Länder that had been opposed to public vaccination campaigns at the beginning of February 1958, such as Salzburg, Upper Austria, Lower Austria, Burgenland, and Vorarlberg, had to surrender to public pressure and carried out vaccination campaigns late in the year.[61] Although all provinces rolled out vaccines by the end of 1958, they did not always succeed in mobilizing the population to the desired extent. For instance, shortly before the vaccination campaign in Graz, in mid-April 1958, medical officials complained that only a few people had registered for vaccination: "It almost seems as if everyone is waiting for their neighbor to take the first step to the registration office."[62] In 1958 and 1959, only 30 percent of the targeted age groups in Vienna were sufficiently immunized.[63]

	1958		
	1st Injection	2nd Injection	3rd Injection
Vienna	39,940	38,023	35,594
Lower Austria		not specified	
Upper Austria	52,908	47,669	5,562
Salzburg	23,567	22,843	17
Styria	131,448	126,575	-
Carinthia	10,807	10,009	7
Tyrol	21,576	20,912	699
Vorarlberg	39,541	35,236	2
Burgenland	13,654	13,445	76
Austria	**333,441**	**314,712**	**41,957**

TABLE 1: Vaccine rollout in 1958[64]

In Vorarlberg, the vaccination coverage rate was significantly higher by the end of 1958, but for a particular reason. Political decision-makers in the westernmost province had shown little interest in general vaccination as late as the spring of 1958, and in the summer of that year, were overwhelmed by a massive wave of polio. Between the beginning of July and the end of November 1958, at least 146 people were hospitalized in Vorarlberg. A total of thirty-five polio-related deaths, mainly among children aged zero to six years, were mourned.[65] No other province recorded such a high mortality rate in 1958. Conflict erupted in the country, largely channeled through the media. According to Elisabeth Dietrich-Daum, the newspaper with the widest circulation, the *Vorarlberger Nachrichten* (VN), sided with the medical profession and the so-called "Family Association" (*Familienverband*), led by general practitioner Dr. Leopold Bischof. In addition to obvious failures in disease prevention (waiving of school closures), the hesitant and apparently purely economically motivated attitude of the provincial government in the matter of vaccination funding was criticized. Governor Ulrich Ilg was quoted as saying that families were responsible for the health of their children and that there was nothing the province could do. In his view, politicians were not to blame. In contrast, large sums of money were allocated each year for the control of animal diseases. In 1958, a total of 900,000 schillings were reserved for the fight against bovine tuberculosis and brucellosis.[66]

Only after several municipalities, above all the provincial capital of Bregenz, declared that they would cover the costs of vaccination from their own modest budgets to quickly offer help to the frightened parents and children did the provincial government relent and approve a vaccination campaign at the end of September.[67] The vaccine was imported from the Detroit plants of Parke Davis, and the hard-won campaign was finally launched at the end of November 1958. The campaign was open to everyone, regardless of age. Minors had to pay a fee of ten schillings, while adults contributed fifteen schillings per injection.[68] The response from the population was huge, as a look at Götzis, the hometown of the vaccination advocate Dr. Bischof, shows: "The physician Dr. Bischof was able to vaccinate over 500 children aged between six months and six years against polio. The 'concert' of the little ones was as grand as the joy of their parents after vaccination. The following day, about 600 children from the Götzner schools were waiting. How seriously parents take this vaccination can be seen from the fact that more than 90 percent of the schoolchildren attended the vaccination campaign. If we add the fact that some had already been vaccinated earlier on their parents' own initiative, we see that there are very few who are not aware of the danger."[69] As polio vaccination was not compulsory, it was still the adults who had to be convinced. By the end of 1958, a total of 70 percent of the toddlers and schoolchildren in Vorarlberg had received double immunization.[70] The willingness to be vaccinated was particularly high in Vorarlberg in the light of the epidemic that the region had just encountered, with numerous deaths and even more seriously impaired children.[71] In addition, the broad media presence in the run-up to the vaccination campaign probably led to increased sensitivity in the affected population. The inclusion of schoolchildren, which was logistically easy, caused vaccination coverage rates to rise even further.

In 1959 and 1960, the administration of IPV was continued in all

Austrian provinces. However, this did not prevent polio epidemics from occurring. Upper Austria was particularly affected in 1959, with over 400 reported cases and more than 50 deaths, even though it ranked second (behind only Styria) in the vaccination statistics in 1958. In the densely populated provinces, however, overall figures reveal little about actual vaccination coverage rates.[72] Throughout Austria, vaccination coverage rates varied considerably, and by 1960, only 40 percent of children and adolescents were sufficiently immunized against poliomyelitis. In terms of the total population, this resulted in a vaccination coverage rate of only 12.5 percent.[73] Although this figure was more than twice as high as in the neighboring country of the Federal Republic of Germany,[74] the massive run expected in 1955, which the opinion polls of the Austrian Poliomyelitis Association had suggested, failed to materialize.[75]

However, this spurred leading representatives of the Austrian medical profession to advocate even more strongly for vaccination. The benefits to the individuals' health were emphasized. Professor Dr. Hermann Zischinsky, head of the Pediatric Infection Department at the Vienna Wilhelminenspital, for instance, warned against a slackening of the current vaccination initiatives: "There is no doubt that poliomyelitis vaccination must be propagated. Petty or even financial concerns must play no role whatsoever here. This is all the more true since we do not know of any significant vaccination damage. One can even say that this vaccination is the most harmless of all. In any case, it is certain that it causes the least reactions."[76]

The OSR, on the other hand, questioned the outcome of the provincial campaigns. Hanns Hoff even condemned IPV as an "Austrian failure." The medical recommendations were not received well by the public, and the information campaign failed in at least one important aspect: "We did not get through psychologically, we were not able to convince the population to be vaccinated," Hoff argued. Another problem was identified regarding the logistics of vaccination. The repeated injections represented not only a financial but also a time commitment for the families. In addition, the mode of administration (via injection) discouraged children. According to Hoff, only about a third of vaccinees returned for their third shot. The responsible department head at the BMfsV also cited the fear of being hurt as one of the main arguments against IPV. Instead of proceeding with annual IPV campaigns, the OSR actively discussed the introduction of oral vaccination with the attenuated live vaccine (OPV).[77] Developed by Albert Sabin in the United States, this alternative method had been successfully tested in the Soviet Union.[78] The experts soon agreed that only OPV would serve as a suitable weapon in the fight against further polio cases in Austria.[79] In 1960,

Austria became the first country in the Western world to enact a federal law regulating the administration of the live vaccine. Austria thus introduced nationwide free voluntary vaccination for all individuals between the age of three months and twenty-one years.[80] However, rapid immunization of the population was out of the question once more. Diplomatic attempts to import vaccines from the USSR failed. Safety concerns prevailed, and the state decided to sign a contract with the British pharmaceutical company Pfizer, whose test protocols provided traceable results and promised the greatest possible transparency. Indeed, every effort was made to prevent a new "Cutter Incident" that would have a lasting impact on public vaccine acceptance.[81] In fact, the Austrian authorities achieved great success with the oral vaccination. Seventy-two percent of those under twenty-one were vaccinated in the first major campaign in November 1961, corresponding to 35 percent of the total population. Although this figure decreased in subsequent vaccination rounds, OPV campaigns still reached about two-thirds of the vulnerable age groups.[82] The number of new infections had already decreased since the introduction of the Salk vaccine, but after the national OPV campaign, virtually no further epidemics occurred. Throughout the 1960s, only isolated cases were reported, and in 1972, Austria was officially declared polio-free by the WHO.[83]

Conclusion

The introduction of IPV in Austria had a bumpy start. It was heavily influenced by the medical disaster known as the Cutter Incident. While leading Austrian experts and even policymakers were initially prepared to allow the costly protection of the population, the news from America forced the government to abandon the initiative in the spring of 1955. Safety concerns mounted, and the OSR did not get around to recommending a large-scale vaccination campaign until late 1957. Private vaccinations in indicated cases, however, were permitted at any time.

Even after the Cutter Incident was clarified by the American authorities and the safety of the vaccine was certified, Austrian politicians refused to conduct a mass campaign. In 1958, however, it was no longer safety concerns but financial considerations that prevented the government from introducing IPV. Officially, the argument of a lack of epidemiological benefit was used to deny public health responsibility for polio prevention. However, poliomyelitis remained a contagious disease, and public demand for effective protection increased. From 1957 onward, the local media increasingly raised the issue of polio vaccination. Criticism of the Austrian government was fueled by the fact that almost all of Austria's neighboring countries had introduced public polio vaccinations regardless of their ideological views. Public discontent put pressure on the provinces to act, and following the lead of Vienna, Tyrol, and Styria, all nine provinces implemented public vaccination in 1958, albeit only after devastating outbreaks of the disease in some cases. These campaigns did not follow a uniform concept but were individually designed. Both the targeted age groups and the cost sharing of those vaccinated varied. The only standard was that two injections were given in quick succession, while a third injection was administered at a greater interval for full immunization. The lack of a state-owned production and testing laboratory had an additional inhibitory effect on the implementation of the vaccination campaigns. The only nationally active, but privately owned, manufacturer struggled with a lack of domestic acceptance. The clumsy information policy of the BMfsV, which decidedly relied on foreign vaccines, probably prevented greater market success.

Although forecasts had predicted a mass rush for vaccination, the uptake of IPV was limited. Vaccination coverage rates varied considerably across regions, with particularly high rates where epidemics had recently occurred. Overall, however, the numbers were disappointing. The blame for the relative unpopularity of IPV was placed primarily on the mode of administration. Injections were unattractive, and even targeted advertising could not sugarcoat the use of needles. However, this argument fell short: unlike the subsequent vaccination campaign with OPV, which was meticulously planned, financed, and implemented by the state, the introduction of IPV was a typical example of federal weakness. The state's lack of commitment must be seen as a strong signal to the population. By refusing IPV distribution, the state downplayed the threat of the disease. Although the implementation of vaccination by the provinces was an ambitious and progressive effort, most of them were unable to offer free vaccination to their population. Economic considerations probably led to social selection, which was detrimental to a high vaccination rate.

In conclusion, however, it is worth noting that also in Austria, there was a general willingness to take advantage of this new public health measure. IPV prevented serious illness in thousands of cases and protected many lives. With the introduction of IPV, a change in the incidence of polio was observed, a trend that intensified with the transition to OPV. Throughout the 1960s, polio was no longer a collective experience but became an individual tragedy.

Endnotes

1. Letter from 1955 enclosed in: Tyrolean State Archive (Tiroler Landesarchiv, hereinafter TLA), Amt der Tiroler Landesregierung (ATLR) 1956, Abteilung (Abt.) Vc, Sanitätsdirektion, Reg. 495, Zl. 561.

2. Alison Day, "An American Tragedy: The Cutter Incident and Its Implications for the Salk Polio Vaccine in New Zealand 1955–1960," *Health & History* 11, no. 2 (2009): 42–61 (here 43).

3. Alfons Labisch, "'Skandalisierte Krankheiten' und 'echte Killer:' Zur Wahrnehmung von Krankheiten in Presse und Öffentlichkeit," in *Propaganda, (Selbst-)Zensur, Sensation: Limits of Press and Economic Freedom in Germany and the Czech Republic since 1871,* ed. Michael Andel et al. (Essen: Klartext, 2005), 273–89.

4. Paul A. Offit, *The Cutter Incident: How America's First Polio Vaccine Led to the Growing Vaccine Crisis* (New Haven-London: Yale University Press, 2005), 31–2.

5. Verordnung vom 11. Jänner 1927 betreffend die Anzeigepflicht bei Poliomyelitis anterior actua (spinale Kinderlähmung) und Encephalitis lethargica epidemica (Schlafkrankheit), *Bundesgesetzblatt für die Republik Österreich (BGBl.)* 38 (1927), 131.

6 Bundesministerium für soziale Verwaltung, ed., *Schluckimpfung gegen Kinderlähmung in Österreich: Versuch einer Bilanz* (Vienna: Europa Verlag, 1967), 113.

7. P. Kraus, "Der derzeitige Stand der aktiven Schutzimpfung gegen übertragbare Kinderlähmung," *Mitteilungen der österreichischen Sanitätsverwaltung (MöSV)* 56, no. 7 (1955): 157–60, (here 157).

8. Paul A. Offit, *The Cutter Incident. How America's First Polio Vaccine Led to the Growing Vaccine Crisis* (New Haven: Yale University Press, 2005).

9. Ibid., 4–10; David M. Oshinsky, *Polio: An American Story* (Oxford: Oxford University Press, 2005), 19–23.

10. John R. Wilson, *Margin of Safety: The Fight against Polio* (Garden City: Doubleday & Company, 1963); John R. Paul, *A History of Poliomyelitis* (New Haven: Yale University Press, 1971); Naomi Rogers, *Dirt and Disease: Polio before FDR* (New Brunswick: Rutgers University Press, 1992); Tony Gould, *A Summer Plague: Polio and its Survivors* (New Haven: Yale University Press, 1995). For more recent research, cf.: Daniel J. Wilson, *Living with Polio: The Epidemic and its Survivors* (Chicago: University of Chicago Press, 2006); Heather Green

Wooten, *The Polio Years in Texas: Battling a Terrifying Unknown* (Austin: Texas A & M University Press, 2009); Gareth Williams, *Paralyzed with Fear: The Story of Polio* (Basingstoke: Palgrave Macmillan, 2013); Richard J. Altenbough, *The Last Children's Plague: Poliomyelitis, Disability and Twentieth-Century American Culture* (New York: Palgrave Macmillan, 2015).

11. Ulrike Lindner, *Gesundheitspolitik in der Nachkriegszeit. Großbritannien und die Bundesrepublik Deutschland im Vergleich* (Munich: R. Oldenbourg Verlag, 2004); Malte Thießen, "Seuchen im langen 20. Jahrhundert: Perspektiven für eine europäische Sozial- und Kulturgeschichte," in *Infiziertes Europa: Seuchen im langen 20. Jahrhundert,* ed. Malte Thießen (Munich: De Gruyter Oldenbourg, 2014), 7–28; Malte Thießen, *Immunisierte Gesellschaft: Impfen in Deutschland im 19. und 20. Jahrhundert* (Göttingen: Vandenhoeck & Ruprecht, 2017); Annette Hinz-Wessels, "Medizinische Verflechtung und Systemkonkurrenz im Kalten Krieg: Poliobekämpfung im geteilten Berlin," *Medizinhistorisches Journal* 55, no. 2 (2020): 132–71.

12. Per Axelsson, "'Do not eat those apples; they've been on the ground!' Polio Epidemics and Preventive Measures, Sweden 1880s–1940s," *Asclepio: Revista de Historia de la Medicina y de la Ciencia* 61 (2009): 23–38.

13. Gareth Millward, "'A Matter of Commonsense': The Coventry Poliomyelitis Epidemic in 1957 and the British Public," *Contemporary British History* 31, no. 3 (2006): 1–23. See also Gareth Millward, *Vaccinating Britain. Mass Vaccination and the Public since the Second World War* (Manchester: Manchester University Press, 2019).

14. Stuart S. Blume, "Lock in, the State and Vaccine Development: Lessons from the History of Polio Vaccines," *Research Policy* 34 (2005): 159–73.

15. Bernardino Fantini, "Polio in Italy," *Dynamis* 32, no. 2 (2012): 329–59.

16 María Isabel Porras Gallo et al., eds., *El drama de la polio: Un problema social y familiar en la España franquista* (Madrid: Los Libros de la Catarata, 2013).

17. Dóra Vargha, *Polio across the Iron Curtain: Hungary's Cold War with an Epidemic* (Cambridge: Cambridge University Press, 2018).

18. Marcin Stasiak, *Polio w Polsce 1945–1989: Studium z historii niępełnosprawności* (Wydawnictwo: Universitas, 2021).

19. The author's habilitation project is dedicated to the history of polio in Austria throughout the twentieth century and focuses on Austria's participation in international science diplomacy in the field of polio control, as well as on Austrian approaches to prevention policy and the medical treatment of polio patients. To date, the following articles have been published: Marina

Hilber, "Vaccine Diplomacy: Austria's Cold War Mission against Polio," *Virus: Beiträge zur Sozialgeschichte der Medizin* 20 (2021): 237–55, https://doi.org/10.1553/virus20s237; Marina Hilber, "Ein unerwarteter Erfolg? Die Geschichte der Poliomyelitis-Schutzimpfungen in Österreich," in *Medicine in Vienna after 1945: Structures, Negotiation Processes, Reflections*, ed. Birgit Nemec et al. (Vienna: Vienna University Press, 2022), 381–402.

20. Day, "American Tragedy," 44; Offit, *Cutter Incident*, 44–57.

21. Offit, *Cutter Incident*, 61–5.

22. Austrian National Archive (Österreichisches Staatsarchiv, hereinafter ÖStA), AdR, BMfsV, Sektion V (Volksgesundheit), 1955, Zl. 69.359-19/1: Oberster Sanitätsrat: Kinderlähmungs-Schutzimpfung, Initiativantrag Prof. Bieling, Niederschrift des Gesundheitsamtes, Vienna, Apr. 16, 1955.

23. Ibid.

24. Ibid. On the implementation of IPV in the countries mentioned, see María-Isabel Porras-Gallo and María-Victoria Caballero, "Different Strategies of Vaccination against Poliomyelitis in the European Region of the World Health Organization," *Virus: Beiträge zur Sozialgeschichte der Medizin* 20 (2021): 257–91 (here 269, 272–3).

25. TLA, ATLR 1956, Abt. Vc, Sanitätsdirektion, Reg. 495, Zl. 180.

26. Offit, *Cutter Incident*; Day, "American Tragedy."

27. ÖStA, AdR, BMfsV, Sektion V (Volksgesundheit), 1955, Zl. 69.359-19/1: Oberster Sanitätsrat: Kinderlähmungs-Schutzimpfung, Initiativantrag Prof. Bieling, May 7, 1955.

28. Ibid.

29. Ibid.

30. ÖStA, AdR, BMfsV, Sektion V (Volksgesundheit), 1955, Zl. 59.450-19/1-55: Zwischenfälle bei Schutzimpfung gegen Poliomyelitis.

31. Offit, *Cutter Incident*; Day, "American Tragedy," 45–8; Nathaniel L. Moir, "To Boldly Remember Where We Have Already Been: Revisiting the Cutter Polio Vaccine Incident during Operation Warp Speed," *Journal of Applied History* 2 (2007): 17–35.

32. The capacity of Behring's production facilities was limited. In Germany, too, American vaccines had to be imported. Lindner, *Gesundheitspolitik*, 246–7.

33. ÖStA, AdR, BMfsV, Sektion V (Volksgesundheit), 1955, Zl. 69.359-19: Oberster Sanitätsrat: Kinderlähmungsschutzimpfung, Initiativantrag Prof. Bieling, May 7, 1955.

34. On risk assessment and safety concerns, cf. Malte Thießen, "On the Interplay between Risk, Vaccinations and Welfare States in Nineteenth and Twentieth-Century Germany," *Historical Social Research* 41, no. 1 (2016): 70–90.

35. ÖStA, AdR, BMfsV, Sektion V (Volksgesundheit), 1956, Zl. 49: Oberster Sanitätsrat, Kommissionsbericht betr. Poliomyelitis-Impfung, Jan. 5, 1956.

36. Porras-Gallo and Cabellero, "Different Strategies," 268.

37. ÖStA, AdR, BMfsV, Sektion V (Volksgesundheit), 1956, Zl. 27.318: Zwischenfälle bei Schutzimpfung gegen Poliomyelitis; ÖStA, AdR, BMfsV, Sektion V (Volksgesundheit), 1956, Zl. 65.860: Notwendigkeit und Durchführung von Prüfungen des Poliomyelitisimpfstoffes, Referat Prof. Bieling erstattet in der 53. Vollversammlung des OSR, June 16, 1956.

38. ÖStA, AdR, BMfsV, Section V (Volksgesundheit), 1957, Zl. 148.957: Einfuhr von Poliomyelitisimpfstoff, Feb. 22, 1957.

39. Cf. among others: Ernst Lorenz, "Zur Klinik und Prophylaxe der Poliomyelitis im Kindesalter," *Mitteilungen der österreichischen Sanitätsverwaltung* (MöSV) 58, no. 2 (1957): 21–3 (here 22); ÖStA, AdR, BMfsV, Sektion V (Volksgesundheit), 1957, Zl. 102.175: Anfrage wegen Schutzimpfung gegen Kinderlähmung, Sept. 3, 1957; ÖStA, AdR, BMfsV, Sektion V (Volksgesundheit), 1957, Zl. 97.492: Poliomyelitis-Schutzimpfung, Import von Impfstoffen, Aug. 1957.

40. "Millionen Kinder schon gegen Kinderlähmung geimpft," *Volksstimme. Zentralorgan der Kommunistischen Partei Österreichs*, July 10, 1957, 5.

41. Hans Hoff and Karl Kundratitz, "Absonderungsmaßnahmen bei Poliomyelitis," *MöSV* 58, no. 12 (1957): 244–5 (here 244).

42. "Immunization Schedule," *Österreichische Ärztezeitung*, Dec. 25, 1957, 1040.

43. Lindner, *Gesundheitspolitik*, 245.

44. Ulrike Lindner and Stuart S. Blume, "Vaccine Innovation and Adoption. Polio Vaccines in the UK, the Netherlands and West Germany, 1955–1965," *Medical History* 50 (2006): 425–46 (here 430).

45. Fantini, "Polio in Italy," 348.

46. Porras-Gallo and Caballero, "Different Strategies," 275–7.

47. TLA, ATLR 1958, Dept. Vc, Sanitätsdirektion, Reg. 495, Zl. 228.

48. A photograph of the press conference on January 22, 1958, has

been preserved in the Austrian National Library (OeNB). Cf. OeNB, Bildarchiv Austria, US 13.032.

49. This information was communicated to the provincial governments in Tyrol and Styria: TLA, ATLR 1958, Abt. Vc, Sanitätsdirektion, Reg. 495, Zl. 105; Styrian Provincial Archives (Steiermärkisches Landesarchiv, hereinafter StLA), Landesregierung, 1958, 024-Po-03: Poliomyelitis-Schutzimpfung 1958.

50. A similar situation existed in the Federal Republic of Germany. Lindner describes Salk vaccinations from 1957 onward as "uncoordinated and inconsistent." Lindner, *Gesundheitspolitik*, 247.

51. ÖStA, AdR, BmfsV, Sektion V (Volksgesundheit), 1957, Zl. 102.467: Durchführung von Poliomyelitis-Schutzimpfungen, Anfrage von Landesrat Univ. Prof. Dr. Koren, Aug. 14, 1957.

52. TLA, ATLR 1958, Dept. Vc, Sanitätsdirektion, Reg. 495, no number.

53 StLA, Landesregierung, 1958, 024-Po-03: Poliomyelitis-Schutzimpfung 1958, Durchführung der Poliomyelitis-Schutzimpfung in Steiermark, Mar. 3, 1958.

54. Ibid.; TLA, ATLR 1958, Abt. Vc, Sanitätsdirektion, Reg. 495, Zl. 105 and Zl. 171.

55. StLA, Landesregierung, 1958, 024-Po-03: Poliomyelitis-Schutzimpfung 1958, Antwort des Amts der Vorarlberger Landesregierung, Mar. 11, 1958.

56. ÖStA, AdR, BMfsV, Sektion V (Volksgesundheit), 1958, Zl. 5719: Durchführung der Poliomyelitis-Schutzimpfung in Steiermark, Informationen für den Herrn Bundesministier, Ansuchen Einfuhrerlaubnis Serotherapeutisches Institut Wien, Feb. 11, 1958.

57. Ibid.

58. TLA, ATLR, Vc Landessanitätsdirektion 1958, Zl. 804.

59. ÖStA, AdR, BMfsV, Sektion V (Volksgesundheit), 1958, Zl. 109.436: OSR, Anfrage des OSR Prof. Dr. Kundratitz betr. Poliomyelitis-Impfstoff österr. Herkunft, Sept. 11, 1958.

60. "Kinderlähmungs-Impfung: "Flohbisse" gegen das lähmende Virus," *Neue Zeit*, Apr. 12, 1958, 3.

61. TLA, ATLR 1958, Abt. Vc, Sanitätsdirektion, Reg. 495, Zl. 105 and Zl.. 171.

62. "Kinderlähmungs-Impfung," *Neue Zeit*.

63. Magistrat der Stadt Wien, ed., Jahrbuch der Stadt Wien 1960 (Vienna, 1961), 96.

64. Source: Werner Anders et al., "Die epidemiologische Situation der Poliomyelitis in der Bundesrepublik Deutschland, der Schweizerischen Eidgenossenschaft und der Republik Österreich," Mitteilungen der Österreichischen Sanitätsverwaltung 62, no. 1 (1961): 1–9 (here 7).

65. Engelbert P. Radmayr, "Zur Phänomenologie der Poliomyelitis-Epidemie 1958 in Vorarlberg," *MöSV* 60, no. 4 (1959): 59–68.

66. Elisabeth Dietrich-Daum, "Impfen erzwingen: Mündige Bürger*innen und säumige Landespolitiker in der Vorarlberger Poliomyelitis-Epidemie von 1958," *Virus: Beiträge zur Sozialgeschichte der Medizin* 20 (2021): 189–212 (here 203–5).

67. *Vorarlberger Nachrichten*, Sept. 20, 1958, 4. Dietrich-Daum, "Impfen erzwingen," 206–7.

68. Ibid.

69. *Vorarlberger Nachrichten*, Nov. 29, 1958, 4.

70. Dietrich-Daum, "Impfen erzwingen," 207.

71. This tendency is also observed by Lindner, *Gesundheitspolitik*, 248.

72. Franz Friza, "Die epidemiologische Situation der Poliomyelitis in Österreich ab 1946," in *Schluckimpfung gegen Kinderlähmung in Österreich: Versuch einer Bilanz*, ed. Bundesministerium für soziale Verwaltung (Vienna: Europa Verlag, 1967), 67–78 (here 71).

73. Ibid., 74.

74. In 1957 and subsequent years, the vaccination coverage rate in the Federal Republic of Germany was less than 5 percent. Lindner, *Gesundheitspolitik*, 249.

75. TLA, ATLR 1956, Abt. Vc, Sanitätsdirektion, Reg. 495, Zl. 180; *Mitteilungsblatt* 1 (1958), ed. Österreichischen Poliomyelitis-Verband.

76. Hermann Zischinsky, "Fragen der Kinderlähmung im Hinblick auf die neuesten prophylaktischen und therapeutischen Möglichkeiten," *MöSV* 60, no. 11 (1959): 205–8 (here 208). This assessment was also confirmed by the director of the Serotherapeutic Institute, Franz Puntigam. Referring to studies from the United States of America and Switzerland, complications after Salk vaccination were extremely rare. However, a national review of vaccine-induced damage in Austria has not been conducted. Franz Puntigam, "Impfschäden," *MöSV* 61, no. 6 (1960): 201–8 (here 204–5).

77. ÖStA, BMfsV, Sektion V (Volksgesundheit), 1960, Zl. 20654: Oberster Sanitätsrat: Orale Schutzimpfung gegen Poliomyelitis; Referat OSR Prof. Dr. Jettmar bei der 72. Vollversammlung des OSR, Oct. 22, 1960.

78. Cf. for further details: Hilber, "Vaccine Diplomacy;" Saul Benison, "International Medical Cooperation. Dr Albert Sabin, Live Poliovirus Vaccine and the Soviets," *Bulletin of the History of Medicine* 56, no. 4 (1982): 460–83.

79. ÖStA, BMfsV, Sektion V (Volksgesundheit), 1960, Zl. 20654: Oberster Sanitätsrat: Orale Schutzimpfung gegen Poliomyelitis; Referat OSR Prof. Dr. Jettmar bei der 72. Vollversammlung des OSR, Oct. 22, 1960.

80. Bundesgesetz vom 28. November 1960 über öffentliche Schutzimpfungen gegen übertragbare Kinderlähmung, *BGBl.* 244 (1960), 2176–7; Richard Havlasek, "Die rechtlichen Grundlagen der Schutzimpfung gegen übertragbare Kinderlähmung," in *Schluckimpfung gegen Kinderlähmung in Österreich: Versuch einer Bilanz*, ed. Bundesministerium für soziale Verwaltung (Vienna: Europa Verlag, 1967), 19–25.

81. Karl Schindl, "Schutzimpfung gegen Kinderlähmung durch Tropfengabe," *Soziale Sicherheit: Zeitschrift für die Österreichische Sozialversicherung* 11 (1961): 393–7.

82. Karl Schindl, "Schluckimpfung gegen Kinderlähmung in Österreich," *Soziale Sicherheit. Zeitschrift für die Österreichische Sozialversicherung* 11 (1962): 439–41.

83. Reinhild Strauss et al., "WHO-Eradikationsprogramm für Poliomyelitis: Status quo und Umsetzung in Österreich," *Wiener Klinische Wochenschrift* 120, no. 7–8 (2008): 210–6.

Gay & Lesbian Movement, Politics, and Media in the Early Days of AIDS in Austria

Andreas Brunner

On March 11, 1983, two men who had died of AIDS in Austria were reported for the first time in the evening journal on the radio station Ö1 of the public broadcaster ORF. A media storm broke out, and the health authorities, but also the gay and lesbian movement,[1] which had so far been reserved with regard to AIDS, felt compelled to react to this "historical break."[2] What was perceived as a catastrophe by those affected is now also the subject of historiographical research. In the USA, for example, Richard McKay investigated the origins of the AIDS epidemic in a wide-ranging study, and Sarah Schulman the resistance to disinterested politics.[3] In recent years, historical research in German-speaking countries has also begun to focus on AIDS. Martin Reichert drew increasingly on contemporary witnesses in his account, which ranges from the early days of AIDS to the immediate present, while Henning Tümmers made the different developments in West and East Germany the subject of his investigation.[4] Prevention policy up to the introduction of combination therapy, on the other hand, was the focus of Sebastian Haus-Rybicki's publication.[5] For Austria, there has been a lack of broader studies to date, with only unpublished master and diploma theses or contributions in anthologies.[6]

The German sociologist and health scientist Rolf Rosenbrock identified four phases of the social and political handling of HIV/AIDS, which can be applied with limitations to the development in Austria. Since AIDS arrives in Austria with a delay, there is a temporal shift, especially in phase one, which Rosenbrock titles the emergence of the AIDS exceptionalism and fixes from about 1981 to 1986. Phase one lasts in Austria from 1983 until the foundation of the Österreichische *AIDS-Hilfe* (ÖAH) in 1985. Phase two, the practice and consolidation of exceptionalism, accordingly extends in Austria from 1985 to 1991; phase three, the dissolution of exceptionalism and first signs of normalization, lasts from 1991 until the introduction of combination therapy in 1996. Phase four from 1996 on represents for Rosenbrock the time of normalization, as AIDS becomes a treatable chronic disease.[7] In his study on AIDS policy in Germany, health scientist Raimund Geene also discusses the connections between the development of the gay and lesbian emancipation movement, AIDS help centers, and self-help groups with health policy.[8] This article focuses primarily on the interactions between politics and the just-forming gay and lesbian movement in Austria and the media in phase one. Further developments can only be outlined in broad strokes.

In many cases, results from American or German researchers can only be transferred to a limited extent, since the political framework conditions as well as the stage of development of the emancipation movement differ. As early as 1981, physicians in the USA had described for the first time a strange accumulation of a rare form of pneumonia that occurred among gay men in large cities like San Francisco and New York. In connection with other rare opportunistic diseases, such as Kaposi's sarcoma, people spoke of Gay-Related Immune Deficiency (GRID), thus also stigmatizing and othering the group of homosexuals, as even medical journals portrayed "without exception [...] AIDS as a 'homo plague' or 'homosexual disease.'"[9] Soon other minorities, such as drug users, Haitians, and hemophiliacs, were identified as disease carriers. In late July 1982, a conference agreed on the name Acquired Immune Deficiency Syndrome (AIDS), but homosexual men remained the main group affected for the time being.

In the German-speaking area, the news magazine *Der Spiegel* first reported on the "shock from over there"[10] at the end of May 1982. In Austria, the bourgeois daily *Kurier* followed at the end of September with a short news item that was quite objective in tone.[11] The representatives of the *Homosexuelle Initiative Wien (*HOSI Wien*)* reacted defensively and upset because of the "anti-homosexual tendency" of the "sensationalist news" with which "the media want to give homosexuals a new stigma," because one could no longer claim that "homosexuality is a disease," but it would be tried to create "a new discrimination: homosexuality MAKES [you] sick!"[12]

Gay and Lesbian Emancipation Movement in Austria

On August 16, 1971, the total ban on homosexual acts was lifted with the so-called *Kleine Strafrechtsreform*. Since 1852, for 119 years, Paragraph 129 I, b had penalized sexual relations between "persons of the same sex" as "fornication against nature." Since the wording of the paragraph was gender-neutral, female homosexuality was also prosecuted in Austria, in contrast with other European legislation. However, the decriminalization of same-sex acts among adults occurred only with "flanking measures,"[13] which were intended to show that homosexuality still remained a socially unwanted behavior. Four new criminal law paragraphs were introduced. Continuing the stereotype of the homosexual corrupter of youth, an age of consent for male homosexual relations was introduced at eighteen years. This Section 209 of the Österreichisches Strafgesetzbuch (StGB) [Austrian Penal Code] was to be the longest lasting. It was not repealed until 2002. The three other Sections prosecuted same-sex male prostitution (§ 210 StGB, repealed in 1989), advertising for fornication with persons of the same sex (§ 220 StGB), and the formation of unions to promote same-sex fornication (§ 221 StGB). Both were repealed only in 1996.

Above all, Sections 220 and 221 were intended to be a stumbling block for the gay movement that was also forming in Austria along American and European lines. Section 220 and the strict Austrian pornography law were also intended to hinder AIDS prevention in Austria. While the first gay emancipation groups began to form in the USA as early as the year after Stonewall in 1970, in France in the wake of the student movement after 1968, and in Germany after the TV broadcast of Rosa von Praunheim's groundbreaking film "*Nicht der Homosexuelle ist pervers, sondern die Situation, in der er lebt*" starting in 1971, new social movements developed in Austria only with a time lag into the mid-1970s.[14] Lesbians and gays initially went their separate ways organizationally. From 1976 on, the lesbian movement gathered within the women's liberation movement in the *Aktion Unabhängiger Frauen* (AUF), while gay men came together in the "informal group" COMING OUT (CO).[15] The ban on fraternization prevented the official founding of an association and thus the establishment of firm structures. The group COMING OUT, which basically saw itself as left-wing but was rejected by the dogmatic left, was committed to the sexual revolution and saw itself as feminist and questioning of the patriarchal social order, broke up a few years after its founding, not only because of a lack of structures but also because of its internal contradictions "between class struggle and integration, between self-realization and political goals."[16]

In March 1979, Wolfgang Förster's attempt to found a "men's group" started as a "non-political self-experience group" with an advertisement in the alternative newspaper *Falter*. Since many members of the group had "left-wing socialization at university behind them," the "step from a private circle [...] to the first legally registered gay group in Austria" was quickly taken.[17] After Sepp Rieder, the press spokesman for Minister of Justice Christian Broda, had assured them in a conversation that there were no reservations on the part of the legislature against founding an association, even with the designation homosexual in the title, the HOSI Wien was officially registered as an association at the beginning of 1980. While the COMING OUT group was politically left-wing but not close to an established party, the HOSI Wien already had good contacts with the *Sozialdemokratische Partei Österreichs* (SPÖ), which ruled with an absolute majority in the federal government and in Vienna during the founding phase of HOSI Wien.

But already in the fall of 1980, it became clear how divided the relationship of the emancipation movement and politics was to be. When, after protests by angry citizens, the city administration of Vienna had demolished an information stand of the HOSI Wien that was part of the *Alternative Festwochen* on Reumannplatz in the proletarian tenth district of Favoriten with excavators, a conflict arose. All the groups participating in the *Alternative Festwochen* showed solidarity with the HOSI Wien, so that the responsible city councilor for culture and later mayor of Vienna, Helmut Zilk, felt compelled to have the information stand rebuilt at the city's expense. This interplay between cooperation and strict rejection was also to characterize the relationship between politics and the gay and lesbian movement during the AIDS crisis.

In 1981, before AIDS became a dominating issue, HOSI Wien took an important step. With the admission of lesbian women to the association, the organization founded by gay men transformed itself, albeit not without conflict, into a non-governmental organization (NGO) supported by lesbians and gays.[18] The following year, a group of gays and lesbians occupied a vacant condemned building on *Linke Wienzeile*, a busy arterial road to the west of the city. The house, owned by the City of Vienna, was used to house apartments, a low-threshold pub, and a counseling center. The Rosa Lila Villa became a visible sign of a young movement that no longer wanted to be pushed into invisibility. What the legislature wanted to prevent in 1971 was a group seeking a way into the public sphere despite the continued threat of criminal prosecution: lesbians and gays who, self-determined and loud, demanded equal rights and social recognition. The operators of the Rosa Lila Villa also came to an agreement with politicians. The City of Vienna supported the counseling center—Vienna's deputy mayor Gertrude Fröhlich-Sandner even attended the opening of the renovated rooms—and eventually gave the association responsibility for the entire house, which to this day is a shining sign of queer visibility in Vienna as Türkis Rosa Lila Villa.[19] Within the squatter scene of the 1980s, the Rosa Lila Villa thus had a unique selling point, as all other squatted houses in Vienna were eventually evicted by the police.[20]

With the HOSI Wien, the young emancipation movement had only just found a mouthpiece, with the Rosa Lila Villa it was gaining visibility in the city when the threat of AIDS became reality in 1983. HOSI Wien had hardly set up structures for future-oriented association work, and the first, albeit fragile alliances with politicians had been made, when the activists had to face a new challenge that was to lead to far-reaching social changes. The media and reporting on AIDS also played a crucial role in this.

AIDS Arrives in Austria

After March 11, 1983, "the first major wave of reporting" about AIDS followed, which, as HOSI activist Kurt Krickler put it cautiously, "was characterized above all by sensationalism and disinformation."[21] Within two weeks (!) "the first information brochure about AIDS in Europe"[22] was produced. With the doctor Reinhardt Brandstätter as vice chairman, HOSI Wien had a well-connected communicator in the Viennese health care system, who was able to win prominent co-authors: the university professors Christian Kunz (Head of the Institute of Virology), Klaus Wolff (Head of the University Skin Clinic), the psychiatrist Walter Dekan and the Vienna City Councilor for Health and Social Affairs Alois Stacher, who did not appear as an SPÖ politician but as president of the *Wiener Arbeitsgemeinschaft für Volksgesundheit* ("Vienna working group for public health"). Stacher, himself a specialist and university professor of internal medicine, financed the printing of the brochure, which was distributed in the gay community in an edition of 8,000.

Knowledge about AIDS was limited; it was not even certain whether a virus caused the disease and how it was transmitted. The authors put together, as they wrote themselves, "causes, theses, assumptions, rumours" about AIDS in five tightly printed columns of a leporello. They used the publications of the US Federal Agency Centers for Disease Control (CDC) as a basis. The thesis formulated by the virologist Christian Kurz that "in the case of transmission by a virus [...] the infection can obviously occur during sexual intercourse and through blood or blood products" also led to the first recommendations of a preventive nature. First, "avoiding sexual contact with people who have or are suspected of having AIDS." It also warned that "the number of sexual partners increases the risk of developing the disease." Members of "risk groups (e.g. homosexuals)" were advised not to donate blood and plasma. "Fear and panic or an exaggerated reduction in sexuality or sexual hostility are not suitable means" to prevent the spread of AIDS, said the doctor and activist Reinhardt Brandstätter, specifying the virologist's suggestions. Because the answer to the fear spread by the media—and with this, Brandstätter addressed the affected homosexual men directly—must be "our personal emancipation, our self-acceptance as homosexuals and the conscious living of our homosexuality."[23]

A few weeks after the beginning of the media hype, important basic principles for the prevention work in the coming years were formulated in this information sheet. While HOSI Wien initially suspected a media conspiracy behind the reporting on AIDS, which "wanted to give homosexuals a new stigma," they now wanted to "guarantee a scientifically and ethically accurate portrayal."[24] At the same time, it was emphasized that the emancipation of homosexuals will be decisive for the success of all measures against the spread of AIDS. This closing of ranks between science, politics, and the emancipation movement was an important statement, because the media were already looking for culprits. It contained the agreement central to the history of AIDS in Austria that future prevention work can only work with the active participation of the homosexual community. All actors involved—science, politics, and movement—had to fight exclusion and stigmatization, which was not an easy task in view of the media agitation.

HOSI Wien also commented on the media "AIDS hysteria" in its quarterly magazine *Lambda Nachrichten* and quoted "a few samples: 'Sex epidemic in Vienna: 3 deaths' ('Blatt am Sonntag,' campaign newspaper of the SPÖ [...]). The *Kurier*, on the other hand, is plagued by sexual envy: 'Many sick people are in the homosexual milieu, [. . .] quite a few have up to 1000 sexual partners a year, hence the name "gay disease."'"[25] The *Basta* magazine, published for the first time in April 1983 by the brothers Wolfgang and Helmuth Fellner, took the same line. They wanted to "put a new, positive attitude towards life on paper for the eighties."[26] With the headline "AIDS. A disease makes headlines: insidious and death certain" the fear was fueled; "AIDS is a fast ticket to the afterlife" was added. According to *Basta*, it is also certain "that three Viennese caught the virus in the USA: in the gay scene in New York, where AIDS has long been raging like a killer."[27]

The direction of the Austrian tabloid media was clear from the first reports: homosexuality, promiscuity, and death were the buzzwords. In addition, there were fear-mongering false reports: AIDS was supposed to be "transmissible through simple droplet infection (like a cough)."[28] Publications such as the news magazine Profil or the trendy Viennese city magazine WIENER reacted with less alarm: "There is helplessness in the bar of the community," wrote Profil, because the "disease is spreading epidemically, its victims are mainly, but not exclusively, homosexual men."[29] A statement by Reinhard Brandstätter in WIENER can also be seen as a sign of uncertainty. Although the AIDS information published by HOSI Wien favored a virus as a possible cause of the infection, the doctor and HOSI activist Reinhard Brandstätter contradicted him "vehemently" in WIENER: "The collapse of the immune system is not caused by a virus, but by constant overloading caused." The immune system would be weakened by infections with "syphilis, hepatitis B, or gonorrhea" and their treatment with penicillin and antibiotics. Since he also brought up "intensive anal intercourse" in the meeting, this came close to a warning to gays about their own way of life.[30]

For Leopold Nenning from the WIENER it was clear: "AIDS is a deadly, incurable disease. Nevertheless, the scaremongering that has been sparked in recent weeks is unfounded." And he also knew: "The fear in the gay scene itself is not as great as one might assume from the newspaper reports. AIDS is 'the' day and night talk, but there are no effects on relevant bars or saunas."[31] The "Magazine for Zeitgeist," as the WIENER called itself, was certainly the most gay-friendly magazine in Austria in the early 1980s. The editor-in-chief was Michael Hopp, who a few years before had been one of the most important activists of the group COMING OUT, but who later renounced his gay past.[32] In August 1983, the WIENER gave AIDS "a face." The story of Kenny Ramsauer had already caused a stir in the USA in May when the gay man, who was marked by dark lesions from Kaposi's sarcoma, appeared on the ABC news show "20/20" during primetime and made an urgent appeal to viewers: "We all know that AIDS is not a gay disease. AIDS can affect anyone." He lamented that "AIDS is only used to discriminate against homosexuals" and "that we [gays] are beginning to distance ourselves from ourselves and our identity because of AIDS."[33] Markus Peichl, alongside Michael Hopp, second editor-in-chief of the WIENER, wrote the most comprehensive article about AIDS in an Austrian medium to date, which reported in detail on the fate of a gay AIDS victim who had already died at the time of publication. Even if he describes Kenny Ramsauer as a promiscuous homosexual, which can be read as discriminatory, he deliberately did not stir up fear. But the uncertainty remained; when pop star Klaus Nomi died from AIDS in September 1983, AIDS again became a topic in the Austrian media, but the artistic achievements of the dazzling star of the New York underground scene prevailed. After that, AIDS disappeared from media coverage until 1985, with the exception of a few brief reports.

On the Way to the *Österreichische AIDS-Hilfe (ÖAH)*

Apart from chronological shifts, the media coverage of AIDS in Austria differed little from that in the Federal Republic of Germany, where Der Spiegel in particular swung to a much-criticized reactionary course. In his early 1987 analysis of the magazine's reporting on AIDS, Eberhard Hübner stated that Der Spiegel "[activated] all its language tricks to make an authoritarian solution appear as the only sensible one."[34] For its seventy-fifth anniversary, Der Spiegel itself published a critical review. "The tenor seemed vile,"[35] said Spiegel editor Enrico Ippolito, characterizing reporting in the 1980s.

In his essay on "the relationship between homosexuality and AIDS," Lukas Engelmann demanded that in a history about AIDS "the traumatizing starting point of this story in the public denunciation of a 'gay epidemic' should not be forgotten," even if in historical accounts the "diverse efforts to destigmatize, to gain political visibility, and to normalize as a result of the history of appropriation by the homosexual community" is central.[36] As Lukas Engelmann asks, can one read the further developments after the initial shock and the reaction of the emancipation movement in Austria as the beginning of the "success story of a broad alliance between social, scientific and political actors?"[37] Or should one rather question it as "the normalization of a state of emergency,"[38] like Hans-Paul Bänziger and Zülfukar Çetin recently did?

The debates in Germany in 1984 and 1985, led by the news magazine *Der Spiegel*, which is also widely read in Austria, met with little response in Austria. Neither articles with sometimes drastic headlines, such as "The Bomb Is Planted,"[39] nor a *Spiegel* contribution by the film director and gay activist Rosa von Praunheim, who caused heated debates in the German gay movement because of Praunheim's criticism of the irresponsible sexual behavior of gay men, left behind any verifiable evidence in the Austrian community.[40] In the gay community, AIDS was a fearful but only marginally discussed topic. Even the discovery of the AIDS virus was skeptically commented on by HOSI activist Kurt Krickler, linking it to Ronald Reagan's US election campaign and the interests of the pharmaceutical industry: "The news from the AIDS front should therefore be treated with great caution."[41]

The intermittent calm may have something to do with Austria's geopolitical situation on the edge of the Iron Curtain and with the fact that Vienna was not a preferred travel destination for gay men. In Austria, for example, in contrast to the USA and Germany, an organized gay movement only developed with a delay of several years, and the gay subculture was also underdeveloped compared to American centers such as San Francisco and New York, but also European cities such as Paris, Amsterdam, Cologne, or Berlin. The sexual liberation that gay men celebrated at extravagant parties elsewhere had not yet arrived in Vienna in this form. It was not until 1983, when the AIDS crisis broke out, that the *Stiefelknecht*, a bar with a darkroom, opened in Vienna. The number of AIDS cases in Austria also increased very slowly at first. By the end of June 1985, sixteen cases had been reported, which, as it soon turned out, were only "the first vanguard of the disease."[42]

Despite all the skepticism towards science and the pharmaceutical industry, HOSI Wien took "an undogmatic and pragmatic line."[43] When the first HIV antibody test was available for testing at the end of 1984, there was an offer to take part in the first HIV antibody prevalence study. HOSI Wien initially hesitated but went on the offensive in terms of publication. In an eight-page article in the *Lambda Nachrichten*, "everything new about AIDS" was laid out. The antibody test was also put up for discussion. In addition to questions about the medical significance of the result, it was above all the psychological consequences of those who tested positive that HOSI Wien focused on. It was still completely unclear whether a positive antibody test led to a disease at all, or how long the incubation period was between infection and the onset of the disease. Could symptomless positives pass on the virus? And what recommendations for action could be derived from a positive test result? Could sexual contact that could lead to infection be prohibited for men who tested positive? The news about the first coercive measures against gay men in the USA was also noticed here. The San Francisco city government closed some gay bathhouses and sex clubs; initial discussions about quarantine measures, the isolation of HIV-positive people, or their tattooing, gained momentum. The activists registered the fears of "a pogrom mood against gays" and quoted the Nuremberg gay magazine *Rosa Flieder*, in which the fear was expressed that forty years after the end of National Socialism "camps for gays would again be legally possible" if epidemic policy regulations were applied to AIDS, which was at least discussed in Germany.[44]

In Austria, the January 1985 issue of the *WIENER* started broader and more aggressive reporting about AIDS. After the AIDS death of the American film star Rock Hudson, "the media ran amok,"[45] as the activist Kurt Krickler put it. The report in the *WIENER* began with a drastic scene: "Bruno R. from Vienna-Währing was just twenty-eight when it was over. He weighed only forty kilograms, could no longer eat or stand freely. The doctors at the Vienna General Hospital fought to the end. In vain. Bruno R. died of AIDS."[46] A description of his promiscuous lifestyle followed. All statistics showed that homosexuals were most frequently affected, but it was also certain that drug use and sexual contact with bisexual men could spread the virus to women. Haemophiles could be infected via contaminated blood supplies, and there was also "a clear epidemiological connection with tropical west and central Africa"[47] in Europe, since a relatively large number of Africans who did not belong to any risk group fell ill. Transmission through blood was considered certain, but HTLV-III (HIV only became mandatory from 1986) was also detected in saliva and semen. Although the virologist also considered transmission through saliva to be unlikely, horrified reports that an infection could be transmitted through a shared drinking glass made the rounds in the tabloid media and increased the stigmatization of those affected. With semen, however, the situation was different, as transmission could occur during anal intercourse with the smallest injury to the intestinal mucosa.

The focus was once again on the sexual behavior of gay men: "Promiscuity increases the risk significantly. You have to educate homosexuals. AIDS is such a dangerous disease that consequences must be taken. A homosexual can think about how to limit his risk,"[48] virologist Christian Kunz was quoted as saying in *WIENER*. Risk minimization as a recommendation for action? The dermatologist Judith Hutterer from the Vienna AIDS clinic of the *Allgemeines Krankenhaus (AKH)* took the same line: "The dangerous thing is anonymous sexual intercourse." Like the virologist Kunz, she did not derive any bans for homosexuals from this, but demanded: "Awareness would be important."[49]

In an interview with *WIENER*, the social-democratic Minister of Health Kurt Steyrer assured that Austria would not have its own "Lex-AIDS," but that it could be included in the existing epidemic law, which would have far-reaching consequences for those affected. AIDS had been a notifiable disease under the umbrella of the Epidemic Act since the spring of 1983, but compulsory examination and treatment, isolation, or the obligation to report by name were also possible measures. Even though the Minister of Health declared "quarantine, protective custody or the closure of homosexual meeting points" to be "inconceivable"—"You can't lock up people"—and also advocated AIDS-awareness, HOSI Wien reacted negatively.[50] Given the current level of knowledge about AIDS, a discussion about extending the epidemic law would be "not justified for reasons related to the epidemic policy."[51]

In the end, HOSI Wien did not give a recommendation for the test, but the activists advertised it by word of mouth. The HOSI Wien found support with two demands from the doctors involved: the test should be anonymous, and an accompanying study should collect possible co-factors for an infection. At the same time, the activists advised: "If someone decides to take the test, he should in any case talk to a trusted person or doctor beforehand about whether he can psychologically cope with the mental stress of a positive test result."[52] However, this advice contained a problematic part: which doctor or friend was even able to provide support? Except for a few specialists, even the bulk of the medical profession knew little more about AIDS than what was being circulated through the media, and what friend could cope with being told of a potential death sentence? A professional support network was needed. Although there was no official appeal, 318 homosexual men participated in the study on HTLV-III antibodies in risk groups in Austria, led by Univ. Prof. Dr. Wolfgang Horak of the Second University Clinic for Heptalogy and Gastroenterology. The results were sobering. Antibodies were detected in 68 (21.4 percent) of the 318 people tested. Evaluation of a questionnaire on possible co-factors revealed "anal intercourse as the main route of transmission, with the receptive (passive) partner far more at risk than the active partner. There were also highly significant correlations between positive antibody findings and the number of sexual partners."[53] The promiscuous lifestyle of many homosexual men, previously dismissed by much of the homosexual movement as an anti-homosexual reflex by the mainstream media, was thus a major factor in HIV infection. Not only did this realization carry the danger of promoting the stigmatization of gay men, but the movement also had to find a position vis-à-vis those homosexuals who believed that AIDS was an invention of reactionary propaganda against their (sexual) liberation.

The *WIENER* reported that "there is no sign of AIDS hysteria in the gay scene." One would get from addressed gays rather the answer: "The probability to die in a traffic accident is nevertheless by far higher." The activist Florian Sommer, resident, social worker, and founder of the Rosa Lila Villa, confessed that "among us organized gays AIDS would not be an issue at all."[54] There were also different opinions within the HOSI Wien. For example, activist Ernst Dummer spread all the usual conspiracy theories about AIDS in an article in *Lambda Nachrichten*. Conjecture about American politics and the interests of the pharmaceutical industry, the destructive potential of the nuclear weapons of the great powers, or the poisoning of our environment led him to the realization that "we live in a time, in a culture, in a society, THAT MAKES US SICK." His appeal represented a counter-position to that taken by Reinhard Brandstätter and Kurt Krickler, who critically questioned the findings of science, but did not fundamentally challenge them. "I don't say: keep fucking as if nothing is wrong, I say: FEAR MAKES SICK / FEAR MAKES SUBJECTIVE / FEAR IS THE MEAN OF SUPPRESSION. My dermatologist says: 'If you want to be afraid, you will always find something to be afraid of.' Therefore, think and don't be afraid!"[55]

One of the conclusions HOSI Wien drew from the test study was that "AIDS is not only a medical problem, but also one of the gay movement." For "all gays in this country," a "strong gay lobby is of eminent importance"[56] because it could influence the health authorities. Participation in the test study proved to be a door opener because it resulted in "cooperation with the doctors, scientists and other responsible parties," and because HOSI Wien was able to participate "in all bodies that have anything to do with AIDS or even have to make decisions in this context."[57] The activists of HOSI Wien made their way to the institutions. Financed by the Ministry of Health, Reinhard Brandstätter and dermatologist Judith Hutterer from the Vienna AIDS Clinic took part in the European Gay Health Conference in London at the end of May 1985 to present the results of the Vienna test study.

The physician and HOSI chairman Brandstätter also succeeded in convincing the responsible section head in the Ministry of Health "that authorities have no chance of getting to the AIDS risk group of homosexual men. [...] The trauma and mistrust in the gays is too deep-seated, after all, [...] if you think of the persecution, oppression and discrimination that continues to this day." Brandstätter therefore proposed the establishment of an Austrian AIDS help organization in the form of a separate association, with representatives of the ministry and the gay movement sitting on its board: "This association should serve as a buffer between the gays and the authorities."[58] The *AIDS-Hilfe*'s tasks would be professional education and information work and professional counseling for gay men, especially after a positive antibody test. The *AIDS-Hilfe* could also offer free and anonymous antibody tests, which is why close cooperation with the AIDS clinic of the AKH and with doctors who treated AIDS patients would also be desirable. A remarkable detail for this early phase in the history of AIDS is that in Brandstätter's paper the organization of voluntary help services for AIDS patients was already considered. Self help groups in particular were later to play an important role in dealing with the AIDS crisis.

The Foundation of the Österreichische *AIDS-Hilfe* (ÖAH)

By Austrian standards, everything happened very quickly. On August 29, 1985, the founding meeting of the Österreichische *AIDS-Hilfe* (ÖAH) took place. Initially, the association was financed mainly by funds from the Ministry of Health; the City of Vienna had refused any participation and was not even willing to provide what the activists considered to be suitable municipal real estate because they feared protests from neighbors. The city government, which two years earlier had supported Europe's first AIDS education brochure and the founding of the Rosa Lila Villa, backed down politically. A balance of interests between science, politics, and the movement was sought in appointments to the committees. A physician and official of the Ministry of Health served as president, homosexual activist Reinhardt Brandstätter as second president, and physician and AIDS expert Judith Hutterer became third president. In addition to a commissioner for drugs and a lawyer from the Ministry, two other activists of the movement were on the board. Due to the incompatibility of their functions in the Ministry and the AIDS-Hilfe, the two representatives delegated by politics withdrew from the AIDS board at their own request after an initial consolidation phase and left their functions to medical professionals.[59]

Even before the AIDS death of US actor Rock Hudson in early October 1985, which came as a surprise to many, media hype set in, prompting Kurt Krickler, as a HOSI and AIDS activist and one of the most eloquent publicists of the Austrian gay movement, to headline "*Der Boulevard läuft Amok*" (The tabloids run amok) in *Lambda Nachrichten* and to reinterpret the acronym AIDS as "Journalists' Disease: Acquired Information Deficiency Syndrome."[60] The realization that AIDS can basically affect anyone led to hysteria whipped up by the media, but instead of focusing their reporting on the known modes of transmission, the media focused on stigmatizing marginalized groups. They also received support from populist, conservative politicians in the Austrian province. In October 1985, for example, the sanitary authorities in Vorarlberg called for compulsory testing of homosexuals, drug addicts, and prostitutes. Against such errant, epidemiologically questionable omnipotence fantasies of regional politicians, a nationwide AIDS law was also supposed to provide protection, which was initially viewed skeptically by representatives of the gay and lesbian movement. After the resolution was passed on May 16, 1986, however, they were satisfied because the reporting of seropositively tested persons, which had been demanded by conservative sides, could be prevented.[61] From the community's point of view, the AIDS law represented a compromise, but it was seen as "a merit of the Ministry of Health" that only mandatory reporting of full-blown AIDS cases and AIDS deaths was introduced. This reporting was to be anonymous with only the initials of the name, the date of birth, and the indication of the sex. In addition, AIDS counseling centers were established by law.[62]

In the face of rising infection and resulting death rates, the ÖAH was thus able to continue and consolidate its counseling activities on a secure legal basis. Kurt Krickler, HOSI activist and secretary/assistant to the management of the ÖAH, noted on the occasion of its fifth anniversary in 1990: "By Austrian standards, this cooperation between the authorities and homosexual associations represented a sensational novelty."[63] It was, however, a success story with an expiration date, because on June 30, 1991, after long-simmering quarrels with the Ministry and the provincial offices over budget cuts and competencies, the association Österreichische AIDS-Hilfe dissolved. The federalization of AIDS prevention and the associated establishment of independent *AIDS-Hilfen* in most of the federal states was a typically Austrian solution. After years of cooperation in the early phase of AIDS in Austria, the fault lines between the emancipation movement and politics became increasingly visible. Since homosexuality was still discriminated against by law, society, and the media, the prevention work of the ÖAH also repeatedly reached its limits. Already the first big poster campaign in 1988, with the slogan "*Schutz aus Liebe*" ("protection out of love"), became a bone of contention. Photographed by the well-known photographer Peter Baumann, it featured three subjects, each in two variations: a young and a somewhat older heterosexual couple, as well as a homosexual male couple. But Franz Löschnak, the Health Minister appointed by the SPÖ (Social Democratic Party of Austria), objected to the homosexual poster because "a scandal would possibly be provoked; moreover, the depiction would violate Section 220 of the Austrian Penal Code (advertising for same-sex fornication)."[64] The billboard companies also refused to post the homosexual poster and a heterosexual poster that was deemed "lewd." However, during a public presentation of all the subjects, the press pounced on the "banned" motifs, helping them gain popularity.

Since Section 220 of the Austrian Penal Code was not abolished until 1996, conflicts between offensive prevention work, as demanded by activists in the gay community, and politics were still programmed. Thus, gay-specific information material that openly addressed and depicted same-sex sexual practices was obtained from the *Deutsche AIDS-Hilfe*. In the summer of 1990, a delivery of brochures to the Rosa Lila Tip counseling center in the Rosa Lila Villa was confiscated by Austrian customs because the pictorial depictions of sexual practices contained therein were deemed "hard pornography" and "advertising for same-sex fornication" under Section 220.[65] A case against the operators of the counseling center was dropped, but it was clear to the community that it had no reliable partner in politics in the fight against AIDS, which is why it increasingly relied on its own initiative in the 1990s and founded self-help groups, as well as relying on political resistance with actionism. The resistance was channeled in the founding of ACT UP Vienna in the fall of 1990. The group protested against the reduction of nursing beds for AIDS patients in Viennese hospitals and against the compulsory testing of all patients in Viennese hospitals, which was decreed as of June 1, 1991.[66] In 1993, the well-known TV presenter Günter Tolar founded the association *Positiv Leben*, which campaigned for unbureaucratic immediate help for HIV-positive people and AIDS patients, and the internet service "Liberty Life," which operated a low-threshold information platform about HIV and AIDS.

In the same year, Gery Keszler and his partner Torgom Petrosian, who was suffering from AIDS, organized the first Life Ball, an AIDS charity supported by the international fashion industry, which took place in Vienna's City Hall, the first event of its kind in the world to be held in an official government building. In 1991, the populist and popular mayor Helmut Zilk had to defend the dramatic undersupplying of AIDS patients and the forced testing of all patients in Viennese hospitals, but now he made the seat of the Viennese provincial government available for a "celebration of life" that was also to become a game changer in the reporting on HIV and AIDS. The increased visibility of homosexual lifestyles also led to increased acceptance in society.

Success Narrative AIDS?

After Chancellor Karl Nehammer "officially" declared the Covid-19 pandemic over in January 2023, journalist Barbara Tóth criticized in a commentary in *Falter* that in Austria "the fight against the virus and its consequences has always been conducted in a party-political way."[67] In the fight against HIV and AIDS, this kind of party-politically oriented health policy was avoided. In contrast to Bavaria, for example, where the catholic-conservative *Christlich-Soziale Union* (CSU) under Peter Gauweiler wanted to make its political mark with coercive measures against HIV-positive people,[68] in Austria, the political disputes were outsourced to the struggle of homosexuals for equal rights. For example, the Österreichische Volkspartei (ÖVP) practically refused all legal reforms. Since the mid-1990s, only the abolition of Section 221 of the Austrian Penal Code (ban on associations) and the Registered Partnership Act (EPG) were passed by political consensus. The abolition of Section 209 (minimum age for male same-sex relationships at eighteen), the introduction of "marriage for all," and the legal recognition of a "third gender" were decreed by the Austrian Constitutional Court against the will of the ÖVP and FPÖ.

Even though legal changes were initially politically impossible to implement, the social confrontation with AIDS and same-sex lifestyles on an unprecedented scale led to a strengthening of the political self-confidence of the gay and lesbian emancipation movement, which first gave rise to demands for legally secured partnerships and more far-reaching anti-discrimination measures. As experts for prevention in the target group that was mainly affected by AIDS in the early phase, health policy accents were set in cooperation with responsible persons in health policy that had an effect far beyond the spheres of life of the queer community. Thus, the strengthening of "risk perception" and "risk management" led to the development of prevention concepts that started with the responsibility of the individual and socially defined groups.[69] This concept of prevention policy became an important criterion for the Jakarta Declaration on health promotion published by the World Health Organization (WHO) in 1997, which was to determine the health policy of the twenty-first century as the "New Public Health." Public health "strives, in contrast to the curative medical model, to prevent disease by influencing behavior (behavioral prevention), but also and above all by improving living conditions (relational prevention), in order to help social groups, but individuals to new resources, which in the salutogenetic model of 'Generalized Restistance Resources' [...] help to produce health-promoting and cope with disease-causing influences."[70]

This success story "between movement, self-help, and professionalization" has also recently come under criticism. Peter-Paul Bänziger and Zülfukar Çetin argued that by telling the AIDS story "as a prime example of a non-discriminatory, 'liberal' form of health policy,"[71] above all "a 'top-down' view is reproduced."[72] Exclusions and connections would thus be obscured. The drug theme, which is closely linked to AIDS, has been left out of the political discourse and remains a stiff-necked child in prevention work as well. At the same time, by concentrating on the AIDS success story, connections to other social movements, such as the anti-globalization movement or autonomous groups, would be overlooked.

The "establishment of the prevention regime and the normalization of AIDS since the 1990s"[73] would have led to history narratives that do not do justice to the complexity of these histories with the "dramatizing juxtaposition of old and new, repressive and liberal, or healthy and sick."[74]

At first glance, it seems obvious to draw parallels between the AIDS pandemic and the Covid-19 crisis. Would a policy that relied less on coercive measures imposed from above have been more successful? But could the successful interaction of affected people and politics against a fear-mongering press in the AIDS crisis have worked under the other media conditions of the 2020s? In any case, the analysis of the relationship between politics and communities in the early years of AIDS shows that positive health policy effects could be achieved with the means of dialogue even, if not always, without conflict.

Endnotes

1. I use the terms gay and lesbian because they were self-chosen identity designations of the actors of the movement.

2. Alexander Garciá Düttmann, *Uneins mit Aids: Wie über einen Virus nachgedacht und geredet wird* (Frankfurt/Main: Fischer, 1993), 40.

3. Richard A. McKay, *Patient Zero and the Making of the AIDS Epidemic* (Chicago: University of Chicago Press, 2017); Sarah Schulman, *Let the Record Show: A Political History of ACT UP New York, 1987–1993* (New York: Farrar, Straus and Giroux, 2021).

4. Martin Reichert, *Die Kapsel: Aids in der Bundesrepublik* (Berlin: Suhrkamp, 2018); Henning Tümmers: *AIDS: Autopsie einer Bedrohung im geteilten Deutschland* (Göttingen: Wallstein, 2017).

5. Sebastian Haus-Rybicki, *Eine Seuche regieren: AIDS-Prävention in der Bundesrepublik 1981–1995* (Bielefeld: Transcript, 2021).

6. Andrea Nussbaum, "Die massenmediale Aufbereitung des AIDS-Diskurses" (PhD diss., University of Vienna, 1994); Ilse Eichberger, "Homosexualität und AIDS: Sozial- und kulturhistorische Aspekte von männlicher Homosexualität und AIDS (1981–2000)" (Diploma thesis, University of Vienna, 2003); Florian Anrather, "Zur Konstruktion und Normierung von Identität und Sexualität im Diskurs der österreichischen AIDS-Hilfen" (Diploma thesis, University of Vienna, 2008); Christine Keplinger, "Österreichische Gesundheitspolitik am Beispiel der AIDS-Hilfen: Eine Politikfeldanalyse. Reaktion der österreichischen Politik auf die AIDS-Problematik von 1983 bis 2010" (Diploma thesis, University of Vienna, 2010); Frank M. Amort, "Über die Topografie von HIV in Wien: Das Unsichtbare sichtbar machen," in *Sex in Wien: Lust. Kontrolle. Ungehorsam*, ed. Andreas Brunner et al. (Vienna: Metroverlag, 2016), 407–412; Katharina Pagitz, "Zwei Smokings mit Message," in *Queer Vienna: Einblicke in ein Bewegungsarchiv, Aether 8*, ed. Andreas Brunner et al. (Zürich: Intercom, 2023), in print; Katharina Kührner and Andreas, Brunner, "AIDS, Trauer und Erinnerung," in *Queer Vienna: Einblicke in ein Bewegungsarchiv, Aether 8*, ed. Andreas Brunner et al. (Zürich: Intercom, 2023), in print.

7. Michael T. Wright and Rolf Rosenbrock, "Aids: Zur Normalisierung einer Infektionskrankheit," in *Handbuch soziale Probleme*, ed. Günther Albrecht and Axel Groenemeyer (Wiesbaden: VS Verlag für Sozialwissenschaften, 2012), 195–218 (here 205–215).

8. Raimund Geene, *AIDS-Politik: Ein Krankheitsbild zwischen Medizin, Politik und Gesundheitsförderung* (Frankfurt/Main: Mabuse, 2000), 225–239.

9. Frank Rühmann, *AIDS: Eine Krankheit und ihre Folgen* (Frankfurt/Main: Edition Qumran im Campus Verlag, 1985), 66; on othering see Haus-Rybicki, *Eine Seuche regieren,* in particular "Teil I: Eine Krankheit der Anderen (1981–1986)," 35–165.

10. Editorial, "Schreck von drüben," *Der Spiegel*, May 30, 1982, 187–189.

11. Editorial, "Amerika zittert vor mörderischem Leiden," *Kurier*, Sept. 29, 1982.

12. Editorial, "Medizin für uns," *Lambda Nachrichten*, Oct. 13, 1982, 33.

13. Wolfgang Stangl, *Die neue Gerechtigkeit: Strafrechtsreform in Österreich, 1954–1975* (Vienna: Verlag für Gesellschaftskritik, 1985), 91.

14. Herbert Gottweis, "Neue soziale Bewegungen in Österreich," in *Handbuch des politischen Systems in Österreich: Die Zweite Republik*, ed. Herbert Dachs and Emmerich Tálos, 3rd ed. (Vienna: Manz, 1997), 342–358.

15. On the lesbian movement within the *Aktion Unabhängiger Frauen (AUF)*, see Ulrike Repnik, *Die Geschichte der Lesben- und Schwulenbewegung* (Vienna: Milena, 2006), 91–103; For the group COMING OUT, see Andreas Brunner, "Sichtbar unter Unsichtbaren: Eine schwule Identität im Spiegel von Politik und Gesellschaft seit den 1970er-Jahren," in *Das "andere" Österreich: Leben in Österreich abseits männlich-weiß-heteronormativ-deutsch-katholischer Dominanz*, ed. Farid Hafez (Vienna: New Academic Press, 2021), 13–26.

16. Wolfgang Förster, "Zwischen Provokation und Integration: Ein Vierteljahrhundert Schwulenbewegung in Österreich," in *Der andere Blick: Lesbischwules Leben in Österreich: Eine Kulturgeschichte*, ed. Wolfgang Förster et al. (Vienna: MA 57 Frauenförderung und Koordination von Frauenangelegenheiten, 2001), 215–224 (here 216).

17. Ibid., 216–217.

18. An independent trans movement did not develop in Austria until the first half of the 1990s, which led to further transformation processes within the leading groups of the emancipation movement, but since these did not happen in the period under study in this article, I use the term gay and lesbian movement, coined by the actors of the time, and not queer movement.

19. In 2012, the Rosa Lila Villa was renamed the *Türkis Rosa Lila Villa* to also reflect the representation of trans people.

20. The City of Vienna came to an agreement with the left-alternative cultural scene after occupations and made free spaces possible with the *Arena*, the *Werkstätten- und Kulturhaus (WUK)*, and the *Amerlinghaus*. However, well-known occupied residential buildings in Ägidigasse/Spalowskygasse or in Gassergasse were cleared with police force. See *Besetzt: Kampf um Freiräume seit den 70ern*, Katalog zur 381. Sonderausstellung des Wien Museums, ed. Martina Nußbaumer and Werner Michael Schwarz (Vienna: Czernin, 2012).

21. Kurt Krickler, "Homosexualität und AIDS(-Politik)," in *Homosexualität in Österreich*, ed. Michael Handl et al. (Vienna: Junius, 1989), 80–90 (here 80).

22. Ibid.

23. All citations in this paragraph from: AIDS Information, Leaflet, ed. Homosexuelle Initiative Wien and Wiener Arbeitsgemeinschaft für Volksgesundheit, March 1983, QWIEN Archive.

24. Editorial, "Medizin für uns," 33; AIDS Information, Leaflet.

25. Kurt Krickler, "Alles über AIDS," *Lambda Nachrichten*, May 30, 1983, 14–21 (here 14).

26. Editorial, *Basta*, Apr. 1984, 6. For the position of the controversial media maker Wolfgang Fellner see Florian Skrabal, "Wer hat Angst vor Wolfgang F.?," *dossier.at* (Dec. 2, 2019), accessed Jan. 3, 2023, https://www.dossier.at/dossiers/korruption/wer-hat-angst-vor-wolfgang-f/.

27. Editorial, "Vergesst HERPES – jetzt kommt: AIDS: Eine Krankheit macht Schlagzeilen: tückisch und todsicher," *Basta*, Apr. 1983, 51.

28. Editorial, *Kurier*, Mar. 16, 1983.

29. Editorial, *profil*, Mar. 16, 1983, 64.

30. Leopold Nenning, "AIDS über Wien," *Wiener*, April 1983, 29.

31. Ibid.

32. For his work as editor of the *WIENER* and his turning away from the gay scene, see Michael Hopp, *Der Mann auf der Couch* (Hamburg: Textem Verlag, 2019).

33. Markus Peichl, "Die letzten Monate des Kenny Ramsauer," *Wiener*, Aug. 1983, 28–31.

34. Eberhard Hübner, "Inszenierung einer Krankheit: Die Aids-Berichterstattung im 'Spiegel'," in *Aids als Risiko: Über den gesellschaftlichen Umgang mit einer Krankheit*, ed. Volkmar Sigusch (Hamburg: Konkret Literatur Verlag, 1987), 218–233 (here 223).

35. Enrico Ippolito, "Wie die fragwürdigen Aids-Berichte immer noch nachwirken," *Spiegel.de* (Jan. 6, 2022), accessed Jan. 3, 2023, https://www.spiegel.de/geschichte/75-jahre-spiegel-wie-die-aids-berichterstattung-immer-noch-nachwirkt-a-c42d2500-64a6-4e41-a1b4-266cc8c74bb3.

36. Lukas Engelmann, "Homosexualität und AIDS," in *Was ist Homosexualität? Forschungsgeschichte, gesellschaftliche Entwicklungen und Perspektiven,* ed. Florian Mildenberger et al. (Hamburg: Männerschwarm, 2014), 271–304 (here 273). The traumatic effects are critically questioned by Patrick Henze-Lindhorst, *AIDS als kollektives Trauma: Über eine Verbundenheit schwuler Generationen* (Berlin: Querverlag, 2022).

37. Ibid.

38. Peter-Paul Bänziger and Zülfukar Çetin, "Die Normalisierung eines Ausnahmezustands? Geschichten der Aids- und der Drogenthematik in der Bundesrepublik Deutschland seit den 1980er Jahren," in *Gewalt, Zurichtung, Befreiung? Individuelle "Ausnahmezustände" im 20. Jahrhundert*, ed. Hannah Ahlheim (Göttingen: Wallstein, 2017), 117–140.

39. Editorial, "Die Bombe ist gelegt," *Der Spiegel*, Nov. 4, 1984.

40. Rosa von Praunheim, "Gibt es Sex nach dem Tode?," *Der Spiegel*, Nov. 25, 1984. For the public dispute between Rosa von Praunheim and the sexologist Martin Dannecker see Martin Dannecker, "Rosa wird evangelisch: Offener Brief an Rosa von Praunheim (1985)," in *Fortwährende Eingriffe: Aufsätze, Vorträge und Reden zu AIDS und HIV aus vier Jahrzehnten*, ed. Martin Dannecker (Hamburg: Männerschwarm, 2019), 13–19.

41. Kurt Krickler, "USA: Für Reagan den AIDS-Virus entdeckt," *Lambda Nachrichten*, July 6, 1984, 40–41 (here 41).

42. Krickler, "Homosexualität und AIDS(-Politik)," 82.

43. Ibid., 84.

44. Kurt Krickler, "Alles Neue über AIDS," *Lambda Nachrichten*, Jan. 11, 1985, 22–28 (here 28). For a discussion of epidemic policy measures in Germany see Hans Haller and Wolfgang Sternsdorff, "'Fünf Jahre in Quarantäne?'," *Der Spiegel*, Dec. 23, 1984, 28–32.

45. Krickler, "Homosexualität und AIDS(-Politik)," 83.

46. Christian Hackl, "Die erste Welle," *Wiener*, Jan. 1985, 62–65 (here 62).

47. Ibid.

48. Ibid., 63.

49. Ibid., 65.

50. Ibid., 67.

51. Krickler, "Alles Neue über AIDS," 28.

52. Ibid.

53. Krickler, "Homosexualität und AIDS(-Politik)," 86.

54. Christian Hackl, "'Sterben muss jeder:' Stimmungsbericht aus der Wiener Schwulenszene," *Wiener*, Jan. 1985, 64.

55. Ernst Dummer, "Was du schon immer über AIDS wissen wolltest," *Lambda Nachrichten*, Jan. 11, 1985, 30.

56. Kurt Krickler, "AIDS: HTLV-III-Antikörper-Untersuchung," *Lambda Nachrichten*, July 12, 1985, 11–13 (here 12).

57. Kurt Krickler, "HTLV-III-Antikörper-Untersuchung," *Lambda Nachrichten*, Apr. 12, 1985, 5–6 (here 5).

58. Krickler, "AIDS: HTLV-III-Antikörper-Untersuchung," 13.

59. Kurt Krickler, "Entstehungsgeschichte der Österreichischen AIDS-Hilfe," in *5 Jahre Österreichische AIDS-Hilfe 1985-1990, Info aktuell 2*, ed. Österreichische AIDS-Hilfe (Vienna: self-published, 1990), 34–35.

60. Kurt Krickler, "AIDS was sonst?," *Lambda Nachrichten*, Oct. 9, 1985, 15–19 (here 17).

61. Bundesgesetz vom 16. Mai 1986 über Maßnahmen gegen die Verbreitung des erworbenen Immundefektsyndroms (AIDS-Gesetz), *Bundesgesetzblatt für die Republik Österreich*, 119. Stück, June 6, 1986.

62. Kurt Krickler, "AIDS in Österreich," *Lambda Nachrichten*, June 27, 1986, 23–25 (here 23). For the further development of the Austrian AIDS law, see Thomas E. Fischer, "HIV/AIDS-Prävention und AIDS-Gesetzgebung in Österreich und Dänemark: Ein empirischer Vergleich" (Diploma thesis, University of Vienna, 2003).

63. Krickler, "Entstehungsgeschichte der Österreichischen AIDS-Hilfe," 35.

64. Dieter Schmutzer, "Informationskampagnen der Österreichischen AIDS-Hilfe," in *5 Jahre Österreichische AIDS-Hilfe 1985-1990, Info aktuell 2*, ed. Österreichische AIDS-Hilfe (Vienna: self-published, 1990), 88–89 (here 88).

65. Frank M. Amort, "Zensur!," *Tamtam 3–4/1990*, 5.

66. Kurt Krickler, "AIDS-Notstand in Wien," *Lambda Nachrichten*, April

16, 1991, 25–28; Kurt Krickler, "HIV-Zwangstestung in den Wiener Gemeindespitälern," *Lambda Nachrichten*, July 16, 1991, 10–13.

67. Barbara Tóth, "Nach der Pandemie ist vor der politischen Aufarbeitung," *Falter*, Jan. 18, 2023, 7.

68. See Haus-Rybicki, *Eine Seuche regieren*, 194–196.

69. Rolf Rosenbrock, "AIDS: Fragen und Lehren für Public Health," in *Wer oder was ist "Public Health"?,* Argument Sonderband AS 198 (Hamburg: Argument Verlag, 1992), 82–114.

70. Geene, *AIDS-Politik*, 94.

71. Peter-Paul Bänziger and Zülfukar Çetin, "Die Normalisierung eines Ausnahmezustands? Geschichten der Aids- und der Drogenthematik in der Bundesrepublik Deutschland seit den 1980er Jahren," in *Gewalt, Zurichtung, Befreiung? Individuelle "Ausnahmezustände" im 20. Jahrhundert*, ed. Hannah Ahlheim (Göttingen: Wallstein, 2017), 117–140 (here 117).

72. Ibid., 118.

73. Ibid., 138.

74. Ibid., 139.

Covid-19: The Constitutional and Legislative Situation in Austria

Maria Bertel
Andreas Th. Müller

Introduction

Although not tailored to a pandemic situation, Austria could count, from the very beginning of the Covid-19 pandemic in March 2020, on a law especially devoted to epidemics. No one doubted that the *Act on Epidemics* of 1950[1] (which originally dates back to 1913 when the "*Gesetz über die Verhütung und Bekämpfung übertragbarer Krankheiten*"[2] had been adopted first) could, in principle, be applied to the situation following the outbreak of the Covid-19 virus.

However, the *Act on Epidemics* from the 1950s quickly proved to be outdated and not fitting the needs and circumstances of a pandemic. In particular, when the outbreak of Covid-19 in the ski area of Ischgl forced people to leave the valley,[3] and hotels and guesthouses had to be closed,[4] those businesses could claim compensation for loss of income, as the authorities had closed them based on the *Act on Epidemics*.[5] Quickly, the Austrian parliament issued the "Covid-19 Act" which consisted of several acts (including the *Covid-19 Measures Act*[6]) and amendments to existing laws.[7] Restrictive measures of the authorities that are based on these new laws, even if they meant that businesses had to be shut down, could not thus rely anymore on the generous rules for the compensation of loss of income of the *Act on Epidemics*.[8] This is just one example of the problems the law-maker faced in the first days of the pandemic in spring 2020.

In the following, we shall discuss the constitutional and legislative situation in Austria with respect to the Covid-19 pandemic. In this regard, we shall address three major fields: the role of the federal state in the pandemic; the legality principle, which is the key provision of the Austrian Constitution when it comes to the division of labor between the legislator and administrative authorities; and fundamental rights since, in the course of the pandemic, the liberty of individuals in Austria has been challenged like probably hardly ever after 1945.

Federal State

Distribution of Competences

Covid-19 challenged the federal state, and some commentators even questioned federalism in general.[9] One of the most important features of a federal state is the (vertical) distribution of powers between different levels of government, resulting in a certain separation of powers.[10] In Austria, as early as 1952,[11] the Constitutional Court confirmed that the distribution of competences, (between the federal level and the constituent units, i.e. the *Länder*), as well as the participation of the constituent units in the legislation at the federal level, were essential to the Austrian federal state (the *Bundesstaat*), which is enshrined in Article 2 of the *Federal Constitutional Act*.[12] According to Article 2 para 2 of the *Federal Constitutional Act*, Austria consists of nine *Bundesländer* (constituent units). The distribution of competences forms part of the Federal Constitutional Act (as laid down in Articles 10–15). It distributes legislative competences and the legal acts adopted subsequently in order to implement them between the federal level and the level of the *Länder*. To that end, numerous competence matters are enumerated in the afore-mentioned provisions. Article 15 of the *Federal Constitutional Act* establishes that those competences not mentioned fall into the competence of the *Länder*.

As far as our topic is concerned, neither epidemics nor pandemics are expressly referred to in Articles 10–15, but "health issues" are mentioned in Article 10 para 1 no. 12 of the *Federal Constitutional Act*. "Health issues" cover care for the general health of the population and regulations to prevent threats to public health.[13] The constitutional provision in question allocates the competence to legislate as well as to execute (i.e., implement) concerning "health issues" to the federal level. The federal legislation adopted during the pandemic thus draws on this competence.

Hence, in Austria, an exclusive legislative competence of the federal (*Bund*) to legislate on Covid-19 existed from the beginning. The question then arises why federalism was questioned in public opinion at all. The answer can be found in the organization of the Austrian administrative system. Competences falling into the responsibility of the federal level are not automatically administered through federal authorities.[14] In fact, in most cases (and also in the case of "health issues," see Article 102 para 1 of the *Federal Constitutional Act*), *Land* authorities, namely the district administrative authorities, the *Bezirksverwaltungsbehörden* (*Bezirkshauptmannschaften*[15]; in municipalities having a special legal status, the *Stadtmagistrate*[16])[17] are responsible for the implementation of the pertinent law (so-called indirect federal administration, *mittelbare Bundesverwaltung*).[18] In those cases, the

Governor (*Landeshauptmann*) under the authority of the competent federal Minister is responsible for the administration.[19] Execution (or implementation) does not only entail setting acts for or against individuals, but also issuing administrative ordinances (*Durchführungsverordnungen*) based on the law, addressing the general public or a certain group within the general public (Article 18 paras 1 and 2 of the *Federal Constitutional Act*). When enacting the law, the legislator decides whether and to what extent administrative ordinances can and must be issued by the competent administrative authorities. Since, compared to enacting laws, issuing administrative ordinances is far less complicated, ordinances allow for reacting faster to changes in real life. During the pandemic, the legislator was therefore rather generous in stipulating the legal basis for ordinances[20] opening up room for action for *Land* authorities to become active on their part.

Apart from the "health issues" competence, "catastrophes/disasters" may also be mentioned in this context. The issue of "catastrophes/disasters" can be split up into "management" and "prevention" of catastrophes. Whereas "prevention" of catastrophes falls into the legislative realm of the federal level, the *Länder* are competent to legislate on the "management" of catastrophes.[21] Even though the pandemic can also be considered a "catastrophe," it was nonetheless covered by the competence of "health issues,"[22] therefore leaving no space for legislation of the *Länder*. A similar line of reasoning applies with respect to the prohibition and regulation of events in the context of the pandemic. Thus, although "the regulation of events" is, generally speaking, a competence of the *Länder* (according to the general clause in Article 15 of the *Federal Constitutional Act*), the prohibition and regulation of events were covered by the federal competence on health issues.[23]

This leads to the following picture regarding legislative and administrative competences in Austria: Whereas the *Länder* did not have any role in the legislation on the Covid-19 pandemic, the *Land* Governor and the *Bezirksverwaltungsbehörden* (the district administrative authorities) were in many fields in charge of the implementation of the *Act on Epidemics* as well as the *Covid-19 Measures Act* in the context of the so-called indirect federal administration (*mittelbare Bundesverwaltung*).[24]

Role of the District Administrative Authorities

The implementation of the pertinent legislative provisions by the *Länder* and the district administrative authorities has the advantage that the execution of the laws can take into consideration regional peculiarities.[25] Since the competent federal minister, within the context of the indirect federal administration, still has the right to issue binding instructions to the *Land* governors (who are, on their part, heading the district administrative authorities), consistency of administration is guaranteed, at least in principle.[26]

The Austrian *Länder* made use, in various ways, of their scope of action regarding the administration of the federal pandemic legislation. This was also due to the fact that the need to administer the pandemic added to the existing tasks of the district administrative authorities, resulting in a very high workload for the staff.[27] One example shall illustrate this: In Vorarlberg, a "*Covid-19 Infektionsteam*" was formed. The staff of all four district administrative authorities together with staff from the *Land* government as well as public health officers (*Amtsärzte/Amtsärztinnen*) combined their forces for purposes of contact tracing and isolation of people suffering from Covid-19 according to § 7 of the *Act on Epidemics*.[28] In contrast, in Tyrol, new staff was hired.[29] Additionally, staff was temporarily assigned to other departments.[30] Moreover, Tyrol set up a "*Corona Zentrum*,"[31] where employees of the *Land* as well as the Austrian army (*Bundesheer*) worked together mainly in contact tracing.[32] In both Tyrol and Vorarlberg, the employee always acted on behalf of a specific district authority, even as they worked in teams consisting of employees of different authorities and institutions. Neither the "*Corona Zentrum*" nor the "*Covid-19 Infektionsteam*" were authorities themselves. Although the pandemic challenged the administration also from an organizational point of view, it did not lead to the creation of new administrative authorities.[33]

Not only was the population challenged by the abundance of legal norms and the fast changes thereof;[34] the district administrative authorities also had to adapt very quickly to these changes, which further added to their workload.[35] Moreover, the district administrative authorities had to still cope with the regular workload.[36] Hence, even though the *Länder* had no share in the pandemic legislation, their authorities were being challenged in manifold ways by the administration of the pandemic.

Legality Principle, Or: How Much Leeway for the Administration?
The Relation between Legal Acts and Administrative Regulations

According to Article 18 para 1 of the *Federal Constitutional Act*, "[t]he entire public administration shall be based on law." Article 18 para 2 of the Federal Constitutional Act stipulates that "[e]very administrative authority can on the basis of law issue ordinances within its sphere of competence." Article 18 of the *Federal Constitutional Act* therefore makes clear that the scope for ordinances is defined by the legislator. It is the task of the legislator not to overstretch the law and not to abandon its responsibilities by using too vague and broad legislative clauses, allowing the administration to regulate matters instead of the legislator.[37] In particular, the legislator must be clear on the core aspects of the regulation in question.[38] Both the requirement of regulating the core aspects as well as to set clear standards regarding the content of ordinances in the law arise from the constitutional requirements as laid down in Article 18 of the *Federal Constitutional Act*.[39] Yet, depending on the subject matter, Article 18 is interpreted more or less broadly. When fundamental rights are at stake, the legislator is required to regulate more specifically and leave less discretion for the administrative authorities than in, say, spatial planning law.[40] In scholarship, this phenomenon is known as "differentiated legality principle" (*differenziertes Legalitätsprinzip*).[41] Therefore, the democratically legitimated legislator is, (also) for reasons of constitutional law, called to guide the administration and provide it with all essential elements so that its role remains to *implement* the law rather than to *define* it.

The relationship between the law and administrative ordinances changed throughout the pandemic. Not only did the law leave space for ordinances of *Länder* authorities, but also for regulations of the Federal Minister of Health. According to Harald Eberhard (who is also referring to the German scholarship), with the pandemic, the "hour of the executive" had come.[42] This becomes manifest in, amongst others, innovative forms of authorizing different administrative authorities to enact ordinances,[43] but also in a shift in the Constitutional Court's jurisprudence on the relation between the legislator and administrative authorities.

Innovative Forms of the Division of Labor between Legislation and Administration in the Pandemic

Whereas the 1950 *Act on Epidemics* follows the "traditional" system (i.e., a certain legal norm defines the space that can be filled by an administrative ordinance issued by the competent administrative authority), in the pandemic the lawmaker created, by virtue of the *Covid-19 Measures Act*, what was called a "cascade system."[44] This means that "unless otherwise provided in an ordinance of the Federal Minister or the governor, additional measures may be established at the regional level by ordinance of the governor or the district administrative authority may establish additional measures at the regional level. Additional measures may be, on the one hand, more stringent measures (such as increasing the minimum distance, additional restrictions on persons, bringing forward curfew hours, extending the obligation to wear mouth and nose protection) and, on the other hand, supplementary measures."[45] The "cascade system" allowed for the reaction to regionally different situations regarding the spread of Covid-19. At the same time, its flexibility also allowed for different reactions in different regions. In this regard, Vienna opted for tighter regulations than the other *Länder*; for instance, the obligation to wear a face mask in public transport ending only in March 2023.[46]

The Constitutional Court's Jurisprudence on Administrative Regulations in the Pandemic

As described above, the legality principle enshrined in Article 18 of the *Federal Constitutional Act* binds both the lawmaker and the administrative authorities. Since the *Covid-19 Measures Act* was rather generous regarding the authorization of the administration to issue further regulations, the first rulings of the Constitutional Court on the *Covid-19 Measures Act* were awaited impatiently. In its judgment of July 14, 2020,[47] the Constitutional Court found that the provision under examination were constitutional. It referred to the situation of crisis and the difficulties of fighting the pandemic and justified, on this basis, the legislator's option for a rather generous legal basis for the administrative ordinances to be adopted subsequently. In particular, the Court decided that "[i]f [...] the legislator leaves it to the administrative authority to decide which of a number of possible measures [... which might] also intensively restrict fundamental rights, it deems necessary according to its prognosis and in consideration of the interests affected, the administrative authority must make its decision based on the level of information about the relevant circumstances on which the law is based that is possible in terms of time and facts in the specific situation [...] and reasonable, and after carrying out the required consideration of interests. In doing so, it must determine these circumstances and document them accordingly in the procedure for issuing the ordinance in order to ensure a review of the legality of the ordinance."[48] Therefore, the Constitutional Court accepted that instead of a more precise determination of the ordinance through the legislator, in the context of the pandemic and its volatility, the administrative authorities can issue administrative regulations, but they have to document the relevant facts guiding their decision. This has to be seen as connected to the fact that the legal reactions to the pandemic depended on scientific facts and the scientific assessment of the development of the pandemic.

This jurisprudence led to different reactions in legal academia: Some commentators were very critical of the leeway granted to the legislator.[49] Others emphasized, however, that the jurisprudence of the Constitutional Court had been quite strict regarding the issuing of ordinances since the administrative authority, as opposed to the legislator, had to explain its regulation and give reasons.[50]

Fundamental Rights

General Observations

As everyone in Austria observed, and painfully experienced, the Covid-19 pandemic entailed an unprecedented restriction of fundamental rights. The impact of the measures taken by the Austrian government was momentous, and for at least three reasons. First, as already indicated, these measures affected each and everyone in the country, although to different extents and degrees. Second, the measures encompassed the full panoply of fundamental rights, from the rights to life and liberty to the freedom of speech, assembly, and religion to property and entrepreneurial freedom.[51] Third, the measures' harshness and suddenness that were characteristic (of at least the first phase) of the Covid-19 pandemic became a further hallmark of the pandemic-induced fundamental rights restrictions.

These three features, in their combination, made the Covid-19 pandemic a unique experience indeed. At the same time, the experience was a shared one given the fact that countries around the globe faced similar challenges. Most international human rights conventions contain special provisions (so-called derogation clauses) that offer governments extra scope of maneuvering in situations of public emergency, for instance, Article 15 of the 1950 *European Human Rights Convention* (ECHR)[52] or Article 4 of the 1966 *International Covenant on Civil and Political Rights* (ICCPR).[53] The same holds true for most domestic constitutions,[54] including the Austrian one where Article 18 paras 3–5 of the *Federal Constitutional Act* authorizes the Federal President to issue emergency regulations under the subsequent control of the parliament.[55] While numerous countries activated the aforementioned derogation clauses in order to obtain additional leeway for taking measures against the pandemic, the Austrian government neither relied on Article 18 para 3 of the *Federal Constitutional Act*[56] nor did it activate the derogation clauses in applicable international human rights instruments (Article 15 ECHR, Article 4 ICCPR). Hence, the constitutional and international legal framework that assessed the lawfulness of fundamental rights restrictions during the Covid-19 pandemic was the "regular" one.

This does obviously not mean, however, that fundamental rights are guaranteed in an absolute manner. Generally speaking, restrictions of fundamental rights, under both the constitution and international human rights law, are lawful if, and to the extent that, they are provided for by law, meet a legitimate objective (i.e., the protection of general interests or the rights and freedoms of others), and are proportionate.[57]

It was widely accepted that the pertinent restrictions pursued a legitimate objective, namely public health as an important public interest as well as the protection of the lives and health of many (in particular elderly or otherwise vulnerable) individuals who would otherwise have been more extensively exposed to serious risks to their physical integrity and life. It is undisputed that fundamental rights do not only have a negative side in the traditional "Lockean" sense of the government being supposed to abstain from interfering with the citizens' lives, liberty, and property. In addition, fundamental rights have a positive side to the extent that the government must actively protect the life and limb of its citizens.[58] It does not come as a surprise that these so-called "positive obligations" can, and often do, conflict with the negative side of fundamental rights, since the government must in certain circumstances limit the fundamental rights of some persons in order to allow the exercise of fundamental rights of others.

The further requirement that the restriction be "provided by law" calls for action on the part of the legislator, i.e. the parliament, in order to provide a heightened amount of democratic legitimacy and oversight (as opposed to purely executive measures) as well as of transparency. Restrictions of fundamental rights shall be decided upon in the privileged place of deliberation that the parliament is supposed to be and before the eyes of the public at large. Yet, as became clear during the Covid-19 pandemic, it was not too difficult to meet this requirement (i.e., the reservation of fundamental rights-restrictive regulation to the legislative body) which is, in essence, a formal one. The pertinent statutory bases (for instance, the *Covid-19 Measures Act*) obtained the blessing of the parliament, often using fast-track procedures.[59] Moreover, they often remained relatively general and vague in authorizing restrictions of fundamental rights by the executive (namely the Federal Minister of Health and the Governors of the *Länder*).[60]

Against this background, the crucial question in assessing the lawfulness of Covid-19-related measures becomes whether the measures in question were "proportionate." This is a substantive criterion calling for an assessment as to whether the adopted measure is fit for promoting the stated objective (public health and/or protection of the rights of other individuals) and whether it is "necessary" in the sense that it is the least harmful measure in order to achieve the said objective and could not have been substituted by alternative measures that would still protect the object in question but would interfere less with the restricted fundamental right.

The proportionality test is not an exercise in logical deduction, but calls for a value judgment on the part of the legislator (and, on the basis of the applicable laws, the competent executive authorities), implying the balancing of interests of the great many persons affected and the various public interests and individual rights at stake (also for education, culture, and the economy). The Constitutional Court—and, subsequently, the European Court of Human Rights—which are mandated to supervise the compliance of the legislation with the standard of proportionality concede a certain margin of appreciation to the State authorities when making this assessment. This signifies that the courts will only intervene in cases of qualified misapplication of the proportionality standard. In addition, judicial control does not operate with the benefit of hindsight but calls for an assessment as to whether, at the time when the decision was made, and on the basis of the information available at this moment in time, the measure in question meets the proportionality test.

In sum, the courts show certain deference toward the legislator when it comes to making the necessary balancing decisions. One important criterion—and instrument of "rationalization" of the value judgment in question—is that the decision to be made is evidence-based, taking due account of the best available scientific insights into the development of the pandemic, the risks posed by the virus to different groups of persons within the population, and the effectiveness of the various instruments to limit the spread of the virus.

If, and to the extent that, the government can establish that its measures were based on the available science, the Constitutional Court will be prone to accept the proportionality of the measures in question. An early example of this approach in the context of the Covid-19 pandemic can be found in the judgment of the Constitutional Court of June 24, 2021, where it extensively cited the projections regarding the risk of infection and its implications for the occupancy of hospital beds as well as intensive care beds.[61] On this basis, the Constitutional Court restricted itself to conclude that "in an overall assessment of the circumstances it cannot object to the administrative authority adopting [the relevant measure] to the extent that the latter, relying on the discretion available to it and in weighing all affected interests qualified [the relevant measure] as indispensable."[62]

Against this background, the Constitutional Court has so far decided, in most cases brought before it, that the government's measures did not breach any fundamental rights. For instance, the Constitutional Court found that the application of the so-called "2G rule," that only persons vaccinated ("*geimpft*") or tested ("*getestet*"), but not persons having recovered from Covid-19 ("*genesen*"), were allowed to access nighttime gastronomy, (as opposed to the otherwise generally applicable "3G rule," where recovered persons could have access), was constitutional given the wide margin of discretion of the legislator and the "epidemiologically particularly unfavorable conditions due to the justifiably assumed increased mixing of a primarily young audience with a low vaccination rate and the increased aerosol emission caused by loud speaking, singing, and dancing."[63] In this and further judgments, the Constitutional Court did therefore accept that far-reaching interferences with the right to private and family life for non-vaccinated persons (including the so-called "lockdown for the unvaccinated" from November 15 to 21, 2021, and at the beginning of 2022) were compatible with the available scientific data and within the margin of discretion of the government.[64]

Of more interest are the cases where the Constitutional Court denied the lawfulness of the restrictive measures for not being compatible with pertinent fundamental right guarantees, which will therefore be at the heart of the subsequent analysis.[65] In view of the broad spectrum of measures the Austrian government adopted during the Covid-19 pandemic and the restrictions to fundamental rights that they entailed,[66] only a narrow selection can be presented here. Among the decisions where the Constitutional Court identified breaches of fundamental rights, the present contribution addresses two judgments that seem symptomatic of the impact of the government's anti-pandemic policy on the fundamental rights situation in Austria. In addition, they testify to the fact that the Constitutional Court, apart from the formal reasoning on the legality principle,[67] has only intervened so far when the government has clearly exceeded the wide margin of discretion conceded to it and, in particular, when the Constitutional Court identified a lack of coherence in the government's treatment of different fundamental rights. In addition, the introduction, and subsequent abolishment, of general compulsory vaccination against Covid-19 deserves closer analysis.

Violation of the Right to Private and Family Life and the Right to Religion

One of the first major judgments of the Constitutional Court regarding the Covid-19 pandemic[68] concerned the right to private and family life and the right to religion, as guaranteed by Articles 8 and 9 of the ECHR, respectively.[69] The *Covid-19 Measures Act*[70] authorized the Federal Minister of Health to regulate entry into certain public places in order to prevent the spread of Covid-19. On this legal basis, the Federal Minister of Health adopted a series of successive administrative ordinances on special protective measures to prevent an emergency situation due to Covid-19 (the so-called "Covid-19 Emergency Measures Ordinances"). With respect to assemblies of persons, § 12 of the Second Covid-19 Emergency Measures Ordinance[71] only allowed for the participation in funerals of up to fifty participants.[72]

The Constitutional Court agreed that this limitation constitutes an interference with both the right to private and family life (Article 8 ECHR) and the right to religion (Article 9 ECHR). At the same time, it stated, without entering into any deeper analysis, that it had no doubt that the measure in question was provided by law, met a legitimate objective, and was fit for promoting the stated objectives.[73] The Court did, however, deny that the measure was proportionate since "the final farewell to loved ones who have died is considered essential by many people and cannot be repeated or substituted."[74] Hence, the interference with the aforementioned fundamental rights was to be considered particularly grave. In addition, the Constitutional Court criticized that the Covid-19 Emergency Measures Ordinance did not provide for analogous restrictions for events falling within the scope of protection of the freedom of assembly (which is equally constitutionally guaranteed, namely by virtue of Article 11 ECHR[75]), thus challenging the coherence of the bundle of Covid-19 measures adopted by the government.

Violation of the Equality Principle and the Freedom of Art

In another case, the applicants complained about a restriction of the equality principle, as enshrined in Article 7 of the *Federal Constitutional Act* and Article 2 of the *Basic Law on the General Rights of Nationals* of December 21, 1867, (Basic Law)[76], as well as of the freedom of art as guaranteed by Article 17a of the Basic Law which has constitutional rank in the Austrian legal order. The applicants were artists and argued that the applicable measures had prevented them from engaging in their artistic activities over an extended period of time.[77]

§§ 7 and 14 of the Fifth Covid-19 Emergency Measures Ordinance[78] restricted the access to cultural institutions to cultural events in fixed composition without any audience and for professional reasons. This means that only rehearsals and the like were possible, but no genuine performances could take place. At the same time, § 18 of the Fifth Covid-19 Emergency Measures Ordinance excluded gatherings for religious reasons from the ordinance's scope of application.

As far as the freedom of art was concerned, the Constitutional Court found that, on the one hand, the measures in question did not focus on the artistic sector and that, on the other hand, the restriction of access to cultural events resulted in a reduction of human interaction that was compatible with the overall objective of the measures aiming at preventing the spread of the Covid-19 virus. On this basis, the Constitutional Court qualified the measure in question as a proportionate restriction of the freedom of art.[79]

As regards the other line of the applicants' argument, the Constitutional

Court considered that the freedom of gathering is protected by several fundamental rights, depending on the purpose of gathering, such as religious gatherings (Article 9 ECHR), (political) assemblies (Article 11 ECHR) or cultural events (Article 17a Basic Law), and that none of these freedoms can *a priori* claim any preeminence vis-à-vis the others.[80] This does not preclude that some of these freedoms deserve special protection in particular circumstances, for instance, the freedom of assembly in the democratic context when it comes to the possibility of civil society to voice their protest against governmental restrictions due to Covid-19. Accordingly, the Constitutional Court confirmed the government's decision not to limit the number of participants in such assemblies (in combination with the fact that they typically take place outside) did not breach the equality principle.[81]

This situation is different, however, with respect to the fact that the ordinance generally exempts religious gatherings from its scope of application with the effect that such gatherings are possible irrespective of the number of participants and irrespective of whether they take place inside or outside. In contrast, cultural events must take place without any audience at all. In the Constitutional Court's view, such discrimination had no objective justification: "Religion and art belong—independently of each other, but in many cases also intertwined with each other—to the basic needs of a civilized society. In both cases, certain fundamental rights are exercised together with or in front of other people."[82] Hence, the categorical difference in treatment of the freedom of religion and freedom of art, which again testifies to a lack of coherence in the regulatory approach taken by the ordinance in question, violated the equality principle of the Austrian constitution.[83]

Compulsory Vaccination

The most hotly debated measure was not the extensive application of the 2G rule, leading to the so-called "lockdown for the unvaccinated," but the adoption, on January 20, 2022, of the "Federal Act on Compulsory Vaccination Against Covid-19" (*Covid-19 Compulsory Vaccination Act*)[84] which obliged all persons above eighteen years to vaccinate themselves against the Covid-19 virus.[85] As is well known, the compulsory vaccination was never really activated as the Federal Minister of Health made use of the authorization under § 19 of the *Covid-19 Compulsory Vaccination Act* and suspended the duty to be vaccinated, before it became operative,[86] and extended the suspension subsequently.[87] Finally, on July 7, 2022, the parliament abolished the *Covid-19 Compulsory Vaccination Act*, without the duty to be vaccinated having actually been operative.[88]

So much ado about nothing? In fact, many consider a duty to be vaccinated the harshest pandemic-induced interference with fundamental rights at all, at least a much harsher one than restrictions of freedom of movement or even lockdowns, as compulsory vaccination does not "only" affect the freedom to move and assemble, but has a direct impact on the personal integrity of the individual. While it is hard to make this comparison in the abstract, i.e. without knowing how extensive the respective restrictions are and how many and what exceptions exist, there is some plausibility to this reasoning. Against this background, many countries have abstained from introducing compulsory vaccination altogether or have restricted the duty to be vaccinated to certain professional groups (e.g. in the health sector, as in France) or to certain age groups (e.g. for the elderly, as in Italy for persons above fifty years).[89] When adopting the general duty of the adult population to be vaccinated against Covid-19, Austria's approach thus received much attention, also internationally, and, depending on the position, was applauded or reprimanded.[90]

To start with, it must be recalled that the legal dimension is only one of several dimensions of the problem. In particular, a measure such as compulsory vaccination raises important questions on the ethical level.[91] As far as the legal debate in Austria is concerned, it was particularly informed by a judgment of the European Court of Human Rights (ECtHR) of April 2021.[92] The case dealt with compulsory vaccination for minors in the Czech Republic, not in the Covid-19 context, but for infectious diseases particularly affecting minors and for which there existed a well-established scientific consensus. In its judgment, the ECtHR concluded that the decision of the Czech parliament to introduce mandatory vaccination for such diseases with respect to minors and to provide financial penalties for parents when not complying with this duty constituted—as in all cases of involuntary medical interventions—an interference with the right to private and family life (Article 8 ECHR) of both the children and their parents. However, the ECtHR acknowledged that the interference had a lawful basis in a parliamentary law and pursued the legitimate aim of protecting the health and the rights of others. With respect to proportionality, the ECtHR conceded the Czech legislator a wide margin of appreciation and took into account that the vaccination duty concerned diseases against which vaccination was considered effective and safe by the scientific community, that the duty allowed for exceptions on grounds of a permanent contraindication or on grounds of conscience, depending on the circumstances of the individual case, that the vaccines in use were continuously monitored, thus checking for possible contraindications in each individual case, as well as that compensation was available in case of injury to health caused by vaccination.[93] In sum, the ECtHR almost unanimously[94] decided that the Czech measures stood in a reasonable relationship of proportionality to the legitimate aims pursued and that the Czech vaccination duty did therefore not breach Article 8 ECHR.[95]

While not directly related to the Covid-19 pandemic and, in many ways, addressing a set of facts that significantly differs from it, the aforementioned ECtHR judgment was received in Austria as a welcome signal that a far-reaching vaccination duty against Covid-19 was also compatible with fundamental rights if it was only designed appropriately, notably by providing for the necessary exceptions and continuously monitoring its effects as well as the epidemiological situation.[96]

This was also the line of reasoning that the Constitutional Court followed when confronted with the need to assess the constitutionality of compulsory vaccination against Covid-19. While the first constitutional complaint against the *Covid-19 Compulsory Vaccination Act* failed for formal reasons,[97] the Constitutional Court decided the second complaint on the merits.[98] It first accepted that compulsory vaccination is to be qualified as a particularly severe interference with the personal integrity of the persons concerned.[99] In addition, it acknowledged that the pertinent rules provided for exceptions due to medical contraindications.[100] In particular, the Constitutional Court expressly and affirmatively referred to the ECtHR's afore-mentioned *Vavřička and Others* judgment.[101] Taking into account that the *Covid-19 Compulsory Vaccination Act* explicitly provided for the possibility of being suspended, the Constitutional Court confirmed that the Federal Minister of Health has a "continuous and strict (control and) reaction obligation with respect to current developments"[102] in this regard and has complied with this duty by making use of the authorization, as explained above. In sum, the Constitutional Court declared the Austrian compulsory vaccination regime against Covid-19 to be compatible with Article 8 ECHR.[103]

Conclusion

While the Covid-19 virus has not disappeared, and while it will continue to be part of our lives in the future, the Covid-19 pandemic has come (almost) to an end.[104] In Austria, hand in hand with the drop of infection numbers, the various restrictive measures have successively been terminated, and the last ones are to be expected to be abolished in the course of 2023.[105] Hence, most of the many special legal provisions introduced as a reaction to the Covid-19 pandemic[106] have meanwhile been abrogated. However, the legal basis for new legal measures against Covid-19, the *Covid-19 Measures Act*, is still in force. It could prove useful to assess the provisions of the *Covid-19 Measures Act* and to implement the provisions that have been proven useful in a further developed *Act on Epidemics*.[107] A new or further developed *Act on Epidemics* would also make it possible to take into account the advantages as well as the disadvantages of the federal structure of Austria, especially with regard to the administration, and would allow for adequate reaction to a new pandemic.

When looking at the reaction of the judicial branch with respect to the restrictive measures taken by the legislative and executive branches in the fight against the Covid-19 pandemic, one can observe a certain preference of a formal as opposed to a substantive approach. Whenever the judiciary could justify the declaration of unlawfulness of restrictive measures by lack of providing sufficient reasons or lack of legal basis, it tended to avoid entering into a more substantive analysis of the Covid-19 measures adopted by the government.

In a similar vein, when dealing with complaints based on alleged violations of fundamental rights, there was a strong tendency to confirm the measures adopted by the government by referring to the wide margin of appreciation of the government. Even when declaring that measures reached too wide and were therefore disproportionate, this was often justified by concluding that the measures in question, while otherwise justifiable, showed a lack of coherence. This might be due to the fact that a substantive approach would have made it necessary to assess scientific facts. The Constitutional Court's jurisprudence therefore also illustrates the position of the Court towards scientific facts, which can be described as cautious.

Endnotes

1. Epidemiegesetz 1950 (EpiG), Federal Law Gazette 186/1950.

2. Gesetz über die Verhütung und Bekämpfung übertragbarer Krankheiten 1913, Law Gazette of the Empire 67/1913.

3. This was broadly covered in the media, see e.g. Walter Mayr, "Corona-Ausbruch in Ischgl: Die Brutstätte," *Spiegel Ausland*, Mar. 17, 2020, accessed Feb. 20, 2023, https://www.spiegel.de/ausland/coronavirus-ausbruch-in-ischgl-die-brutstaette-a-8f56e5a2-635f-473a-96e9-300b6cbf4180; Ivo Mijnssen, "In einem österreichischen Skiort infizierten sich Hunderte von Gästen aus halb Europa mit dem Coronavirus – nun steht ganz Tirol unter Quarantäne," *Neue Zürcher Zeitung*, Mar. 19, 2020, accessed Feb. 20, 2023, https://www.nzz.ch/international/corona-virus-in-tirol-infektion-beim-apres-ski-in-ischgl-ld.1546680?reduced=true.

4. For all the administrative regulations covering the first days of the pandemic in the Paznaun valley, see Bruno Hersche et al., "The experts commissions report on the management of Covid-19 in Tyrol," Oct. 12, 2020, accessed Feb. 20, 2023, https://www.tirol.gv.at/fileadmin/presse/downloads/Presse/Bericht_der_Unabhaengigen_Expertenkommission.pdf (page 232 et seqq).

5. See § 32 Epidemiegesetz 1950 (EpiG), Federal Law Gazette 186/1950.

6. Bundesgesetz betreffend vorläufige Maßnahmen zur Verhinderung der Verbreitung von Covid-19 (Covid-19-Maßnahmengesetz – Covid-19-MG), Federal Law Gazette I 12/2020 (last amendment: Federal Law Gazette I 103/2022).

7. See Bundesgesetz über die Errichtung des Covid-19-Krisenbewältigungsfonds (Covid-19-FondsG), Federal Law Gazette I 12/2020; Bundesgesetz betreffend vorläufige Maßnahmen zur Verhinderung der Verbreitung von Covid-19 (Covid-19-Maßnahmengesetz), Federal Law Gazette I 12/2020; Gesetzliche Budgetprovisorium 2020; Bundesfinanzrahmengesetz 2019 bis 2022; Bundesgesetz über die Einrichtung einer Abbaubeteiligungsaktiengesellschaft des Bundes (ABBAG-Gesetz), Federal Law Gazette I 51/2014; das Arbeitsmarktpolitik-Finanzierungsgesetz, Federal Law Gazette I 101/2000; das Arbeitsmarktservicegesetz und das Arbeitsvertragsrechts-Anpassungsgesetz geändert werden (Covid-19 Gesetz), Federal Law Gazette I 12/2020.

8. For an overview on the numerous legal acts, amendments to laws as well as administrative regulations see Reinhard Klaushofer et al., "Ausgewählte unions- und verfassungsrechtliche Fragen der österreichischen Maßnahmen zur Eindämmung der Ausbreitung des Covid-19-Virus," *Zeitschrift für öffentliches Recht* 75, no. 4 (2020): 649–771; Reinhard Klaushofer et al., "Unions- und verfassungsrechtliche Fragen der österreichischen Maßnahmen zur Eindämmung der Ausbreitung des Covid-19-Virus (II)," *Zeitschrift für öffentliches Recht* 76, no. 3 (2021): 613–750; Reinhard Klaushofer et al., "Unions- und verfassungsrechtliche Fragen der österreichischen Maßnahmen zur Eindämmung der Ausbreitung des Covid-19-Virus (III)," *Zeitschrift für öffentliches Recht* 77, no. 4 (2022): 937–1096.

9. Konrad Lachmayer, "Muddling through Mutation Times or the Return of Federalism," Verfassungsblog 2021, accessed Feb. 20, 2023, https://verfassungsblog.de/muddling-through-mutation-times-or-the-return-of-federalism-in-austria/; "Studie: Föderalismus war in Krise hinderlich," Österreich ORF, May 31, 2021, accessed Ferbruary 20, 2023, https://oesterreich.orf.at/stories/3106207/; Daniel Bischof, "Die Pandemie als föderale Zerreißprobe," *Wiener Zeitung*, Feb. 14, 2021, accessed Feb. 20, 2023, https://www.wienerzeitung.at/nachrichten/politik/oesterreich/2092710-Die-Pandemie-als-foederale-Zerreissprobe.html; Petra Stuiber "Corona-Maßnahmen: Wie Föderalismus nicht funktioniert," *Der Standard*, Nov. 9, 2022, accessed Feb. 20, 2023, https://www.derstandard.at/story/2000131001556/wie-foederalismus-nicht-funktioniert and in comparative perspective Yvonne Hegele and Johanna Schnabel, "Federalism and the management of the Covid-19 crisis: centralisation, decentralisation and (non-)coordination," *West European Politics* (2021): 1052–76.

10. Anna Gamper, *Staat und Verfassung*, 4th edition (Vienna: Facultas, 2018), 38.

11. Constitutional Court of the Republic of Austria, Judgment, December 16, 1952, G17/52.

12. Bundes-Verfassungsgesetz, Federal Law Gazette 1/1930 (last amendment: Federal Law Gazette I 235/2021). All translations of acts, unless otherwise stated, are provided by the Austrian Legal Information System RIS, https://ris.bka.gv.at/Englische-Rv/. Please note that the translations regarding the Bundes-Verfassungsgesetz (B-VG) (Federal Constitutional Act), are sometimes referring to it as Federal Constitutional Law and sometimes as Federal Constitutional Act.

13. Matthias Lukan, Article 10 para 1 no. 12, in: "Kommentar zum Bundesverfassungsrecht B-VG und Grundrechte," ed. Arno Kahl et al. (Vienna: Jan Sramek Verlag: 2021), margin no 1.

14. Arno Kahl and Karl Weber, *Allgemeines Verwaltungsrecht*, 7th edition, (Vienna: Facultas, 2019), 92 et seq., 185 et seq.

15. Ibid., 191.

16. Ibid., 196.

17. For the indirect federal administration, see ibid., 92 et seq., 185 et seq.

18. Ibid., 92 et seq.

19. Ibid., 185.

20. See below.

21. See, e.g. Peter Bußjäger and Jakob A. Egger, "Verfassungs- und verwaltungsrechtliche Grundlagen staatlicher Krisenkommunikation," *Österreichische Jurist:innenzeitung* 8, no. 2 (2021): 63–71 (here 65).

22. Ibid., 65.

23. Felix Reimann, "Die Gesundheitskrise und die Interpretation der bundesverfassungsgesetzlichen Kompetenzbestimmungen," *Zeitschrift für Verwaltung 19*, no. 1 (2021): 113–6 (here 116).

24. Covid-19-Maßnahmengesetz; see supra note 16.

25. Philipp Abbrederis, "Pandemiebekämpfung aus Sicht der Landesverwaltung. Ein Erfahrungsbericht aus der Praxis," *Journal für Rechtspolitik* 29, no. 3 (2021): 145–51 (here 147).

26. Ibid., 146 et seq.

27. Mathias Egger and Daniel Wachter, "Die Bezirksverwaltungsbehörden als Schaltzentrale in der Pandemiebekämpfung – Vollzugsprobleme und deren mögliche Ursachen mit besonderem Blick auf den Covid-19-Vollzug der Bezirkshauptmannschaften in Tirol," in *Öffentliches Recht Jahrbuch 2021*, ed. Gerhard Baumgartner (Vienna: NWV, 2021), 47–68 (here 56).

28. Philipp Abbrederis, "Pandemiebekämpfung aus Sicht der Landesverwaltung. Ein Erfahrungsbericht aus der Praxis," *Journal für Rechtspolitik* 29, no. 3 (2021): 145–51 (here 147).

29. Eller and Wachter, "Die Bezirksverwaltungsbehörden als Schaltzentrale in der Pandemiebekämpfung," 56.

30. Ibid.

31. "Corona-Zentrum Innsbruck; Lokalaugenschein mit LH Platter und Verteidigungsministerin Tanner," Land Tirol, Sept. 18, 2020, accessed Feb. 20, 2023, https://www.tirol.gv.at/meldungen/meldung/corona-zentrum-innsbruck/

32. Eller and Wachter, "Die Bezirksverwaltungsbehörden als Schaltzentrale in der Pandemiebekämpfung," 57.

33. Abbrederis, "Pandemiebekämpfung aus Sicht der Landesverwaltung," 147, in footnote 18; Eller and Wachter, "Die Bezirksverwaltungsbehörden als Schaltzentrale in der Pandemiebekämpfung," 57.

34. Mathis Fister, "Kommunikation und Fehlkommunikation von Recht. Am Beispiel des Covid-19-Rechts," *Österreichisches Anwaltsblatt* 257, no. 10 (2020): 552–4 (here 552).

35. Eller and Wachter, "Die Bezirksverwaltungsbehörden als Schaltzentrale in der Pandemiebekämpfung," 60.

36. Ibid., 61.

37. Theo Öhlinger and Harald Eberhard, *Verfassungsrecht*, 13th edition (Vienna: Facultas, 2022), 270.

38. Ibid., 271.

39. Ibid., 270 et seq.

40. Ibid., 272 et seq.

41. Richard Novak, "Das "differenzierte Legalitätsprinzip" in der verfassungsgerichtlichen Rechtsprechung," in *Staatsrecht und Staatswissenschaften in Zeiten des Wandels: Festschrift für Ludwig Adamovich zum 60. Geburtstag*, ed B.-Ch. Fink et al., (Vienna: Springer-Verlag 1992), 491–501; Öhlinger and Eberhard, *Verfassungsrecht*, 272 and 274 et seq.

42. Harald Eberhard, "Alte und neue verfassungs- und verwaltungsrechtliche Strategien zur Ermöglichung und Bändigung von Verwaltungsspielräumen in der Krise," *Zeitschrift für öffentliches Recht* 77, no. 1 (2022): 137–52 (here 138) referring to Tristan Barczak, "'Die Stunde der Exekutive' – Rechtliche Kritik einer politischen Vokabel," *Recht und Politik*, no. 4 (2020): 458–68; Maryam Kamil Abdulsalam, "Die Stunde der Exekutive: Ein Wendepunkt im Umgang mit Tatsachen?," *Jahrbuch des öffentlichen Rechts der Gegenwart* 69, no. 1 (2021): 481–504.

43. See § 7 *Act on Epidemics* 1950.

44. IA 826/A XXVII. GP 12, available here https://www.parlament.gv.at/dokument/XXVII/A/826/fname_826305.pdf; Peter Bußjäger and Friederike Bundschuh-Rieseneder, "Der rechtliche Rahmen regional differenzierter Covid-19-Bekämpfung," Zeitschrift für Gesundheitsrecht 120, no. 4 (2020): 120–4 (here 120 et seq.).

45. IA 826/A XXVII. GP 12, available here https://www.parlament.gv.at/

dokument/XXVII/A/826/fname_826305.pdf.

46. "Übersicht der aktuellen Corona-Regeln," Stadt Wien, February 8, 2023, accessed Feb. 20, 2023, https://coronavirus.wien.gv.at/neue-corona-regeln/#:~:text=F%C3%BCr%20Besucher*innen%20gilt%20PCR,d%C3%BCrfen%20die%20Einrichtungen%20nicht%20betreten. See in this regard also Klaushofer et al., "Unions- und verfassungsrechtliche Fragen (III)," 1058 et seq.

47. Constitutional Court of the Republic of Austria, Judgment, July 14, 2020, V411/2020 (V411/2020-17); V396/2020 ua; V395/2020 ua.

48 Constitutional Court of the Republic of Austria, Judgment, July 14, 2020, V411/2020 (V411/2020-17); V396/2020 ua; V395/2020 ua.

49. Klaushofer et al., "Ausgewählte unions- und verfassungsrechtliche Fragen (I)," 761.

50. Eberhard, "Alte und neue verfassungs- und verwaltungsrechtliche Strategien," 145 et seq.; Christian Ranacher, "Politisches Krisenmanagement und Rechtsstaat – die Perspektive der Verwaltung," *Journal für Rechtspolitik* 29, no. 3 (2021): 263–8 (here 265).

51. See Klaushofer et al., "Ausgewählte unions- und verfassungsrechtliche Fragen (I)," 681 et seq.; Klaushofer et al., "Unions- und verfassungsrechtliche Fragen (II)," 693 et seq.

52. See, for instance, Jens Meyer-Ladewig and Roman Lehner, Article 15, in: *EMRK Europäische Menschenrechtskonvention – Handkommentar*, 4th edition, ed. Jens Meyer-Ladewig et al. (Baden-Baden: Namos, Helbing-Lichtenhahn, Manz, 2017).

53. See, for instance, William A. Schabas, Article 4, in: *Nowak's CCPR Commentary: U.N. International Covenant on Civil and Political Rights*, 3rd edition, (London: N.P. Engel, 2019).

54. A research for "emergency provisions" in a database of all national constitutions worldwide, finds pertinent references in 187 constitutions; https://constituteproject.org/constitutions?key=em&lang=en.

55. Article 18 paras 3–5 of the Federal Constitutional Act.

56. See Konrad Lachmayer, "Austria: Rule of Law Lacking in Times of Crisis," Verfassungsblog, Apr. 28, 2020, accessed Feb. 20, 2023, https://verfassungsblog.de/rule-of-law-lacking-in-times-of-crisis/.

57. See Article 8 para 2, Article 9 para 2, Article 10 para 2, and Article 11 para 2 ECHR.

58. Öhlinger and Eberhard, *Verfassungsrecht*, 311 et seq.

59. The legislative proposal for the Covid-19 Act was introduced on 14 March 2020 and already adopted by the National Council (*Nationalrat*), i.e. the first chamber of the Austrian Parliament, on 15 March 2020. The second camber, the Federal Council (*Bundesrat*), gave its green light on the same day, as did the Federal President. By signing it into law, the Covid-19 Act could still be promulgated on 15 March 2020; https://www.parlament.gv.at/gegenstand/XXVII/A/396?selectedStage=105.

60. See above.

61. Constitutional Court of the Republic of Austria, Judgment, June 24, 2021, V 2/2021-12, paras 73–75.

62. Ibid., paras 76, 88.

63. Constitutional Court of the Republic of Austria, Judgment, March 3, 2022, V 231/2021-15, para 74.

64. See Judgment, March 17, 2022, V 294/2021-19; Judgment, April 29, 2022, V 23/2022-25; Judgment, April 29, 2022, V 35/2022-22. See in this regard also Klaushofer et al., "Unions- und verfassungsrechtliche Fragen (III)," 1050 et seq.

65. At this moment in time, we have not any pertinent decision from the European Court of Human Rights in Strasbourg since it takes much longer to decide than the Constitutional Court; see e.g. *Thevenon v. France*, no. 46061/21, ECHR 2021-V.

66. See for a comprehensive overview notably Klaushofer et al., "Ausgewählte unions- und verfassungsrechtliche Fragen (I)," 681 et seq; Klaushofer et al., "Unions- und verfassungsrechtliche Fragen (II)," 693 et seq.; Klaushofer et al., "Unions- und verfassungsrechtliche Fragen (III)," 999 et seq.

67. See supra note 61.

68. Constitutional Court of the Republic of Austria, Judgment, June 24, 2021, V 2/2021-12.

69. The ECHR has the status of constitutional law in Austria, Federal Law Gazette 59/1964. Accordingly, individuals can complain to the Constitutional Court by arguing that a domestic statute or administrative ordinance is incompatible with guarantees of the ECHR.

70. See supra note 6.

71. Federal Law Gazette II 598/2020.

72. See on this also Klaushofer et al., "Unions- und verfassungsrechtliche Fragen (II)," 724 et seq., 728 et seq.

73. Constitutional Court of the Republic of Austria, Judgment, June 24, 2021, V 2/2021-12, paras 44–5.

74. Ibid., para 46.

75. See on this further Susanne Gstöttner and Konrad Lachmayer, "Versammlungsrecht in Zeiten der Pandemie. Eine verfassungsrechtliche Analyse der neuen epidemierechtlichen Bestimmungen," NetV, (2020), 124.

76. Staatsgrundgesetz vom 21. Dezember 1867 über die allgemeinen Rechte der Staatsbürger für die im Reichsrate vertretenen Königreiche und Länder, Law Gazette of the Empire 142/1867.

77. Constitutional Court of the Republic of Austria, Judgment, June 30, 2022, V 312/2021-15.

78. Federal Law Gazette II 475/2021.

79. Constitutional Court of the Republic of Austria, Judgment, June 30, 2022, V 312/2021-15, para 47.

80. Ibid., para. 54.

81. Ibid., para. 55.

82. Ibid., para 58.

83. See in this regard also Klaushofer et al., "Unions- und verfassungsrechtliche Fragen (II)," 710 et seq., 725 et seq., 729 et seq.

84. Bundesgesetz über die Impfpflicht gegen Covid-19 (Covid-19-IG), Federal Law Gazette I 4/2022.

85. See § 1 Bundesgesetz über die Impfpflicht gegen Covid-19 (Covid-19-IG), Federal Law Gazette I 4/2022; for exceptions see § 3 leg cit. See in this regard also Klaushofer et al., "Unions- und verfassungsrechtliche Fragen (III)," 1073 et seq.

86. Federal Law Gazette II 103/2022.

87. Federal Law Gazette II 198/2022.

88. Federal Law Gazette I 131/2022.

89. For an overview on vaccine mandates in Europe, see Rosa Hodkin, "Vaccine mandates," Institute for Government, Dec. 23, 2021, accessed Feb. 20, 2023, https://www.instituteforgovernment.org.uk/article/explainer/vaccine-mandates.

90. See, for instance, Katrin Bennhold, "Austria's sweeping Covid vaccine mandate is becoming law," New York Times, Feb. 3, 2022, accessed Feb. 20, 2023, https://www.nytimes.com/2022/02/03/world/europe/austria-covid-vaccine-mandate.html; Philip Oltermann, "Austria passes Covid vaccine mandate, but question marks linger over enforcement," The Guardian, Feb. 4, 2022, accessed Feb. 20, 2023, https://www.theguardian.com/world/2022/feb/04/austria-passes-covid-vaccine-mandate-but-question-marks-linger-over-enforcement.

91. See e.g. Deutscher Ethikrat zur Covid-19 Impflicht, Nov. 22, 2021, accessed Feb. 20, 2023, https://www.ethikrat.org/mitteilungen/mitteilungen/2021/deutscher-ethikrat-empfiehlt-ausweitung-der-gesetzlichen-impfpflicht/?cookieLevel=not-set

92. See *Vavřička and Others v. the Czech Republic*, nos 47621/13 and 5 others, ECHR 2021.

93. See ibid., paras. 291 and 302.

94. The Grand Chamber decided the merits of the case by 16 votes to 1; see ibid., para 347.

95. See ibid., para 309.

96. See along these lines, for instance, the First Report of the Commission set up by § 19 Bundesgesetz über die Impfpflicht gegen Covid-19 (Covid-19-IG), Mar. 8, 2022, available at https://www.bundeskanzleramt.gv.at/dam/jcr:fe92b07a-19a3-402d-91f6-fbfe37e4ac5a/bericht_monitoring-kommission_080322.pdf. See also Second Report of the Commission set up by § 19 Bundesgesetz über die Impfpflicht gegen Covid-19 (Covid-19-IG), May 23, 2022, available at https://www.bundeskanzleramt.gv.at/dam/jcr:075a29b6-0b01-4b1d-ba2d-ee20fbfb35e6/monitoringkommission_23052022.pdf.

97. Constitutional Court of the Republic of Austria, Ordinance, Apr. 29, 2022, G 29/2022.

98. Constitutional Court of the Republic of Austria, Judgment, June 23, 2022, G 37/2022-22, V 173/2022-11.

99. Ibid., paras 208, 224–5, 232.

100. Ibid., para 209.

101. Ibid., paras 211, 222 et seq.

102. Ibid., para 214.

103. Ibid., para. 235.

104. "WHO: Das Ende der Covid-19-Pandemie ist in Sicht," accessed Feb. 20, 2023, https://unric.org/de/150922-covid/.

105. Simon Rosner, "Regierung legt den Fahrplan für Ende der Corona-Regeln fest," Wiener Zeitung, Feb. 1, 2023, accessed Feb. 20, 2023, https://www.wienerzeitung.at/nachrichten/politik/oesterreich/2176597-Ende-der-Corona-Massnahmen.html. "Austria's sweeping Covid vaccine mandate is becoming law," New York Times, Feb. 3, 2022, accessed Feb. 20, 2023, https://www.nytimes.com/2022/02/03/world/europe/austria-covid-vaccine-mandate.html.

106. See the overview in https://www.oesterreich.gv.at/themen/coronavirus_in_oesterreich/Rechtliche-Grundlagen.html.

107. Ranacher, "Politisches Krisenmanagement und Rechtsstaat," 267. This proposal goes back to a request of the Land governors, Leitantrag "Covid-19-Pandemie," Beschluss der Landeshauptleutekonferenz vom 19. November 2021 (VSt-265/127).

Everyday Life during Corona Lockdown: Community, Retrotopia, and Distance Learning

Silke Meyer

This chapter will give insights into everyday life in Austria during the Covid-19 pandemic with a special focus on the first lockdown in 2020. After a short timeline of events in Austria, I will explore the narratives of community and retrotopia and their role of making sense of the lockdown experience. A defining caesura during lockdown was the closure of schools: I will therefore examine the impact of distance learning with a focus on social class and educational inequality in the first lockdown and its aftermath. To conclude, I will discuss an unexpected turn of events after the lockdowns, which is a boom in homeschooling, in the context of alienation from politics and the state.

Methodologically, I will draw on ethnographic material collected through the first lockdown and contextualize these individual perspectives with Austrian surveys on distance learning and its impact on pupils.

"When I knew that everything was going to be different": A Timeline of Covid-19 Provisions and Regulations in Austria

> My older son had his skiing week which was a big deal at his school. I mean, everywhere else was starting to close down, it was on the news that they were all going to be closed down, restaurants and cafés and everything, but the school kept going to the slopes and carried on with their skiing week. We had been laughing about this at home, like skiing is everything in Tyrol. But then, on the Thursday, I heard him coming come up the stairs in his boots with heavy steps and then I knew that everything was going to be different.
>
> Female author, living in Innsbruck with two children age four and ten.

The Coronavirus took hold of Austria slowly at first but, as in most other countries, to a great effect. The first news reports from China about a strange virus affecting the lungs were noticed at most, but the topic hardly made it into everyday conversations in 2019. The term "Coronavirus" was not used until January 2020, when virologists identified the virus as part of the corona family. When the events in China were observed, the Foreign Ministry advised against traveling to the Province of Hubei in China, and the air carrier AUA stopped flights to China.

On January 25, 2020, the first two cases of the illness were reported in Innsbruck. The couple affected had previously spent time in Bergamo, where a devastating outbreak was to be reported later on. Only three days later, the Department of Health established a uniform approach to the enforcement of the epidemic law. Tyrol continued to play a role in the events: in March 2020, Icelandic authorities declared Tyrol as a risk area, after it was discovered that hundreds of tourists had left the skiing resort Ischgl with symptoms of Covid-19 and thus contributed to the spread of the disease throughout Europe. The local authorities had not regarded it as necessary to caution people about the high risks of contagion and had not issued any warnings. As a result, 48 percent of the infections in Germany and more than 11,000 cases worldwide could be traced back to Ischgl.[1]

People in Austria and worldwide witnessed a number of unprecedented events with an enormous impact on everyday life. On March 10, 2020, restrictions on travels took effect: passenger planes from Northern Italy, South Korea, and Iran were banned from landing in Austria; arrivals from risk areas outside the EU were required to provide a medical certificate documenting that they did not carry the virus. This requirement was extended to incoming travelers from the neighboring country of Italy, where health checks were introduced at the borders. Checks at border crossings were reinforced with soldiers from the Austrian Armed Forces, road service staff, and firefighters. In Tyrol, as an area of transit with close transnational relations to Germany and Italy, these restrictions were experienced as huge repercussions. People were prevented from commuting to work and from seeing and caring for family members and friends across the borders.

On March 10, 2020, it was further announced in a press conference that events in enclosed spaces of 100 people and outdoors of 500 people would be banned. Cinemas and theaters were closed, concerts were cancelled, and football matches were carried out as ghost events without an audience. Private festivities like weddings and birthday parties had to be postponed. People were generally asked to reduce their social life in order to prevent the disease from spreading and to protect the elderly and sick from the risk of contagion.

A day later, on March 11, the closing of schools and universities was announced for March 16, 2020. Onsite teaching was to be replaced by distance learning until Easter. Schools offered care options care for younger children whose parents had to go to work but without teaching. Kindergartens and elementary schools also remained open, but parents were urged to leave their children at home whenever possible. Educational institutions hurried to make use of learning platforms or send out learning materials and assignments via email but to a limited effect.

The most drastic restrictions in everyday life came with nationwide lookdown, which started on March 16, 2020. This meant a general exit restriction and a ban on entering public places. Shops, restaurants, and cafés were closed, and playgrounds and sporting fields were cordoned off. The only exceptions from the prohibition were imminent danger, taking care of persons in need of assistance, caring for animals, meeting basic needs like going shopping for groceries or medication, or professional purposes. Going for short walks was allowed as long as one did not meet people from other households. This regulation included an obligation to work from home, if possible, which was later on interpreted as a recommendation. With the exception of those working in systemically relevant jobs, people were homebound.

The first nationwide lockdown lasted until May 2, 2020. When shops, hotels, and restaurants gradually re-opened in May 2020, masks became compulsory in public transportation and commercial establishments. Curfews until 10 p.m. were supposed to contain and control private meetings. Border controls were kept in place until June 15, 2020. Universities remained closed and continued to mostly teach online. In the schools, the graduating classes returned on May 4, 2020, while younger pupils (around age fourteen and below) followed two weeks later and older pupils four weeks after that. On June 3, 2020, schools in Austria had resumed teaching on site only to close again from November 3 until December 6, 2020, in a so-called "light lockdown," which had shops and service institutions remain open but schools, restaurants, tourist hotels, cinemas, and theaters closed. By the end of 2020, younger Austrian pupils had spent fifty-three school days, and older pupils eighty-three school days, in distance learning.[2] A third lockdown shut down Austria again from December 26, 2020, until February 7, 2021, to be followed by a fourth nationwide lockdown on November 22, 2021, which was lifted on December 12, 2021, for those people who were vaccinated or recovered from the virus.

Furthermore, from January 2021 to April/June 2022, masks covering nose and mouth in buildings had to be worn. From June 2021 onwards, a green pass as verification for the status of vaccinated, tested, or recovered (the three Gs of "*geimpft, getestet oder genesen*"). Schools tested their pupils three times a week, which naturally led to a high number of cases and quarantines. When infected with Covid-19, parents had to collect their children who then had to stay home for ten days. Other provisions, like social distancing, masks, and curfews, were taken. Generally, it was the lockdown that had the most impact on everyday life and shall thus be the focus in this contribution.

Making Sense of the Crisis: Narratives of Community and Good Old Times during the First Lockdown in 2020

That the first lockdown was an extraordinary caesura is evident from the timeline of restrictions.[3] The Austrian government even felt compelled to issue a pamphlet with guidelines on how to cope with everyday life during the first lockdown in April 2020 (Fig. 1).

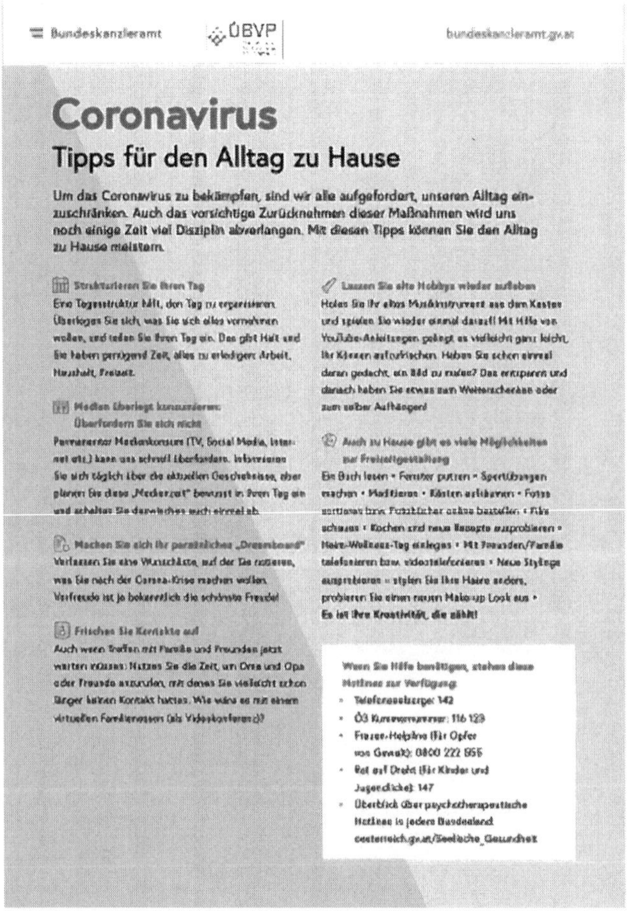

Bundeskanzleramt ÖBVP bundeskanzleramt.gv.at

Coronavirus

Tipps für den Alltag zu Hause

Um das Coronavirus zu bekämpfen, sind wir alle aufgefordert, unseren Alltag einzuschränken. Auch das vorsichtige Zurücknehmen dieser Maßnahmen wird uns noch einige Zeit viel Disziplin abverlangen. Mit diesen Tipps können Sie den Alltag zu Hause meistern.

FIGURE 1: Source: https://www.oesterreich.gv.at/dam/jcr:e0db-2cc6-3a32-48bc-b0ac-8f6eadcd00a6/200420_Covid_Merkblatt_Alltag_A4_BF.pdf

Here, they acknowledge the unusual restrictions and ask for discipline in order to manage daily conflicts, feelings of cabin fever, and isolation. Tips include structuring the day with time slots for work, housework, and leisure activities; acknowledging what has been achieved in the day; consuming media consciously (and not constantly); putting together a "dreamboard," a list of things to do after Corona; making time for family (e.g., a virtual family dinner with grandparents) and hobbies (painting, playing or learning an instrument); and doing all the things for which one does not find time under normal circumstances (sorting photos, trying new recipes, cleaning the windows and trying out new fashion stylings). The pamphlet closes with the appeal, printed in bold: "It is your creativity that counts!" and a list of helplines for counseling in crisis. The pamphlet is accompanied by one for couples in lockdown (find time for each other but also time for yourself, be forgiving, have a sense of humor). Special advice for dealing with children and teenagers is not given. What we can derive from the publication is that many people were in dire need of support in coping with everyday life during lockdown.

Corona, Community and Communitas: "*Tirol haltet Zsamm*"

In such a situation of insecurity and fear, people tried to make sense of the crisis through narrative. In narrative analysis, this purpose of stories is well established: stories transform events into meaningful experiences that create order and constitute social identities for the individual subject. This sense-making functions at the level of the individual and the collective: individually, because stories are told, performed, and appropriated by individuals; collectively, because sense-making works best when meaning can be shared intersubjectively.[4]

During the first lockdown in 2020, the official narrative was one of solidarity: people were asked and forced to change their daily ways of living in order to protect the elderly and the vulnerable. The corresponding narrative was one of standing together and looking out for each other. The Austrian government issued an information campaign with the slogan: "*Schau auf dich, schau auf mich. So schützen wir uns.*" ("Look after yourself, look after me. This is how we protect ourselves.") In this way, coping with everyday life was tackled through a heightened sense of community. Digital care activism, like Facebook groups and other virtual forms of neighbor communities, sprang up like mushrooms, with offers to go shopping for others, take over repair work (contact-free), to take care of pets, and to help with Covid-related paperwork.[5] Their aim was to bring together those who were stuck at home with nothing to do with those who could not leave home due to infections or risk of them. Generally, the groups were also used to pass on opinions and information from legal advice to psychological support lines.[6]

The story accompanying these initiatives was one of crisis and a corresponding momentum for community building, which echoed Corona narratives on broader scale. Crisis literally means turning point, and this turning point is often interpreted as a solution to problems related to this specific crisis. The optimistic spin on the pandemic, health risks, isolation, and economic decline was the narrative through which people were reminded that, through the crisis, the only help and hope lies in solidarity and in togetherness. The county of Tyrol also picked up on the narrative and, in August 2020, published a song to thank the citizens of Tyrol for their cooperation and sense of community. The launch was announced in a leaflet sent to every household in Tyrol by the Governeur Günther Platter and his party, the Austrian People's Party. Platter thanked the citizens for their discipline and for standing together in difficult times. The song, commission by the County of Tyrol, was titled "*Tirol haltet Zsamm*," translated as "Tyrol stands together" or "Tyrol united," with a dialectal spelling "*Zsamm*" adding local color.[7]

Platter earned some praise but more criticism for the initiative. Oppositional parties referred to the economic crisis in many Tyrolean businesses, most of all in tourism, which caused many people to lose their jobs and even their existence. Taxpayer's money, so they claimed in the *Tiroler Tageszeitung* from August 10, 2020, should be used to help them rather than to self-promote the leading party ÖVP.[8] According to the ORF, the campaign cost more than 200,000 Euro.[9]

The song was in the tradition of Alpine folk songs with harmonica, percussion, harp, guitar, and tympanon or Hackbrett and singing. The video follows the conventional iconography of snowy mountains from bird's eye perspective and a rising sun in a blue sky. The musicians with a noticeable diversity in age, ethnicity and gender are shown recording the song in different studios—singing together but keeping their distance, as everybody was supposed to do. The text tells a story of a sudden and eerie silence, empty streets, closed borders, and restricted mobility and freedom. There is no normality, and days stretch for too long. After the description of bleakness and isolation, the melodious and spirited refrain suddenly turns the narrative around with a change of tune and the tradition of community. The text states: "*Denn do war a Kraft, ma hat gspürt, dass man's kann, dass man des schafft, Tirol haltet zsamm.*" ("For there was a power, you could sense that we can manage, as long as Tyrol stands together," my translation). The message is clear: with the power of community in crisis, Tyrol will follow tradition and stand together. The song was the official voice of the county government acknowledging fear and isolation but also trying to spread hope and a spirit of community.

This group feeling works on a personal level but also as an imagined community. People shared the experiences of a sudden change of everyday structure but also the feeling of fear and insecurity. The anthropologist Victor Turner has described this liminal state as resulting in the formation of communitas: In ritual theory, communitas describes the state between two social statuses before and after the ritual practices. Communitas as a liminal phase is characterized by its transitionary quality and by anti-structure, i.e., the fact that social structures and hierarchies are temporarily suspended: "[S]ince this condition and these persons elude or slip through the network of classifications that normally locate states and positions in cultural space. Liminal entities are neither here nor there; they are betwixt and between the positions assigned and arrayed by law, custom, convention, and ceremonial."[10] Communitas is "a 'moment in and out of time' and in and out of secular social structure, which reveals, however fleetingly, some recognition (in symbol if not always in language) of a generalized social bond that has ceased to be and has simultaneously yet to be fragmented into a multiplicity of structural ties." Liminal society is therefore "unstructured or rudimentarily structured and relatively undifferentiated comitatus, community, or even communion of equal individuals who submit together to the general authority of the ritual elders."[11] Katharina Eisch-Angus has described the Austrian society as "locked in liminality": everyday life was unhinged, and the prevalent mood was one of insecurity and disorientation. But the formation of communitas beyond social structures resulted in many personal and imagined communities through symbolic acts like the Tyrolean song, Facebook support groups, or in newly established neighborhood talks across the fence. Talking about the news, the daily numbers of infections and new regulations for quarantine or school closures, served a re-structuring purpose. Fear was tamed by getting together, phoning friends and family, and by physical everyday tasks like cooking and cleaning. It was not by accident that baking bread and washing hands had become a new routine during lockdown. Beyond the practical and medical necessity, they can be read as liminal practices of embodiment, a physical self-assurance in this state of "betwixt and between."[12]

Turner also refers to the creative moment in liminality and to individual agency. Corona communitas has had many of those effects: from secret open-air parties instead of clubs to digital meetings not only in the work place but also at home in order to see grandparents or friends, sharing a glass of wine through the screen.

Eisch-Angus also points out the close relationship between liminality, communitas and humor: during the first lockdown, endless memes, jokes and anecdotes shortage of toilet paper and more were shared in conversations and on social media.[13] Liminality brings about a carnivalesque mood: between fear and humor, linguistic creativity in new word coining like distance stressing for distance learning or word crossings like "coronoia" (Corona and paranoia), coronials and pandemials (Corona/pandemic and millennials), "*Alleinachten*" (*allein* and *Weihnachten*, alone and Christmas) and "Virol" instead of Tirol, referring to the events in February and March 2020 in Ischgl and Innsbruck.[14]

"Corona Biedermeier": Lockdown and Retrotopia

Another narrative trying to boost morale during lockdown was, at first sight, a rather unexpected one: retrotopia, or the story of good old times. When the discipline of European Ethnology at the University of Innsbruck launched a call for stories about lockdown experiences, we received many accounts of stress and chaos, but also of nostalgia and childhood memories in the entries.[15]

One example is from a female writer, thirty-eight years old, who lives in Innsbruck with her husband and her two children. She writes about her lockdown experiences in retrospect:

> At first I had a lot of respect for the lockdown. I didn't know what to expect, I mean, nobody knew. Schools and shops closed, no more going to work, even the borders are closed! And then the children at home all day? I panicked just thinking about it. And then it started and it was completely different from what I thought: it was spring and we were all at home, we baked and cooked, everyone was home for lunch. I only remember that from my childhood, a family having a cooked lunch together. Then we could send the children cycling alone, the streets were empty, it was so wonderfully quiet outside. We sneakily went for short walks, quite aimlessly, just strolling around the neighborhood. We also talked a lot with the neighbors, which we never do otherwise, and it was really nice to get to know them better. It turned out that we studied the same course at university: "It took a lockdown for us to figure that out," we said. So, it wasn't all that bad, actually the break was good for us. (My translation).

The structure of the story is clear: the narrator begins with an unknown and potentially fearful situation of lockdown, which, in retrospect, surprisingly turns out to be positive. The narrative pattern of the story about the good old days serves her as a structure. This pattern is based on the nostalgic vision of an idealized past, against which a negatively experienced present is delineated. The cultural scientist and psychologist Bernd Rieken explains the tendency to put the past in a positive light in biographical terms because childhood memories are free of responsibilities, pressure and stress. The good old days are one's own childhood, directly addressed in the excerpt: "I only remember that from my childhood." The motifs of riding a bicycle without parental supervision and strolling around "aimlessly" also fit in here. One's own life story is transferred to general life circumstances and the time of childhood is positively reinterpreted in memory.[16]

Obviously, this positive spin in times of a global health crisis requires some narrative effort but is no exception: Memory frequently manages to mark periods that were characterized by existential hardship as good old times. Examples can be found in biographical research for the post-war period, which at first glance hardly lends itself to idealization. Nevertheless, in retrospect, this historical epoch is narrated as a good time of great communality, neighborly help, and social cohesion. Corona retrotopia follows the trodden paths of twentieth century war-stories about the breakdown of the health system and the economy, about ambivalent and confusing information, food rationing, hoarding, and female needlework like sewing masks. Although politics and media were careful not to use the terminology of emergency rule "*Ausnahmezustand*," the discussion about parliamentary legislative and governing through special enactments was reminiscent of enabling acts and emergency regulations of Europe during World War I and its aftermath.[17] War and the pandemic were short-circuited in the collective memory in Austria, and the war-like images and metaphors promoted this imaginary.[18]

Sociologist Zygmunt Bauman names the longing for continuity and solidarity as characteristics of retrotopia and interprets the revaluation of the national as a quest for tradition and a return to a tribal mentality.[19] While closed borders were a concrete economic problem in the tourist region of Tyrol, photos of empty motorways and clear skies without contrails during the Easter holiday in 2020 were celebrated on social media (Fig. 2).

FIGURE 2: Kronenzeitung, April 15 2020: An empty Europa-Bridge, photographed in March during Lockdown (credit: Christof Birbaumer / Kronenzeitung)

These images represent the memorability of the lockdown moment but they also show an appreciation of tranquility and a time-out from the constant and stressful transit traffic in the Inn valley. According to Bauman, people are no longer willing to pay for their freedom with the price of security and well-being; a new tribalism and aggression towards foreigners and sharing of resources are the consequences. In the retrotopia of the lockdown, deceleration and time travel into the past are important motifs and were termed a new Biedermeier, "we baked and cooked," central to the narrative: "like in the old days." The world seems to have shrunk into a manageable and comfortable size. The narrative of community also fits in with this: Society moved tangibly closer together, making solidarity a national duty in the campaigns. Our Corona author also only "really gets to know" her neighbors in the lockdown, and she marks the significance of this event in direct speech: "It takes a lockdown for us to find that out." Immediately afterwards, she draws a conclusion: "It wasn't all that bad." In the coda, the crisis becomes a "break" that is "good for everyone." In this reinterpretation, we can see how she derives meaning from the lockdown experience: the crisis reminds us of positive pasts and thus causes us to question the present. In this narrative, the Covid-19 pandemic serves as a warning against a hectic lifestyle, against anonymity, against a confusing globalized world. Of course, the narrative message heavily collides with the reality of global delivery services like Amazon, which thrived during lockdown. Still, the author succeeds in positioning herself as middle-class, family-oriented, educated, and endowed with critical and ecological consciousness, a person who recognized the signs that it has all become too much and that she—we—could do with a break. Turning events into narrative thus serves to overcome contingency: the narrative structure brings order into chaos and purpose into confusion.

Challenges in Everyday Life during the Pandemic: The Multiple Effects of School Closures

While narratives of community and change are part of coping techniques in crisis, people still faced challenges in everyday life up to an existential degree. Out of many areas of crisis, e.g. isolation, violence at home, lack of money due to short-time work, I will focus on the closures of schools and the impact this had on children, teenagers, and their parents.[20]

First of all, it is noticeable how the closure of schools and universities brought the everyday life of families in accordance with the crisis management by the Austrian government. It was a moment when a nationwide crisis governance protruded into family space, when individual perceptions of health risks and regulations intersected with state and expert views.[21] Our female author heard her son coming up the stairs in his boots, which he would have left at school if the skiing week was to be continued, and knew: "Everything was going to be different." With lockdown rules and quarantine regulations, national governance seeped into everyday life: checking the news in order to plan ahead became part of a daily parental routine, and infection numbers, seven-day-incidences (giving the number of infected people in relation to the population of an area) and quarantine regimes were key topics of parental WhatsApp groups and telephone conversations in lockdown.

Family life during the first lockdown was a challenge. Parents describe their daily routines as chaotic, like this single mother of three who sent in a description of her day:

> It is chaos from the moment I get up till I go to bed again. With one kid at *Gymnasium*, one at elementary school and one kindergartener, I am dealing with three different systems, three different routines or lack of routines. When I sit down, like I do now to order my thoughts, I can still hear them shouting out in my head "I need you, Mom," "Where is my something, Mom?" and "I am so bored, Mom!" I don't understand the math problem of my eldest and I don't have the patience to do craftwork with my youngest. There is always shouting, and I am in the middle like a hamster in his wheel: cooking, and helping with school, and cleaning and cooking again. Honestly, the trip to the supermarket feels like a holiday. [...] And no one to talk to, I have never been so in demand and so lonely at the same time.

This short sequence shows the mental and physical overload that parents, and mostly mothers, suffered during lockdown. She is concerned that she fails her children not being able to provide the education, patience, and psychological support. With the additional worries about income, rent and spending costs, crowded housing space, and cabin fever, the situation can easily lead to burnout and psychological damages. It is important to note that lockdown experiences are not all about baking bread and chatting with the neighbors across the fence, as we saw in the first account. Families with young children dealt with time, space, and money problems due to short-time work, housing situations, and lack of support networks. Children missed their friends and school. Lockdown and distance learning showed that schools are not only places of education but also—and even more so—of social learning. While physics and geometry can be studied at home, social learning like exercising empathy and tolerance is much more effective outside of a family context. During distance learning, pupils missed out on the opportunity to enjoy or endure their peers' company and the diversity they bring to the table. However, social learning was only one field of learning losses during the first lockdown in 2020.

Learning Losses and Educational Inequality during the First Lockdown in 2020

School closures and pandemic-related distance learning resulted in learning losses in variable degrees. A study for Austria, Germany, and Switzerland showed that learning routines and outcomes changed considerably. From a sample of 8,344 pupils, about a third declared that they kept up their daily routines and spent twenty-five hours a week on studying and school matters. They further stated that they felt that they learned more than they did in during classroom teaching; were at ease with planning their day independently; and spent time with sports, reading, and activities other than computer games. Generally, they did not feel like they were on a school break. At the other end of the spectrum, eighteen percent stated that they spent nine hours or less a week on learning, that they had difficulties getting up in the morning, found it hard to structure their day, and played computer games for twenty-five hours or more per week. Psychological problems of feeling lonely, violent behavior in families, and economic difficulties were added to academic ones: the number of pupils with depression rose significantly, by 15 percent. In spring 2020, one out of four youths in Germany between sixteen and nineteen showed signs of depression.[22]

While initial studies emphasized that the availability of digital devices and the knowledge how to use them for successful distance learning was one of the main problems during the first lockdown,[23] later studies showed that the difficulties were not primarily related to technological resources. More important factors were the age of the pupil, living situations, space and the number of (younger) siblings to share it with, and language competences from pupils and parents. The most significant factor, however, was the academic support, supervision, and motivation from parents and other family members, which was lacking in the group of pupils who did not cope well with learning at home.[24] Parents with academic qualifications were more successful in guiding their children during school closures, whereas socially disadvantaged pupils experienced more academic problems during school closures.

In educational sciences, the relationship between socio-economic background and academic achievements is argued with Bourdieu's theory of capital forms:[25] economic capital describes the financial resources of a family, for example living space and having a room to oneself, owning a digital device, but also being able to afford private tutoring. Cultural capital captures the academic resources of middle- and upper-class parents, which coincide with teacher's and school's expectations, cultural competences like reading books and newspapers, watching the news, and cultural goods like owning books. Social capital refers to membership to a group that can provide academic and other forms of support. All forms of capital contribute to learning success at school as well as in distance learning, but during lockdown and outside of school, family capital had become the only resource for pupils. This resulted in lower learning successes, a lower motivation to learn, less time invested in school issues, lower levels of self-organization, less digital instruction and support with digital learning material at home, fewer interactions with teachers, less or poorer equipment, and less parental support and motivation due to lack of time and academic skills.[26] Teachers reported that, during lockdowns, they lost touch with pupils from disadvantaged families much more often than with those from a privileged background.[27] Similarly, those pupils rarely see teachers as confidential contact persons and generally feel alienated from the school. This sentiment increased significantly during lockdown, especially when pupils from poor socio-economic backgrounds experience learning problems. Taken together, lockdowns operated like a focal glass onto the dynamics between socio-economic background and academic success. Thus, school closures during lockdown reinforced educational inequality and strengthens the hypothesis that educational success is inherited rather than earned individually.[28]

Further Lockdowns in 2020 and 2021

The relationship between learning success and social background became even more apparent in the following lockdowns. During the first lockdown in spring 2020, the school closures caused a feeling of helplessness and chaos. Schools and families were unprepared, teachers went into survival mode, mainly aiming to keep up the communication with their pupils.[29] Many different ways of communication were used: Some sent tasks via the school learning platforms, some sent emails, some did very little, but the overall message was to somehow keep in touch with the pupils. Attendance was dealt with generously, and exams were stopped and grades did not matter.

However, teachers, pupils, and parents felt much more under pressure in following lockdowns. From fall 2020 onwards, most schools had managed to set up online learning tools, and teachers resumed their curricula, exams, and grading. This put pupils under great pressure, especially those who had fallen behind during the first lockdown, as a longitudinal survey with thirty-two parents between March and October 2020 showed.[30] Furthermore, because the first lockdown affected most jobs and professions, most parents were at home and could help their children with learning tasks. However, the divide in parental support enlarged in the following lockdowns, because more and more blue collar workers were called into work, which meant that their children dealt with school work on their own, whereas white collar workers and highly qualified professionals worked from home and could offer academic help, time, and support. It is no surprise that educational inequality widened suddenly and abruptly during the lockdowns in autumn 2020 and in 2021 when the two factors coincided: parents with higher educational qualifications, who were more able to help their children with school matters anyway, now worked from home and devoted time to support their children in distance learning. Thus, it became clear that parental help and support was the most important resource during distance learning. Of course, access to laptops and tablets and the knowledge of how to use them efficiently were essential tools during homeschooling too.[31] But digital equipment existed in most households or was organized by schools rather swiftly. What could not be organized during the lockdowns was academic support. Schools offered a daycare system but did not do any teaching there.

With regard to distance learning and beyond, the virus was not "the big leveler." In Austria, it showed social inequality under a magnifying glass: children from less privileged backgrounds fell behind in school and suffered from psychological stress and depression more than their peers from better socio-economic backgrounds. They also suffered from physical handicaps like falling ill more often and living unhealthy lifestyles with sleep deprivation and weight gain.[32] Crowded living space meant a higher risk of infection when one family member was ill, especially during lockdown. Commuting on public transport posed a higher risk than home office.[33] Corona society was not equally vulnerable, but the virus favored the rich and discriminated against the poor.[34]

On a macro-scale, Julia Bock-Schappelwein and Ulrike Famira-Mühlberger point to the economic consequences of school closures for the labor market. Long-time school closures over weeks have been shown to have negative effects on the subsequent success of the labor market. In Austria, education is the most important determinant of the development of economic growth. The disruption in education caused by the education policy during the Covid-19 crisis, with school closures and subsequent losses in the quality of learning, will reduce economic growth in the long term.[35]

Homeschooling after the Pandemic

When schools went back to teaching onsite in 2021, Austria witnessed a peculiar development: the number of voluntary homeschoolers rose steeply in 2021 and 2022. From an average of 2,100 in the years 2010 to 2019, it rose to 7,500 in the school year 2020/2021, which is the year when distance learning was stopped and most pupils returned to school after four lockdowns.[36] So, after being exposed to distance learning, a surprisingly high number of families decided that this was a better way of educating their children.

Homeschooling is possible in Austria for children between six and fifteen years since 1867, when it was laid out in the Constitution. Originally, the possibility to homeschool can be traced back to Empress Maria Theresia, who introduce compulsory schooling in 1774. To avoid forcing the children of the aristocracy and upper classes to go to the same school as everybody else, they were allowed to be educated at home by teachers. The bourgeois movement enshrined the right to homeschool in the Constitution in 1867, which is still valid today.[37] As long as children pass an annual external test (*Externistenprüfung*), they can be taught at home.

Parental motives for homeschooling are mainly educational and social: they are discontent with school curricula and the ways topics are taught, and they are afraid of mobbing in the classroom. However, these were all reasons for being taught at home before the pandemic, and they do not explain the sudden rise in numbers. Current research assumes that the new homeschoolers in the aftermath of the pandemic find additional reasons in an increasing alienation from the state and dismissal of its educational politics and practices. This skepticism is rooted in an anti-state attitude and had been expressed most vigorously in protests against Covid-19 regulations.

Homeschooling as an expression of protesting against the state is not new.[38] It includes an unusual specter from progressive left-wing and conservative right-wing positions who become "strange bedfellows"[39] in their criticism of state education politics. Political sociologists have found a similar unlikely combination of political attitudes in the group of Corona protestors and their public demonstrations against Covid-19 regulations. They can be described as a highly diverse crowd brought together by a deep alienation from the state's political system. Amlinger and Nachtwey term this new phenomenon "libertarian authoritarianism," delineating a new position of rebellion favoring individual freedom above solidarity and community.[40] This position of challenging authority combines rightwing, esoteric, and fundamentalist ideas, and it is widespread in reform-educational milieu.[41]

In the school year 2021/22, the number of homeschooled students fell to 6,353 due to stricter controls in the annual exam and perhaps also due to an awakening in the everyday life of homeschoolers.[42] Still, numbers in autumn 2022 are twice as high as in 2019. This social field of unlikely alliances across the political spectrum, only united in its skepticism against official politics, provides an interesting research field for the future.

Conclusion

It is definitely too early to analyze "the new normal" in post-pandemic society in Austria. Whether the experimental mode of DIY and sustainable growth and the corresponding social groups will remain productive after the pandemic is to be seen.[43] Our field data from the first lockdown in March 2020 showed that the narratives of community and retrotopia served to make sense of the crisis. But we can observe that their dominance wore down quickly, and they became much less influential in everyday conversations and in daily practice. Even in 2021, during the time when the number of infections rose above the level of the first lockdown in Austria and many people suffered and died from Covid-19, the tune of "*Z'sammen*" had faded.[44] The narratives helped people to derive meaning in a challenging situation, but they had little effect on the post-pandemic reality.

What has remained real is the social inequality in pandemic and post-pandemic society in Austria. With regard to educational inequality, we saw a rise after the first lockdown, and we saw that the level of mental and physical overload in families has kept aligned to differences in socio-economic background. The Coronavirus was no leveler but reinforced structural inequality in education.

Endnotes

1. Gabriel Felbermayr et al. "Aprés-ski: The Spread of Coronavirus from Ischgl through Germany," 2020, accessed Feb. 6, 2023, https://www.ifw-kiel.de/fileadmin/Dateiverwaltung/IfW-Publications/Gabriel_Felbermayr/Apres-ski__The_Spread_of_Coronavirus_from_Ischgl_through_Germany/coronavirus_from_ischgl.pdf.

2. Julia Bock-Schappelwein and Ulrike Famira-Mühlberger, "Covid-19-bedingte Schulschließungen: ökonomische Herausforderungen für Kinder, Eltern, Unternehmen und Gesellschaft," in *Ein Jahr Corona: Ausblick Zukunft der Arbeit*, ed. Ursula Filipič and Annika Schönauer (Vienna: ÖGB-Verlag, 2021), 77–86 (here 78), accessed Feb. 5, 2023, https://nbn-resolving.org/urn:nbn:de:0168-ssoar-72650-2.

3. With regard to everyday life in Austria during Corona times, there are many collections of experiences, images, objects, and stories that are not examined in this chapter, but are worth exploring for more context, for example the online collection of objects at the Wienmuseum here: https://www.wienmuseum.at/de/corona-sammlungsprojekt (accessed Feb. 5, 2023) or the Addendum stories about everyday life here: https://www.addendum.org/coronavirus/podcast-corona-alltagsgeschichten/ (accessed Feb. 5, 2023); the collection of photographs in Kathrin Pallestrang, "Fotostrecke: Corona-Lockdown," *Österreichische Zeitschrift für Volkskunde*, 74, no. 1–2 (2020): 173–186. Nadja Kerschhofer-Puhalo analyzes the visibility of the Corona discourse in urban landscapes in Viennese street art and advertising, Nadja Kerschhofer-Puhalo, "Corona is here! Zeichen der Pandemie in der Wiener Stadtlandschaft. Eine diskursanalytische Skizze," *Wiener Linguistische Gazette* 90 (2021): 217–264. The Corona blog of the Corona Data Panel by the University of Vienna contains short glimpses on questions of everyday life during the pandemic here: https://viecer.univie.ac.at/coronapanel/ (accessed Feb. 5, 2023).

4. Silke Meyer, "Narrativität," in *Kulturtheoretisch argumentieren: Ein Arbeitsbuch*, ed. Timo Heimerdinger and Markus Tauschek (Münster: Waxmann, 2020), 294–322; Jerome Bruner, *Making Stories. Law, Literature, Life* (New York: Farrar Straus & Giroux, 2002).

5. Andrea Baier and Christa Müller, "Die Do-it-Yourself (DIY)-Community in Zeiten von Corona. Plädoyer für eine demokratisierte Daseinsvorsorge," in *Die Corona-Gesellschaft: Analysen zur Lage und Perspektiven für die Zukunft*, ed. Michael Volkmer and Karin Werner (Bielefeld: transcript, 2020), 383–393.

6. For example, the Facebook group "Corona Nachbarschaftshilfe Tirol – Wir unterstützen euch!" (Corona neighborhood help Tirol – we support you!) with more than 3,600 members in Innsbruck and surrounding areas, see https://www.facebook.com/groups/1546921968807715/permalink/1547072105459368 (accessed Feb. 5, 2023).

7. The official campaign can be found here: https://www.tirol.gv.at/tirol-europa/protokoll/tirol-haltet-zsamm/ (accessed Feb. 5, 2023).

8. Corona-Dankeslied vom Land Tirol: Z'sammhalten sorgt für Misstöne, August 19, 2020, accessed Feb. 5, 2023, https://www.tt.com/artikel/17218703/corona-dankeslied-vom-land-tirol-z-sammhalten-sorgt-fuer-misstoene.

9. Liste Fritz: CoV-Dank kostet 200.000 Euro, November 19, 2020, accessed Feb. 5, 2023, https://orf.at/stories/3190432/.

10. Victor Turner, *The Ritual Process: Structure and Anti-Structure* (Ithaka, New York: Cornell UP, 1991 [1966]), 95.

11. Ibid., 96.

12. Katharina Eisch-Angus, "Locked in liminality: Angst und Methode in der Krisenerfahrung der Gegenwart," *Zeitschrift für Empirische Kulturwissenschaft*, 118 (2022): 78–103, https://doi.org/10.31244/zekw/2022.05. Searches for the word "sourdough" quadrupled in 2020, see Lydia Maria Arantes, "Das pandemische Brotbacken: Liminalität und Communitas in Corona-Zeiten," in *Covid-19: Sinn in der Krise*, ed. Jan Beuerbach et al. (Berlin, Boston: De Gruyter, 2022): 267–282 (here 267), https://doi.org/10.1515/9783110734942.

13. For online forms of communication during the pandemic see Paul Eisewicht, Nico Steinmann and Pauline Kortmann, "Die globale Corona-Pandemie im Spiegel persönlicher Postings – Plattformbezogene Kommunikationsmodi in sozialen Medien," *Österreichische Zeitschrift für Soziologie* 46 (2021): 353–384, https://doi.org/10.1007/s11614-021-00465-w.

14. Oksana Havryliv, "Sprache und Corona," *Linguistische Treffen Wroclaw*, no. 20 (2021): 69–81 (here 72), accessed Feb. 5, 2023, https://linguistische-treffen.pl/articles/20/04_havryliv.pdf.

15. We launched this call for stories over social media and local newspapers in April 2020 and received eighty-seven entries from people in Tyrol through email. The stories vary in length from about 200 to 4,500 words and give interesting insights into the everyday lives and self-perception of their authors. People did not share many details about their socio-economic

background, but it is evident that many of them are educated and, during the first lockdown, stayed at home and found the time and zest to write their story. The fact that nostalgia and retrotopia feature prominently in these accounts is certainly linked to this social setting.

16. Bernd Rieken, *Wie die Schwaben nach Szulok kamen: Erzählforschung in einem ungarndeutschen Dorf* (Frankfurt/Main: campus, 2000), 85.

17. Manfred Matzka, "Husch-pfusch-Gesetze, zahllose Erlässe: Das Virus im Maßnahmengesetz," Der Standard, Apr. 4, 2020, accessed Feb. 6, 2023, https://www.derstandard.at/story/2000116589247/husch-pfusch-gesetze-zahllose-erlaesse-das-virus-im-massnahmengesetz.

18. Katharina Eisch-Angus, "Kontrolle und Verwundbarkeit: Das institutionelle Subjekt im Deadlock der Sicherheitsgesellschaft," *Hamburger Journal für Kulturantrophologie* 13 (2021): 96–124 (here 121–122), https://journals.sub.uni-hamburg.de/hjk/article/view/1727/1546.

19. Zygmunt Bauman, *Retrotopia* (Berlin: Suhrkamp, 2017), 65.

20. For surveys on social problems during Corona in Austria, see *Die österreichische Gesellschaft während der Corona-Pandemie: Ergebnisse aus sozialwissenschaftlichen Umfragen*, ed. Wolfgang Aschauer et al. (Wiesbaden: Springer, 2022), accessed Feb. 5, 2023, https://library.oapen.org/bitstream/handle/20.500.12657/53363/978-3-658-34491-7.pdf?sequence=1#page=35.

21. Anna Weichselbraun, "Chronotopos Corona," *Österreichische Zeitschrift für Volkskunde* 75, no. 1 (2021): 81– 85 (here 82).

22. Martin Bujarda et al., *Belastungen von Kindern, Jugendlichen und Eltern in der Corona-Pandemie* (Wiesbaden: Bundesinstitut für Bevölkerungsforschung, 2021), 26, https://doi.org/10.12765/bro-2021-02.

23. For example Carolin Bergheim, "Wie gut gelingt Homeschooling in der Corona-Krise?," *Corona Blog 47*, May 28, 2020, https://viecer.univie.ac.at/corona-blog/corona-blog-beitraege/blog47. The data was collected from May 1 to 6, 2020.

24. Stephan Gerhard Huber and Christoph Helm, "Lernen in Zeiten der Corona-Pandemie. Die Rolle familiärer Merkmale für das Lernen von Schüler*innen: Befunde vom Schul-Barometer in Deutschland, Österreich und der Schweiz," *DDS – Die Deutsche Schule* 16 (2020): 37–60, https://doi.org/10.31244/9783830992318.02; Helm, Christoph, Stephan Gerhard Huber and Alexandra Postlbauer, "Lerneinbußen und Bildungsbenachteiligung durch Schulschließungen während der

Covid-19-Pandemie im Frühjahr 2020: Eine Übersicht zur aktuellen Befundlage," in *Schule und Schulpolitik während der Corona-Pandemie. Nichts gelernt?*, ed. Detlef Fickermann et al. (Münster: Waxmann, 2021), 59–81, https://doi.org/10.25656/01:23872.

25. Hans-Peter Blossfeld et al., "Soziale Ungleichheiten und Bildungsentscheidungen im Lebensverlauf: Die Perspektive der Bildungssoziologie," *Journal for Educational Research Online,* 11, no. 1 (2019): 16–30; Rolf Becker, "Entstehung und Reproduktion dauerhafter Bildungsungleichheiten," in *Lehrbuch der Bildungssoziologie*, ed. Rolf Becker (Wiesbaden: Springer, 2017), 89–150, https://doi.org/10.1007/978-3-658-15272-7_4.

26. Christoph Helm et al., "Was wissen wir über schulische Lehr-Lern-Prozesse im Distanzunterricht während der Corona-Pandemie? – Evidenz aus Deutschland, Österreich und der Schweiz," *Zeitschrift für Erziehungswissenschaften* 24 (2021): 237–311, https://doi.org/10.1007/s11618-021-01000-z.

27. Mario Steiner et al., "LehrerInnenbefragung Zwischenergebniss: Was tun, damit aus der Gesundheitskrise nicht auch eine Bildungskrise wird?," IHS Blog (2020), accessed Feb. 5, 2023, https://www.ihs.ac.at/index.php?id=1176.

28. Christoph Helm et al., "Lerneinbußen und Bildungsbenachteiligung durch Schulschließungen während der Covid-19-Pandemie im Frühjahr 2020: Eine Übersicht zur aktuellen Befundlage," *DDS – Die Deutsche Schule*, 18 (2021): 59–81, https://doi.org/10.31244/9783830994589.03. This review also mentions that some studies suggest a lesser or no relation between school closures and learning losses, especially in German-speaking areas. However, the authors conclude that the data base is too small and too diverse here and that more research is needed.

29. Benjamin Dreer and Bärbel Kracke, "Lehrer*innen im Corona-Lockdown 2020 – Umgang mit der Distanzbetreuung im Spannungsfeld von Anforderungen und Ressourcen," in *Das Bildungssystem in Zeiten der Krise: empirische Befunde, Konsequenzen und Potentiale für das Lehren und Lernen*, ed. Christian Reintjes et al. (Münster: Waxmann, 2021), 45–62.

30. See Kammer für Arbeiter und Angestellte, *Corona: Arbeit und Care: Forschungsbericht* (Vienna, 2021).

31. Isabell van Ackeren et al., "Chancenausgleich in der Corona-Krise: Die soziale Bildungsschere wieder schließen," *DDS – Die deutsche Schule* 112, no. 2 (2020): 245–248, https://doi.org/10.25656/01:19333.

32. Evelyn Dawid, *Armutsbetroffene und die Corona-Krise: Eine Erhebung zur sozialen Lage aus der Sicht von Betroffenen* (Vienna: Österreichische Armutskonferenz/Bundesministerium für Gesundheit, Soziales, Pflege und Konsum, 2020).

33. Katharina Manderscheid, "Über die unerwünschte Mobilität von Viren und unterbrochene Mobilitäten von Gütern und Menschen," in *Die Corona-Gesellschaft: Analysen zur Lage und Perspektiven für die Zukunft*, ed. Michael Volkmer and Karin Werner (Bielefeld: transcript, 2020), 101–110.

34. Jürgen Manemann, "Gleichheit vor dem Virus! Verwundbarkeiten und das Tragische in der Corona-Krise," in *Die Corona-Gesellschaft: Analysen zur Lage und Perspektiven für die Zukunft*, ed. Michael Volkmer and Karin Werner (Bielefeld: transcript, 2020), 349–356.

With regard to migrant population, this can be seen in Judith Kohlenberg et al., Covid-19 und Migrationshintergrund. Erreichbarkeit, Umgang mit Maßnahmen und sozioökonomische Herausforderungen von Migrant/inn/en und Geflüchteten. Vienna 2021, https://www.sozialministerium.at/dam/jcr:d9df0617-5bae-4e5d-a30e-d00712428018/Covid-19%20und%20Migrationshintergrund.pdf

35. Bock-Schappelwein and Famira-Mühlberger, "Covid-19-bedingte Schulschließungen."

36. Veronika Hofinger et al., "Homeschooling in Österreich in problematischen Kontexten," *Zeitschrift für Bildungsforschung* 12 (2022): 535–552. https://doi.org/10.1007/s35834-022-00359-1.

37. Rainer Palmstorfer, "Häuslicher Unterricht in Österreich: Das Grundrecht auf 'Homeschooling,'" *Recht der Jugend und des Bildungswesens* 60, no. 1 (2012): 115–22, http://doi.org/10.5771/0034-1312-2012-1-115.

38. Mourão Permoser et al., "Reframing Human Rights: The Global Network of Moral Conservative Homeschooling Activists." *Global Networks. A Journal of Transnational Affairs* 21, no. 4 (2021): 681–702.

39. Martha Albertson Fineman "Home Schooling: Putting Parental Rights Over Children's Best Interest," in *The Wiley Handbook of School Choice*, ed. R. A. Fox and N. K. Buchanan (Hoboken: John Wiley & Sons, Inc., 2017), 362–376.

40. Carolin Amlinger and Oliver Nachtwey, *Gekränkte Freiheit: Aspekte des libertären Autoritarismus* (Berlin: Suhrkamp, 2022).

41. Julia Mourão Permoser and Kristina Stoeckl, "Reframing Human Rights: The Global Network of Moral Conservative Homeschooling Activists," *Global Networks* 21, no. 4 (2021): 681–702, http://doi.org/10.1111/

glob.12299; Matthias Pöhlmann, *Rechte Esoterik: wenn sich alternatives Denken und Extremismus gefährlich vermischen* (Freiburg: Herder, 2021).

42. To date, there hardly any studies on the phenomenon with the notable exception of Hofinger, Reisinger and Walter, "Homeschooling in Österreich."

43. Sophie Karmasin et al., "Das neue Retro? Österreich nach der Corona-Krise – wie sich unser Land verändern wird," available online: https://irihs.ihs.ac.at/id/eprint/5328/7/karmasin-gangl-walter-spitzer-kocher-2020-das-neue-retro.pdf, Vienna 2020 (accessed Feb. 5, 2023).

44. Wolfgang Aschauer et al, eds., *Die österreichische Gesellschaft während der Corona-Pandemie: Ergebnisse aus sozialwissenschaftlichen Umfragen* (Wiesbaden: Springer, 2022), 15, https://library.oapen.org/bitstream/handle/20.500.12657/53363/978-3-658-34491-7.pdf?sequence=1#page=35 (accessed Feb. 5, 2023).

The Covid-19 Pandemic and its Influence on Austria's Tourism Industry

Mike Peters
Robert Steiger

Introduction

The Covid-19 crisis has hit tourism in Austria badly and has changed the demand and supply conditions. Until the pandemic tourism in Austria was characterized by a steady growth. This paper outlines this development and the status quo of tourism in Austria before Covid-19. The next section then shows what happened during the Covid-19 crisis: in addition to the chronological events, it illustrates which topics were also discussed by tourism researchers during the crisis. Thereafter the paper looks at the time after Covid-19 and discusses the extent to which the crisis might have a lasting effect on demand and supply. The conclusion focuses on necessary and future research initiatives.

Tourism before Covid-19

Austria is a mature tourism destination with small annual growth rates in the long-term (Fig. 1). Decadal growth rates were 9.2% in the 1980s, followed by a decline of 7.3% in the 1990s, a recovery in the 2000s of 9.6% and an accelerated growth of 20.1% in the 2010s. While in 1974 the focus of overnight stays was in the summer season (72%), seasons were almost balanced (52% summer share) in 2019, the last pre-Covid-19 year. Nevertheless, on a regional level, there are both summer-dominated destinations, like lake regions in Carinthia (e.g., 98% in St. Kanzian/Klopeiner See) and winter-dominated ski destinations in Western Austria (e.g., 92% in Ischgl). The average length of stay declined by 38% between the 1980s and the 2010s. In this time period, arrivals increased by 89% suggesting a remarkable increase of tourism-related traffic.[1]

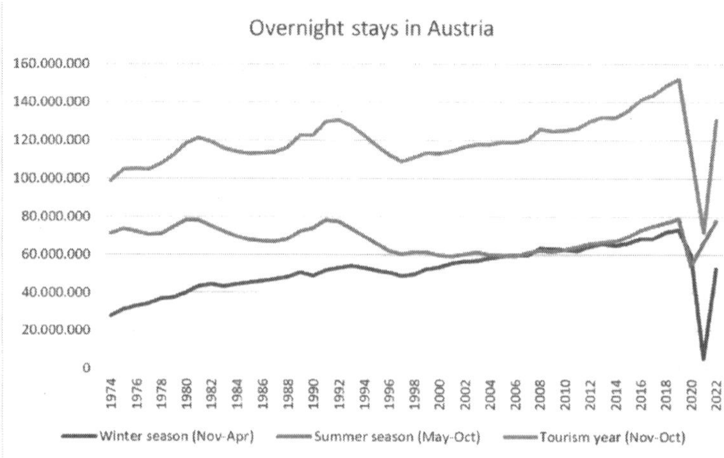

FIGURE 1: Development of overnight stays in Austria since 1974)[2]

Tourism intensity (tourist overnights per inhabitant) is high in many Austrian destinations, suggesting a high economic importance but also potential negative externalities. The federal state of Tyrol in Western Austria is ranked 4th among European regions with a tourism intensity of 43 overnights per inhabitant.[3] On a municipality level, some even exceed values of 500.[4] This has given rise to growing public debate on reaching or exceeding carrying capacity limits of the socio-ecological system. One example of that debate are projects on lift-links of existing ski areas that aim to improve competitiveness[5] in the stagnating ski tourism market.[6] A citizens' initiative against a proposed lift-link between two glacier ski areas in Tyrol gained 168,000 support signatures and a local referendum rejected the project.[7] Another example is a referendum about the candidacy of Tyrol for the 2026 Winter Olympics that was rejected by the majority of voters. In a subsequent experiment, sustainable renovation of sports infrastructure and using the Olympic village for public housing after the Games turned out to be the most important factors for potential support of the candidacy.[8]

The tourism industry in Austria is characterized by a high share of SMEs, especially family firms.[9] Historically, tourism developed predominantly endogenously, controlled by local entrepreneurs and capital.[10] Nowadays, concern grows that embeddedness and control is shrinking due to the problem of succession in many locally owned hotel establishments. With more and more internationally acting companies stepping in, part of control and value added might be transferred to regions outside of the Alps.

A positive consequence of endogenous development was that where tourism was able to provide alternative income for the farming population, emigration from rural alpine valleys was prevented during the transition from an agrarian to a service society in the twentieth century.[11] However, recent migration flows show that some tourism destinations are starting to lose population.[12] This might be in part due to a higher education level of the young population combined with an only limited local market of high qualification jobs. A consequence of an increasing level of education are better job opportunities, which is in turn intensifying labor shortage in the tourism industry.[13] The Austrian Court of Auditors noted a labor shortage in about one third of all labor market districts in 2018.[14]

Even before Covid-19 climate change was considered as a mid-term but grand challenge for Austrian tourism. In Austria, temperatures increased by 1.8°C since the end of the nineteenth century, about 20% more compared to warming over global land areas. A further warming of 1.3° C (compared to 1971-2000) is projected for the next three decades, and 2.1-4.0°C until the end of the century, depending on the development of global greenhouse gas emissions.[15]

For summer tourism, a warmer climate allows a prolongation of the season for many tourist activities, representing a potential for tourism.[16] Nevertheless, some activities, e.g., climbing might also be negatively affected due to destabilizing slopes in high alpine areas. More pronounced droughts may impact golfing, as about one third of all golf courses in Austria are located in areas facing water shortages in the future.[17]

For winter tourism, a remarkable decline of snow cover duration and snow depth represents a serious challenge.[18] Climate change will shorten potential ski seasons and declining availability of snow will require more intense snowmaking. By the 2050s, about 20% of ski areas would not be able to guarantee a sufficiently long ski season despite snowmaking, because conditions have become too warm in these locations. During the economically important Christmas-New Year holiday period, 34% of ski areas are projected to face high risks of closures.[19] Furthermore, required higher volumes of technically produced snow in the remaining ski areas means higher costs and resource consumption.[20]

Another challenge in tourism before Covid-19was the falling demand on the labor market. Studies worldwide point to an image problem in the industry[21] especially among young job seekers: poor working hours, low pay and a poor working atmosphere are just some of the reasons given.[22] Austrian tourism companies are essentially small businesses and/or family businesses that find it very difficult to offer long-term career options within a company.[23]

Tourism and Covid-19: A Chronology

Tourism has been among the hardest hit of all the economic sectors affected by the pandemic. To control the spread of the Covid-19 virus, almost all countries imposed containment measures including travel restrictions, border closures, prohibition of public events, total or partial quarantines, confinement and physical distancing. "Travel restrictions led to a global collapse in international tourism arrivals, which fell 74 per cent worldwide from 1.5 billion in 2019 to 381 million in 2020. (…) arrivals fell 70 per cent in Africa, 69 per cent in the Americas, 71 per cent in Europe and 76 per cent in the Middle East" (Organization, 2022, pp. 12-13) [24]

The first phase of the crisis was characterized by playing down the rise of Covid-19. The winter season 2019/2020 was quite successful until the Covid-19 crisis hit the industry dramatically in March 2020. Usually, the winter season lasts until April and in some glacier regions until mid-May. At the end of February 2020, first cases were reported (in Innsbruck) but hardly commented by the tourism industry. Although some hotel managers received notice from former Icelandic guests (on March 5/2020 reporting their infections when returning to their home country), hotels in the destination of Ischgl did not take prevention measures and did also not inform hotel guests and were not asked to and did not shut down immediately.[25] However, on the weekend of March 13th 2020 all tourism businesses in Tyrol immediately had to close down due to several Covid clusters in fully booked tourism destinations. Taking advantage of existing contingency and crises communication plans, hoteliers directly communicated with police and district administration but also with the Tyrolean chambers of commerce. Thus, hotel owners relied on directives and rules published by destination management organisations and district administration offices. During that phase many hoteliers thought this might be a short-term crisis evaluating the situation critical but they were glad that the crisis hit them after they already ran a major part of the winter season. They assumed to repair the loss during the remaining year if the government supports the industry with immediate funding. A major challenge for hotel managers was the management of their workforce.[26] Various travel warning and travel ban announcements in the tourism sending markets and in Austria emerged. Strict border controls did not allow border crossings neither for vacation nor for any other visit purposes.[27]

Mid-March 2020, the so-called "*Kurzarbeit*" (short-work) regulation was introduced promising a large amount of the employees' salary paid by the government with no or only partial work in March.[28] However, in the first months not many hoteliers took advantages of that support and dismissed workforce. Although, many hotel managers cared about their seasonal workers who had to stay in quarantine and supported them with accommodation and locals cost coverage.

In the months from June to October 2020 tourism demand increased again. Tourism managers took advantage of funding and support opportunities of the government. Although, travel was restricted in Austria's main tourism markets (e.g., Germany), domestic tourism contributed to sound tourist arrival numbers for rural and lake-side destinations, whereas urban tourism suffered strongly.[29] The summer season developed well for restaurant managers claiming that they do not feel like being in a crisis as although many borders to sending countries remained closed, domestic demand was high. Many tourism businesses profited from the testing initiative "secure hospitability"[30] to regularly test their employees, others refrained from taking advantages of such measures and did not open their businesses. While several leading businesses in the industry voted for a strategic change after Covid-19 in order to mobilize regional markets and circular economies, others postulated to rebuild the industries pre-Covid-19 conditions.

Overnight stays were 42.6% below 2019 and about at the same level as in 2001. The most affected federal state was Vienna (-82%) (Fig. 2). In general, tourists avoided densely populated areas[31] in that year likely due to a higher risk of infection. Furthermore, urban tourism suffered from a very restrained business tourism and still strict international travel regulations. The least affected federal states in Austria are located in the Southeast with Burgenland, Styria and Carinthia with losses between 18-21% (Fig. 2). All three federal states offer lake tourism, the latter two also mountain tourism.

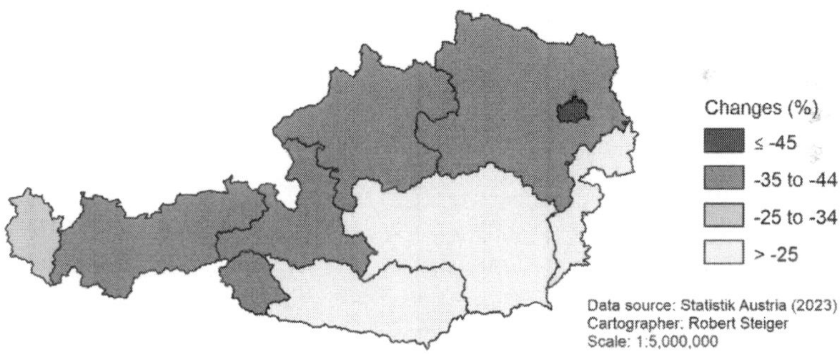

FIGURE 2: Change of overnight stays in summer 2020 compared to 2019

From November 2020 to April 2021 the second wave of Covid-19 infections evolved. Although, the new lockdown started in October 2020, the cable car industry demanded to re-open their lifts for the winter season 20/21. During Christmas, they were able to open again with several further safety regulations. However, in this third phase, many cableway companies applied for several funding and support initiatives such as lock-down sales substitution and short-work options. Especially those who did not re-open as they are dependent on international markets took advantage of these subsidies. The cableway industry perceived this phase of the crisis as a "catastrophe."[32] Overall, several industry players called for a rethinking of well-known tourism growth paths and asked for responsible tourism strategies post-Covid-19. The results of the WIFO tourism analysis for the first four months of winter 2020/21 (November 2020 to February 2021) already showed a total loss (arrivals -95.1%, overnight stays and income - nominal and real - each -93.5%)[33]. Furthermore, with the beginning of 2021, vaccination against Covid-19 started with the first dose, in April one could take the second dose. Therefore, the situation was improving. In June 2021 restrictions were relaxed again and, in addition to the obligation to wear masks, the 3G rule was applied: those who had recovered ("*genesen*"), been vaccinated ("*geimpft*) or tested ("*getestet*") were allowed, for example, to go to restaurants or shops. Further easing in July, for example, did not foresee any upper limits of visitor numbers for events. Entry into certain regions was regulated using the "High Incidence Decree" and from time-to-time certain villages could only be visited with a novel proof of a negative Covid-19 test. The rules during this summer were quite complicated but allowed tourism to slightly recover.

During November 2021, the highest number of Covid-19 infections was reached, and a second hard lockdown was announced on the 17th of November 2021. In February 2022 shops and restaurants and hotels were allowed to open again. However, several regulations made it hard for consumers, e.g., negative Covid-19 test were demanded in close-contact service industries (e.g. hair cutters) and masks were demanded mostly in all shops and restaurants. In the beginning of 2022 vaccination measures were introduced and during the year the number of the very serious infections decreased.

In contrast to the lockdown-related total loss of the 2020/21 winter season in Austria (overnight stays -92.4%), demand in winter 2021/2022 increased steadily after renewed closures at the beginning of the season, so that the backlog increased from November 2021 to April 2022 to the pre-crisis level of 2018/19 to an average of almost 28% for overnight stays and a good 19% in terms of nominal tourism income[34], being on the level of the year 2003.

Like in the summer season, the most affected federal state was Vienna (-62%) (Fig. 3). The least affected federal state was Vorarlberg (-22%). A potential reason is that travel restrictions imposed by Switzerland on Austria were less strict than those imposed by Germany and the share of Swiss guests is traditionally higher in Vorarlberg compared to other federal states.

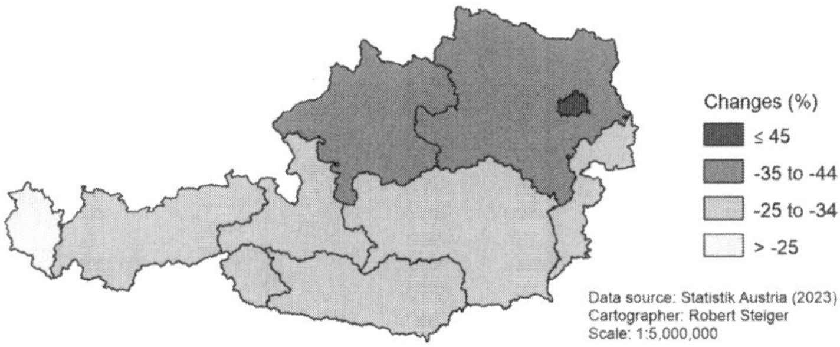

FIGURE 3: Change of overnight stays in winter 2021/22 compared to 2018/19

The vaccinations were becoming more and more effective and severe Covid-19 cases fell drastically after mid-march 2022. The summer of 2022 was almost a normal travel summer. However, after the summer season and at the end of 2022 many provinces in Austria were considering light lockdowns and tightened the rules (e.g., masks were demanded again in supermarkets and public buildings).

The winter season 2022/23 has provided an example of what the climate future holds for the Austrian winter tourism industry: the Russian war against the Ukraine has caused energy prices to soar, putting pressure on the cost side. Furthermore, in fall 2022, the feared energy crisis in the upcoming winter sparked a public debate whether ski areas should be allowed to operate, as they cannot be considered as critical infrastructure. Although the energy crisis could be averted, the warm winter season with increased need for snowmaking together with high energy prices fueled a discussion about the suitability of winter tourism in Austria.

The tourism industry in Austria faced various challenges during the above presented chronology:

- Due to several travel bans in the first years of Covid-19 many international tourism sending markets broke down. Especially long-haul markets like China, India or the United States decreased dramatically and only slowly recovered.

- Because of restricted travelling crossing borders, domestic tourism was increasing. Residents discovered local recreation areas not only for short holiday excursions but also for their overall vacations. Overtourism challenges in regional demand were reported and camping holidays became more popular.

- The demand structure varied during the crisis: tourists asked for apartments instead of hotel accommodation, the convention and business traveler market was almost non-existent for about two years.
- International travels and thus the flight market broke down and many flight-routes were cancelled.

During the crisis, a substantial number of scientific research papers tried to shed more light on the changes both on the demand and on the supply side. Especially in tourism research and in the first year of the pandemic, we find contributions dealing with changing travel behaviour or travel risk perceptions[35] of international and domestic travelers, analyzing potential impacts of the crisis on tourism sustainability and resilience,[36] discussing new paths of tourism development and tourism research,[37] and identifying the crisis' impact on specific stakeholders in tourism, e.g. such as employees,[38] residents[39] or destination management and marketing organizations.[40] Especially in the year 2020 in which drastic lockdown measures and[41] travel ban but also closed borders hindered traveling, these researchers observed current changing behaviors, tourism industry global challenges[42] and anticipated future paths of tourism development:

Travel behaviour and risk perceptions during the crisis: One of the first studies conducted in the early phase of Covid-19 analyzed data collected at two points of time, in the beginning of March and at the end of March 2020. In the European Covid-19 outbreak phase more than 1300 questionnaires were collected among travelers in Germany, Austria and Switzerland. Due to travel bans and worldwide media coverage reporting rising death tolls during that time certainly increased the risk perception of Covid-19 and travel risk perception. Interestingly, the authors found clusters of travelers in period 1 and 2: in period one, "the nervous" were younger and had less travel experiences, the "reserved" did indicate a willingness to drastically change travel behavior, while the "relaxed" were older and had more travel experience. This cluster was only found in phase 1, the first survey. Two weeks later, the second survey revealed the following clusters: the "reserved" and the "nervous" were quite similar, the third cluster was labelled as the "anxious" showing very high levels of risk perception of the virus, of the travel risk perception and of travel behavior. Further research tried to forecast international visitor arrivals amid Covid-19 (Liu, Vici, Ramos, Giannoni, & Blake, 2021; Qiu et al., 2021),[43] novel travel behaviors,[44] and pandemic affect and customers' perceived travel benefits.[45]

Domestic tourism demand: Since it was no longer possible to cross borders or to travel to other countries, the demand for domestic leisure and holiday offers increased. Marketing campaigns by the Austrian Tourist Board focused on local summer holidays, and in the summer of 2020 and 2021 there was particularly strong demand for offers in lake and mountain regions. Many Austrians have come to appreciate local recreation areas that were previously not a holiday alternative. Even in winter, the locals learned to appreciate the cable car companies in particular: According to the regulation, cable cars did not have to close completely in winter 2020/2021 either and were available to the locals even though there were no economic advantages to be gained due to the absence of international guests. It was already apparent at the end of 2021 that the outbreak of Covid-19 in the ski resort of Ischgl in Tyrol did not cause any lasting damage to its image in the main sending market Germany.[46] The critical debates by local interest groups regarding the dominance and profit-making of cable car companies in Austria's ski areas also diminished during the Covid-19crisis. The opening of many cable car companies, which was economically difficult but important for the quality of life of the locals, also contributed to this image recovery.[47] Interestingly, the increased demand for local recreational areas led to time- and location-related demand peaks: although international tourism collapsed, the challenge of overtourism was discussed again in many communities.[48] Due to a lack of alternatives, lakes, gorges (e.g. Vomper Loch in Tirol), or other natural treasures became so popular that some regions restricted access.[49]

Covid-19 and future sustainability: Another stream of literature published during the pandemic was discussing the impact of the crisis on sustainable tourism development in the future. While for instance Ioannides & Gyimóthy (2020)[50] call for a redesign of training, educational and curricula in tourism, Higgins-Desbiolles (2020)[51] highlight that "the Covid-19 crisis inspired transformational thinking among some tourism academics as a moment of great potentiality" (p.16). Other interpret the Covid-19 crisis as a possibility to bundle the industries' power to address the climate change challenges.[52] "Covid-19 will accelerate transformations (...)" (p.670) needed to further develop a novel way of thinking to initiate innovative models of economically, ecologically but also socio-culturally sustainable tourism. A re-discovery of complex constructs such as resilience and responsible tourism in tourism research but also in tourism policy was one further result of the Covid-19 crisis. Resilience refers to change but not (only) as a reaction but as using a triggering event as an opportunity to "improving performance post-disturbance (bouncing forward)" (Prayag, 2020, p. 181).[53] Some authors especially refer to the importance of community resilience[54] which is of particular importance for small tourism businesses embedded in rural destinations. Tourism research regards the Covid-19 crisis as a stimulus for a paradigm shift in sustainable tourism development.[55] In a recent review paper,

Gössling and Schweiggart (2022)[56] explored what has already been studied in the last two years of the Covid-19 pandemic, arguing for a consensus among tourism research and practitioners about the crises serving as turning point to "build tourism back better", in avoiding to return to overtourism phenomena – therefore it requires tourism research to study optional adaptions.[57]

Covid-19 and its impact on the tourism workforce: More than 330 million jobs were accounted to the travel and tourism worldwide for the tourism and travel industry, this equals about 10.6% of the total global employment. Looking at the indirect and induced effects we see that one created tourism job creates 1.5 additional jobs. The most important subsector is the accommodation and food service sector that provide about 144 million tourism jobs worldwide. Certainly, this economic disruption caused millions of job and income losses: almost 62 million jobs were lost and in the accommodation and food sector service more than 20% of the workforce got lost.[58] Many workers left the industry during the crisis and very few new entrants were recorded. For instance, in Austria, usually, 40,000 new workers enter the industry, but in the years 2020-2021 there were only 20,000. Therefore, after 2020, a job record was set in 2021 and 2022 on the Austrian labor market – mainly in the accommodation, food, and gastronomy sector.[59]

Covid-19 and digitization in tourism: The Covid-19 crisis is often attributed an innovative effect on digitization in the tourism industry. In fact, studies show that communication processes between various stakeholders in destinations have been significantly optimized through digital communication technologies. As observed in schools, training and further education institutions, the crisis is pushing managers and entrepreneurs to use a wide variety of virtual communication software to initiate digital meetings (e.g., Zoom, BBB, Microsoft Teams).[60] Little is known about the effect of this particular crisis on long-term digitization or digital transformation efforts, but in the short-run, many technologies were developed during the crisis in a very fast time, e.g., "digital health passports, tracking of vaccination or Covid-19 test results and Covid-19 tracing apps" (Becken & Loehr, 2022, p. 5).[61]

The Legacy of Covid-19

The Covid-19 crisis has accelerated several changes in Austrian tourism:

Travel demand increased significantly with the reduction of Covid-19 regulations in 2022: Nevertheless, the current research indicates that travelers are using sustainability attributes to a much greater extent to plan their trip. Although before the crises research assumed that sustainability plays a greater role in the travel decision and the travel behaviour during the trip, this assumption could be confirmed for several traveler segments.[62] Besides tourism, the demand for organic products increased significantly after the crisis.[63]

As early as 2022, it became apparent that the desire to travel after two years of abstinence is enormous. The rapidly emerging and high demand in summer 2022 led to many *resource bottlenecks* (e.g., at airports, airlines), in particular there was a lack of skilled workers in almost all areas along the tourism value chain. This labor shortage was already being discussed as a challenge before the crisis,[64] however, far-reaching measures are only being taken now as the shortage is worsening. Some destinations are developing destination-wide employer branding measures and recognizing the importance of a quality workforce. These measures also help small and medium-sized companies that are struggling on the labor market due to their size disadvantages.

Before the crisis, there were critical debates about *rethinking the previous growth paradigms* (e.g., arrivals and overnight stays) and instead including attributes such as quality of life and environmental quality in the strategy development. During the Covid-19 crisis, tourism policy and destination management started to radically revise existing tourism development strategies. After just one year of crisis, this has been done in many federal states in Austria and strategy papers have been adjusted and re-written. Furthermore, these strategies were provided with a concrete request to develop indicators for measuring sustainability in the near future (see e.g., strategy papers in Tyrol and Upper Austria).[65] In addition, resources were requested in some federal states to provide specialist personnel for these activities. For example, sustainability coordinators have been installed in all 34 Tyrolean tourism destinations. These managers take care of concrete initiatives that are allowed to only benefit the sustainability of tourism.

The public debate about planned mergers of ski areas has perished since the Covid-19 crisis. As mentioned above, residents no longer support the previously often propagated paradigm of economic growth. Recently Schönherr et al. (2023, p. 4)[66] identified that "demanders of sustainable tourism are characterized by a shift in residents' positive economic perceptions towards critically questioning tourism development" (2023, p. 4).[67] In addition, strict nature conservation regulations and negative image effects that reach into the main tourism markets of Austria (e.g., Germany and the Netherlands). Cableway companies are often seen as the main drivers of this growth, and the expansion of ski area boundaries and the construction of new cableway systems are ecologically not sustainable. Furthermore, cableway managers in Western Austria do not want to jeopardize the positive image effects built up among the residents during the Covid-19 crisis through new protests against ski area expansion plans.

Also driven by the war in Ukraine and the health crisis, long-discussed *sustainability projects* are now being implemented. Photovoltaic systems are built in mountain regions and even wind turbines in the mountains are no longer banned and are being recommended by former critics.

Crises can stimulate innovation. The management literature shows that in times of crisis, companies often implement long-planned initiatives or ask themselves clearly relevant questions.[68] This also applies to the tourism industry in Austria. Current studies underline that, for example, small and medium-sized companies form networks and collaboratively tackle challenges in the field of digitization, sustainability, and human resource management.[69]

Conclusion

The Covid-19 crisis has abruptly stopped the long-term growth of Austrian tourism. Besides short-term challenges related to managing the pandemic and its associated regulatory requirements as well as demand losses, the pandemic will have longer lasting impacts even if demand is back at the old level again. These impacts require further research to better understand the underlying phenomena and to support the industry in sustainable development.

Due to the crisis, Austrian tourism which is dominated by small- and medium-sized enterprises has further come under financial pressure. More research is also required regarding the creeping potential loss of control due to foreign investments. No official numbers are available monitoring the anecdotally reported 'sellout' of some tourism destinations. To evaluate the magnitude of the potential problem, reliable numbers are required, e.g. on a case study basis. It can be further investigated, how local entrepreneurs could be supported to take over vacant accommodation businesses and (if necessary) how to adapt regulations in order to support locally controlled community-based tourism.

Concerning labor shortage, there is already a vast body of research investigating potential causes and solutions to that problem (e.g., regarding employer attractiveness and employer branding). However, given the demographic change with low birth cohorts and an increasing shortage in almost all sectors of the economy, it is questionable if labor shortage in the tourism industry can be solved solely by improving working conditions and the sector's image. Considering the critical public debates about overtourism and exceeded carrying capacity, a rather radical approach could be to investigate what tourist volume could be handled in the destinations with the available workforce. Subsequently, new forms of tourism could be developed and discussed that require less workforce, less tourist volumes with fewer negative externalities.

Furthermore, one central question to be addressed will be what share of regional value creation can be sustained for the local population? Even if the aim of lower tourist levels with the same value creation would not be reachable, a discussion of these topics might help in progressing towards more sustainable tourism development by breaking up old thought patterns.

Climate change needs to be considered in all future tourism strategies and development paths. To do so, practitioners need reliable evidence on potential impacts and especially on potential feedback loops within the tourism industry. While physical impacts are strongly investigated (e.g., climate change impact on ski season length and suitability of snowmaking), there is only very limited scientific information on how the changing environmental conditions (e.g., less natural snow in winter, white ski slopes in green landscape; or glacier loss and increasing natural hazards and heat stress in summer) might affect tourism demand. Therefore, an important research gap are more integrated assessments of climate change impacts on the tourism industry combining both physical and societal impacts and reactions.

Finally, to learn from the Covid-19 crisis, further analyses are needed: We have to understand whether and how the Covid-19 support measures for tourism companies have had a lasting effect. In addition, locals must be more involved in future tourism development. One the one hand, strategy development in tourism also affects other industries and locals who do not benefit directly from the industry. On the other hand, better and fact-based communication measures are needed to inform all stakeholders in tourism destinations about the potential contribution of sustainable tourism in their region.[70]

Endnotes

1. Statistik Austria, "Statcube Database," Feb. 2023, accessed Feb. 28, 2023, https://www.statistik.at/datenbanken/statcube-statistische-datenbank.

2. Ibid.

3. Eurostat, "Eurostat Jahrbuch Der Regionen 2010: 11 – Tourismus," 2011, accessed Feb. 28, 2023, https://ec.europa.eu/eurostat/documents/3217494/5725865/KS-HA-10-001-11-DE.PDF.pdf/9baf973e-0f9c-48e9-9c34-869a6afbfd70?t=1414775809000.

4. Statistik Austria, "Statcube Database."

5. Martin Falk, "Gains from horizontal collaboration among ski areas," *Tourism Management 60,* (2017): 92–104, https://doi.org/10.1016/j.tourman.2016.11.008.

6. Robert Steiger and Daniel Scott, "Ski tourism in a warmer world: Increased adaptation and regional economic impacts in Austria," *Tourism Management* 77, 104032 (2020), https://doi.org/10.1016/j.tourman.2019.104032.

7. APA, "Volksbefragung Brachte Knappe Mehrheit Gegen "Gletscher-Ehe"," *Der Standard* (Jul. 17, 2022), accessed Feb. 28, 2023, https://www.derstandard.at/story/2000137527403/projekt-tiroler-gletscher-ehe-endgueltig-abgesagt.

8. Elisabeth Feilhauer et al., "What residents of potential Olympic cities want: using conjoint analysis to deal with dominant and heterogeneous preferences," *Current Issues in Tourism* (2022): 1–14, https://doi.org/10.1080/13683500.2022.2067030.

9. Andreas Kallmuenzer et al., "Trade-offs between dimensions of sustainability: exploratory evidence from family firms in rural tourism regions," *Journal of Sustainable Tourism 26,* no. 7 (2017): 1204–21, https://doi.org/10.1080/09669582.2017.1374962.

10. Werner Bätzing, *Die Alpen: Geschichte Und Zukunft Einer Europäischen Kulturlandschaft* (München: 2015, C.H. Beck).

11. Ibid.

12. Peter Čede et al., "The Eastern Austrian Alps: Their Exceptional Demographic Status in the Alpine Region," *European Countryside* 10, no. 4 (2018): 634–51, https://doi.org/10.2478/euco-2018-0035.

13. Andrea Hausold, "Austria's Tourism Needs Tens of Thousands of

Employees," accessed Feb. 28, 2023, https://www.tourism-review.com/austrias-tourism-lacks-thousands-of-staff-news12233.

14. Rechnungshof Österreich, "*Bedarf an Fachkräften Im Tourismus. Bericht Des Rechnungshofes*," 2000, accessed Feb. 28, 2023, https://www.rechnungshof.gv.at/rh/home/home_1/home_2/Anhang_2_Bedarf_an_Fachkraeften_im_Tourismus.pdf.

15. Marc Olefs et al., "Past and future changes of the Austrian climate – Importance for tourism," *Journal of Outdoor Recreation and Tourism* 34, 100395 (2021), https://doi.org/10.1016/j.jort.2021.100395.

16. Ulrike Pröbstl-Haider et al., "Climate change: Impacts on outdoor activities in the summer and shoulder seasons," *Journal of Outdoor Recreation and Tourism* 34, 100344 (2021), https://doi.org/10.1016/j.jort.2020.100344.

17. Ibid.

18. Olefs et al., "Past and future changes of the Austrian climate."

19. Steiger and Scott, "Ski tourism in a warmer world."

20. Robert Steiger et al., "Impacts of climate change on mountain tourism: a review," *Journal of Sustainable Tourism* (2022): 1–34, https://doi.org/10.1080/09669582.2022.2112204.

21. Andreas Mölk et al., "Radicalization and attenuation in the construction of tourism employment images: a multi-level frame analysis," *International Journal of Contemporary Hospitality Management* 34, no. 2 (2021): 457–81, https://doi.org/10.1108/ijchm-12-2020-1490.

22. Tom Baum, "Sustainable human resource management as a driver in tourism policy and planning: a serious sin of omission?" *Journal of Sustainable Tourism* 26, no. 6 (2018): 873–89, https://doi.org/10.1080/09669582.2017.1423318; Jill M. Poulston, "Working Conditions in Hospitality: Employees' Views of the Dissatisfactory Hygiene Factors," *Journal of Quality Assurance in Hospitality & Tourism* 10, no. 1 (2009): 23–43, https://doi.org/10.1080/15280080902716993.

23. Mike Peters et al. "Hospitality entrepreneurs managing quality of life and business growth," *Current Issues in Tourism* 22, no. 16 (2018): 2014–33, https://doi.org/10.1080/13683500.2018.1437122.

24. International Labour Organization "The future of work in the tourism sector: Sustainable and safe recovery and decent work in the context of the Covid-19 pandemic," accessed Jan. 10, 2023, https://www.ilo.org/wcmsp5/groups/public/---ed_dialogue/---sector/documents/meetingdocument/wcms_840403.pdf.

25. Marius Mayer et al., "Media discourses about a superspreader destination: How mismanagement of Covid-19 triggers debates about sustainability and geopolitics," *Annals of Tourism Research* 91, 103278 (2021), https://doi.org/10.1016/j.annals.2021.103278.

26. Oliver Fritz and Sabine Ehn-Fragner, "Covid-19-Krise stoppt dynamische Expansion im Tourismus," 2020, accessed Feb. 28, 2023, https://www.wifo.ac.at/jart/prj3/wifo/resources/person_dokument/person_dokument.jart?publikationsid=66655&mime_type=application/pdf.

27. Kir Kuščer et al., "Tourism organizations' responses to the Covid-19 pandemic: an investigation of the lockdown period," *Current Issues in Tourism* 1–14 (2021): https://doi.org/10.1080/13683500.2021.1928010.

28. Cornelia Ritzer, "Tausende Anträge auf Kurzarbeit: AMS prüft Hilfe massiv," *Tiroler Tageszeitung*, Mar. 27, 2020, acce sed Feb. 27, 2023, https://www.tt.com/artikel/16801773/tausende-antraege-auf-kurzarbeit-ams-prueft-hilfe-massiv.

29. Fritz and Ehn-Fragner, "Covid-19-Krise stoppt dynamische Expansion im Tourismus."

30. Bundesministerium für Arbeit und Wirtschaft, "Sichere Gastfreundschaft," accessed Feb. 28, 2023, www.sichere-gastfreundschaft.at.

31. Martin Falk et al., "Uneven domestic tourism demand in times of pandemic," *Tourism Economics* (2022), https://doi.org/10.1177/13548166211059409.

32. ORF Tirol (Producer). "Weiterer Lockdown für Walser "Katastrophe"," Dec. 18, 2020, accessed Feb. 26, 2023, https://tirol.orf.at/stories/3081356/.

33. Oliver Fritz, "Tourismusanalyse: Nach Totalausfall der Wintersaison drohen empfindliche Verluste für das gesamte Jahr 2021," 2021, accessed Feb. 26, 2023, https://www.wifo.ac.at/jart/prj3/wifo/resources/person_dokument/person_dokument.jart?publikationsid=67061&mime_type=application/pdf.

34. Oliver Fritz and Anna Burton "Stetige Erholung im österreichischen Tourismus seit Jahresbeginn, Teuerung trübt weitere Erwartungen," 2022, accessed Feb. 28, 2023, https://www.wifo.ac.at/jart/prj3/wifo/resources/person_dokument/person_dokument.jart?publikationsid=69685&mime_type=application/pdf.

35. Larissa Neuburger and Roman Egger, "Travel risk perception and travel behaviour during the Covid-19 pandemic 2020: a case study of the DACH region," *Current Issues in Tourism* (2020): 1–14, https://doi.org/10.1080/13683500.2020.1803807.

36. Girish Prayag, "Time for Reset? Covid-19 and Tourism Resilience," *Tourism Review International* 24, no. 2 (2020): 179–84, https://doi.org/10.3727/154427220x15926147793595; Francesc Romagosa, "The Covid-19 crisis: Opportunities for sustainable and proximity tourism," *Tourism Geographies* 22, no. 3 (2020): 690–4, https://doi.org/10.1080/14616688.2020.1763447.

37. Marianna Sigala, "Tourism and Covid-19: Impacts and implications for advancing and resetting industry and research," *J Bus Res 117* (2020): 312–21, https://doi.org/10.1016/j.jbusres.2020.06.015.

38. Tom Baum et al., "Covid-19's impact on the hospitality workforce – new crisis or amplification of the norm?," *International Journal of Contemporary Hospitality Management* 32, no. 9 (2020): 2813–29, https://doi.org/10.1108/ijchm-04-2020-0314.

39. Jun Wen et al., „Covid-19: potential effects on Chinese citizens' lifestyle and travel," *Tourism Review* 76, no. 1 (2021): 74–87, https://doi.org/10.1108/tr-03-2020-0110.

40. Kir Kuščer et al., "Tourism organizations' responses to the Covid-19 pandemic," 247–60.

41. Neuburger and Egger, "Travel risk perception and travel behaviour during the Covid-19 pandemic 2020."

42. Stefan Gössling et al., "Pandemics, tourism and global change: a rapid assessment of Covid-19," *Journal of Sustainable Tourism* 29, no. 1 (2020): 1–20, https://doi.org/10.1080/09669582.2020.1758708.

43. Anyu Liu at al., "Visitor arrivals forecasts amid Covid-19: A perspective from the Europe team," *Ann Tour Res* 88, 103182 (2021), https://doi.org/10.1016/j.annals.2021.103182; Richard T. R. Qiu et al., "Visitor arrivals forecasts amid Covid-19: A perspective from the Asia and Pacific team," *Ann Tour Res* 88, 103155 (2021), https://doi.org/10.1016/j.annals.2021.103155.

44. Jun Wen et al., "Covid-19: potential effects on Chinese citizens' lifestyle and travel," *Tourism Review* 76, no. 1 (2021): 74–87, https://doi.org/10.1108/tr-03-2020-0110.

45. Friedericke Kuhn et al., "The impact of the SARS-CoV-2 pandemic on tourists' personal prestige – an experimental study," *International Journal of Culture, Tourism and Hospitality Research* 16, no. 1 (2021): 238–58, https://doi.org/10.1108/ijcthr-02-2021-0035.

46. imark, "Aktuelle imark Studie: Wahrnehmung Tirols bleibt positiv stabil," 2021, accessed Feb. 21, 2023, https://imark.at/de/markenwahrnehmung-tirol/.

47. Robert Steiger et al., "Die Covid-19 Pandemie als Treiber von Innovationen in der Tourismusbranche? Ein Fallbeispiel der niederösterreichischen Bergbahnen," *Zeitschrift für Tourismuswissenschaft* 13, no. 3 (2021): 405–22, https://doi.org/10.1515/tw-2021-0030.

48. Jeetesh Kumar and Anshul Garg, "Covid-19 Vs. Overtourism: Challenges or Opportunities for Tourist Destinations: Theoretical Perspective," in *Overtourism as Destination Risk,* ed. Anukrati Sharma and Azizul Hassan (Bingley: Emerald Publishing Limited, 2021), 263–74.

49. Hans Hopfinger and Nadine Scharfenort, "Overtourism: Ein wegen der Covid-19 Pandemie aus der Zeit gefallenes Phänomen?," *Berichte: Geographie und Landeskunde* 94, no. 3 (2021): 179–85.

50. Dimitri Ioannides and Szilvia Gyimóthy, "The Covid-19 crisis as an opportunity for escaping the unsustainable global tourism path," *Tourism Geographies* 22, no. 3 (2020): 624–32, https://doi.org/10.1080/14616688.2020.1763445.

51. Freya Higgins-Desbiolles, "The "war over tourism:" challenges to sustainable tourism in the tourism academy after Covid-19," *Journal of Sustainable Tourism* 29, no. 4 (2020): 551–69, https://doi.org/10.1080/09669582.2020.1803334.

52. Bruce Prideaux et al., "Lessons from Covid-19 can prepare global tourism for the economic transformation needed to combat climate change," *Tourism Geographies* 22, no. 3 (2020): 667–78, https://doi.org/10.1080/14616688.2020.1762117.

53. Girish Prayag, "Time for Reset? Covid-19 and Tourism Resilience," *Tourism Review International* 24, no. 2 (2020): 179–84, https://doi.org/10.3727/154427220x15926147793595.

54. Seongsoo Jang and Jinwon Kim, "Remedying Airbnb Covid-19 disruption through tourism clusters and community resilience," *J Bus Res 139* (2022): 529–42, https://doi.org/10.1016/j.jbusres.2021.10.015.

55. Higgins-Desbiolles, "The "war over tourism";" Marianna Sigala, "Tourism and Covid-19: Impacts and implications for advancing and resetting industry and research," *J Bus Res* 117 (2020): 312–21, https://doi.org/10.1016/j.jbusres.2020.06.015.

56. Stefan Gössling and Nadja Schweiggart, "Two years of Covid-19 and tourism: what we learned, and what we should have learned," *Journal of Sustainable Tourism* 30, no. 4 (2022): 915–31, https://doi.org/10.1080/09669582.2022.2029872.

57. Nikos Ntounis et al. "Tourism and Hospitality industry resilience during the Covid-19 pandemic: Evidence from England," *Current Issues in Tourism* 25, no. 1 (2021): 46–59, https://doi.org/10.1080/13683500.2021.1883556; David Weaver et al., "Pragmatic engagement with the wicked tourism problem of climate change through 'soft' transformative governance," *Tourism Management* 93, 104573 (2022), https://doi.org/10.1016/j.tourman.2022.104573.

58. International Labour Organization, "The future of work in the tourism sector."

59. Nadine Grieger et al., "Die Arbeitsmarktlage in der Gastronomie," 2022, accessed Mar. 6, 2023, http://www.ams.at/content/dam/download/arbeitsmarktdaten/österreich/berichte-auswertungen/001_spezialthema_0522.pdf.

60. Susanne Becken and Kenneth F. Hughey, "Impacts of changes to business travel practices in response to the Covid-19 lockdown in New Zealand," *Journal of Sustainable Tourism* 30, no. 1 (2021): 108–27, https://doi.org/10.1080/09669582.2021.1894160.

61. Susanne Becken and Johanna Loehr, "Asia–Pacific tourism futures emerging from Covid-19 recovery responses and implications for sustainability," *Journal of Tourism Futures* (2022), https://doi.org/10.1108/jtf-05-2021-0131.

62. Mauricio Carvache-Franco et al., "Motivations and Loyalty of the Demand for Adventure Tourism as Sustainable Travel," *Sustainability* 14, no. 14 (2022), https://doi.org/10.3390/su14148472; Karolin Schmidt et al., "Covid-19 – A window of opportunity for the transition toward sustainable mobility?," *Transp Res Interdiscip Perspect* 10, 100374 (2021), https://doi.org/10.1016/j.trip.2021.100374.

63. Federal German Ministry of Food and Agriculture, "Trend zur Steigerung der Nachfrage nach Bio-Produkten hält weiter an," 2022, accessed Feb. 28, 2023, https://www.bmel.de/SharedDocs/Pressemitteilungen/DE/2022/20-oeko-barometer-2021.html; Federal Austrian Ministry of Agriculture, Forestry, Regions and Water Management, "Nachfrage nach Bio-Lebensmitteln steigt," accessed Jan. 9, 2023, https://info.bml.gv.at/themen/lebensmittel/lebensmittel-in-oesterreich/biowachstum.html.

64. Mölk et al., "Radicalization and attenuation in the construction of tourism employment images."

65. Amt der Oberösterreichischen Landesregierung, "Oberösterreich – Tourismusstrategie 2022," accessed Jan. 9, 2023, https://www.land-oberoesterreich.gv.at/101574.htm; Hubert Siller et al., "Der Tiroler Weg:

Perspektiven für eine verantwortungsvolle Tourismusentwicklung," 2021, accessed Feb. 2, 2023, https://www.tirolwerbung.at/_Resources/Persistent/f/a/b/7/fab7b0004fcf117a589b4bd8622d57568ecc7d23/Tiroler%20Weg%20NEU.pdf.

66. Sarah Schönherr et al., "Attitudes not set in stone: Existential crises changing residents' irritation," *Tourism Management* 96, 104708 (2023), https://doi.org/10.1016/j.tourman.2022.104708.

67. Ibid.

68. Birgit Pikkemaat et al., "Needs, drivers and barriers of innovation: The case of an alpine community-model destination," *Tourism Management Perspectives* 25, (2018): 53–63, https://doi.org/10.1016/j.tmp.2017.11.004.

69. Steiger et al., "Die Covid-19 Pandemie als Treiber von Innovationen in der Tourismusbranche?"

70. Ibid.

Conspiracy Theories in Austria during the Pandemic

Claus Oberhauser

Conspiracy theories are much more visible in times of crisis and are one means of understanding the world.[1] It is probably all too human to explain the inexplicable through the actions of secret powers in the underground and background. The Covid-19 crisis was and is a great challenge for society, politics, and living together in solidarity. Families split over discussions about vaccinations and the question of who is to blame for the disaster. People took to the streets worldwide to protest against measures and demand freedom of speech. Others have accused these people of acting anti-democratically. In Austria, reports of antisemitic incidents have increased in the wake of these protests.[2] Observers of the protests were aware that a radicalized group compared measures to the Nazi regime and grossly trivialized the Holocaust.[3] By no means did all protesters go that far, and by no means were all of them conspiracy theorists. The demonstrators are a very heterogeneous grouping, held together not by one conspiracy theory but by their rejection of the measures and criticism of the government based on discontent, distrust, and various conspiracy theories. However, many people were and still are driven by what is known in research as the underlying cognitive paradox of "believing in nothing, believing in everything." This distrust mindset consists of trusting so-called official facts less than "alternative facts," relying more on one's intuition, and lacking intellectual humility. These people also believe more in conspiracy theories.[4]

Distrust was also the dominant topic in political communication in Austria in the last few years. The resignation of Chancellor Sebastian Kurz due to allegations of corruption and political pressure in connection with social discord over the measures shows a pronounced and empirically measurable distrust in Austrian democracy.[5] Almost inevitably, this development led not only to the founding of a new party (MFG), but also, at least in terms of rhetoric, to a radicalization of a populist opposition party, namely the Freedom Party of Austria (FPÖ). Right-wing populism and conspiracy thinking seem to go hand in hand in Austria.

This essay aims to describe what constitutes conspiracy thinking in general and in Austria. Furthermore, the role of the different actors and the conspiratorial discourses will be analyzed as well as the connection between conspiracy thinking and populism in Austria.

Conspiracy Theory—Definition?

There are a variety of definitions of the concept of conspiracy theory and also different discourse positions: scientific definitions, popular scientific explanations, journalistic interpretations, and counter-definitions of people who are branded conspiracy theorists. I was a member of the COST-Action COMPACT with over one hundred active participants and co-author of a guide on conspiracy theories.[6] I define conspiracy theories as interpretations of developments, conditions, and events that can be traced back to a conspiracy. Accordingly, the current crisis for a conspiracy theorist results from the implementation of a secret plan devised by evil forces or agents. In research, following Michael Barkun, three constants are distinguished: one, nothing is as it seems; two, everything is connected; and three, nothing happens by accident.[7]

The goal is to track down the secret plan and expose the evil forces. Conspiracy theories question a so-called official narrative based on the constant "nothing is as it seems." Conspiracy believers are convinced system media promulgates an official narrative that is not true. Accordingly, these media can be assumed to be lying ("*Lügenpresse*"). In German-speaking countries, a debate has arisen since March 2020 about whether the addition of "theory" has validity. The debate has been going on in research for quite some time, but it was only a side issue.[8] Due to the Covid-19 crisis and the resulting rejection of vaccinations by a part of the German-speaking population that tends to believe in conspiracy theories, a debate arose about the scientification of a phenomenon that, according to the opinion of journalists in particular, is directly opposed to scientific knowledge. Notable here is the role of Ingrid Brodnig, an expert in social media who is very well-known in Austria and Germany. She is the author of a widely acclaimed popular science book on talking to conspiracy believers.[9] She is a vehement advocate of the approach that the addition of theory suggests scientificity. She advocates using the term conspiracy myth. Also strongly received in Austrian media is Pia Lamberty, a psychologist. In a popular science book written by her and Katharina Nocun, they argued for the term conspiracy narrative for the same reasons as Brodnig.[10]

This confusion of terms is problematic. Following the German expert Michael Butter, he suggests continuing to use the term in order to not promote a split in society. Those who "speak of 'conspiracy theories' acknowledge that conspiracy theorists and non-conspiracy theorists alike are concerned with understanding the world."[11] Moreover, if someone stops using the term because it suggests scientificity, he/she argues against the scientific consensus. That should never be the case, especially in times of scientific skepticism.

Peter Knight, who is one of the most renowned experts in the field of research on conspiracy theories, points out the major problem regarding the use of "conspiracy theory" in the following statement: "The term 'Conspiracy Theory' often acts as an insult itself, an accusation of unsophisticated … thinking that verges on the mentally disturbed."[12] This means that the term has a negative connotation and is therefore in no way an upgrade.

People resist being called conspiracy theorists because of this negative bias. It is precisely this fact that can be exploited to reinterpret the term. One example is the microbiologist Sucharit Bhakdi, one of the best known opponents of measures in Germany and Austria. At the pandemic's beginning, he became prominent through a public letter to the then-German Chancellor Angela Merkel. In the Austrian public, he was very present on the private television station servusTV. With his wife, a university professor of biochemistry, Bhakdi wrote a bestseller in which he confronted the political handling of the pandemic. In the book, which sold very well in Austria, the authors wrote about the term conspiracy theory, saying that it means nothing other than knowledge that does not suit the government.[13]

Another example concerns the most effective Austrian alternative medium in terms of reach during the pandemic: the internet television station AUF1. Its founder Stefan Magnet, no stranger to the Austrian right-wing extremist scene, is trying to position his station as an alternative medium that, unlike the system media, guarantees freedom of opinion. Critics accuse Magnet and his station of making antisemitic and conspiratorial statements. He counters this by calling the terms "antisemitism" and "conspiracy theory" a framing to suppress him and his station.[14]

In summary, there are various approaches to defining the concept of conspiracy theory. Apart from the terminology, it is essential to evaluate the phenomenon similarly. The more accurate the description of the phenomenon, the more likely one is to face the described reinterpretations.

Salient Conspiracy Theories in Austria

Were there any conspiracy theories in the pandemic that were specifically Austrian? That can be answered in the negative with certainty. Overall, the conspiracy theory discourse was very similar in Western countries, which means that the main strands were stable. In a more extensive study, the authors found, however, that the respective context or the reaction of the persons to conspiracy theories was quite different depending on the cultural context.[15]

The most dominant conspiracy theories in Austrian discourse build on pre-pandemic antecedents. In this respect, the pandemic is a catalyst for previously developed ideas. Conspiracy theories do not simply fall from the sky but dock onto discourses. That means that a cultural archive of conspiracy theories can be retrieved at a given time.[16] Here one should speak of the so-called occasion relatedness of conspiracy theories. Furthermore, this cultural archive was less socially and medially present and visible before the pandemic. That is why many people were surprised by the sudden emergence of these thoughts.[17]

One of the most discussed conspiracy theories of the pandemic, which received broad approval in Austria based on quantitative studies, is the most controversial one.[18] Many people were concerned about what and where the origin of the pandemic was. Very soon, rumors about the coronavirus as a bioweapon arose. That builds on the fact that a laboratory in Wuhan studied coronaviruses. The exciting aspect of this theory is its epistemic status. When US President Trump vaguely announced in 2020 that he had received intelligence indications that China was withholding the truth about the origin, the uproar was tremendous, and Trump was accused of spreading a conspiracy theory. When Biden became president in January 2021, some scientists commented in prominent journals that the possibility that the virus originated in the lab should not be ruled out. As a result, a delegation of scientists was sent to China by the WHO to investigate the various theories of the origin of the virus. The authors of the report about their findings classified the laboratory theory as extremely unlikely.[19] Nevertheless, various studies and scientists continued to suggest that studies on the laboratory theory should be pursued. This theory only becomes conspiratorial if one assumes that the virus is deliberately directed against the (European) population as a bioweapon. Consequently, conspiracy theorists would interpret the pandemic as a hoax to distract from the true intentions of the powerful who invented the weapon.

Hoax and Liars

A widespread conspiratorial view in Austria, Germany, and Switzerland was and is the conviction that the virus is not dangerous, that vaccination is harmful, and that there may not be a pandemic at all. Conspiracy theories about vaccination have been on the rise for quite some time. Historically, they have antecedents in the late eighteenth century.[20] Such theories are widespread in esoteric groups and alternative media platforms. Even before the pandemic, the Bill and Melinda Gates Foundation was suspected of operating secretly.[21]

Concerning these conspiracy theory beliefs, some scientists played a prominent role. In particular, the aforementioned Sucharit Bhakdi became a VIP in this scene in Austria. It should be emphasized that it is not science per se that is being questioned all the time; instead, people claim that the virologists working for the government are either lying or bought agents. The same conviction can be applied to the harsh questioning of what conspiracy believers call the system press or the lying press. These media are accused of being bought and of spreading disinformation. Although the term lying press has a historical equivalent, its current form derives from the usage of members of the PEGIDA protest movement about the European refugee crisis.[22]

Globalists, Plans, and Replacements

According to the 2020 GLOBSEC study shortly before the pandemic, Austria did well in terms of conspiracy thinking compared to other Central and Eastern European countries.[23] However, the study authors highlighted that one specific conspiracy theory had a high approval rate in Austria: 42 percent of respondents assumed Austria is insidiously and secretly Islamized. The Freedom Party of Austria has fueled this discourse for several years. During the protests from 2020, especially in Vienna, it became clear that far-right groups were docking their conspiracy theories to this belief. For many years, the belief that the white European population is being replaced has been a powerfully effective conspiracy theory in German-speaking right-wing extremism.[24] Initially, the concept of "*Umvolkung*," based on the so-called "Kalergi Plan," played a significant role in right-wing extremism after 1945. In 2011, the publication of the book *Le Grand Remplacement* by the French author Renaud Camus brought the new term into the vernacular of the New Right.[25] Mainly due to the so-called refugee crisis from 2014/15, the term the Great Replacement has become virulent. Depending on the context, various collectives, such as the EU or the Davos Economic Forum, as well as investors such as George Soros or diffuse Jewish bankers, are named as the originators of this alleged exchange. The umbrella term "globalists" has become established as a code word. For an outsider, globalists seems not to be a far-right term. Only through the context does it become clear what or who this cipher refers to.

Strongly associated with this discursive strand are conspiracy theory notions of a so-called "*Plandemie*." Supporters of this theory assume that the pandemic has been planned by global elites for some time in order to bring about changes that are in their interests. Among other things, fears of (state) surveillance, disciplining, and punishment become visible. These are old ideas regarding the allegedly endangered individual's freedom. Ideas about the so-called Great Reset, blamed on the Davos Economic Forum, trend in the same direction. The Great Reset is interpreted as a secret plan to subjugate (Austrian) society.[26] These ideas are based on conspiracy theories that emerged in Western societies in the 1990s referring to the so-called New World Order, which allegedly takes the place of the Cold War order. The New World Order is seen as a secret elite world government that seeks to bring people under its control. This conspiracy theory has roots in religious movements in the USA and was carried into the German-speaking countries through books of the right-wing esoteric Jan Udo Holey.[27]

QAnon has not been out of the public eye since the pandemic. This movement emerged in 2016/17 and assumes a worldwide conspiracy driven by (Democratic Party) pedophiles. At its core, it comes to a revival of antisemitic blood legends. Donald Trump functions as a savior in this movement. During the pandemic, belief in this conspiracy theory rose in Germany and Austria, but it does not occupy an extraordinarily prominent position.[28] The *lieu de mémoire* of this grouping was the attack on the Capitol in Washington on January 6, 2021, during which the so-called QAnon Shaman attracted international attention. Flags of QAnon were omnipresent at the Austrian protests.[29]

This list and description of Austria's most common conspiracy theories during the pandemic illustrates a wide variety of groupings that by no means have a homogeneous political core. The only thing holding the groups together is the belief that the official version of the pandemic is inaccurate and that certain elites are up to something else. Research shows that these convinced conspiracy believers tended to reject the vaccination and, since fall 2021, became quite radicalized, and the overall mood became more extreme than before.[30]

Austrian Conspiracy Theorists and the Protests

First, conspiracy theorists were only one group among the protesters against the measures. That is an important finding that has often been overlooked in the discourse. Research on populist movements has already shown that conspiracy theorists and so-called "normal" citizens protested side by side.[31]

Second, right-wing extremists did not infiltrate the protests, but these groups were there from the beginning and loudly used their media presence. No demonstration came without a report about the right-wing extremist slogans and flags. Particularly highlighted in the media were the repeatedly convicted Holocaust denier Gottfried Küssel and the right-wing extremist Martin Sellner, founder of the Identitarian Movement Austria.[32]

Third, protests, so-called "hygiene demonstrations" against the measures, began very early in the pandemic in Germany. The "*Querdenker*" Movement, which was the driving factor behind the protests, became the focus of public attention.[33]

After the large demonstrations in Berlin in the second half of 2020, the movement also began to pick up speed in Austria in the fall. The large demonstrations were held in Vienna. Initially, the demonstrations were not organized by political parties but by individuals. Several groups were working together. In addition to Küssel and Sellner, for example Martin Rutter, a former politician and founder of a group of "*Querdenker,*" and Hannes Brejcha, who is known for his conspiratorial statements, should be mentioned. A bus company that organized trips to demonstrations, esoteric associations, and sects also played a role.[34] These groupings were never self-contained, and the founders of the respective subgroups also fell out several times. Due to the interventions by the parties mentioned above, the demonstrations developed in a radical direction. The Freedom Party of Austria, in particular, gave those individuals and groupings a stage. That was an attempt to exploit this electoral potential, which is described in more detail below.

The protests became more aggressive after the announcement by then-Chancellor Alexander Schallenberg in November 2021 that mandatory vaccination would be implemented due to under-vaccination rates. In this process, the discourse changed. Conspiracy theories were even more in the foreground, and during the weekly demonstrations, people were aggressive. The law would have gone into effect on February 5, 2022, after most of the members of the National Council voted in favor of it. However, it was not implemented, and the law was temporarily suspended. In June 2022, it was repealed entirely. After the suspension of the law, the demonstrations suddenly became fewer. However, some people from these groups started to defend Putin concerning Russia's war of aggression on Ukraine since February 2022. It turns out that the war by no means has the same appeal for conspiracy believers as Covid-19 and, especially, the vaccination policy.

A study by sociologists at the University of Basel of protesters in southern Germany and to some extent Austria clearly shows what was formative for these people. Right-wing extremism was not the initial focus here, but protesters were often disappointed Green Party voters. These people no longer saw themselves represented by their actual party.[35] Some stated that they would vote for another party in the next election. Furthermore, conspiracy theories were the driving force behind these attitudes. The study also addressed the very present esoteric groups, which felt particularly challenged about mandatory vaccination. Due to the increasing radicalization in 2021, leftists, rightists, and esotericists came together more and more. They formed a movement that can best be described as a new *Querfront*, as Michael Butter put it.[36] That term can be used to describe a movement characterized, above all, by the fact that it is assumed as common ground that democracy in this form no longer functions.

In addition, this agreement and the strong rejection by the opposing side led to a group polarization and a move to more extreme opinions. Butter assumes that the measurably increasing antisemitic incidents can be traced back to this narrative. Accordingly, wearing the Nazi's yellow star forced on Jews with the word "unvaccinated," equating the measures with persecution under Nazism, and comparing the measures to Nazi policies would be extreme examples of this group expressing that democracy seems to be abolished for them. It is obvious that right-wing extremists used this stage: relativizations of the Nazi regime were on full display, and much more publicly than before, under the guise of the freedom of speech. The many court cases in Austria against the *National Socialism Prohibition Act* ("*Verbotsgesetz*") clearly show that the convicted persons are often not aware of the seriousness of their expressions and assume that they are simply making their displeasure known.[37] In response, the *Prohibition Act* will be amended in the future in Austria.[38]

Furthermore, the surveys of demonstration participants in Austria within the framework of the Austria Corona Panel project should be highlighted. Within this group, it is clear that the approval of conspiracy theories is high (regarding Bill Gates's involvement, for example, 39 percent). Conspiracy theorists downplay Covid-19 and its consequences. They firmly pronounce esoteric thinking and hostility to science, and the disapproval of populist parties against measures is high. As stated at the beginning of the text, the surveys confirm that these people rely on their intuition. Furthermore, the findings indicate that people trust so-called anecdotal evidence more than official narrative statistics.[39] Concerning the (social) construction of truth, conspiracy theorists equate the subjective/anecdotal with statistics, whose goal is the dissolution of the individual. This anecdotal evidence is the antagonist of Covid-19 politics based on the advice of virologists.[40]

The Role of Alternative and Social Media

Since March 2020, alternative and social media have become more of a focus in Austria. In particular, politically right-wing and extreme right-wing media gratefully took up the heated Covid-19 discourse and established themselves as media that offered a stage for conspiracy theories. Among others, the magazine or internet portal *Wochenblick* deserves special mention. The transition from reports about the allegedly false Covid-19 policy to the conspiracy-theoretical interpretation of the war in Ukraine was seamless. *Wochenblick* focuses strongly on the Great Reset and links, for example, the UN's Sustainable Development Goals to the New World Order.[41]

Of course, this is only one example among many; during the pandemic, a tangled network of associations, party-affiliated organizations, and activities on social media formed.[42] At the beginning of the pandemic, when there were more rumors than conspiracy theories, WhatsApp, Facebook, and YouTube were still important media for spreading disinformation. Later on, however, these forums shifted to Telegram channels after the de-platforming of offensive content from the major media providers. Overall, social media and the internet help disinformation spread quickly; people can exchange information much more rapidly and find a group that shares their thoughts. The shift to Telegram channels has had two effects: on the one hand, group polarization can be determined by analyzing the content of the messages. On the other hand, authorities easily monitor such groups.[43]

During the pandemic, the private television station servusTV took on a unique role. In contrast to the public media, it styled itself as the only critical voice regarding Covid-19 policy and the danger of the virus. Controversial guests such as the aforementioned Sucharit Bhakdi were invited to the studio for discussion. When the latter was awarded the mockery prize "*Das Goldene Brett vorm Kopf*" for unscientific downplaying of the pandemic in December 2020, a significant discussion about so-called false-balancing, i.e., the scientific majority opinion not accurately represented in media by inviting people who disagree, arose in Austria as a result.[44] Despite all the criticism of servusTV, ratings rose during the pandemic.[45] In debates based on a recently published book, the philosopher Richard David Precht, who is very well known in Germany and Austria, argued that there was a lot to be learned from servusTV in terms of reporting, as critical voices were not heard enough during the pandemic.[46] Although there is some merit to this argument, it cannot be denied that people who believe in conspiracy theories about the pandemic increasingly drew their information from servusTV, as the Austria Corona Panel project can show.[47]

The aforementioned private internet TV station AUF1, founded by Stefan Magnet in 2021, occupies a prominent position. From the start, AUF1 was characterized by radicalized false balancing, presenting only opinions that differed from the scientific consensus. AUF1 also applies this to their coverage of the war in Ukraine. In addition, those responsible for the program are more concerned with pointing out possible mistakes made by the public media than with informing the audience.

In his comments, Magnet styles himself as a fighter for freedom of expression. Several analysts point out that he frequently uses antisemitic code words in ciphers. During the Covid-19 protests in Austria, it became increasingly clear that AUF1 appealed greatly to conspiracy believers: banners, posters, and stickers could be found anywhere at the demonstrations in

2021. CeMAS, a German think tank that monitors right-wing conspiracy theorists, showed in an analysis that AUF1 quickly became one of the most followed alternative media in the German-speaking regions.[48] Due to lawsuits, however, the station's future is in doubt.

Alternative media and servusTV thus positioned themselves as diametrically opposed to the official narrative, which, it was claimed, was presented by the "mainstream media." ServusTV opened the discourse to critical and, as it turned out, highly problematic voices. Other alternative media went a step further and radicalized the discourse.

Politics and Populism

Michael Butter recently assumed that the German-speaking countries, Germany, Austria, and Switzerland, have been shaped by the German discourse in the majority and show very similar strands.[49] This argument has to be modified insofar as the political exploitation of the Covid-19 protests was much more robust in Austria than in Germany due to the longer populist tradition. Austria's Freedom Party was and is a model for German opposition parties. The second modification concerns the Austrian corruption scandal. During the Covid-19 protests, the slogan "Kurz must go" could already be heard everywhere. In the course of the investigation into the 2019 Ibiza affair, referring to the publication of a video showing the then-Vice Chancellor of the Republic and federal party chairman of the Freedom Party of Austria Heinz Christian Strache and Johann Gudenus negotiating influence peddling in Austrian politics and media with a fictitious Russian oligarch's daughter, cell phones of actors allegedly involved were seized by the judiciary.[50] The analysis of chats led to the indictment of leading politicians of the Austrian People's Party (ÖVP) and employees of ministries for corruption. Among others, Chancellor Sebastian Kurz resigned as a result of the accusations. Accordingly, the support in society for the current government was and is not strong. Studies indicate that, overall, trust in democracy has declined as a result of these two problematic situations— Covid-19 and the political scandal.[51] That is a crucial factor in terms of belief in conspiracy theories.[52] Whether the decline of democratic consciousness goes hand in hand with the poorly developed scientific consciousness in Austrian society is currently the subject of a large-scale study. Conspiracy theories certainly play a role to be determined in detail.[53]

The opposition parties were not opposed to the given political discourse at the pandemic's beginning. For example, representatives of the Freedom Party of Austria even called for faster action concerning a general lockdown. It very soon became clear that the then-*Klubobmann* Herbert Kickl, in particular, was willing to take a radical course about the government's Covid-19 policy since 2021.

Outside these circles, however, a new party developed in Austria that deliberately targeted protest voters with regard to the handling of Covid-19 politics. The MFG (People, Freedom, Fundamental Rights) party was founded in February 2021. For example, the medical doctor Christian Fiala, who had already spoken out publicly at the beginning of the pandemic as a significant critic of the measures and founder of interest groups in this regard, is a prominent member of the new party.[54] Initially, the established parties did not take the MFG seriously, as it was assumed that more than the counter-position against measures alone would be needed to achieve success. However, the Upper Austrian Election in September 2021 changed the attitude towards the party: MFG succeeded in winning three mandates, which caused shock waves among the established parties and media. After minor successes in further local elections, the trend is now emerging that members are falling out among themselves and that building up a functioning structure is nearly impossible. Since its founding, the party has also had to contend with the fact that some supporters express conspiracy theories and radical and inhumane positions on social media.[55]

The Freedom Party of Austria seems to be uniting the protesting electorate under their command. That is strongly linked to the rise of Herbert Kickl. He was a speaker at a large demonstration in March 2021, which marked the beginning of the radicalization of the demonstrations. In his speech, Kickl expressed solidarity with people the government allegedly branded as those with "tin foil hats"—a disrespectful, satirical designation of conspiracy theorists. In a highly populist expression, Kickl contrasts these individuals with the executive organs of the government as wearers of "steel helmets."[56] This closing of ranks with conspiracy theorists meant that the extreme right-wing groups within the demonstrations were endorsed. Observers of this and later speeches stated that antisemitic remarks were heard in the audience.[57] The radical course of the Freedom Party of Austria, driven by Kickl, was criticized in the strongest terms by other major parties. After federal party chairman Norbert Hofer resigned, Kickl became his successor on June 19 2021, cementing this course. At the demonstrations in the fall and winter of 2021, it became increasingly apparent that the Freedom Party of Austria was claiming leadership of the movement. In addition, Kickl reclaimed the repulsion of the mandatory vaccination law because of his interventions and the pressure built by the Freedom Party of Austria.

Kickl's rise is a lesson in the connection between populism and conspiracy theories.[58] Kickl styled himself as the leader of a strongly anti-elitist movement. He insinuated that the elites collaborated with foreign powers to act against their people. In his speeches, Kickl repeatedly invoked will and intuition as the guiding principles of the common man: the virus is not a dangerous disease, but the system that makes the common man sick. Since this movement does not correspond to a precise political classification and there are several groups, such as esoteric conspiracy theorists or right-wing extremists among them, Kickl operated with what Ruth Wodak called calculated ambivalence by deliberately addressing various code words and not rejecting radical statements in the audience.[59] Of course, whether this will lead to success is written in the stars. However, the survey results suggest that the Freedom Party of Austria can count on success in the next elections.

Paranoia Paradigm

During the pandemic, it became clear that a discourse of conspiracy theory research, which is quite important, is hardly mentioned anymore. There is a connection between conspiracy theory panic and conspiracy panic.[60] There is the side that immediately shouts "conspiracy theory!" without questioning. Moreover, there is the other side, which behind the scenes and under the surface, always sees conspiracies. Both sides are mutually exclusive. Conspiracy theory panic can have disastrous consequences, following Räikkä and Basham[61] or Dentith.[62] First, real conspiracies and corruption may no longer be uncovered. Second, it can prevent vigilance against or justified criticism of the state and government actions. Third, intellectuals could be silenced because people no longer dare to say anything to express something deviant. The third point, in particular, is problematic: it is also a question of who is considered an expert and who is not. Räikkä and Basham claim that conspiracy theories are not a de-plausibility from the outset but should be examined according to scientific and, thus, objective standards.[63]

Many views on conspiracy theories in society assume that a critique takes on a "normal" position. Calling someone a conspiracy theorist can solidify such a position following the sociology of knowledge. Understanding conspiracy theorists as bearers of heterodox knowledge, they appear stigmatized and de-legitimized. One of the essential texts in conspiracy theory research cited as a reference by many journalists in recent years takes a look at this: Richard Hofstadter's *The Paranoid Style in American Politics* (1964)[64] has become an iconic text. In his analysis, he stated that conspiracy theorists follow a paranoid style and are a phenomenon at the fringes of society. Mark Fenster criticized Hofstadter for taking the position of a liberal consensus historian and marginalizing an entire group of people while accusing them of paranoid thinking.[65] According to Dentith, studies and many journalistic texts on conspiracy thinking are still based on Hofstadter's concept.[66] In a recent article in *Nature*, the anthropologist Elżbieta Drążkiewicz shows that scientists in this field still tend to follow the paranoia paradigm by being interested in what traits conspiracy believers exhibit that distinguishes them from the "normal" person defined by the scientist: "Many, myself included, want to defend democracy and science, so it is easy to define those who embrace conspiracy theories as a threat or enemy. However, that deflects researchers' attention to individuals and their beliefs and stops them looking at the systems that push people towards conspiratorial circles." This stigmatization of the alleged conspiracy believer as a threat to society and democracy was a significant issue in the Austrian discourse. The fact that conspiracy theories, radicalization, and extremism go hand in hand has been proven by various studies. However, simply stating that conspiracy theories are dangerous is problematic because it can further drive social polarization. It is essential to examine why different people turn away from established media, politicians, and social conventions. Advice centers and helplines in Austria have registered that they have received significantly more reports of conspiracy believers in the family environment since March 2020. In this regard, the factor of media popularity should not be underestimated: conspiracy theories have been omnipresent in media discourse since the start of the pandemic in Austria. Quantitative studies generally do not find a significant increase in conspiracy believers compared to pre-pandemic studies. Thus, the more the phenomenon was reported, the more conspiracy believers became visible. Michael Butter assumes that conspiracy theory thinking was already present in many people before the pandemic without being noticed in the family.

Conclusion

Although the alternative media mentioned in the text primarily uses the Russian war of aggression as an opportunity to spread Russian propaganda, downplay, or even justify the war, the grouping that constituted the Covid-19 protests has noticeably become much smaller. Does this now mean that the suspected radicalization of the group of protesters driven by conspiracy theories was exaggerated by the media, concerned scientists, and intelligence agencies? No, this is by no means true. We as a society must learn that conspiracy theories are now more visible and are not an exception but are more common than we would like to admit. The general solution to the problem is by no means to draw a red line between one side and the other.

First, instead of specifying a conspiracy theorist's psychological characteristics in contrast to a "normal" person, focusing on the social conditions that lead people to believe in conspiracy theories is necessary. That is an urgent task of ethnographic, historical, sociological, and political research.

Second, suggesting that someone believes in a conspiracy theory and is on the other side of society is far too shallow an analysis. In this context, taking a closer look at qualitative gradations is vital. What strategies do right-wing extremist conspiracy theorists use? How do they use social and alternative media? Why do they appeal to parts of society?

Third, the connection between conspiracy theories, discontent in society due to disconnectedness and no political equivalent, and the rise of right-wing populism in Austria need to be much more closely examined by researchers and society. Conspiracy theories are widespread in (political) extremism. It must be a common goal of a democratically minded society to expose radical ideas and prevent people from incorporating them into their lives.

Fourth, alternative media and extremist positions should be given much less space in public discussion. Strengthening independent so-called quality media should be a priority goal of a democratic society. Coverage of the protests was characterized by an often merely general assessment of the situation as conspiratorial and an emphasis on far-right representations. Alternative media used this and showed a different truth, accusing the established media of lying. Strengthening quality media, especially critical and reflective attitudes, and teaching media literacy, should be valued and worth protecting for society. The pandemic should be a lesson on how to avoid alarmism and sensationalism in the future.

Endnotes

1. Jan-Willem van Prooijen and Karen M. Douglas, "Conspiracy Theories as Part of History: The Role of Societal Crisis Situations," *Memory Studies* 10 no. 3 (2017): 323–333, https://doi.org/10.1177/1750698017701615.

2. "Noch nie so viele Übergriffe," *Öffentliche Sicherheit* 7–8 (2022): 60.

3. Vanessa Gaig and Johannes Pucher, "Zehntausende bei Demo gegen Coronamaßnahmen: Rechtsextreme als Anführer," *Der Standard*, Nov. 20, 2021, accessed Jan. 27, 2023, https://www.derstandard.at/story/2000131307965/zehntausende-bei-demo-gegen-corona-massnahmen-rechtsextreme-als-anfuehrer.

4. Devora Newman et al., "Believing in Nothing and Believing in Everything: The Underlying Cognitive Paradox of Anti-Covid-19 Vaccine Attitudes," *Personality and Individual Differences* 189 (2022): 111522, https://doi.org/10.1016/j.paid.2022.111522.

5. SORA, *Multiple Krisen: Demokratie unter Druck* (2022), https://www.demokratiemonitor.at/wp-content/uploads/2022/11/2022_SORA_Presseunterlage_Demokratiemonitor.pdf.

6. COMPACT Education Group, *Guide to Conspiracy Theories* (2020), https://conspiracytheories.eu/_wpx/wp-content/uploads/2020/03/COMPACT_Guide-2.pdf.

7. Michael Barkun, *A Culture of Conspiracy: Apocalyptic Visions in Contemporary America* (Berkley: University of California Press, 2003), 3–4.

8. Armin Pfahl-Traughber, ""Bausteine" zu einer Theorie über "Verschwörungstheorien:" Definitionen, Erscheinungsformen, Funktionen und Ursachen," in *Verschwörungstheorien: Theorie – Geschichte – Wirkung*, ed. Helmut Reinalter (Innsbruck: Studienverlag, 2002), 30–45.

9. Ingrid Brodnig, *Einspruch! Verschwörungsmythen und Fake News kontern – in der Familie, im Freundeskreis und online* (Vienna: Brandstätter, 2021).

10. Katharina Nocun and Pia Lamberty, *Fake Facts: Wie Verschwörungstheorien unser Denken bestimmen* (Cologne: Quadriga, 2020).

11. Michael Butter, "Verschwörungstheorien: Eine Einführung," *Aus Politik und Zeitgeschichte: Verschwörungstheorien* 71, no. 35–36 (2021): 4–11 (here 7). "Wer dagegen von "Verschwörungstheorien" spricht, erkennt an, dass es

Verschwörungstheoretiker*innen wie Nichtverschwörungstheoretiker*innen darum geht, die Welt zu verstehen (my translation)."

12. Peter Knight, *Conspiracy Culture: From Kennedy to the X Files* (New York: Routledge, 2000), 11.

13. Sucharit Bhakdi and Karina Reiß, *Corona Fehlalarm? Zahlen, Daten und Hintergründe* (Berlin: Goldegg, 2020).

14. Florian Zeller, "TV-Sender Auf1: Antisemitismus ist Programm," *Der Standard*, Nov. 2, 2022, accessed Jan. 27, 2023, https://www.derstandard.at/story/2000140238998/tv-sender-auf1-antisemitismus-ist-programm.

15. Elisa J. Sobo and Elżbieta Drążkiewicz, "Rights, Responsibilities and Revelations: Covid-19 Conspiracy Theories and the State," in *Viral Loads Anthropologies of Urgency in the Time of Covid-19*, ed. Lenore Manderson et al. (London: UCL Press, 2021), 67–88.

16. Michael Butter, "Conspiracy Theories in Germany, Austria, and Switzerland," in *Covid Conspiracy Theories in Global Perspective*, ed. Michael Butter and Peter Knight (London / New York: Routledge, 2023), 208–221.

17. Butter, "Verschwörungstheorien," 11.

18. Stephan Lewandowsky et al., "Leak or Leap? Evidence and Cognition Surrounding the Origins of the SARS CoV-2 Virus," in *Covid Conspiracy Theories*, ed. Butter and Knight, 26–40.

19. Jon Cohen, "Call of the Wild: Why So Many Scientists Say It's Unlikely that SARS CoV-2 Originated from a 'lab leak'," *Science* 373 (2021): 1072–1077.

20. Marina Hilber, "Preventing Paralysis: The Use of Inactivated Poliomyelitis Vaccine in Austria, 1955–1960," in *Covid-19 and Pandemics in Austrian History*, ed. Marc Landry and Dirk Rupnov (CAS 32) (New Orleans: UNO Press – innsbruck university press, 2023), pages.

21. Butter, "Conspiracy Theories," 210.

22. Markus Beiler and Johanna Kiesler, ""Lügenpresse! Lying Press!" Is the Press Lying?," in *Trust in Media and Journalism*, ed. Kim Otto and Andreas Köhler (Wiesbaden: Springer VS, 2018), 155–179, https://doi.org/10.1007/978-3-658-20765-6_9.

23. GLOBSEC, *Voices of Central and Eastern Europe Perceptions of Democracy & Governance in 10 EU Countries* (2020), https://www.globsec.org/what-we-do/publications/voices-central-and-eastern-europe-perceptions-democracy-governance-10-eu.

24. Andreas Önnerfors, "'Der Grosse Austausch': Conspiratorial Frames of Terrorist Violence in Germany," in *Europe: Continent of Conspiracies: Conspiracy Theories in and about Europe,* ed. Andreas Önnerfors and Andre Krouwel (London: Routledge, 2021), 76–96.

25. Mattias Ekman, "The Great Replacement: Strategic Mainstreaming of Far-Right Conspiracy Claims," *Convergence* 28, no. 4 (2022): 1127–43, https://doi.org/10.1177/13548565221091983.

26. Clare Birchall and Peter Knight, "A Perfect Storm: Covid-19 Conspiracy Theories in the United States," in *Covid Conspiracy Theories*, ed. Butter and Knight, 335–50 (here 347–48).

27. Eduard Gugenberger, "Die Verschwörung der Außerirdischen," in *Typologien des Verschwörungsdenkens*, ed. Helmut Reinalter (Innsbruck: Studienverlag, 2004), 115–128.

28. CeMAS, *Q Vadis? Zur Verbreitung von QAnon im deutschsprachigen Raum*, (Berlin: 2022), https://cemas.io/publikationen/q-vadis-zur-verbreitung-von-qanon-im-deutschsprachigen-raum/CeMAS_Q_Vadis_Zur_Verbreitung_von_QAnon_im_deutschsprachigen_Raum.pdf.

29. Colette M. Schmidt, "Corona-Demos: Unter gefährlichen Flaggen," *Der Standard*, Nov. 12, 2022, accessed Jan. 27, 2023, https://www.derstandard.at/story/2000133302828/corona-demos-unter-gefaehrlichen-flaggen.

30. Eric Allen Jensen, Axel Pfleger, Lisa Herbig, Brady Wagoner, Lars Lorenz and Meike Watzlawik, "What Drives Belief in Vaccination Conspiracy Theories in Germany?," *Frontiers in Communication* 6 (2021): 1–7, https://doi.org/10.3389/fcomm.2021.678335.

31. Butter, "Conspiracy Theories," 213.

32. Markus Sulzbacher, "Gottfried Küssel, verurteilter Neonazi, als regelmäßiger Teilnehmer bei Corona-Demos," *Der Standard*, Feb. 15, 2021, accessed Jan. 21, 2023, https://www.derstandard.at/story/2000124196510/gottfried-kuessel-verurteilter-neonazi-als-regelmaessiger-teilnehmer-bei-anti-corona.

33. Butter, "Conspiracy Theories," 212.

34. Vanessa Gaig et al., "Die Köpfe hinter den Querdenker-Demos," *Der Standard*, Jan. 15, 2021, accessed Jan. 27, 2023, https://www.derstandard.at/story/2000123339446/die-koepfe-hinter-den-querdenker-demos.

35. Nadine Frei and Oliver Nachtwey, "Wer sind die Querdenker_innen?," in FES E-Papierreihe "Demokratie im Ausnahmezustand. Wie verändert die Coronakrise Recht, Politik und Gesellschaft?" (2021), http://library.

fes.de/pdf-files/dialog/18030.pdf; Nadine Frei and Oliver Nachtwey, "Quellen des 'Querdenkertums:' Eine politische Soziologie der Corona-Proteste in Baden-Württemberg," (2021), http://doi.org/10.31235/osf.io/8f4pb.

36. Michael Butter, "Linke und rechte Verschwörungsgläubige: Die neue Querfront," *Der Spiegel*, Jan. 8, 2021, https://www.spiegel.de/politik/deutschland/linke-und-rechte-verschwoerungsglaeubige-die-neue-querfront-a-00000000-0002-0001-0000-000174784614.

37. "Wiederbetätigung: Freispruch für Angeklagten," Jan. 24, 2023, accessed Jan. 27, 2023, https://salzburg.orf.at/stories/3191519/.

38. "Verbotsgesetz soll reformiert werden," Nov. 14, 2022, accessed Jan. 27, 2023, https://www.derstandard.at/story/2000140796480/regierung-praesentiertreform-des-verbotsgesetz.

39. Noelle S. Lebernegg and Jakob-Moritz Eberl, "Coronavirus Verschwörungstheorien: Gekommen um zu bleiben?," Jun. 7, 2021, https://viecer.univie.ac.at/corona-blog/corona-blog-beitraege/blog118/.

40. Alexander Bogner, *Die Epistemisierung des Politischen: Wie die Macht des Wissens die Demokratie gefährdet* (Stuttgart: Reclam, 2021).

41. "Presserat rügt "wochenblick.at" für Corona Berichterstattung," *Der Standard*, Mar. 11, 2022, accessed Jan. 27, 2023, https://www.derstandard.at/story/2000134021827/presserat-ruegt-wochenblickat-fuer-corona-berichterstattung.

42. Vanessa Gaigg et al., "Anwälte für Aufklärung, Corona-Volksbegehren und "Querdenker": Der organisierte Maßnahmenwiderstand," *Der Standard*, Mar. 10, 2021, accessed Jan. 27, 2023, https://www.derstandard.at/story/2000124786247/das-dichte-netz-der-corona-massnahmenkritiker-und-wer-dahintersteckt.

43. Miro Dittrich and Josef Holnburger, "Nur einen Klick vom Rechtsterror entfernt," Jun. 30, 2021, https://cemas.io/blog/naidoo-telegram/.

44. Srdjan Govedarica, "Ein Sender für Corona-Leugner?," Dez. 20, 2021, accessed Jan. 27, 2023, https://www.tagesschau.de/ausland/europa/servus-tv-corona-101.html.

45. "2021 – Das bislang stärkste Jahr für ServusTV," Dec. 31, 2021, accessed Jan. 27, 2023, https://presse.servustv.com/news-2021-das-bislang-staerkste-jahr-fuer-servustv-?id=147726&menueid=18705&l=öster-

reich. This trend is also evident in 2022.

46. Richard David Precht and Harald Welzer, *Die vierte Gewalt – Wie Mehrheitsmeinung gemacht wird, auch wenn sie keine ist* (Frankfurt/Main: S. Fischer, 2022).

47. Jakob-Moritz Eberl and Noelle S. Lebernegg, "Die alternativen Covid-Realitäten des österreichischen TV-Publikums," Aug. 6, 2021, https://viecer.univie.ac.at/corona-blog/corona-blog-beitraege/blog125/.

48. Jan Rathje, "Verschwörungsideologische Positionierungen zum russischen Angriffskrieg gegen die Ukraine," Mar. 11, 2022, https://cemas.io/blog/positionen-ukraine/.

49. Butter, "Conspiracy Theories."

50. Bastian Obermayer and Frederik Obermaier, *Die Ibiza-Affäre: Innenansichten eines Skandals: Mit einem Vorwort von Armin Wolf* (Cologne: Kiepenheuer & Witsch, 2019).

51. SORA, "Multiple Krisen." Furthermore, the problematic economic situation, the war in Ukraine, and the climate crisis should be mentioned.

52. Jan-Willem van Prooijen, "Empowerment as a Tool to Reduce Belief in Conspiracy Theories," in *Conspiracy Theories and the People Who Believe Them*, ed. Joseph E. Uscinski (New York: Oxford University Press, 2019), 432–442.

53. *Studie zu den Ursachen von Wissenschafts- und Demokratieskepsis in Österreich: IHS legt dem BMBWF vorläufige Ergebnisse vor*, Jan. 3, 2023, https://www.ots.at/presseaussendung/OTS_20230103_OTS0044/studie-zu-den-ursachen-von-wissenschafts-und-demokratieskepsis-in-oesterreich-ihs-legt-dem-bmbwf-vorlaeufige-ergebnisse-vor.

54. Irene Brickner, "Christian Fiala: Ein Arzt läuft gegen den Lockdown Sturm," *Der Standard*, Apr. 27, 2020, accessed Jan. 27, 2023, https://www.derstandard.at/story/2000117128778/ein-arzt-laeuft-gegen-den-lockdown-sturm.

55. Markus Sulzbacher, "Antisemtismus im Umfeld der Impfgegnerpartei MFG," *Der Standard,* Feb. 23, 2022, accessed Jan. 27, 2023, https://www.derstandard.at/story/2000133520111/antisemitismus-im-umfeld-der-impfgegnerpartei-mfg.

56. "Kickl wettert bei Corona-Demos über "Corona-Stahlhelmen" und "Schmuddel-Typen"," Mar. 6, 2021, accessed Jan. 27, 2023, https://www.puls24.at/news/politik/kickl-wettert-bei-corona-demos-ueber-corona-stahlhelmen-und-schmuddel-typen/228741.

57. "Corona-Demos: Zahlreiche Anzeigen und Kickl-Rede bei Jesuitenwiese," OÖ Nachrichten, Mar. 6, 2021, accessed Jan. 27, 2023, https://www.nachrichten.at/panorama/chronik/corona-demos-zahlreiche-anzeigen-und-kickl-rede-bei-jesuitenwiese;art58,3362990.

58. Eiríkur Bergmann and Michael Butter, "Conspiracy Theory and Populism," in *Routledge Handbook of Conspiracy Theories,* ed. Michael Butter and Peter Knight (London: Routledge, 2021), 330–43. Populism research is currently focusing strongly on the connection between the two phenomena.

59. Ruth Wodak, *The Politics of Fear: The Shameless Normalization of Far-Right Discourse*, 2nd ed. (Los Angeles: Sage, 2020).

60. Jack Z. Bratich, *Conspiracy Panics: Political Rationality and Popular Culture* (New York: State University of New York Press, 2008).

61. Juha Räikkä and Lee Basham, "Conspiracy Theory Phobia," in *Conspiracy Theories*, ed. Uscinski, 178–86.

62. Matthew R. X. Dentith, "The Problem of Conspiracism," *Argumenta* 3, no. 2 (2018), 327–343.

63. Claus Oberhauser, ""'Verschwörungstheorie:" Genealogie eines problematischen Begriffs," in *Zwischen Wahn und Wahrheit: Wie Verschwörungstheorien und Fake News die Gesellschaft spalten*, ed. Michael C. Bauer and Laura Deinzer (Berlin: Springer, 2021), 57–79.

64. Andrew McKenzie-McHarg, "From Status Politics to the Paranoid Style: Richard Hofstadter and the Pitfalls of Psychologizing History," *Journal of the History of Ideas* 83, no. 3 (2022): 451–75.

65. Mark Fenster, *Conspiracy Theories: Secrecy and Power in American Culture*, rev. ed. (Minneapolis: University of Minnesota Press, 2008).

66. Dentith, "The Problem."

67. Elżbieta Drążkiewicz, "Study Conspiracy Theories with Compassion," *Nature* **603**, no. 765 (2022), *https://doi.org/10.1038/d41586-022-00879-w.*

68. Roland Imhoff et al., "Conspiracy Mentality and Political Orientation across 26 Countries," *Nat Hum Behav* 6 (2022): 392–403, https://doi.org/10.1038/s41562-021-01258-7.

69. Butter, "Verschwörungstheorien," 10–11.

Populism and the Pandemic in Austria: The Role of Radical Political Attitudes on Feeling Affected by the Covid-Pandemic –The Results of a Survey

Reinhard Heinisch
Amélie-Jacqueline Apke

Introduction

In this chapter, we address both theoretically and empirically the relationship between feelings of being physically and economically affected by Covid-19 and subjective political variables that imply alienation from the political establishment. In particular, these feelings include populism, authoritarianism, and lack of trust in government. This chapter draws on an extensive theoretical discussion to test the argument that voters' political dispositions have an effect that goes beyond physiological conditions, such as a medically diagnosed illness, and objectively measurable economic circumstances. The empirical findings discussed in this chapter are based on an original survey conducted in Austria in 2020 with a representative sample of 1,200 individuals. The analysis shows that populism and associated anti-establishment leanings have a significant impact on people's perception of their health and economic well-being. Our work intends to contribute to understanding the demand side of Covid-19 politics, which has generally been overshadowed by the focus on the supply side in the form governments and their policies.

In our work, we find that authoritarian and populist attitudes indeed shape an individual's perception of the pandemic, both in how much they feel affected in their own health and to a lesser extent in their economic well-being. These results show that such attitudes shape individuals' subjective perception beyond objectively measurable levels of illness and economic hardship.

Our chapter is organized as follows: first, we provide a general introduction to the topic. Subsequently, we discuss the literature and theoretical approaches connecting populism and related sentiments to the Covid-19 crisis, developing our hypotheses about how such attitudes should influence how individuals perceive the effect of the pandemic on their lives. Then, we introduce our original survey and provide information about the context in which it took place and the Austrian case. In the final part, we present our two analyses and findings along with a discussion of their implications for future research.

The Covid-19 Pandemic as a Political Challenge: A Theoretical Introduction

The Covid-19 pandemic will certainly be considered the most devastating public health crisis the world has faced in the past century. It has had far-reaching social, political, and economic impacts. The direct consequences of contracting the new type of virus and its impact on the healthcare system have been the focus of public debate for over three years. Citizens were faced with unprecedented government interference in individual freedoms and rights, with most mitigation policies affecting the individual well-being of people around the globe. However, there appears to be a cost associated with essential quarantine, social distancing, and other Covid-19 interventions: the objective impacts of the pandemic may include job loss, reduced wages, increased take-home costs, and other serious mental and physical health consequences. This raises the question of how the experience of being exposed to Covid-19 has affected the population and how subjective perceptions can be demonstrated. A subjective experience can be explained not only by physical or socioeconomic features but also by attitudes that influence one's perception of a given situation: political attitudes can greatly influence individual and subjective concerns and perceptions, especially if these are attitudes that express distrust of the political mainstream, such as populist and authoritarian positions.

As a corollary of different crises, the resurgence of social vulnerabilities is one of the realities experienced everywhere on the planet in recent decades. The moral and material fragility to which individuals are more and more exposed is accompanied by the (re-)appearance of populist leaders, who are using sovereigntist discourses and translating generalized frustrations into social forces with the aim of gaining political power. This shows that vulnerability is no longer just an issue that can be addressed in exploring the lack of extension of individual rights or the improvement of democracy but has become a fundamental element in thinking about political representation. This is especially relevant in the context of a universal crisis experienced individually and collectively.

The politicization of pandemics and infectious disease outbreaks can be explained by the political nature of public health itself.[1] In Europe, the nature of this pandemic almost invited populist actors to oppose any kind of political status quo and to reclaim power over decision-making processes held by elites and professionals: the coronavirus initiated a global public policy emergency with implications in almost all policy sectors.[2] Different waves of containment and mitigation policies followed, including lockdowns, curfews, and different emergency measures that limited people's freedom of movement, and rights to association, education, mobility, and work. An unprecedented crisis, its ramifications are still very present across all policy sectors on national and European Union levels. The pandemic posed enormous social and political challenges, with governments everywhere facing significant opposition and criticism of almost all decisions about lockdown and standoff measures, financial support for business, and testing and vaccination efforts. In an environment of considerable skepticism regarding mitigation measures, a widespread lack of trust, and high pressure to (re-)act, debates on public health and scientific measures were highly politicized. Increased media visibility of political institutions and scientific experts emphasized irregularities and inconsistencies in policy decisions across the European Union, often characterized by unpredictability and uncertainty.[3] Yet parties, political actors, experts, and governments had to react quickly to scientific uncertainties, to legitimize measures and political discourses, without always knowing the outcomes of these decisions. Consequently, most policies responding to the virus seem top-down, untransparent, and elite-driven in their execution, with low levels of parliamentary debate.[4] Hence, political attitudes become even more relevant during universal crisis situations, where knowledge and science constitute the very basis of policy decisions.

The pandemic changed political agendas, and some of the most important issues in politics were temporarily marginalized. For opposition parties, in particular, the first lockdown was the most difficult moment to align with the government's position.[5] At the beginning of the pandemic and during the rally 'round the flag effect,[6] many opposition parties moderated the political debate by positioning themselves as "respectable" actors. As the crisis continued, however, they tended to use the crisis as a weapon against the government and established parties, accusing them of being incapable of responding to the pandemic, as cases from France, Spain, and Italy show.[7] Particularly populist actors can use a crisis instrumentally as a discursive political opportunity. By identifying failures from the opposition in government or previous regimes, populist actors often describe a situation as having reached a certain threat level and crisis moment that demands the use of force. Crises can be framed as a critical threat or as a critical opportunity, depending on the rejection or diffusion of responsibility and blame. In response to a crisis-infused uncertainty, populist actors in Western Europe have generally shown a tendency to adopt chameleonic attitudes and ambiguous positions regarding public health policies, therapies, and vaccines with the aim of decontextualizing and politicizing science.[8] As a result, conflicts over Covid-19 policy increased on many levels. In Austria, contention increased after the first wave, with not only the government and the opposition being critical of each other, but also increasingly the state governments and the federal government, often represented by the Green Minister of Health.

From the Supply Side to the Demand Side in Politics Related to Covid-19

Populism can be analyzed through the attitudes of its supporters on the "demand-side" and among its providers on the "supply-side."[9] In contrast to the focus in the media and academia on decision-makers and political party actors[10] and on the effectiveness of policies,[11] the role of affected citizens was initially much less discussed. The relationship between individual feelings of being affected by the pandemic and political as well as sociocultural attitudes seemed particularly unclear. However, initial studies conducted in the summer and fall of 2020 show that economic fears related to the Covid-19 pandemic tend to lead people to vote for right-wing nationalist and populist parties.[12]

A survey of Austrian citizens conducted in May 2020 showed that individuals with populist attitudes tend to have low trust in political institutions and in science and research and that these orientations correlate positively with Covid-19 conspiracy beliefs.[13] This research thus highlights the special role of experts in the pandemic and points to the importance of the different reception of scientific discourses by the public.

However, what is the situation in Austria? Here, we first pose the question of the population's subjective impact from the Covid-19 pandemic. We know from research that self-interest and experience become dominant factors in individuals' decision-making when public policy is associated with such immediate, individual threats.[14] Therefore, in our study, we focus on two types of Covid-19-related impacts that seem to be most important: health and economic security. There are few things more valuable to a person than their health, which is ultimately linked to their physical survival. However, the pandemic can impact health in several ways. First, there is the immediate impact of the coronavirus, which can lead to severe illness; and second, there is the experience of fear that particularly vulnerable groups experience, even if they do not become ill. In addition, there is the negative impact on the health of people who suffer from other diseases but whose treatment has been postponed due to limited hospital capacity or who suffer from psychological problems because their freedom of movement has been restricted. Therefore, we emphasize the importance of the subjective feeling of being affected in one's health because we must leave it to the respondents to determine the effect that the pandemic has had on them, however "objectively" ill a person may be. It is the mental state that determines attitudes and behavior.

The other important and widespread impact is economic, as people lost their jobs, had to go on short-time work, or were otherwise economically affected, leading to existential fears for many. Again, there is a strong subjective component, as some people are more resilient than others in the same situation and therefore assess the level of impact differently. Thus, our notion of impact is not limited to the disease itself or the loss of a job or business, but remains on a subjective level, which is thus open to political influence and public debate.

Theory and Empirical Approach

In our survey, we investigate the extent to which certain political attitudes intensify the subjective concern caused by the pandemic. This is based on the idea that the experience of Covid-19 does not simply depend on the experience of a disease, i.e. a physiological or physical phenomenon, but essentially also on the social and political environment. Especially in the case of a pandemic, it is not a single experience of fate but a collective experience, whereby collective dynamics occur in humans as group creatures. People compare their experience of a crisis-like phenomenon with that of others, the latter being closely related to the collective behavior of the affected society. If one believes that policymakers have the interests of citizens at heart, if one believes their judgment to be reasonable, or if one even shares their worldview, then the subjective feeling of being affected by the pandemic may be different than if policymakers are perceived differently or if one distrusts them. In this situation, the feeling of being left alone with problems and worries may aggravate subjective consternation.

Populism in particular is a current phenomenon that expresses a very strong skepticism toward elites, and not only political elites: i.e., the government and the established parties but also social elites, such as those in science and medicine. Especially during health crises, it is not only political leaders who make decisions, but experts from many scientific fields who call for action in the media or visibly advise political decision-makers. Therefore, the question arises to what extent elite skepticism plays a role in perceived concern. Subsequently, we present here our theoretical approach and definition of populism.

The crucial influence of populist ideas in this context stems from the fact that this ideologically assumes a supposed opposition between "the people" and "the elite."[15] Indeed, scientific knowledge production, with its long-established gatekeepers and formal criteria, is often part of the populists' stereotype of "aloof elites."[16] The antagonistic relationship between "ordinary people" and the "academic elite" can be defined as a struggle for epistemic authority, i.e., for sovereignty over how "true knowledge" is produced. For populists, knowledge produced by experts and elitist professionals represents an uncontrollable constraint on popular power.[17]

The populist antagonism can also be defined as a struggle for decision-making authority, i.e., for sovereignty over how political power is produced. Populist actors can turn crisis situations politically and electorally into an opportunity wherein they can frame a crisis as a failure of representation, a failure that is portrayed as a direct result of incapable elites and other "mainstream" actors to provide the promised change to the people. Populism works very well when a collective imagination of a virtuous and homogenous people is created that emphasizes morality, the system's neglect, and threats to the people's well-being, health, and safety. Populism is characterized by a belief in an antagonistic relationship between the good people and the corrupt elite, whose power must be broken.[18] Since "the people" are always right in the populist imagination, common sense forms the basis for many decisions. A crucial element in this context are moral panics, a concept that has influenced the study of social reactions during crisis situations since the 1970s.[19] Moral panics can be used to justify decisions and alter the individual perception of crisis situations and feelings of being affected. When populist actors compose a certain discourse that represents them as the true and moral representatives of the virtuous people, defending peoples' sovereignty, honor, and promises of change, it might also improve their effectiveness and impact in claim-making.

Populist crisis performances also often devalue complexity through the forging of new divisions, anti-intellectualism, and the simplification and emotional dramatization of health crises.[20] Throughout the Covid-19 crisis, different and common responses shaped populism around the globe, such as pharmaceutical messianism,[21] anti-science and alt-science attitudes, or the simplification, dramatization, and blaming of specific parts of society. Yet, rather than being an individual experience, medical populism has led populists to naturally develop new political agendas and policy priorities but also new collective identities and transnational movements, such as the alt-science network.[22] However, it is important to note that alternative knowledge claims and inefficient, anti-scientific, or harsh strategies proposed by populist actors are not necessarily populist in nature, nor are they sufficient indications for a populist character. Populism across the board is "not primarily characterized by hostility to scientists"[23] since anti-scientific solutions[24] to the pandemic have also been part of non-populist agendas.

However, even without such elite skepticism and criticism of scientific positions, the pandemic poses an unprecedented challenge to society as a whole, where people dealing with a potentially deadly disease must respond to a plethora of complex and expert- and politician-mediated information that is often situational and subject to a changing overall situation.[25] In the context of the Covid-19 pandemic, governments introduced stringent measures that severely restricted the lives of many citizens, but primarily based on expert and political assessments of the situation rather than popular demands[26] and often selective in their application.[27] At the same time, there is no comprehensive scientific consensus on the proper management of the coronavirus.[28] In particular, the scientific practice of mutual criticism and the formulation of statements based on probabilities and risk assessments are very unfamiliar to a population with a high need for safety. Moreover, access to alternative information, especially via social media, is very easy, so experts' prescriptions can be constantly questioned and seemingly easily refuted.[29]

Despite possible similarities, such populist ideas are conceptually distinct from attitudes based on distrust of government, political and ideological disagreements, and/or differences in interests.[30] Yet, feeling unrepresented or abandoned by the government or distrusting its judgment can also be cause of negative feelings that, while different from populist rejection of elites, can still lead a person to feel negatively affected compared to others. For these reasons, several of the above motivations may also apply to people with low trust in government or to people with authoritarian tendencies. Lack of trust in government implies a lack of trust in the political process to find a solution, which especially exacerbates an individual's sense of being negatively affected. In contrast, people with high levels of trust in governments would probably feel less affected, all other things being equal. Moreover, the unpredictability of the pandemic and the controversy surrounding government responses are likely to have a particular impact on people with authoritarian tendencies, who typically prefer order and hierarchy. Thus, we will closely examine authoritarianism and trust in government, along with populism, as attitudinal factors that we hypothesize to contribute significantly to feelings of being affected.

Hypothesis Formation and Rationale

Previous research has shown that people respond to basic health risks by turning to medical experts rather than politicians and supporting policy changes that mitigate their risks.[31] Moreover, when public policy is linked to such immediate individual threats, self-interest and experience become dominant factors in individuals' decision-making.[32] Thus, the fundamental response to a crisis such as the Covid-19 pandemic, where both health and financial risks can be easily attributed to segments of society, can be expected to depend on whether or not individuals belong to these risk groups. Thus, how people perceive their own exposure to the pandemic should have a clear objective side. Clearly, one's own health may be affected by the pandemic either by becoming ill with the coronavirus or by having one's health affected by a lack of resources to treat health problems not related to Covid-19, such as when medical procedures cannot be performed. The objective financial impacts of the pandemic may range from job loss to reduced work hours, reduced wages, and increased take-home costs.

Therefore, these objective consequences are likely to be unevenly distributed across demographic groups. We would expect (working) young people to be more affected financially than (retired) older people, while the opposite should be true for health, with the more vulnerable older people feeling more affected. We would expect men to feel more affected by the health aspects of the pandemic because their relative mortality is higher, while we would expect women to feel more affected financially because they are more likely to be employed in an economic sector that has had to close (retail, hospitality, tourism, etc.). Income and education are likely to have an impact, as both influence the resources available to individuals to cope with the pandemic. Higher income protects against potential financial risks and is usually associated with a less vulnerable job situation. It also means that an individual has more options for accessing health resources when needed. Similarly, a higher level of education is often associated with a less vulnerable and fluctuating work situation and also provides greater access to resources that can help mitigate health risks.

In summary, our first overarching hypothesis, H1, is based on the expectation that objective assessments of individual risk are based on social groups. We further specify our expectations for such groups in the following sub-hypotheses.

H1: Different social groups feel more or less affected by a crisis depending on their objective risks.

The dependent variable, feelings of being affected, is measured by the two indicators, health and economic, and the independent variables, i.e. the socio-demographic characteristics, are age, gender, education, and income.

Another set of factors concerns the political congruence of citizens and the government, where we focus on the following hypothesis.

H2: Political support for government affects how much people feel impacted by a crisis. Specifically, government supporters will feel less impacted.

Here we also take into account whether respondents are voters of the governing parties or of the opposition. In contrast to the anti-establishment factors examined below, this hypothesis examines merely the importance of political support between government and voters as a factor influencing feelings of being affected. Non-support of the government is understood as an expression of one's political or ideological preference rather than a rejection of government and the political establishment in general.

Finally, we turn our attention to populist and associated attitudes and, for the reasons described in the theory section, formulate the following three hypotheses as follows:

H3: Individuals with populist attitudes are more likely to feel negatively affected by the Covid-19 pandemic than individuals without such attitudes do.

Regarding trust in government as a factor in explaining feelings of being affected, it should be noted that trust in government and populism are distinct yet related concepts. Trust corresponds to a sense of apprehension about political processes that are likely seen as opaque, possibly corrupt, and potentially ill-intentioned. Nevertheless, for all the skepticism about government, low trust does not necessarily mean the presumed abuse of power and betrayal of the people that populist attitudes typically convey.[33] Indeed, in the history of measuring populism, trust in government has often been used as a proxy measure.[34] Nonetheless, the above arguments that apply to the relationship between populism and feeling affected by Covid-19 would thus also underpin the closely related concept of trust.

H4: People's trust in government is likely to impact whether they feel affected by the Covid-19 pandemic.

The last hypothesis assumes a motive that leads people to support radical politics because they prefer authority, hierarchy, and discipline. In contrast, the new situation of the pandemic, along with governments and intuitions that react in contradictory and confusing ways, as well as the context of social and political backlash to the government's measures, may cause people with strong authoritarian tendencies to feel negatively affected.

H5: Individuals with authoritarian attitudes are more likely to feel negatively affected by the Covid-19 pandemic than individuals without such attitudes do.

Data and Methods

To analyze the subjective feeling of being affected, we designed our own survey, which went into the field at the beginning of September 2020. Importantly, this survey was able to capture public opinion before the more specific discussions about vaccine procurement and vaccination skepticism arose, which have since dominated public and scientific discourse. It therefore provides a rather unvarnished, rare insight into the views of the Austrian public on the relationship between perceptions of the pandemic and government action on the one hand, and those individually affected on the other, before one specific aspect, vaccination, began to overshadow other issues. The survey was fielded online through the survey company *Market Institut*, which randomly sampled 1,200 respondents from their respondent pool of 25,000–30,000 Austrians.[35]

The survey contained several questions about the respondents' feeling of being affected in different ways by the Covid-19 crisis. The two questions that matter for our analysis here asked people to what extent they felt affected in their own health and their own financial situation. Here, we focus exclusively on the subjective perception of people, so that the health impact is not limited to having contracted Covid-19 and financial impact is not limited to have lost one's job, but it is left to the respondents and their subjective assessment whether and to what extent they felt affected.

On a scale of 0 to 10, how much did you feel negatively affected [in your health well-being OR economically] by the Covid-19 crisis?

While populist attitudes have been measured in a range of ways and a battery of up to eighteen questions has been identified as the most reliable way of measurement,[36] the same research shows that all of these questions correlate very highly. Thus, our approach—given the constraints of a survey tapping into various aspects of the pandemic—was to measure populism using one item proxy that combines the three central characteristics of populism: the common people, the bad elites, and a Manichean conflict between them. Our item asks for respondents' agreement with the following statement, with the response scale ranging from 0 (do not agree at all) to 10 (agree very much):

In our country, the powerful listen far too little to the common people.

We define as "populists" those respondents who agree with the above statement with a value of 7 to 10 on the scale. Both the average and median value of responses is 7, making this a logical cut-off point.[37] All other variables are more normally distributed; thus, we split these scales in the middle (e.g., scale values of 0 to 5 as a perception of coping with one's income, values of 6 and higher as not coping with one's income). We are confident that this proxy measures populism for several reasons: First, it captures the main conceptual ingredients of a populist sentiment. Second, 82% of FPÖ voters among our respondents are populists, while only 62% of all other respondents fall into this category. This lends face-validity since the FPÖ is Austria's dominant populist party.[38]

Third, we include conceptually related items like trust in government and authoritarianism, which have independent effects on respective dependent variables. These items were captured by the following two questions on the survey. In each case, respondents were asked to rate their position on a scale from 0 (do not agree at all) to 10 (agree very much):

Trust in government: *On the whole, you may trust that the government wants only the best for the country.*

Authoritarian attitude: *The country would be better off if the young people were educated for obedience and discipline.*

The timing of our survey had the advantage of measuring the degree of subjective concern before the political party discussions between government and opposition or between the radical right Freedom Party of Austria (FPÖ) and other parties regarding an effective anti-Covid-19 policy. This means that the results of that survey allow a direct look at the population's sense of concern under the relatively most favorable circumstances in the course of the pandemic.

In this study, we first compare whether there are striking differences in subjective concern, focusing first on the demographic categories of age, education, and gender. Subsequently, we want to analyze the attitudes toward trust in government and society, authoritarianism, and populism.

Conducting the Survey: Context in Late Summer 2020

Regarding the background of the survey, the situation of the pandemic in Austria in the run-up to the survey can be summarized as follows: at the beginning of the pandemic in Austria, the federal government initially reacted quite decisively and imposed a strict lockdown as early as the beginning of March 2020. This was mainly due to the worsening situation in neighboring Italy. The conservative-Green governing coalition under Chancellor Kurz clearly saw this as an opportunity to demonstrate determination and leadership, while Germany, which had always been the most important reference country for Austria, initially reacted in a rather disorganized manner. Since the 2015 refugee crisis, the Austrian chancellor had criticized both German and EU leadership in dealing with crises, and this time was no exception. Kurz also portrayed the virus as a threat coming into Austria from abroad, so border closures and a strict lockdown became the first means of combating the pandemic.

The relative success in coping with the first wave and Austria's disproportionate dependence on tourism led to a rapid and almost complete opening of the country in June, making it difficult to take strict measures when, in early fall, the number of daily incidents exceeded even the highs of the first wave. The government seemed paralyzed and unsure of how to respond. A structural problem for the government was that the Austrian Constitutional Court had retroactively declared several of the adopted anti-Covid measures unconstitutional. In addition, the fact that the Ministry of Health was controlled by the Greens caused friction the longer the pandemic lasted.

Coalition messages were increasingly confused, and in the context of the state elections, conservatives blamed the Social Democratic government in Vienna for exacerbating the pandemic. This not only ignored similar problems in conservatively governed provinces, but also further politicized the pandemic. The opposition no longer saw any need to exercise restraint, and the FPÖ in particular went on the offensive. While the Social Democrats accused the government of doing too little, too late, and the Freedom Party protested incompetence, the FPÖ took the opposite approach, criticizing what it saw as the arrogant and authoritarian nature of the decisions. This was the context in which we conducted a survey on political attitudes and their impact on perceptions of Covid-19 shortly before the second wave.

Survey Findings and Analysis

The first step of our analysis compares the different variants of the feeling affected among the 1,200 respondents of our survey. Figures 1a and 1b show the results by type of impact: the left panel displays the impact of the pandemic on individuals' health and economic well-being, while the right panel shows the impact on threats to personal safety at home due to more conflict and restrictions on personal choice. We added this to provide a richer contextual picture of the way in which people felt affected. Figure 1a indicates that about a quarter of respondents do not feel that their own health has been affected by the Covid-19 pandemic. Conversely, this means that almost 75% feel that their health was affected in some way and to some extent. This is remarkable given the extremely low incidence rate, consisting of at most a few thousand in a country of nine million even when undercounting and misreporting are taken into account, during the first wave of Covid-19 in Austria. It is also completely immaterial whether the disease in a medical or physiological sense genuinely affected these individuals; all that matters for the political consequences is that people make this subjective attribution. The findings for economic impact are similar, although there one did expect relatively much higher numbers, given the economic fallout from the first lockdown. In fact, about 25% of Austrians indicate that their health is affected with values greater than 5 and their economic well-being with values greater than 6. The average values are 3.2 (health) and 3.7 (finances).

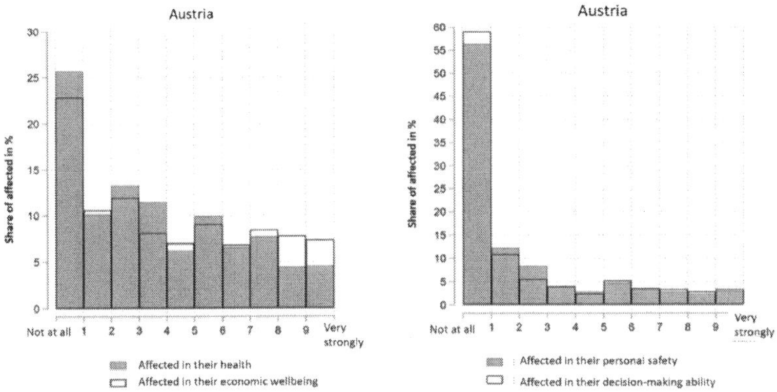

FIGURE 1ab: Degree to which people felt affected by Covid-19 in their health, economic well-being, security in their own homes, freedom of personal decision-making ability. Source: own survey, n = 1,200 people, conducted by the Market Institute, Linz, September 2020.

By comparison, we notice in Figure 1b that overall, the percentage of people feeling affected in their personal security and in their decision-making ability is much lower. There, the averages are 1.6 and 1.7 respectively. About 5% of respondents each gave a score above 8 for personal safety and freedom of choice (and 10% each gave a score of 6 and above). While these values seem small, at least 5% of the population felt little security and freedom in their households as a result of the pandemic.

We present the findings on our hypotheses tests in Table 1. It lists the results of four logistical regression models (Models A1, 2 and B1, 2), two for each of the two types of impact. The models A1 and B1 include the independent variable government supporter but not trust in government, whereas A2 and B2 do not feature the variable government supporter but do incorporate trust in government. Due to the potential similarity of these two variables, we opted for this approach.

We first address the demographic characteristics discussed above as possible influencing variables, in particular gender, age, education, and social status as measured by monthly income. Subsequently, we analyze the influence of the political attitudes discussed above, in particular whether voters support or oppose the government and then the potentially more extreme political determinants, whether respondents are populist, trust the government, or are authoritarian. To test whether voters who support the government might evaluate the Covid-19 situation differently than respondents who oppose the government, we identify respondents who voted for one of the governing parties (ÖVP or Greens) in the last election.

As we see in Table 1, there are first no significant differences between the Models A1 and A2 and B1 and B2. We may thus interpret the findings as follows: while gender is not significant, we see a clear negative effect for the variables age and high income. This is quite plausible, as both groups can be assumed to have higher material security. Although other people may have a greater risk of being adversely affected by Covid-19, they have felt less impacted due to their ability to ride out both the illness and its economic consequences when compared with younger respondents. For high education levels, we find that this leads to a lower subjective health concern but leaves economic concern unaffected.

Turning to the political variables, we find that supporting or opposing government has no bearing on feelings of being affected, neither in health nor economic well-being. By contrast, populist attitudes turn out to be significant predictors of feeling affected in one's health, which is shown by both Models A1 and A2. It is also a significant factor in Model A2, measuring the effect of populism and feelings of economic impact. However, it is not significant in Model B2 when the variable trust in government is included, which appears to pick up this effect and is significant. This means that people who trust the government feel significantly less negatively affected in their economic well-being. This seems to be quite defensible in theory. In contrast to the health domain, where partisan or ideological differences in policy are less relevant, how the economic impact of Covid-19 is managed makes a difference in economic policy. Thus, confidence in the government's competence and goals matters more in the economic impact dimension than in the area of health impact. A strong predictor of impact are authoritarian attitudes. In all four models and in all configurations, such tendencies increase the probability of feeling negatively affected in both health and economic well-being.

Overall, we can confirm hypotheses H1 (demographic characteristics) and H5 (authoritarian views), partially confirm H3 (populist attitudes about health outcomes) and H4 (confidence in economic well-being), and reject H2 (support for government).

	Affected in Health				in Economic Wellbeing			
	Model A1		Model A2		Model B1		Model B2	
Female	-0.15	●	●	●	●	(0.20)	-0.21	●
Age	-0.01**	●	●	●	●	(0.01)	-0.05***	●
Education (re.. low)								
medium	0.03	●	●	●	●	(0.26)	0.11	●
high	-0.56*	●	●	●	●	(0.33)	-0.25	●
Income (re. less than €1500)								
€1500 - €2099	-0.21	●	●	●	●	(0.39)	-0.35	●
€2100 - €2699	-0.34	●	●	●	●	(0.38)	-0.54	●
€2700 - €3599	-1.15***	●	●	●	●	(0.36)	-0.99***	●
€3600 +	-0.85***	●	●	●	●	(0.34)	-1.68***	●
Government supporter	-0.26	●			●	(0.19)		
Trust in government			●	●			-0.18***	●
Populist attitudes	0.46**	●	●	●	●	(0.20)	0.26	●
Authoritarian attitudes	0.73***	●	●	●	●	(0.19)	0.81***	●
Constant	4.16***	●	●	●	●	(0.52)	7.30***	●
N	938		938		●		938	
R^2	0.07		●		●		0.15	

standard errors in ( ) *** p<0.01, ** p<0.05, * p<0.1

TABLE 1: Influence of demographic characteristics and political attitudes on feelings of concern in one's health and economic wellbeing. Source: own survey, n = 1,200 people, conducted by the Market Institute, Linz, September 2020.

In summary, we may conclude that different social groups are affected to different degrees, with the category of gender never appearing as a factor. Age and income, on the other hand, have significant influences on feelings of both health and economic impact. These effects remain robust even in a modified model configuration (A1,2/B1,2). This confirms the assumptions underlying H1. H2, tested in two configurations, shows us that voting preferences for government parties have no effect on feelings of concern. For the populist attitudes, there is confirmation of H3 with respect to health concern and only partial confirmation for economic concern. This supports the theoretical assumptions that populism and trust (H4) are overlapping factors and matter especially in the economic dimension. The strongest effect among the political variables is that of authoritarian attitudes. This remains robust in all model configurations and can be confirmed for all dependent variables. Thus, we can accept H4, that authoritarian attitudes have an effect on how much people feel affected by the Covid-19 pandemic. It must be acknowledged, however, that in this study, the populism factor was measured via a single indicator question, which leaves some room for interpretation and may not have been as precisely specified as that for authoritarian attitudes. The findings clearly point to the subjective political attitudes as having an important impact on what appears to be a physical state—feeling healthy or sick, which was the goal of this study.

Conclusion

This study addressed the influence of certain political attitudes on various forms of individual impact in the context of the Covid-19 pandemic. Underlying this project was the idea that such individual feelings of impact can be explained not only by physical characteristics or material conditions, but also by political attitudes that significantly influence one's evaluation of a given situation, especially in the collective experience of a pandemic. The focus was on attitudes that express alienation from the political system or distance from the political mainstream, including populist and authoritarian positions and (lack of) trust in government. These were combined in various regression models with other variables such as support for government, party preference, and various demographic determinants to calculate the relative net effects on two types of impact. We focused on health and economic impact, which have dominated public debate in Austria for months and for which the influence of political variables can best be theoretically justified.

In general, the models show that radical attitudes such as authoritarian and populist positions increase health and economic impact. Only in the model configuration with the variable "trust in government" do populist attitudes show attenuated significance for economic impact. Authoritarian attitudes have a strong and significant influence on how affected people feel in all dimensions and model configurations. Overall, our results underscore the role of political attitudes in people's assessment of a crisis's impact on their own lives, even in areas that would be considered apolitical or objectively determined per se. It is also important to note that these causal relationships were already manifest, and thus clearly demonstrable, at a time when Austria appeared to have weathered the pandemic well. However, the results already provide a first indication of why the discussions about lockdowns, school closures, and compulsory vaccination subsequently polarized society, which manifested itself in numerous protest rallies and even in the founding of a new political party against compulsory vaccination. If these causal mechanisms are better understood, public debate can also be conducted by policymakers in a way that can better address political alienation and related emotions such as moral panics and fears. This work also calls for future research on the connection between radical political attitudes on feelings of affectedness, especially in other country cases and other circumstances.[39]

Endnotes

1. Jacky Chambers et al., "Reflections on the UK's Approach to the 2009 Swine Flu Pandemic: Conflicts between National Government and the Local Management of the Public Health Response," *Health & Place* 18, no. 4 (2012): 737–45, https://doi.org/10.1016/j.healthplace.2011.06.005; Michel Foucault, "The Politics of Health in the Eighteenth Century," *Foucault Studies* 18 (2014): 113–27, https://doi.org/10.22439/fs.v0i18.4654; Ian Harper and Melissa Parker, "The Politics and Anti-Politics of Infectious Disease Control," *Medical Anthropology* 33, no. 3 (2014): 198–205, https://doi.org/10.1080/01459740.2014.892484.

2. Sarah Wolff and Stella Ladi, "European Union Responses to the Covid-19 Pandemic: Adaptability in Times of Permanent Emergency," *Journal of European Integration* 42, no. 8 (2020): 1025–40 (here 1025), https://doi.org/10.1080/07036337.2020.1853120.

3. Silvio O. Funtowicz and Jerome R. Ravetz, "Science for the Post-Normal Age," *Futures* 25 (1993): 739–55.

4. Jakob-Moritz Eberl et al., "From Populism to the 'Plandemic': Why Populists Believe in Covid-19 Conspiracies," *Journal of Elections, Public Opinion and Parties* 31, sup1 (2021): 272–84 (here 274).

5. Giuliano Bobba and Nicolas Hubé, "Between Mitigation and Dramatization: The Effect of the Covid-19 Crisis on Populists' Discourses and Strategies," in *Populism and the Politicization of the Covid-19 Crisis in Europe*, ed. Giuliano Bobba and Nicolas Hubé (Cham: Palgrave Macmillan, 2021): 131–44.

6. Sylvia Kritzinger et al., "'Rally Round the Flag': The Covid-19 Crisis and Trust in the National Government," *West European Politics* 44, no. 5–6 (2021): 1205–31.

7. Martin Baloge and Nicolas Hubé, "France: Two Separate Populist Parties, Two Separate Networks and One Go-between Group," *Demos National Reports in the WP* 6 (2021); Jaume Magre et al., "Spain: Is Ideology Back in Populist Discourse?," in *Populism and the Politicization of the Covid-19 Crisis in Europe*, ed. Giuliano Bobba and Nicolas Hubé (Cham: Palgrave Macmillan, 2021): 31–44; Daniele Albertazzi et al., "The Right-Wing Alliance at the Time of the Covid-19 Pandemic: All Change?," *Contemporary Italian Politics* 13, no. 2 (2021): 181–95.

8. Carlo Berti and Carlo Ruzza, "Populism, Science and Covid-19 as a Political Opportunity: The Case of the European Parliament," in *Populism and Science in Europe*, ed. Hande Eslen–Ziya and Alberta Giorgi (Cham: Palgrave Macmillan, 2022): 91–115 (here 111).

9. Kirk A. Hawkins et al., eds., *The Ideational Approach to Populism: Concept, Theory, and Analysis* (New York: Routledge 2018).

10. Alexi Gugushvili et al., "Votes, Populism, and Pandemics," *International Journal of Public Health* 65, no. 6 (2020): 721–22; Martin McKee et al., "Are Populist Leaders Creating the Conditions for the Spread of Covid-19?," *International Journal of Health Policy and Management* 2020, 1–5; Yannis Stavrakakis and Giorgos Katsampekis, "Populism and the Pandemic: A Collaborative Report," *Populismus Interventions* 7 (2020): 1–56; Jakub Wondreys and Cas Mudde, "Victims of the Pandemic? European Far-Right Parties and Covid-19," *Nationalities Papers* 50, no. 1 (2022): 86–103; Kerim Can Kavakli, "Did Populist Leaders Respond to the Covid-19 Pandemic More Slowly? Evidence from a Global Sample," (Working Paper, 2020), available online, accessed Jan. 12, 2023, https://kerimkavakli.com/research/; Brett Meyer, "Pandemic Populism: An Analysis of Populist Leaders' Responses to Covid-19," *Tony Blair Institute for Global Change* (2020), accessed Jan 12, 2023, https://institute.global/policy/pandemic-populism-analysis-populist-leaders-responses-Covid-19.

11. Paolo Nicola Barbieri and Beatrice Bonini, "Populism and Political (Mis-)Belief Effect on Individual Adherence to Lockdown during the Covid-19 Pandemic in Italy," *Economia Politica* 38, no. 2 (2021): 483–504.

12. Gilles Ivaldi and Oscar Mazzoleni, "Economic Populism and Sovereigntism: The Economic Supply of European Radical Right-Wing Populist Parties," *European Politics and Society* 21, no. 2 (2020): 202–18.

13. Eberl et al. 2021, "From Populism to the 'Plandemic'."

14. Dennis Chong et al., "When Self⊠Interest Matters," *Political Psychology* 22, no. 3 (2001): 541–70.

15. Eric Merkley, "Anti-Intellectualism, Populism, and Motivated Resistance to Expert Consensus," *Public Opinion Quarterly* 84, no. 1 (2020): 24–48; Daniele Caramani, "Will vs. Reason: The Populist and Technocratic Forms of Political Representation and Their Critique to Party Government," *American Political Science Review* 111, no. 1 (2017): 54–67.

16. Niels G. Mede and Mike S. Schäfer, "Science-Related Populism: Conceptualizing Populist Demands toward Science," *Public Understanding of Science* 29, no. 5 (2020): 473–91.

17. Stephen Turner, "What Is the Problem with Experts?," *Social Studies of Science* 31, no. 1 (2001): 123–49; Harry Collins et al., "Introduction: Pluralist Democracy, Populism and Expertise," in *Experts and the Will of the People*, ed. Harry Collins et al. (Cham: Palgrave Macmillan, 2020), 1–9; Paul Saurette and Shane Gunster, "Ears Wide Shut: Epistemological Populism, Argutainment and Canadian Conservative Talk Radio," *Canadian Journal of Political Science/Revue canadienne de science politique* 44, no. 1 (2011): 195–218; J. Eric Oliver and Wendy M. Rahn, "Rise of the Trumpenvolk: Populism in the 2016 Election," *The ANNALS of the American Academy of Political and Social Science* 667, no. 1 (2016): 189–206.

18. Cas Mudde, "The Populist Zeitgeist," *Government and Opposition* 39, no. 4 (2004): 541–63; Hawkins et al. 2018, *The ideational approach to populism*; Paul Taggart, "Populism and Representative Politics in Contemporary Europe," *Journal of political ideologies* 9, no. 3 (2004): 269–88; Matthijs Rooduijn, "The Nucleus of Populism: In Search of the Lowest Common Denominator," *Government and Opposition* 49, no. 4 (2014): 573–99; Cas Mudde and Cristóbal Rovira Kaltwasser, "Studying Populism in Comparative Perspective: Reflections on the Contemporary and Future Research Agenda," *Comparative Political Studies* 51, no. 13 (2018): 1667–93.

19. Stanley Cohen, "Whose Side Were We On? The Undeclared Politics of Moral Panic Theory," *Crime, Media, Culture* 7, no. 3 (2011): 237–43.

20. Gideon Lasco and Nicole Curato, "Medical Populism," *Social Science and Medicine* 221, no. 1 (2019): 1–8.

21. Gideon Lasco and Vincen Gregory Yu, "Pharmaceutical Messianism and the Covid-19 Pandemic," *Social Science and Medicine* 292, no. 1 (2022): Article 114567.

22. Guilherme Casarões and David Magalhães, "The Hydroxychloroquine Alliance: How Far-Right Leaders and Alt-Science Preachers Came Together to Promote a Miracle Drug," *Revista de Administração Pública* 55, no. 1 (2021): 197–214.

23. Jan Werner Müller, "Why Do Rightwing Populist Leaders Oppose Experts?," *The Guardian* (Mar 26, 2020), accessed Jan. 12, 2023, https://www.theguardian.com/commentisfree/2020/mar/26/rightwing-populist-leaders-oppose-experts-not-elites.

24. Mede and Schäfer 2020, "Science-Related Populism."

25. Gabriel S. Lenz, *Follow the Leader? How Voters Respond to Politicians' Policies and Performance* (Chicago–London: University of Chicago Press, 2012); John R. Zaller, *The Nature and Origins of Mass Opinion* (Cambridge: Cambridge University Press, 1992).

26. Rogers Brubaker, "Paradoxes of Populism during the Pandemic," *Thesis Eleven* 164, no. 1 (2020): 73–87; Stavrakakis and Katsampekis 2020, "Populism and the Pandemic."

27. Brubaker 2020, "Paradoxes of Populism during the Pandemic."

28. Stavrakakis and Katsampekis 2020, "Populism and the Pandemic."

29. Brubaker 2020, "Paradoxes of Populism during the Pandemic;" Stavrakakis and Katsampekis 2020, "Populism and the Pandemic;" Mede and Schäfer 2020, "Science-Related Populism."

30. Caramani 2017, "Will vs. Reason."

31. Bethany Albertson and Shana Kushner Gadarian, *Anxious Politics: Democratic Citizenship in a Threatening World* (Cambridge: Cambridge University Press, 2015).

32. Chong et al. 2001, "When Self Interest Matters."

33 Bram Geurkink et al., "Populist Attitudes, Political Trust, and External Political Efficacy: Old Wine in New Bottles?," *Political Studies* 68, no. 1 (2020): 247–67; Eberl et al. 2021, "From Populism to the 'Plandemic.'"

34. Pippa Norris and Ronald Inglehart, *Cultural Backlash: Trump, Brexit, and Authoritarian Populism* (Cambridge: Cambridge University Press, 2019); Armin Schäfer, "Cultural backlash? How (Not) to Explain the Rise of Authoritarian Populism," *British Journal of Political Science* 52, no. 4 (2022): 1977–93.

35. n = 1,200 interviews, representative of the defined target group. The max. statistical margin of error is +/-2.90 percent for n = 1,200 respondents.

36. Agnes Akkerman et al., "How Populist Are the People? Measuring Populist Attitudes in Voters," *Comparative political studies* 47, no. 9 (2014): 1324–53; Bruno Castanho Silva et al., "An Empirical Comparison of Seven Populist Attitudes Scales," *Political Research Quarterly* 73, no. 2 (2019): 409–24.

37. Splitting the scale at the theoretical mid-point of five attributes 74 percent of Austrian respondents to the category of populist. As we aim to differentiate between populist and non-populist respondents relative to their own system, we chose the measure that better discriminates between the target categories.

38. We also checked that the regression results are similar for our first analysis when replacing populism with FPÖ vote, though the results in health show that the two measures are distinct.

39. Additional bibliographical reference:

Luiza Bialasiewicz and Christina Eckes, "'Individual Sovereignty' in Pandemic Times: A Contradiction in Terms?," *Political Geography* 85, no. 2 (2021): Article 102277.

Tereza Capelos and Alexia Katsanidou, "Reactionary Politics: Explaining the Psychological Roots of Anti-Preferences in European Integration and Immigration Debates," *Political Psychology* 39, no. 6 (2018): 1271–88.

Gabriele Magni, "It's the Emotions, Stupid! Anger about the Economic Crisis, Low Political Efficacy, and Support for Populist Parties," *Electoral Studies* 50 (2017): 91–102.

Cas Mudde, *Populist Radical Right Parties in Europe* (Cambridge: Cambridge University Press, 2007).

Cas Mudde, "The Populist Radical Right: A Pathological Normalcy," *West European Politics* 33, no. 6 (2010): 1167–86.

Jens Rydgren, *The Oxford Handbook of the Radical Right* (New York: Oxford University Press, 2018).

Mikko Salmela and Christian von Scheve, "Emotional Roots of Right-Wing Political Populism," *Social Science Information* 56, no. 4 (2017): 567–95.

Amy Skonieczny, "Emotions and Political Narratives: Populism, Trump and Trade," *Politics and Governance* 6, no. 4 (2018): 62–72.

Non-topical Article

The *Österreichische Gemeinschaft* in the Early Second Republic: Contrasts and Contradictions in Defining Austrian Identity[1]

Katja Maierhofer

Introduction

Since the Second Republic of Austria was proclaimed in 1945, questions of national identity have shaped the trajectory of its ongoing history.[2] Especially in the early phase after WWII, the dispute over independence offered potential for conflict. The present paper aims at contributing to the examination and reevaluation of nation building and identity formation by assessing the activities of the patriotic association *Österreichische Gemeinschaft*.[3] This organization was dedicated to affirming Austrian sovereignty and positioned itself as a key player in the discourse over independence and Austrian identity in the early Second Republic. Despite a large number of publications disseminating these ideas, the *ÖG* has not yet been the focus of scholarly interest. The present paper addresses this apparent gap by analyzing the association's positionings in the early phase after WWII, which proves to be crucial for identity and collective belonging.

The statements of the *ÖG* are not only worth a closer look due to the numerous texts it contributed to the public discourse about the Austrian nation since 1947.[4] This intellectual lobby also must be attributed a considerable role in the formation of identity because of good connections to governing parties. Nevertheless, the *ÖG* was clearly not among the main decision makers in identity politics. It was not a party organization but rather a fringe group aiming to affirm the sovereignty of the Austrian nation. Due to this objective, however, the *ÖG* is still of high interest for research on early initiatives of Austrian identity formation.

This collective of intellectuals set itself the goal of contributing "to the ideational construction of an inwardly renewed Austria"[5] from the beginning of the Second Republic. As is evident from well-known examples of political decisions at the highest level, such as the renaming of the school subject German to *Unterrichtssprache* ("teaching language") or the publication of a specifically Austrian dictionary (*Österreichisches Wörterbuch*),[6] these early attempts to argue for independence were primarily symbolic actions. The *ÖG* also contributes to these efforts with its ideas and comes up with the most diverse justifications to demarcate the sovereign Austrian nation from any concept of the German.

In examining these lines of argument, the present paper mainly aims to show which concepts were used in the attempt of consolidating a still unstable identity. Contrasting some divergent or even contradictory perspectives will provide proof of the rather unsystematic and arbitrary character of the early approach. The statements of the *ÖG* serve as symptomatic evidence for the search for an Austrian identity in this early phase of uncertain conceptualizations.

The intentions are clear from the very beginning. When the group of intellectuals gathered as *ÖG* in 1947, its aim was to consolidate Austria as a new national entity. This becomes evident from the first issue of their periodical, the front page of which reads:

> The human community has gone haywire. … And yet there is a longing for peace through the peoples of the world … [but] many peace efforts are only hypocrisy, deceiving the neighbor as a wolf in sheep's clothing. The Austrian people fell victim to this hypocrisy in 1938. … The thousand-year-old community of the Danube region must come together peacefully against new desirability. … That is the guiding principle of the "Österreichische Gemeinschaft" that publishes this humble paper.[7]

In these few lines, we can already find countless narratives that say a lot about the position of this community. They express the desire for peace; the "neighbor" Germany is described as an aggressor, while Austria is seen as a victim.[8] Moreover, there is a clear idea of a re-united Danube region. What is remarkable here, however, is the fact that within the numerous publications of this association we can also find completely different, sometimes contradictory, statements about their mission that lead to a tension regarding the positions on peace and democracy, war and hegemony. For instance, the *ÖG* also sees one of its main goals in "fighting against the traitors of their homeland."[9]

Even the earliest declarations are thus caught in a seemingly irresolvable conflict between peace narratives and militant-aggressive slogans. This effect, which becomes even more apparent in subsequent publications of the *ÖG*, shall be explored in order to showcase the poorly thought-out way of dealing the formation of Austrian identity after 1945. As far as the *ÖG* is concerned, the diffuse simultaneity of narratives must also be looked upon in connection with the history of the association. Since its roots reach back to the year 1925, its core principles were stated under completely different ideological conditions. The *ÖG* eventually emerged from initiatives of reuniting the members of an association that had already existed in the First Republic.[10] Precisely because of their self-imposed ambition to re-establish a prewar organization and seamlessly continue its activities, a retrospective is necessary to understand the effects in the Second Republic.

History of the *ÖG*

The Association(s) before 1938

The prehistory of the *ÖG* begins in the midst of the politically unstable conditions after WWI. In 1925, the *Großösterreichische Jugend* was founded as an association of Catholic students. It was expanded in 1928 to become the *Großösterreichische Gemeinschaft*.[11] This association was to exist until 1938, and then it was forced to dissolve. After the war, its remaining members gathered again and established the *ÖG*.[12] In both the First and the Second Republic, the leaders were Wilhelm Schmid, who also owned the publishing house (*Österreichischer Kulturverlag*) that disseminated the association's ideas, and Ernst Josef Görlich, an "educator, historian, and poet"[13] working in Vienna.

At the beginning, the *Großösterreichische Jugend* was still a small circle of just ten to twelve people. Its activities were strongly linked to the probably better-known collective *Österreichische Aktion*, which has already been subject to research by historian Janek Wasserman.[14] The connection to this group is evident from the fact that the key texts of both initiatives were written by the same people. The *Großösterreichische Jugend* spread its ideas in a magazine called *Das Vaterland*, published by Wilhelm Schmid. Various articles in this periodical, whose name refers to a newspaper from the nineteenth century, clearly evoke a monarchist tradition and are authored by Ernst Karl Winter, Karl Zeßner-Spitzenberg, Alfred Missong and Schmid himself.[15] Together with August M. Knoll, the aforementioned are the theorists who published the manifesto of the *Österreichische Aktion* in 1927.[16]

The *Aktion* was committed to the Catholic sociological tradition after Karl von Vogelsang and aligned its convictions with a "sociology of fathers and princes."[17] The *ÖG* also reports of itself that in the First Republic it had been shaped by the Christian social doctrines influenced by Vogelsang and Anton Orel.[18] When they founded the *Großösterreichische Jugend*, Schmid and Görlich also exchanged ideas with Alfred Missong, August M. Knoll, and Ernst Karl Winter.[19] That the preceding *Großösterreichische Gemeinschaft* perceived itself as part of the *Aktion* is apparent from its two most important manifestos.[20] By publishing the periodical *Vaterland*, which has already been the focus of previous studies by Miechowiecki und Papiór,[21] the *Gemeinschaft* contributed to the dissemination of the ideas of the *Österreichische Aktion*.[22] Its program is centered on a monarchist and Catholic concept of *Großösterreich*, while German nationalism, National Socialism, and any concept of *Preussisch* are vehemently opposed. Also, Antisemitic tendencies are clearly visible.[23]

Since the assessments spread by these groups in the First Republic have already been addressed by scholarship, they shall not be focused on in the present studies. However, some core principles are to be mentioned in order to contrast them with the statements made in the Second Republic.

The main goal of the *Gemeinschaft* was to reclaim Austria's former importance. It opposed any Anschluss initiatives and condemned ideas of *Großdeutschtum*. The vision was to "think and live a European Austria."[24] Despite its reduced size, Austria "should get out of its narrowness and again become … patron and representative of the idea of international reconciliation in the heart of Europe."[25] This desire for building up a "peace alliance"[26] is clearly linked to the concept of regaining Austrian hegemony. "Loyalty to the imperial family"[27] is expressed. The *Gemeinschaft* wanted to be a 'young guard' for the exiled *Landesvater* and sees its task in preparing a so-called "coming empire" which is imagined as the continuation of the Habsburg monarchy.[28] In perceiving itself as a 'disciple of authority,' it explicitly opposed democracy because the opinion was that "democracy has burned the bridges between today and yesterday. The revolutionary, non-authoritarian approach ... stands in open contradiction to the clearly authoritative institution of the Church of Christ and the family."[29]

The ÖG after 1945: Conflicts of Reorganization and Continuity

The clearly monarchist program propagated by this interest group of the First Republic is more than evident from its statements. However, these views could obviously not be continued in the Second Republic. This tension is what makes the history of the *ÖG* particularly interesting. The efforts to rebuild an association that had spread such ideas before WWII seem even more remarkable given the fact that the connection to its own past was to be drawn as seamlessly as possible.[30] This can be seen from the fact that the period between 1938 and its re-establishment in 1947 is referred to as the "catacomb period."[31] Also, the members of the *ÖG* directly proceeded to holding meetings again in the usual way.[32] Most evidently, they always list 1925 as the founding year of the *ÖG*.[33] In light of those signals for an explicit continuation of prewar activities, the highly interesting question arises as to how far its continuation could be brought into line with the completely different political circumstances. Further investigation of this issue also addresses an apparent gap in research, since there have not been any more detailed studies on the ÖG in the Second Republic so far.

But it is the activities after 1945 that prove particularly interesting, as the organization had to abandon many of its former principles to continue to exist. At the same time, however, it took its Austria-patriotic activities of the First Republic as an argument to ascribe to itself an important role in identity and cultural politics. By emphasizing that it had already carried "the main burden of the struggle for independence"[34] in the First Republic, the *ÖG* claimed its place in the discourse about Austrian sovereignty after 1945. As is stated retrospectively in 1977, the *ÖG* had "always ... advocated the idea of full autonomy and independence of the Austrian fatherland."[35] Especially in the politically decisive period until the State Treaty, it was intensively committed to conceptualizing the uniqueness of an "Austrian people" or "Austrian man."[36] The *ÖG* also claims to have used the expression "Austrian nation" (*Österreichiche Nation*) for the first time."[37]

As the objectives needed to be adapted to the new circumstances, the *ÖG*'s core narrative is shifted towards a "commitment to the Austrian nation and culture" and a strong emphasis on sovereignty and peace.[38] The clearly stated Catholic orientation persists as a main principle. Also, the particularly vehement rejection of any pan-German ideology was continued after WWII. More remarkably, the *ÖG* still adheres to the idea of a united Danube region. By far the greatest contradiction to the ideas of the First Republic, however, is the attitude toward democracy. While the association had openly positioned itself as anti-democratic before WWII, it now wanted to "achieve a true democracy and rejects ... any dictatorship."[39] This reorientation seems to be a necessary consequence from the rejection of authoritarian forms of government, which was now even more deeply anchored in the collective memory. The fact that this attitude was demanded by the occupying powers might play a role here as well. Any monarchist sympathies have disappeared from the statements of this association formerly longing for a return of the Kaiser. However, some might not have had a complete change of mind as will become evident from the examples given in this paper. While 'on the surface' it was clearly emphasized that the *ÖG* now supported democracy, presumably not all members had abandoned their former principles and become 'good democrats.'

With its core objective of standing up for Austrian independence, however, the *ÖG* clearly struck a chord within the early Second Republic. The public debate about Austrian identity probably also favored its expansion. By the early 1950s, the ÖG with its various regional and local groups, some of which even operated on a small-scale basis in smaller towns, had already spread over most federal provinces. At the twenty-fifth anniversary celebrations in 1950, the association counted 600 members.[40] Although the rapid growth is always emphasized, especially in this early phase after 1945, this is the only absolute figure given. The documented records of the *ÖG* (which are archived in the *Dokumentenarchiv der Österreichischen Gesellschaft für Zeitgeschichte*[41]) do not contain membership statistics. The reports of the annual conferences only contain vague information, stating that the number of members had "increased by one hundred," "doubled," or "tripled."[42] Thus, neither the number of members around 1938 nor of those re-assembled in 1947 is known. From the sparse information, it can only be roughly estimated that around fifty gathered for its re-establishment.

Shortly after having been re-established, the *ÖG* made an effort to create a periodical again to spread its ideas.[43] In 1948, seven issues were published under the title *Die Gemeinschaft*, followed in 1949 and 1950 by *Die Nation*. Both bore the subtitle *Blätter für österreichische Erneuerung*. From 1951, the magazine was named *Die Österreichische Nation*[44] (and continued to exist under this name until the dissolution of the *ÖG* in 2004). Wilhelm Schmid again served as the editor of the association's journal, which became a monthly periodical in 1955. Moreover, a number of books published in Schmid's *Österreichischer Kulturverlag* supported the dissemination of the *ÖG*'s ideas. In 1947, a volume of poems *Mein Österreich, mein Vaterland* was published; in 1948 *Die Sprache des Österreichers* and *Lachendes Österreich*; in 1949 the *Handbuch des Österreichers*; and in 1952 a biography of Anton Orel as well as the *Kulturgeschichte und Wirtschaftsgeschichte Österreichs*.[45]

The *ÖG*'s Contribution to the Discourse of Austrian Sovereignty and Identity: An Analysis

Material and Method

For the study, into which the present paper shall offer an insight, mainly journal texts from the fifty-one issues between 1947 and 1955 were examined. Some textual evidence was also drawn from the works *Die Sprache des Österreichers*, *Handbuch des Österreichers* and the *Kulturgeschichte*. The texts were analyzed using an open, non-category-based approach. In line with the discourse-semantic perspective of Wolfgang Teubert,[46] no quantifying steps were taken. Instead—fully aware of the arbitrary shape of the discourse that comes about through the reorganization of knowledge—I have engaged with the all-encompassing question of how Austria's role as a nation was imagined in the context of hostile disputes and peaceful dialogue and especially in foreign policy relations with other states in Europe. Here, it was of particular interest to examine the (attributed) relation to the people of the Danube region and of course to Germany, (for which the question of the common language played a particularly important role), but also the depiction of Austria as mediator between 'East' and 'West.'

Moreover, I observed the constructions of identity (e.g., connotations associated with an 'Austrian type of person' and corresponding attributes to its 'opponents') and how the association does position itself and its own role/

responsibility in relation to the nation of Austria.

Throughout the investigation of the statements made by the *ÖG* in the early Second Republic, vast amounts of textual evidence on these questions could be found and compared to ideas from earlier and later phases. As already indicated, these statements are often characterized by contradictory positions. These ambiguities emerge from the tension between the *ÖG*'s history and its new objectives, but also from the still rather uncertain concepts of Austrian identity. A brief overview of the results shall now precede the more detailed discussion of examples illustrating the main lines of argumentation.

Ambiguities and Irritations

Regarding the arguments used to justify the Austria's independence, the *ÖG* was constantly walking a tightrope, both in terms of its image of the Austrian nation and its self-image. In a very remarkable way, the statements oscillate between war and peace, between aggressiveness and tolerance, between hegemonic narratives and victim roles. Austria is sometimes described as powerful, superior, strong, and independent, but then again as innocent, passive, peaceful—culminating in the depiction of a victim who was robbed and cheated. This ambivalence of representation also mirrors how Austria was seen by various political decision makers. The "victim's doctrine" was the official narrative set by the government.[47] Dealing with the occupying powers, it was also necessary to emphasize independence from Germany and demonstrate independent viability.[48] However, ideas of returning to the Habsburg hegemony could clearly not be voiced under the Allied occupation. Even when referring to their own role in the discourse over Austrian independence, the *ÖG*'s members got caught up in contradictions: on the one hand, they claim to be Christian-tolerant in their approach to others and pacifist. On the other hand, they act aggressively and hatefully toward Germans. Of course, these arguments serve the same purpose, namely to argue independence. Nevertheless, direct comparisons will show that these positions are strongly divergent and difficult to reconcile.

The first example, by which this becomes apparent, concerns ideas of 'greatness' in opposition to the depiction of the small, innocent Austria becoming a victim. The *ÖG* frequently portrays Austria as an important nation that outshines other countries due to the great relevance of the Habsburg Empire to European history. Since it is claimed that the reduced size of territory should not be understood as a reduction in power or influence, this major line of argumentation from the First Republic is continued.[49] The idea of imagining Austria as a 'peace community' of the Danube region peoples prevailed. On the one hand, it testifies to the existing orientation towards a more powerful and influential Austria, and on the other hand, Austria is depicted as tolerant and cosmopolitan. Furthermore, there are constant references to its unifying and mediating power. These are claimed to be a result of its past. A very important narrative concerns the 'mixture of peoples' (*Völkermischung*), from which the moderate and peaceful 'Austrian character' was formed. A shared history of experience is declared an important factor bonding Austria with the countries of *Altösterreich*. The idea of a 'linguistic unity' (*Sprachgemeinschaft*), which is repeatedly used as an argument of belonging by the Greater Germans, is vehemently rejected.

Every opportunity is used to draw a differentiation from Germany while clearly deviating from peaceful profile and acting aggressive and hostile. As the Germans are blamed for their 'brutal' and 'reckless' behavior during WWII, this also contributes to their portrayal as perpetrators and thus indirectly underlines the role of Austria as a victim. It is particularly alarming that the *ÖG* even speaks about a specific 'national character' of the Germans which it describes pejoratively. While Germany is portrayed as 'bad' and 'inferior,' Austria is supposed to appear 'better' and 'superior.' Here, the *ÖG* uses harsh and highly problematic lines of argumentation and clearly does not act in the spirit of the claimed Christian values, since there is no forgiveness for the Germans. Nor does it behave according to the role as a 'moderate' mediator but deliberately provokes public ideological debates and conflicts.[50] This aggressive conduct against the Germans is particularly irritating due to the intentions of stylizing Austria as harmless in other statements. The narrative of victimhood, according to which Austria was invaded by the superior Germans, is stressed again and again. But this idea, strongly anchored in the self-image of many Austrians, is linked to the portrayal of Austria as innocent and defenseless. Only Germany is blamed for the fact that Austria was denied its independence. Complaints about unequal treatment and heteronomy are expressed.[51] The argumentation focused only on the German claims to power over Austria. No comparable criticism was voiced against the occupying powers.[52] Traces of 'Greater German' sentiment were, however, also and especially denounced within Austria. The *ÖG* did not shy away from accusations against other Austrians. Therefore, even more critical perspectives afar from any glorified mythology of 'victimhood' can be found in the texts.

A further contrast arises given the *ÖG*'s longing to influence political decisions. As the Grand Coalition was seen as a crucial factor in maintaining independence, the non-partisan *ÖG* constantly urged the SPÖ and ÖVP to unite and to fight against any sympathies for the Anschluss that still must have existed. Like the occupying powers, it considered the cooperation of the two major parties an important protection against the forces that had been unleashed after their disruption in the First Republic.[53] In its periodical, the *ÖG* frequently asked political decision makers to take action against opponents of Austrian independence. With some concerns, it even directly addressed the government and the Federal President. The *ÖG* obviously valued its own importance very highly. However, it was by no means a "mass movement" but wanted to distinguish itself as an elitist group. Strict admission criteria are emphasized in texts from different decades.[54] The fact that they obviously justified the importance of their opinion by qualitative rather than quantitative criteria also fits in with the elitist views that the group had already held in the First Republic. The magazine was also not available for street sale, as the editors were convinced that it was "more useful in the right places."[55] The exact circulation is not known for either the periodicals or the books. However, their wide reach and relevance, both in Austria and internationally, is repeatedly emphasized.[56] It may be surprising that such a significant interest is attributed to a journal that was most likely read exclusively by members of the *ÖG*.[57] It was presumably only through the good contacts of the influential circle around Wilhelm Schmid and Ernst Karl Winter[58] that the periodical was able to gain some resonance, including among Austrians abroad. The amount of donations made for its expansion supports the thesis that the *ÖG*'s ideas were indeed widely received and considered worth funding. Within two years (1953–1954), a total of more than 18,000 Schillings were collected to make the monthly publication possible.[59]

Arguments and Narratives in Detail

One of the main topics that the *ÖG* had always emphasized in the First Republic and continued to argue with in the Second Republic is the idea of Austria's strong relation to the peoples in the Danube region. The *ÖG* still associated the Austrian identity with this area, which is naturally united through mountains and waters. The unified Danube region, which for the most part consists of "the territory of the old Austro-Hungarian monarchy," is used as a symbol for a European orientation but also evokes Austria's historical hegemony.[60] The *ÖG*'s mission concerns the commitment to Austria and to the "community of all peoples," especially those with whom it is connected by history and geography. To the *ÖG*, being Austrian means being European.[61] However, this argument is no longer used to openly demand a return of the Habsburg Empire but mainly undermines any idea of belonging to Germany. Perceiving Austria as part of the Danube region in contrast to the German region is seen as "one of the strongest pillars" on which Austrian sovereignty is based.[62] Countless textual evidence refers to the importance of this connection, which, in contrast to the *Sprachgemeinschaft* invoked by the Greater Germans, had lasted for centuries.

However, the question of a language-related national identification marks a core problem the *ÖG* had to deal with. As the German language was used as an argument for Austria's belonging to Germany by the Greater Germans, the *ÖG* made the linguistic unity with Germany responsible for the disaster of the war.[63] Equating language with nation or people is stated to be dangerous and a fallacy that had become fatal to Austria.[64] Instead of language, the common fate (*Schicksalsgemeinschaft*[65]) is considered to be decisive in terms of national belonging. Precisely from the question of whether language does or does not make a nation, another remarkable contradiction in perspectives arises within the *ÖG*'s periodical and books. On the one hand, any nation-building character of language is vehemently denied, as long as the common language with Germany is at stake. On the other hand, the *ÖG* claims the exact opposite whenever the peculiarities of Austrian German are discussed. When it comes to characteristics that distinguish German in Austria from German in Germany, the essential importance of language for identity and nation building is emphasized. Language is described as a "mirror of the character, an expression of a people's imagination, thoughts and feelings." This approach in explaining "the difference of the German and Austrian language use by the difference of the German and Austrian national character ... and furthermore the effect of the German national character in the intellectual life" is explicitly referred to as "ethnological."[66] The distinction between Austria and Germany is argued with the nature of the two different 'types of people'.[67] The *ÖG* claims that the 'Austrian character' has been shaped by the 'blood mixture.'[68] The concept of Austria being composed of a diversity of tribes, including Celts, Romans, and Slavs, justifies its sovereignty and refutes the argument that it is "purely German."[69] This unique national character, which is described as "harmonically balanced," even affects thinking and the "more logical, more meaningful, more correct way of expression."[70] Another important argument concerns the Austrian "willingness to communicate, receptivity to the nature of other peoples"[71] and the ability to act as a "mediator in the diversity of nations."[72] This characteristic is seen as very significant and is considered to be reinforced by the geographical location in the middle of Europe. The *ÖG* claims that the political path of Europe might have developed quite differently, and even the war could have been forestalled, if the importance of Austria "as the keystone of the European equilibrium had been adequately recognized."[73] This shows how remarkably high the *ÖG* valued Austria's role in foreign policy. This role is, however, not perceived as a passive one, as it was during the Cold War, when questions of Austrian belonging were negotiated in the midst of the interests of East and West. Instead, Austria is claimed to serve as a mediator (*Vermittler*) and therefore is assigned a decisive and active role. This is also expressed by the architectural metaphor of the "keystone," (*Schlußstein des europäischen Gleichgewichts*), which means that without Austria, the European balance would collapse.

This role as a *Vermittler* is also seen as an obligation. Austria's mission and its traditional vocation consisted in bringing about "supranational peace"[74] and becoming a bridge or "the shortest and most important link"[75] between West and East. The tradition of the 'cosmopolitan empire' is meant to be continued in the 'new' Austria, since the Second Republic is also referred to as a "historic key point at the crossroads of major economic and cultural routes."[76] Because of its achievements in business, art, music, literature, and science, its importance and capability of standing independently is undeniable.[77] From these positions in particular, it becomes evident that the *ÖG* attempted to invoke the narrative of 'Austrian exceptionalism' as often as it could. Emphasizing Austria's independence most evidently wasn't enough, as it is constantly portrayed as unique and extraordinary.

The *ÖG* keeps claiming that Austria is incomparable to any other state, but above all, it is stressed that Austrians can have nothing in common with the Germans, because the latter are brutal and brash. As the *ÖG* points out, this bad 'national character' even becomes manifest from their way of speaking, since it appears to be artificial and lacking any sentiment.[78]

As mentioned, the texts are full of clear devaluation of the Germans. Portraying them as evil and spoiled helps to depict Germany as a perpetrator and Austria as an overly "credulous victim."[79] The ruthlessness and unscrupulousness of the Germans is a major argument, while Austrians are attributed with a more reserved and subtle nature.[80] Solidarity, selflessness, moral integrity, and humanity are identified as characteristics of the people in the center of the Danube region. Austrians were respected all over the world for their politeness, whereas the German influence had distorted their character.[81]

According to the *ÖG*, the Austrians' overly tolerant nature walks hand in hand with the danger of being influenced. Due to their too selfless adaptability and the high consideration for others, Austrians had become prone to abandoning their peculiarities, which is identified as their "national error."[82] For they tend to behave "honorably even towards one's enemies," and they betray their own people.[83] This tendency of letting one's own interests and character fade into the background was to be observed especially when dealing with the Germans. Too benevolent motives prevent the populace from asserting itself as Austrian. It is argued that Austrians have always lacked self-confidence and, without justification, felt inferior to the overly self-confident and preponderant Germans. As a result, they are partly to blame for becoming a victim of the German dominance.

Along with this rather unusual way to handle the narrative of victimhood, there are yet a few more interesting statements about the role of Austrians in WWII. Besides the typical depictions of a violent attack and the inaccurate idea of a general resistance to the Anschluss,[84] there are also indications to be found in the texts that there had been misconduct on the Austrian side. For instance, "conscious betrayal of some and the naivety of others"[85] are given as reasons for the outbreak of WWII right at the beginning of the *Gemeinschaft*'s first issue. Although characterizing Austrians as naive still fits with the notion of an innocent victim, this attribution at least acknowledges that both the betrayers did something wrong. Those who allowed themselves to become 'instruments' are to blame eventually as well.[86]

The ÖG spoke out very clearly in favor of excluding those who were "ideationally or factually" incriminated from cultural and political life.[87] It accordingly also disapproved of the too moderate dealing of the Grand Coalition with former Nazis. The *ÖG* repeatedly criticized the fact that the ÖVP and SPÖ were, for fear of losing votes, not taking tougher action against those who were still sympathizing with Nazi ideas.[88] In addition to combating any threats 'from outside,' the association obviously set itself the goal of defending the nation's freedom and independence against any Nazi tendency inside Austria.[89] For this purpose, even a new *Österreichische Aktion* was founded, which is explicitly identified as a united combat front formed by various organizations.[90]

One threat that was particularly fought against was the *VdU* (*Verband der Unabhängigen*), founded in Salzburg. Because they wanted to prevent this party from gaining strength, the ÖG is said to have intensified its activities there. The publications of the *Kulturverlag* were perceived as a counterpoint to the Anschluss initiatives, which were tending to be strong in Salzburg. The journal was intended to provide "an intellectual foundation for the restoration of Austria."[91] Presumably, the vehement opposition to the *VdU* was more of an attempt to avert the impending loss of power to the governing parties (especially the ÖVP[92]). The *ÖG*, however, stylized its fight against this party to be a resistance movement against Nazi ideologies.

Nevertheless, the *ÖG* emphasized that this 'war' it was waging was an intellectual one, fought only "against ideas, but not against people."[93] The fact that the members themselves were probably aware of the ambivalence in the appearance of their statements is expressed pointedly within the claim that they want to "act like a lamb among other lambs but as a wolf to any other wolf" (as the Latin saying *Agnus cum agnis, lupus in lupos* expresses).[94]

The ÖG apparently saw its calling and task in pointing out grievances—which is why, in retrospect, its members claim to have always been the "conscience of the nation."[95] For example, the *ÖG* claims to have pointed out the dangers in the face of Austrofascism—although it is referred to as the "Dollfuß Schuschnigg era" and always considered with a certain ambiguity within the texts—and to have warned about WWII before anyone else.[96] They insist that if the politicians at the time had heard them, Austria would have been spared from the "bitterest ordeal of its history."[97] The conviction that the *ÖG* should therefore be seen as a "pioneer of the resistance movement"[98] marks just another attempt to intentionally reinterpret history in its own favor and to assign itself a more significant role in the discourse on Austrian identity. Since it considered itself an important monitoring instance, it also sent conference reports and memoranda to politicians, informing them about its activities and assessments. The *ÖG* made urgent recommendations for strengthening Austrian identity and commented on official initiatives in education as well as denazification.[99]

After some years of denouncing anything that seemed *Großdeutsch* and claiming to be the conscience of the nation, the *ÖG* developed a remarkable interest in clarification and reappraisal—also in terms of the victim doctrine. Although it undoubtedly took an idealized view of Austria in a vast part of its statements, efforts of assessing the war events with "ruthless openness"[100] appear as early as 1963. In a so-called "Austrian manifesto," the view of WWII as the defense of the homeland was opposed. In 1976, the *ÖG* eventually addressed a memorandum to the government, demanding that a clear position on Austrian soldiers in the *Wehrmacht* be officially stated. Firstly, the *ÖG* wanted the government to declare that those soldiers had done their military service against Austria, regardless of whether it was voluntary or forced. Secondly, they demanded an official confirmation that, from an Austrian point of view, the war was not lost and the Allies had not come as enemies but as liberators. Not being clear on this issue would, according to the *ÖG*, be equivalent to subliminal propaganda.[101] These views, expressed ten years before the Waldheim affair triggered a public discourse, must have been considered strong and unusual demands. However, this is not the only call for action from that period.

The *ÖG* states that since 1970 it had seen its explicit task in taking stand on issues of state, cultural, and economic policy. Therefore, concrete proposals were drawn up and subsequently communicated to political decision makers and public figures.[102] For instance, the closing statement of the 1978 conference was addressed to the Federal President, the presidents of the National Parliament and the chairpersons of the Federal Council, the Chancellor and the members of the federal government, as well as all governments of the federal provinces. The leaders of the two major parties at federal level and in the provinces, high-ranking officials in the authorities concerned, media houses, related organizations, as well as friends and members of the *ÖG* also received the document.[103]

There is a small amount of evidence for reactions on those letters, in which the politicians state their recognition of the work of the association and assure that its considerations would deserve and also receive attention.[104] For instance, the *ÖG* stated in 1954 that sending its periodical free of charge to those responsible for political development in Austria and Europe was worthwhile. It is noted with satisfaction that its voice is heard and heeded.[105] Even Chancellor Kreisky confirms this view with his letter to the *Bundesobmann* of the time, Walter Schwarzer, in which he responds in great detail to a memorandum. He concludes by assuring the *ÖG* "that its comprehensive deliberations on the fields of economic, social, and cultural policy will be given due consideration in the work of the federal government."[106] Still, it is difficult to assess whether these ideas had any actual impact on political decisions.

As the *ÖG* was convinced that the Grand Coalition was a necessity, it repeatedly urged unity—reminding of the fact that inner conflict, contradictions and 'party strife' had led to serious consequences in the First Republic.[107] Therefore, the association itself wanted to serve as an example "that it is possible for socialist and conservative people to work together in the spirit of *Österreichertum*."[108] It is constantly stressed that socialist and conservative views are equally welcome and represented in the *ÖG*.[109]

The idea of putting aside substantive debates and consolidating contradictory opinions in favor of Austria's independence even affected concepts about the form of government. In several examples, it becomes evident that many members were still following a tradition of the former *Großösterreichische Gemeinschaft* and holding monarchist attitudes. As was already pointed out, not all of them had come around to being 'good democrats' despite the clear pro-democratic profiling on the outside. Apparently, there was in no way an intention of excluding or scaring this group away.[110] On the contrary, in order to avoid stepping on their toes, it was preferred to ignore the question of the form of government. In 1953, the *ÖG* still decreed "full freedom in the question of the form of government."[111] As long as the monarchists put Austria first and the republicans did not disregard the history before 1918, these two groups were considered equal within the *ÖG*. Instead of dealing with this debate, it was regarded more important to "work together on the *österreichische Ideologie*."[112] This term refers to the underpinning of Austria's independence, which should be approached cooperatively, while positions on the form of government should only be discussed "in private."[113] Incidentally, the fact that these identity policy efforts are described as work on an 'Austrian ideology' (*österreichische Ideologie*) is remarkable as the *ÖG* was, after all, interested precisely in ensuring that the concept of a sovereign Austria no longer had the status of an ideology, but was regarded as a fact. Overall, however, this example makes it particularly clear that the main argumentative strategy of the *ÖG* was to unite those who 'think Austrian' in any way—regardless of the striking differences.

Like several examples given so far, this line of argumentation also shows that the *ÖG* had an interest in affirming the Austrian nation by all means. Despite any contradictions arising from the sometimes divergent approaches, they contributed to the discourse over Austrian identity from all possible directions.

Conclusion

The *ÖG* deserves attention as an intellectual lobby or 'think tank' that helped to build Austrian identity at the beginning of the Second Republic. As a non-partisan association, which most likely stood close to the ÖVP due to its history, it acted as a partner of the Grand Coalition in the initiatives to consolidate Austria's national sovereignty. However, with regard to the fight against persistent Greater German ideas, it also profiled itself as a control body. Because of its good connections to personalities in politics and the fact that its statements were taken note of at the highest level, the *ÖG* played a role in the discourse on identity. With the concepts it negotiated, this intellectual group contributed to the ideational construction of the Second Republic.

Even though the *ÖG*, whose publications may have been received primarily within a circle of intellectuals with similar interests, probably had little direct influence on the negotiation of public or elite opinion, its perspectives are worth a more detailed study. Their extensive contributions testify to the way in which the construction of Austrian identity was carried out. The results show that especially in the early phase after WWII, Austria profiled itself mainly through a clear distinction from Germany.[114] This narrative was also promoted by the occupying powers and was seen as crucial to the international acknowledgement of Austrian sovereignty, which is also stressed Matthias Pape and Michael Gehler.[115] For the *ÖG*, arguing Austria's emancipation meant devaluing anything German. However, while it finds very clear, often harsh words for the portrayal of Germany, the depiction of Austria in the texts of the *ÖG* is often characterized by contradictory concepts. The fact that the lines of argumentation are sometimes divergent (e.g., divided between peace narratives and combative positions) says a lot about the identity discourse of the time. The ambivalence in which the *ÖG* gets entangled in its attempt to characterize Austria can be seen as symptomatic for the disorientation concerning the notion of Austrian identity. Although the members of the *ÖG* represented a very clear political goal, even they did not have a stable idea of what concepts to attribute to Austria nor were they sure about what role they themselves wanted to take on in propagating those concepts. This reflects the uncertainty of Austrians about their national self-image in the early Second Republic. Given the fact that even today views of Austria and the interpretation of its role in international relations is subject to public debates, it is understandable that at that time there were no solid concepts of national identity.

As a result, intellectual groups like the *ÖG* instrumentalized everything that seemed suitable for the purpose of identity formation. The diffuse juxtaposition of narratives in the examined texts underlines this impression of the *ÖG* trying to utilize any idea for the purpose of affirming Austrian independence and sovereignty—if not Austrian "exceptionalism."[116] The question of how its sovereignty was reinforced was obviously seen as secondary and hardly reflected on. Instead of setting up a coherent perspective that would serve as a policy for all of its publications, arguments were collated loosely, regardless of contradictions.

In this process of reconstructing an Austrian identity, it seems like any suitable component that could be found in the ruins of Austria after WWII was used for the building of a new nation. As the study of the *ÖG*'s positions suggests, the emphasis may not have laid so much on whether those components all fit together as on the fact that the rebuilt state was seen as capable of standing on its own.

Endnotes

1. This paper was first delivered at the Annual Meeting of the Austrian Studies Association in New Orleans, April 12–15, 2022.

2. On the earliest official efforts of building an Austrian identity, see Emil Brix, "Zur Frage der österreichischen Identität am Beginn der Zweiten Republik," in *Die bevormundete Nation: Österreich und die Alliierten 1945–1949*, ed. Günter Bischof and Josef Leidenfrost (Innsbruck: Haymon-Verlag, 1988), 93–104; Peter Thaler, *The Ambivalence of Identity: The Austrian Experience of Nation-Building in a Modern Society* (West Lafayette: Purdue University Press, 2001), 58–63. The research described in the present paper serves as a piece of evidence for many of the processes Thaler identifies in the discourse over a sovereign national identity after WWII.

3. Henceforth abbreviated as *ÖG*.

4. The *ÖG* continued to exist until 2004, but lost importance as the consolidation of Austrian sovereignty proceeded.

5. *Nation: Blätter für österreichische Erneuerung* 2, no. 4 (1950): 51.

6. In 1945, the school subject was renamed in order to avoid the term *Deutsch*; Wolfgang Pollak, *Was halten die Österreicher von ihrem Deutsch? Eine sprachpolitische und soziosemiotische Analyse der sprachlichen Identität der Österreicher* (Vienna: ÖGS/ISSS, 1992), 61. Brix provides a copy of a school report that includes the subject *Unterrichtssprache*; Brix, "Zur Frage der österreichischen Identität," 104. The decision to publish a new Austrian dictionary (*amtliches Wörterverzeichnis*) was made in 1947; Amtliche Regeln und Wörterverzeichnis: Vereinfachung der Rechtschreibung, Erlaß vom 28. Mai 1947, Z. 23.580-IV/12, Verordnungsblatt für den Dienstbereich des Bundesministeriums für Unterricht, Jul. 1, 1947, ALEX/Österreichische Nationalbibliothek, Wien, 90, accessed Dec. 31, 2022, https://alex.onb.ac.at/cgi-content/alex?aid=vcu&datum=1947&size=35&page=96.

7. *Gemeinschaft: Blätter für österreichische Erneuerung* 1, no. 1 (1948): 1.

8. More precisely, the image of Austria being the "first victim" of National Socialism, which was to shape the nation's self-depiction for decades, is evoked here. This issue is described in detail by Heidemarie Uhl, "Das 'erste Opfer': Der österreichische Opfermythos und seine Transformationen in der Zweiten Republik," *Österreichische Zeitschrift für Politikwissenschaft* 30, no. 1 (2001): 19–34, accessed Dec. 31, 2022, https://nbn-resolving.org/

urn:nbn:de:0168-ssoar-59626. On the question of how this "victim's doctrine" was used in Austria's dealings with the occupying powers, see endnote 47.

9. *Nation* 2, no. 4 (1950): 51.

10 *Gemeinschaft* 1, no. 2 (1948): 8.

11. Roland, *Großösterreichische Gemeinschaft* (Vienna: Großösterreichische Gemeinschaft, 1930), 22.

12. *Nation* 2, no. 3 (1950): 35.

13. *Österreichische Nation: Zeitschrift der staats-, kultur- und gesellschaftspolitischen Vereinigung "Österreichische Gemeinschaft" – Bundesverband* 27, no. 5/6 (1975): 63.

14. Janek Wasserman, *Black Vienna: The Radical Right in the Red City, 1918–1938* (Ithaca: Cornell University Press, 2014), 132–57, accessed Dec. 31, 2022, https://doi.org/10.7591/9780801455223-008; Janek Wasserman, "Österreichische Aktion: Monarchism, Authoritarianism, and the Unity of the Austrian Conservative Ideological Field during the First Republic." *Central European History* 47, no. 1 (2014): 76–104, accessed Dec. 31, 2022, https://doi.org/10.1017/S0008938914000636. Heer also briefly discusses the *Aktion* but doesn't mention the *ÖG*; see Friedrich Heer, *Der Kampf um die österreichische Identität* (Vienna: Böhlau, 2001), 397–8.

15. Jan Papiór, "Die "österreichische Idee" als Redaktionsgrundlage der Zeitschrift "Vaterland"," in *Schöpferische Begegnungen*, ed. Norbert Honsza (Wrocław: Wydawnictwo Uniwersytetu Wrocławskiego, 2000), 101–26 (here 105–7). Precisely, Zeßner-Spitzenberg, Winter and Schmid were among the staff of the *Vaterland*. Missong and Görlich had only written individual contributions.

16. August M. Knoll et al., *Die österreichische Aktion: Programmatische Studien* (Vienna: self-published, 1927).

17. Knoll et al., *Österreichische Aktion: Programmatische Studien*, 9. Vogelsang was a publicist who paved the way for a Christian *Arbeiterbewegung*. Also, many ideas of the later *Christlichsoziale Partei* are based on his social theory. Therefore, Heer refers to him as *geistiger Vater* of the party; see Heer 2001, *Kampf um die österreichische Identität*, 279.

18. The ideas of Anton Orel, a social reformer who profiled himself as a successor of Vogelsang's theory, were still discussed by the *ÖG* in the Second Republic; see August M. Knoll et al., eds., *Anton Orel: Leben und Werk* (Salzburg: Österreichischer Kulturverlag, 1952).

19. *Österreichische Nation* 27, no. 5/6 (1975): 64.

20. Roland, *Großösterreichische Gemeinschaft*; Wilhelm Schmid, "Großösterreichische Jugend," in *Die österreichische Aktion: Programmatische Studien*, ed. August M. Knoll et al. (Vienna: self-published, 1927), 270–84.

21. Papiór, "Redaktionsgrundlage der Zeitschrift 'Vaterland'"; Adam Miechowiecki, "Die recycelte Monarchie: Die "Österreichische Aktion" und ihre Vorstellungen eines neuen, alten Österreich" (Master's thesis, University of Vienna, 2021); Ursula Prutsch and Klaus Zeyringer, eds., *Leopold von Andrian (1875–1951): Korrespondenzen, Notizen, Essays, Berichte* (Vienna: Böhlau, 2003). As Leopold Andrian was also a contributor to the *Vaterland*, it is also discussed in the volume published by Prutsch/Zeyringer on this writer and diplomat.

22. Roland, *Großösterreichische Gemeinschaft*, 37; The *Vaterland* was published from 1927 to 1938 but was probably not available for sale publicly. Besides the *Österreichische Aktion*, it also served the *Katholische Aktion* and the *Vaterländische Aktion*; see Papiór 2000, "Redaktionsgrundlage der Zeitschrift 'Vaterland,'" 102–3.

23. Miechowiecki, "Recycelte Monarchie," 57; Papiór 2000, "Redaktionsgrundlage der Zeitschrift "Vaterland"," 101–2; Prutsch/Zeyringer 2003, *Leopold von Andrian*, 497; Roland, *Großösterreichische Gemeinschaft*, 12–3. Papiór also notes that, compared to the Christian Social weekly periodical *Das Neue Reich* (from 1932, before that *Schönere Zukunft*), the *Vaterland* was much more vehement in its advocacy of the Austrian idea and much more conservative in its outlook. At the same time, however, what was propagated in the *Vaterland* also served social democratic and monarchist principles.

24. Knoll et al., *Österreichische Aktion: Programmatische Studien*, 10.

25. Roland, *Großösterreichische Gemeinschaft*, 24.

26. Miechowiecki, "Recycelte Monarchie," 54–6, 70–78, 303.

27. Schmid, "Großösterreichische Jugend," 284.

28. Roland, *Großösterreichische Gemeinschaft*, 12–3, 20.

29. Schmid, "Großösterreichische Jugend," 281.

30. With the founding of the *ÖG*, the *Großösterreichische Gemeinschaft* was continued but there was no direct equivalent to the *Österreichische Aktion* after 1945. Because of the strongly overlapping circle of people, however, it can also be argued that the former *Aktion* was continued with the new *ÖG* as well.

31. *Nation* 2, no. 3 (1950): 35.

32. *Gemeinschaft* 1, no. 2 (1948): 8.

33. *Österreichische Nation* New Series 16, no. 3 (1998): 3.

34. *Gemeinschaft* 1, no. 1 (1948): 4.

35. Österreichische Gemeinschaft, *Was die österreichische Gemeinschaft ist und will* (Innsbruck: Österreichische Gemeinschaft 1977) DO 616, Inv. Nr. 480/14. OR/*ÖG* Organisationen, Parteien, Vereine: Österreichische Gemeinschaft (Vienna, Archiv Österreichisches Institut für Zeitgeschichte [henceforth abbreviated as AÖIZG], 2021), 1.

36. *Österreichische Nation* 27, no. 5/6 (1975): 64.

37. Österreichische Gemeinschaft, *Was die österreichische Gemeinschaft ist und will* (AÖIZG), 1.

38. *Gemeinschaft* 1, no. 1 (1948): 4. The objectives summarized in the main text are described as follows in the German original:

Die Wiederbelebung der österreichischen Idee auf katholischer Grundlage.

Bekenntnis zur österreichischen Nation.

Pflege österreichischer Kultur.

Friedliche Zusammenarbeit der Völker des Donauraumes.

Ablehnung jeder volks- und gesamtdeutschen Ideologie.

Eintreten für die kulturelle und politische Selbstständigkeit und für soziale Gerechtigkeit.

39. Ibid.

40. *Gemeinschaft* 1, no. 1 (1948): 4; *Nation* 2, no. 4 (1950): 54, 84.

41. This collection comprises only a small selection of documents published by the ÖG under *Bundesobmann* Walter Schwarzer in the 1970s. In addition to the already cited mission statement (see endnote 35), a conference report from 1978 (see endnote 103), a memorandum from 1976 including a response by Chancellor Kreisky (see endnotes 101 and 106), the archive holds three further documents from 1979 in which the association positions itself on history and current politics, and a blank membership form from the 1970s.

42. *Gemeinschaft* 1, no. 3 (1948): 12.

43. In the first issue, it is noted that they had wanted to continue immediately with the magazine *Vaterland*, but this was impossible due to a lack of resources; *Gemeinschaft* 1, no. 1 (1948): 1.

44. The periodical bears the same title as a brochure written by Alfred

Missong. Missong, who was part of the *Österreichische Aktion* in the First Republic and thus also belongs to the circle of the *ÖG*, was one of the founders of the ÖVP after the war and served as editor-in-chief of *Österreichische Monatshefte*. The brochure "Die Österreichische Nation" was published as a supplement to this party organ in 1946. The fact that the *ÖG* highly recommended it and wished for a wide distribution testifies to a close connection between the *ÖG* and leading ÖVP functionaries. Due to the high appreciation of the text (e.g., in *Gemeinschaft* 1, no. 1 (1948): 4), it is likely that the later title of the journal was inspired by Missong.

45. Ursula Kramml, "Salzburger Verlagsgeschichte von 1945 bis 1959" (Master's thesis, University of Salzburg, 2002), 243.

46. Wolfgang Teubert, "Die Wirklichkeit des Diskurses," in *Linguistische Diskursanalyse: neue Perspektiven*, ed. Dietrich Busse and Wolfgang Teubert (Wiesbaden: Springer Fachmedien Wiesbaden, 2013), 55–146, accessed Dec. 31, 2022, https://doi.org/10.1007/978-3-531-18910-9.

47. Despite a blatant contradiction of the historical facts, according to which Austrians must also be attributed the role of perpetrators, the perspective of Austria as a victim of the Nazis was insisted on in order to secure the political favor of the occupying powers. On the circumstances of building up and adhering to this narrative, see Günter Bischof, "Die Instrumentalisierung der Moskauer Erklärung nach dem 2. Weltkrieg," *Zeitgeschichte* 20, no. 11/12 (1993): 345–366 (here 348–350). The fact that Austria, despite its longing for independence, had been emphasizing this victim role, with which it actually states its own 'lack of freedom,' anticipates the contradictions that are to be developed in this paper. The paradox that precisely this self-image "has been used again and again to mobilize national identity forces" is particularly evident in the debate on the question of neutrality – which has flared up again since the Russian invasion of Ukraine; Berthold Molden, "Österreichs hundertjährige Opferdoktrin," *science.orf.at*, Mar. 27, 2022, accessed Dec. 31, 2022, https://science.orf.at/stories/3212192/.

48. These efforts on the ideational level reflect the factual demarcation as any relations to Germany, including economic cooperation, were cut off during the occupation; Otmar Höll, "Die Außenpolitik gegenüber Deutschland, der Schweiz und Liechtenstein," in *Handbuch Außenpolitik Österreichs*, ed. Martin Senn et al. (Wiesbaden: Springer Fachmedien Wiesbaden, 2023), 447–79 (here 453, 456), accessed Dec. 31, 2022, https://doi.org/10.1007/978-3-658-37274-3_22.

49. Roland, *Großösterreichische Gemeinschaft*, 24.

50. *Österreichische Nation* 7, no. 10 (1955): 153.

51. *Nation* 1, no. 1 (1949): 4; *Österreichische Nation* 4, no. 4 (1952): 73–4.

52. The *ÖG*'s statements on the occupation were not the focus of the examination discussed in the present paper as the debate about identity is mainly shaped by conflicts with Germany. The *ÖG* did not criticize cultural influences from the occupying powers in the same way that is, for example, evident from the fact that Anglicisms appear sporadically in the texts, while any language imports from Germany are vehemently rejected; *Österreichische Nation* 11, no. 12 (1959): 182.

53. Because of the serious consequences the disruption of the socialist and conservative parties had brought in the First Republic, the Grand Coalition was also supported by the Allies. The cooperation between the two major parties, which was established as a political consensus in the early years after WWII, was of great interest and demanded to be maintained throughout the occupation period; Manfred Rauchensteiner, *Die Zwei: Die Große Koalition in Österreich 1945–1966* (Vienna: ÖBV, 1987), 128–129.

54. Roland, *Großösterreichische Gemeinschaft*, 27; *Österreichische Nation* 4, no. 2 (1953): 39; *Österreichische Nation* 27, no. 5/6 (1975): 65.

55. *Österreichische Nation* 5, no. 2 (1953): 40.

56. *Österreichische Nation* 3, no. 3 (1951): 47.

57. Members were obliged to subscribe to the *ÖG*'s periodical; *Österreichische Nation* 2, no. 4 (1950): 82.

58. Although the former deputy major of Vienna, who is known for his attempt to reconcile right-wing and left-wing views, stayed in America after WWII, he continued to contribute to the *ÖG*'s actions; *Gemeinschaft* 1, no. 4 (1948): 16. For further information on Winter's activities after 1945, see Christian Stifter, *Zwischen geistiger Erneuerung und Restauration: US-amerikanische Planungen zur Entnazifizierung und demokratischen Reorientierung und die Nachkriegsrealität österreichischer Wissenschaft 1941–1955* (Vienna: Böhlau, 2014), 386–92.

59. *Österreichische Nation* 5, no. 6 (1953): 104; *Österreichische Nation* 6, no. 1 (1954): 16; *Österreichische Nation* 6, no. 3 (1954): 48; *Österreichische Nation* 6, no. 8 (1954): 128.

60. *Österreichische Nation* 5, no. 5 (1953): 74. The natural borders of this territory (such as the Engadine, Lake Constance, the Carpathians, the Sava, the Danube, and the Adriatic Sea) are described in great detail to argue that its coherence is destined by nature.

61. *Gemeinschaft* 1, no. 3 (1948): 9.

62. *Österreichische Nation* 5, no. 5 (1953): 87.

63. *Österreichische Nation* 6, no. 1 (1954): 6–10.

64. Görlich, *Handbuch des Österreichers*, 193–4.

65. *Österreichische Nation* 7, no. 1 (1955): 10–11; *Nation* 2, no. 3 (1950): 45.

66. *Österreichische Nation* 3, no. 1 (1952): 8.

67. *Nation* 2, no. 4 (1950): 53.

68. *Gemeinschaft* 1, no. 3 (1948): 10–11; *Österreichische Nation* 3, no. 1 (1951): 2.

69. *Nation* 2, no. 5 (1950): 91. Each of the supposed 'substrates' is even attributed a characteristic of its own. Accordingly, in the 'Austrian nature' one finds Illyrian tenacity, Celtic lust for life, Slavic musicality, and Roman-Germanic *Staatswille*.

70. *Österreichische Nation* 4, no. 1 (1952): 9–10.

71. *Nation* 2, no. 6 (1950): 103.

72. *Österreichische Nation* 3, no. 4 (1951): 59.

73. *Nation* 1, no. 6 (1949): 77.

74. *Österreichische Nation* 3, no. 5 (1951): 80.

75. *Nation* 1, no. 6 (1949): 78.

76. Reiter, *Kultur- und Wirtschaftsgeschichte*, 258.

77. *Nation* 1, no. 5 (1949): 77; Reiter 1952, *Kultur- und Wirtschaftsgeschichte*, 259–73.

78. *Nation* 1, no. 4 (1949): 43–4; *Österreichische Nation* 4, no. 1 (1952): 8–9; *Österreichische Nation* 6, no. 6 (1954): 95.

79. *Nation* 1, no. 4 (1949): 44.

80. *Nation* 1, no. 4 (1949): 43–4; *Nation* 2, no. 4 (1950): 68.

81. *Gemeinschaft* 1, no. 1 (1948): 1; *Nation* 1, no. 1 (1949): 3; *Nation* 1, no. 4 (1949): 43–4; *Nation* 2, no. 4 (1950): 68.

82. *Nation* 1, no. 4 (1949): 43–4.

83. Hrauda, *Sprache des Österreichers*, 5–6.

84. Görlich, *Handbuch des Österreichers*, 16, 77; *Österreichische Nation* 6, no. 7 (1954): 98.

85. *Gemeinschaft* 1, no. 1 (1948): 1.

86. *Nation* 2, no. 1 (1950): 3–4.

87. *Nation* 1, no. 1 (1949): 7.

88. Precisely, the *ÖG* accused the two major parties of an "undignified hunting for voters," see *Nation* 1, no. 2 (1949): 24. As Rauchensteiner explains, they were especially concerned with pulling the *Minderbelastete* (not heavily incriminated former Nazis) to their side, as soon as the *Sühnefolgen* (consequenses of atonement) were ended for this group; see Rauchensteiner, *Die Zwei*, 129.

89. *Österreichische Nation* 6, no. 4 (1954): 61.

90. *Gemeinschaft* 1, no. 5 (1948): 17; *Nation* 2, no. 1 (1950): 3–4. It is unlikely that this initiative was intended to tie in with the principles of the earlier *Aktion*. Presumably, this name, marked by tradition, was chosen to gather as many like-minded people as possible.

91. *Nation* 2, no. 1 (1950): 9–10 (Nachdruck aus dem *St. Galler Tagblatt*).

92. Given its prehistory, the fact the *ÖG* stood close the ÖVP cannot be denied (see also endnote 44). The thesis that an association like the *ÖG* consisted mainly of ÖVP sympathizers is also supported by the aspect that conservatives and communists were particularly concerned with nation-building, but not so much the Social Democrats; Thaler, *The Ambivalence of Identity*, 59. Still, the *ÖG* profiled itself as non-partisan and repeatedly referred to proportional representation. It is possible that precisely because of its strong sympathies with the ÖVP, it always emphasized the equality of the two major parties, see *Nation* 2, no. 2 (1949): 24. The intention may have been to prevent their periodical from being seen as a party medium.

93. *Nation* 2, no. 4 (1950): 55.

94. *Österreichische Nation* 3, no. 4 (1951): 50.

95. *Österreichische Nation* 27, no. 5/6 (1975): 65.

96. *Nation* 2, no. 4 (1950): 52–4. More specifically, the *Großösterreichische Gemeinschaft* had warned against Prussian belligerence, which brought it into conflict with a youth movement called *Neuland*.

97. *Nation* 2, no. 3 (1950): 35.

98. *Österreichische Nation* 27, no. 5/6 (1975): 64.

99. In 1949, the *ÖG* participated in a memorandum on the removal of the incriminated literary scholar Josef Nadler, and in 1952 it commented on a decree by the Ministery of Education concerning *staatsbürgerliche Erziehung*; see *Nation* 1, no. 2 (1949): 24; *Österreichische Nation* 4, no. 1

(1952): 3; *Österreichische Nation* 4, no. 6 (1952): 94.

100 . *Österreichische Nation* New Series 17, no. 4 (1999): 16.

101. Walter Schwarzer et al., *Memorandum über die Notwendigkeit einer politisch richtigen Wertung und Sprachregelung für die Teilnahme von Österreichern als Soldaten der großdeutschen Wehrmacht im Zweiten Weltkrieg* (Innsbruck: Österreichische Gemeinschaft, 1976) DO 616, Inv. Nr. 811/2. OR/*ÖG* Organisationen, Parteien, Vereine: Österreichische Gemeinschaft (Vienna, AÖIZG, 2021), 3.

102. Österreichische Gemeinschaft, *Was die ÖG ist und will* (AÖIZG), 2. The fact that these efforts to actively participate in political discourse only began with the Kreisky era gives the impression that the *ÖG* was more critical of this government led by the Social Democrats. This seems plausible because of the close ties to the ÖVP. However, a change in the *ÖG*'s leadership could also be responsible for the increased activism. The uncertain documentation situation (see endnote 41) must also be taken into account.

103. Österreichische Gemeinschaft, *Tagungsabschlußerklärung* (Innsbruck: Österreichische Gemeinschaft, 1978) DO 616, Inv. Nr. 480/7–9. OR/*ÖG* Organisationen, Parteien, Vereine: Österreichische Gemeinschaft (Vienna, AÖIZG, 2021), 1.

104. *Nation* 1, no. 1 (1949): 3; *Österreichische Nation* 5, no. 5 (1953): 87; Österreichische Gemeinschaft, *Was die ÖG ist und will* (AÖIZG), 2.

105. *Österreichische Nation* 6, no. 4 (1954): 61.

106. Bruno Kreisky, *Brief des Bundeskanzlers an den Bundesobmann der Österreichischen Gemeinschaft, Walter Schwarzer.* Wortgetreue Abschrift von Walter Schwarzer (Wien, Nov. 14, 1977) DO 616, Inv. Nr. 480/11–3. OR/*ÖG* Organisationen, Parteien, Vereine: Österreichische Gemeinschaft (Vienna, AÖIZG, 2021), 5.

107. *Gemeinschaft* 1, no. 6 (1948): 21; *Österreichische Nation* 5, no. 2 (1953): 40; *Österreichische Nation* 6, no. 5 (1954): 78–9; Görlich, *Handbuch des Österreichers*, 324.

108. *Österreichische Nation* 5, no. 2 (1953): 39.

109. *Österreichische Nation* 5, no. 2 (1953): 39; *Nation* 1, no. 2 (1949): 24.

110. Nevertheless, this must be considered a rather small interest group that disappeared over time, since the majority of Austrians shows a strong acceptance of democracy as the preferred form of government in the Second Republic; Fritz Plasser and Gilg Seeber, "The Europeanization of Austrian Political Culture: Austrian Exceptionalism Revisited," in *Global Austria:*

Austria's Place in Europe and the World, ed. Günter Bischof and Fritz Plasser (CAS 20) (New Orleans: UNO Press, 2011), 225–228.

111. *Österreichische Nation* 5, no. 2 (1953): 39.

112. *Österreichische Nation* 5, no. 5 (1953): 87.

113. *Österreichische Nation* 27, no. 5/6 (1975): 65.

114. It seemed to pay off for Austria to orient its identity policy toward the demarcation from its neighbor at least until 1989, as is pointed out by Gabriele Holzer, *Verfreundete Nachbarn: Österreich – Deutschland: Ein Verhältnis* (Vienna: Kremayr & Scheriau, 1995), 49. For the impact this position had on their political relations, see also Engelbert Washietl, *Österreich und die Deutschen* (Vienna: Ueberreuter, 1987).

115. Matthias Pape, *Ungleiche Brüder: Österreich und Deutschland 1945–1965* (Köln: Böhlau, 2000), 65–73; Michael Gehler, ""Kein Anschluß, aber auch keine chinesische Mauer:" Österreichs außenpolitische Emanzipation und die deutsche Frage 1945–1955," in *Österreich unter alliierter Besatzung 1945–1955*, ed. Alfred Ableitinger et al. (Vienna: Böhlau, 1998), 205–68 (here 206–7).

116. For further details on how those narratives of Austria being exceptional evolved (and to what extent they are applicable to the often claimed *Sonderweg* ("special path") in political terms), see Anton Pelinka, "Austrian Exceptionalism," *Austrian History Yearbook* 33 (2002): 1–14, accessed Feb. 10, 2023, https://doi.org/10.1017/S0067237800013795.

Review Essay

Nazism in Austria in the University, in Sports, in Monuments and National Memory

Günter Bischof

Herbert Posch and Martina Fuchs, eds., *Wenn Namen leuchten: Von der Universität Wien 1938 bis 1945 vertriebene Geschichte-Studierende und -Lehrende: Ein Denkmal* (Vienna: LIT Verlag, 2022)

Andreas Praher, *Österreichs Skisport im Nationalsozialismus: Anpassung – Verfolgung – Kollaboration* (Berlin: De Gruyter, 1922)

Heidemarie Uhl, Richard Hufschmied, and Dieter Binder, eds., *Gedächtnisort der Zweiten Republik: Das Österreichesche Heldendenkmal im Äußeren Burgtor der Wiener Hofburg* (Vienna: Böhlau, 2021)

More than three quarters of a century after the end of World War II, Austria is still grappling with the legacies of the war. As these books under review here demonstrate, just about every national institution was affected by the Nazi regime in Austria, be it higher education, popular sports, or the national memory regime. Austrians have long lived with the notion that they were "victims" of Hitlerite Germany. These books demonstrate that they were perpetrators too, on every level of society, and deeply implicated in Hitler's terror regime.

The various history departments of the University of Vienna recently installed a memorial in their sacred hallways to the Jewish and politically persecuted 128 students and 8 faculty that were excluded from continuing their studies and expelled ("*Vertreibung*") from the university after the "Anschluss" of Austria to the Third Reich in March 1938. The editors lay out the bureaucratic process of terminating an entire group of students from continuing to study and/or finishing their studies at the university. By the same token, Jewish faculty, or faculty members married to Jews, lost their jobs and often their pension (or parts of their pension) too. The University of Vienna was closed from March 12 to April 25, 1938. Jews were no longer allowed to step on university grounds after April 24. Altogether, 322 faculty members lost their jobs in March 1938 (236 for "racial" reasons, 86 for "political" ones). Hundreds of students were expelled. The Minister of Education Oswald Menghin, who spearheaded this expulsion administratively, was a Professor of Prehistoric Studies at the University of Vienna and a colleague of the expellees. A considerable number of faculty members were ideological pan-Germanists and underground Nazis and supported Menghin.

What stands out in this book is the fact that 128 biographies of expelled Jewish students have been carefully researched. Some of them are hair-raising World War II stories, like that of Ida Piepes. Hailing from Galicia, she studied history and Romance languages at the University of Vienna, starting in 1931; she finished her dissertation and exams in 1937; however, due to faculty resistance, she did not graduate until 1946. Herself a Communist, she eventually married the Communist Felix Margulies. After spending time in Switzerland and Belgium, they ended up in France, where they fought in the resistance. She was betrayed and ended up in the Drancy Camp with a death sentence; the camp was liberated before her execution. Now married and with children, she and Margulies returned to Vienna.

Leopold Weinberger was terminated at the University in his fourteenth semester. He lost everything and was deported to the Theresienstadt Camp, where he died. He was one among eight Jewish students who were murdered in the Nazi Concentration Camps. The lucky ones, like Osias Heschel Babad and Jakob Josef Bachstitz, both from Galicia, found refuge in the United States and Palestine respectively.

Of the eight Jewish faculty members who lost their jobs, two ended up in the United States, one in Great Britain. The historian of Modern History Friedrich Engel-Jánosi, a specialist on the Vatican, taught at Catholic University in Washington, DC for most of the war. He returned to teach at the University of Vienna in the late 1950s, never to receive a full professorship. The Medievalist Gerhart Ladner managed to get to London and then to Toronto in Canada. He ended up teaching at the University of California in Los Angeles and after his retirement as a Visiting Professor at UC Berkeley. Alfred Frances Pribram taught Modern History as a full professor and was also a corresponding member of the Austrian Academy. From 1924 to 1928, he selected Austrian fellows for the Rockefeller Foundation. He retired in 1930, lost his teaching privileges after the "Anschluss" and resigned from the Austrian Academy before he could be fired. He went to Great Britain and taught for a brief while at the London School of Economics before he passed away in 1942.

At the end of the book, the competition for the memorial is explained. A crucial element was the individual naming of all the expelled History students from the University (along the lines of historian Saul Friedländer's call of "*Gebt der Erinnerung Namen!*"). Of the four invited submissions, Iris Andraschek's project "*Wenn Namen leuchten*" won the artistic competition. She aimed at "allowing the names of the expelled students and faculty to become visible and shining from the darkness of the past and oblivion." On four panels of glass, the individual names of 128 students and eight faculty members are inscribed and shining through LED lights in the back. Additionally, the memorial inscription heads the panels: "In memory of those persecuted by National Socialism 1938–1945, who studied and taught at the previous [History] institutes of the University of Vienna." The memorial panels are installed in a long hallway, next to a traditional large lecture hall for History Department now named after the famous American gender historian and Jewish refugee from Vienna "The Gerda Lerner Lecture Hall."

This memorial to expelled Jewish students and faculty of the History departments comes as one in a long line of memorial initiatives of the University of Vienna dating back to the 1980s. The History departments had been contemplating such a memorial since 2010, culminating in the "Working Group Memorial Places History," which succeeded in getting the memorial discussed here built.

Andreas Praher's sports history of skiing under National Socialism is a prosopography of sorts, a collective biography of numerous Austrian skiing champions who launched careers in the National Socialist sports system. Similarly, sports functionaries continued their careers after the "Anschluss" in March 1938 under National Socialism. The "Austrian Skiing Association" (*Österreichischer Skiverband*, or ÖSV) easily blended into the Nazi Sports organizations. Praher also looks at those who migrated overseas before or after the "Anschluss." When World War II ended, the many Nazi skiing "heroes" managed to escape denazification and easily blended into the skiing world of the Second Republic.

Praher stresses the continuity from prewar to war to postwar. The ÖSV had a national "*völkisch*" great-German tradition going back to pre-World War I times and continued it in the First Republic. It passed an "*Arierparagraph*" in its basic constitution as early as 1923, excluding all Jewish members from its organization and its constituent ski clubs all over Austria (115ff). Even before the Nazis were in power in Germany, the ÖSV demonstrated "*vorauseilender Gehorsam*" (201ff, 417), anticipating that society-at-large might act on its Antisemitism in the future. Many of the ski stars and sport functionaries joined the Nazi party (NSDAP), the SA, and the SS for similar opportunistic reasons already in the early 1930s (135f). "The road from the local ski club to the SA was a short one" (154), argues Praher.

Among many ski champions, the case of the downhiller Hellmut Lantscher from Innsbruck is telling. The early SA-man fled to Germany and joined the Austrian Legion. By 1937, he entered competitions for Germany. After the Anschluss, he managed to stay away from the frontlines by continuing to train for Nazi organizations and compete, winning the world championship in 1939. After the war he claimed to always have been "unpolitical" (154), irrespective of the fact that his whole family was serving the Nazi Party in various functions. His cousin Gustav Lantschner was an early Party and SS member. He also fled to Hitler's Third Reich before the Anschluss and skied in international competitions for Germany. He acted in skiing films and became a camera man for Leni Riefensthal in her "mountain films" (280ff). After the war he fled to Argentina to escape denazification efforts. He settled in the Andean skiing town San Carlos de Bariloche along with his brother Fritz, who had been a high Nazi Party functionary in the *Gau Tirol-Vorarlberg*, and his family (289, 376ff). Tyrolean ski instructors settled there before the war and welcomed their old skiing pals.

After the "Anschluss," Austrian skiing sports came "home" ("*Heim ins Reich*") (187ff). The ÖSV was discontinued (197) and its functionaries now served the National Socialist cause. Austrian skiing was integrated into the Nazi organization DRL (*Deutscher Reichsbund für Leibesübungen*) and was brought under the heel of state control by the NS-regime. National Socialism used skiing "to prepare young men physically and psychically for war" (181). Skiing became a "*Volkssport*" and was supposed to strengthen the "*Volkskraft*." The "*Ostmark*" star skiers were admired and heroized in Nazi Germany and started for Germany in international competition. Many launched their careers in Nazi Party formations, supporting Nazi propaganda efforts. Wilhelm Köstinger, born in Leoben, Styria, was an especially egregious case. A skiing champion since the mid-1930s, he was "politically reliable" (337) and joined the state police in 1939. He most likely was involved in Jewish deportations in Innsbruck and joined the *Einsatzgruppe I* in the campaign against Poland as an elite SS-soldier and probably was involved in the shooting of Polish intelligentsia (339). The extent of his involvement in war crimes in Poland is not known. He was never tried after the war even though he was a POW of the British. He entered various skiing competitions in the early 1930s and ended up working for the SD of the SS in Oslo, Norway, where he was involved in deporting Jews to Auschwitz (343).

Not all skiing champions served the Nazi regime. In the course of the 1930s, many left to become ski instructors in the United States, looking for a better life. They became involved in building up American ski resorts and the skiing industry. Some resisted the Nazi regime, like Hannes Schneider, the inventor of the "Arlberg method" of skiing. He also was a popular movie star of sorts, next to Leni Riefensthal, working in the skiing film productions of Arnold Franck (227). After the "Anschluss," he was incarcerated by the Nazis, whose propaganda machinery denounced him, and then put him under "house arrest." He managed to emigrate to the United States in 1938 and started his own skiing school in North Conway, New Hampshire (238f). He was celebrated in the USA as a film star and "The World's Foremost

Ski Expert" (227). Many of his St. Anton ski instructors, like Friedl Pfeiffer and Benno Rybitzka, had come to the USA before him; others, like Anton "Toni" Matt and Ludwig Föger, followed Schneider. They ended up in the 10th Mountain Division of the US Army and continued their careers as ski instructors and skiing entrepreneurs after the war.

Schneider's Jewish friend Rudolf Gomperz helped St. Anton reconstruct its winter tourism industry. He was killed by the Nazis in Maly Trostinec, Belarus, where many Viennese Jews were killed. Other Jewish skiiers, like Paula Kann, managed to get to the USA. She taught in Hannes Schneider's Skiing School in North Conway and became a well-known ski racer for the USA during the war (241f). Praher dedicates his book to those persecuted by the Nazis: Hannes Schneider and Rudolf Gomperz.

Praher concludes his book with chapters on the "failed denazification" after the war and the skiers' and functionaries' "reintegration" into the postwar sports world of the Second Republic. The return of the Nazi skiing champions from the "*Ostmark*" to the slopes, and functionaries such as Alfred Rössner, who had joined the SA in 1931 and trained the *Hitler Jugend* after the "Anschluss", to their former roles (or their flight to Argentina), were made possible with professions of their "Austrian patriotism" and "their success in the sports world for Austria" (384). Like the rest of their Austrian compatriots, they all claimed to have been "victims of National Socialism" (382). Their "illegal" activities before the war were thus excused and swept under the carpet. The ÖSV was restarted in December 1945. Since Austria wanted to restart its winter tourism industry, it began to court the former Nazi skiing stars. Rössner was let go from the American internment camp Glasenbach in 1947 to train the Austrian olympic team for St. Moritz in 1948 (402). Thus Austrian skiiers began to win Olympic gold medals again after the war to make Austria a "sports nation," buttressing Austria's postwar identity.

Praher's study is based on meticulous archival research, thus bringing Austrian sports history to a mature level.

The hefty and richly illustrated book on the Vienna "Heroes Memorial" (*Heldendenkmal*) illustrates the difficulty of constructing a broadly acceptable Austrian post-World War II memory. The Ministry of Defense (BMLV) has been responsible since 1963 (331) for the *Heldendenkmal* at the *Äussere Burgtor* on Vienna's central *Heldenplatz* (Heroes Square), where Hitler gave his famous speech on March 15 and also viewed a parade on the *Ringstrasse* and laid a wreath on the tomb of the dead soldier in the crypt of the *Heldendenkmal* (283–86).

This book was commissioned by the BMLV from an advisory group of scholars, who in 2014 presented a new concept for the use of the *Heldendenkmal* and wrote a good part of this book. This occurred on the advice of the German scholar of memory Aleida Assmann, who argued that the controversial memorial also served as an Austrian "history book for the past 100 years" on the *Heldenplatz*, which was a "central stage of the Republic." Therefore it should be maintained but not be removed (432). It rather should become a "place of learning" (433).

The *Heldendenkmal* indeed has a long history as a central place of Austrian memory— military memory, to be precise. It was first erected in the Napoleonic era in 1824 to glorify the Habsburg soldiers who were humiliated and defeated by Napoleon's Army and in the end were victorious (42–46).

It was reconstructed in 1934 as a prestige project of the Austrofascist Regime to commemorate the fallen soldiers of World War I and all the Habsburg soldiers of previous wars. Anna Stuhlpfarrer presents all the projects submitted to the architectural execution of the site. The winning project included the crypt with the monument to the dead soldier by the sculptor Wilhelm Frass, an illegal member of the National Socialist Party since 1933. He secretly included into the monument a letter dedicated to the Nazi soldiers and the German people (173). After many attempts, Frass's monument was finally lifted in 2012 and his dedication was found, along with a pacifist letter by his assistant Alfons Riedel; nobody had known about this counter-statement (427f). As Heidemarie Uhl points out, Austria's leading politicians and visiting dignitaries, who had deposited wreaths at the feet of Frass monument for a generation, thus had "bowed before Nazi symbols" (427).

The meat of this volume is in Peter Pirker's fifty-page essay on the *Heldendenkmal* "as a symbol of post-National Socialist democracy in Austria" (309–59).[1] Pirker looks at the use of the *Heldendenkmal* in the post-World War II era and in the process deconstructs "the myth" of the Austrian *Opferdoktrin* .[2] He argues that the "victim's theory," proffered by the Provisional Renner Government in the Austrian "Declaration of Independence" of April 27, 1945 (fashioned after the 1943 Allied Declaration on Austria) did not explain the heroic memory of Austrian World War II *Wehrmacht* soldiers, whose memory was included in the 1950s in the commemoration of the heroic Austrian soldiers of previous wars. The "Declaration of Independence" did not mention the Austrian resistance either, called for in the Allied Moscow Declaration. The government quickly corrected this lacuna by passing the *Opferfürsorgegesetz*, giving resistance fighters public financial support as "victims" of the war, and publishing the *Red-White-Red* book in 1946, celebrating the deeds of the Austrian World War II resistance (313). "*Opfer*" in German means both "victim" and "sacrifice" in English. Pirker distinguishes between the "sacrificial" and "victimological" forms, "*Aufopferung*" and "*Opferwerdung*."[3] The memory of the World War II soldiers proffered in ceremonies pushed by the veterans' lobby (*Kameradschaftsbund*) increasingly stressed their heroic sacrifices in the war: they did not consider themselves victims.

So the state's victim's theory, designed to integrate all Austrian victims, did not include soldiers and resistance fighters; nor did it explicitly include Jews, the "real victims" (313). In July 1959, politicians of the grand coalition revealed a new inscription on the façade of *Heldendenkmal*: "*Im Gedenken an die Opfer im Kampfe für Österreichs Freiheit*" (Commemorating the victims who fought for Austrian Freedom). Even though this memorial was dedicated to the Austrian resistance, representatives from the resistance organizations were not invited; it was a "sneaky action" (330–32). In 1965 a separate "*Weiheraum*" (sacred room) was dedicated to the Austrian resistance inside the *Heldendenkmal*. It was not architecturally inviting, nor was it open to the public like the crypt, where the heroic soldiers were commemorated. From 1966 to 2010, politicians laid wreaths on the Austrian national holiday on October 26 in both the crypt and the *Weiheraum*, honoring both *Wehrmacht* soldiers and the resistance fighters and commemorating the sacrifices (*Aufopferung*) of both groups (340). This represents a "dualism in the Austrian politics of history" (311). Kurt Waldheim, in his 1986 election campaign spoke of having "done his duty" like hundreds of thousands of Austrian soldiers, promoting the sacrificial rhetoric used by the veterans' lobby since the 1950s.[4] After Waldheim, the Austrian World War II memory regime was reconstructed and came to speak of Austrian perpetrators too, next to the victims. It is doubtful whether Pirker's complex redefinition of the postwar Austrian memory regime centered on the *Heldendenkmal* will replace the old "victim's myth," designed to distance postwar Austria from (Nazi) Germany. University professors and skiers may have made "sacrifices" for the Nazi fatherland, being "victims" after the war gave them a means to reintegrate into their professions and the Austrian nation.

Endnotes

1. Pirker had first published the theses of his long essay in a shorter version in these pages, see Peter Pirker, "The Victim Myth Revisited: The Politics of History in Austria up until the Waldheim Affair," in *Myths in Austria History: Construction and Deconstruction*, ed. Günter Bischof, Marc Landry and Christian Karner (CAS 29) (New Orleans: UNO Press – innsbruck university press, 2020), 151–172.

2. On the Austrian victim myth, see also Simon Blount, "The Victim Myth: The Reinvention of Austria in the Postwar Years," *Journal of Austrian Studies* 55, no. 3 (Fall 2022); 71–76.

3. Pirker acknowledges that Cathleen Giustino (next to Aleida Assmann) made the distinction of "victim" and "sacrifice" in English for "*Opfer*" in the pages of CAS 26, Pirker, "The Victim Myth Revisited," 153, 168n6.

4. Pirker, "The Victim Myth Revisited," to 155.

Book Reviews

David S. Luft, *The Austrian Dimension in German Intellectual History: From Enlightenment to Anschluss*. (London: Bloomsbury Academic, 2021)

Janek Wasserman

In his 1981 article, "What is German History? Reflections on the Role of the Nation in German History and Historiography," James Sheehan observed that the Kaiserreich and the Reichsgründung loomed over subsequent German historical scholarship even long after its disappearance. He argued that the boundaries of the German nation-state need not dictate the contours of German history while urging scholars to consider German affairs in their multiplicity. In The Austrian Dimension in German Intellectual History, David Luft applies this lesson in a different context: the book "presents a new way of thinking about Austrian intellectual history – one that neither concentrates on Vienna nor encompasses the whole of the Habsburg Monarchy. It is an intellectual history of German-speaking Austria..." (1) By considering this "Austrian dimension" in relation to German intellectual history on one hand and Habsburg traditions on the other, Luft strives for a new, unified picture of Austria's contributions to German and European culture. Warning against "teleological, essentialist accounts of what is German by pointing to another 'Germany'" (1), Luft seeks a "less reductive understanding of the European past" (2). To accomplish this, the author presents the political and cultural conditions in German-speaking Austria, i.e. Cisleithanian Austria, as the backdrop for an intellectual history of Austrian philosophy, literature, and the human sciences between 1740 and 1938. This slender yet ambitious book takes aim at many of the leading figures in twentieth-century Austrian history and European intellectual history, respectively: H. Stuart Hughes, William Johnston, Pieter Judson, Robert Kann, Carl Schorske, inter alia. While it offers a useful conceptualization of the Austrian cultural space and its distinctive values, the book provides less guidance for new pathways in Austrian intellectual history, however.

The introduction and conclusion make clear that Luft believes the intellectual history of Austria is unfamiliar to the Anglophone world and is occluded by its German counterpart. He wishes to tease that distinctive Austrian tradition out. Looking at modern Austrian history, he sees the German and Bohemian hereditary lands as linked intellectually, political, and culturally. He distinguishes the experiences of those territories from Hungarian and Galician ones, justifying their exclusion from this "Austrian" story. Peering inside the Austrian "box" (8) reveals a German tradition indebted to the Enlightenment yet skeptical of idealism and Romanticism, committed to individuality but invested in what we share as human beings, interested in religion while committed to modern science. It also possesses the following unique attributes: "a resistance to reductionism and ideological polarization, the emphasis on ethics and inner experience, and respect for unconscious energies and what we cannot control" (139). These traits distinguish Austrian cultural life from contemporary northwestern German and Central European contexts.

Chapters One and Two provide a schematic narrative of historical developments from the Middle Ages until the Anschluss, demonstrating the "long historical connection between Austria and Bohemia" (15). This effort redirects attention away from either the story of the Habsburg dynasty or the lands near Vienna, two general preoccupations of Austrian historiography. These chapters provide few new historical details and seem a curious detour away from the core intent of the book, yet they do establish the many commonalities between Austrian and Bohemian lands in Cisleithenia. They also present Vienna and Prague as complementary – and competing – centers of Central European German life. Luft stresses reform Catholicism and centralized political authority in Austria and Bohemia as underlying conditions for intellectual development. Chapter Two provides a quadripartite division of the modern period (1740–1792, 1792–1866, 1867–1900, 1900–1938/1939), yet it is interested in continuities and ruptures across those divisions. The Enlightenment and Josephinism characterized the first era, with Sonnenfels and Dobrovsky as leading lights. The conservative early nineteenth century saw the emergence of figures like Bolzano, Grillparzer, and Stifter. A skepticism of German idealism and Romanticism emerged then, which was not to subside. The liberal late nineteenth century saw the flourishing of Viennese fin-de-siècle modernism but also the emergence of new, illiberal political trends. In perhaps the most controversial periodization, Luft chooses 1900 rather than 1918 as the dividing line. He argues that the "generation of 1905" possessed decidedly different traits than its predecessors (and the generation of 1927) and therefore merited separate consideration, even though Austria and Bohemia ceased to share a common fate after 1918.

After this historiographical and conceptual spadework, Luft applies his model to three areas of Austrian intellectual history: philosophy, literature, and the human sciences. As he stresses, this book "can only be provisional" (12) and "is meant to be heuristic rather than encyclopedic (139), and the case studies are more suggestive than comprehensive. The philosophy chapter treats Bernard Bolzano, Franz Brentano, Ernst Mach, Ludwig Wittgenstein, and the Vienna Circle within a mere twenty-eight pages. For those familiar with the work of Johnston, Barry Smith, Rudolf Haller, John Blackmore, and Friedrich Stadler, there is little new here. Luft stresses the Austrian interest in nominalism and a modest form of positivism. The literature chapter is the finest in the book, reminding the reader of Luft's unsurpassed contributions on Musil, Stifter, Hoffmannsthal, Weininger, and others. At the center of the current inquiry are Grillparzer, Stifter, Kraus, Musil, Hoffmannsthal, Broch, Rilke, and Kafka. The text sings as Luft discusses Stifter, inviting the reader into the Austrian's "state of calm, of presence, of awareness of the world, appreciation for the world" (98). Luft shows the shared ethical concerns of these Austrian writers, which he contends separates it from the German tradition. The final—and oddest—chapter deals with the human, or social, sciences by looking very briefly at psychoanalysis and Austrian economics. Whether these disciplines are exemplary or representative of Austrian Geisteswissenschaften is not well established, and the summary treatment of such rich disciplinary traditions leaves little room for even scratching the surface. After skimming across the cameralist tradition and the German historical school, the parlous state of fin-de-siècle social sciences briefly comes into focus. Following Bruce Caldwell, Luft sees the defining feature of the economics of Menger and Hayek as an emphasis on "what we do not know and what we cannot control: the unanticipated consequences of human action and conscious attention" (123). Freudian psychoanalysis, per Luft, demonstrated "commitments to science, civilization and nineteenth-century liberalism" (135). He lauded Freud's valorization of self-knowledge and critical inquiry and his contribution to our understanding of human nature. A reader barely gets her bearings in this brief discussion.

There is much to recommend this book, and it achieves many of its core aims. Like Sheehan, Luft has made the case convincingly that Austrian, German, and European historians need to be more intentional (in a Brentanian sense) about their object of study: Austrian intellectual history refers to a German-speaking space distinct from "Germany" or the Habsburg Empire yet intimately connected to Western (and Central) Europe. For a lay, Anglophone audience, the essay carves out a larger space for Austrian ideas and thinkers in a broader "Western" canon.

Questions emerge, however, when the readers shifts away from the "Austrian" descriptor and considers the historical account offered. Does the book's conceptualization fundamentally alter our understanding of Austrian intellectual history or how it is practiced? That is unclear. The Austrian Dimension offers the same canonical figures that have been studies for seventy years, and this "new" understanding of Austrian-ness does not lead to new interpretations of any of their works. Moreover, it does not open new pathways for Austrian intellectual history. Women are treated as an afterthought. Conservative, Catholic, nationalist, and idealist thought receives little attention. So does socialist, leftist, and heterodox thought. It is disappointing to see a major work of Austrian historiography make little substantive use of twenty-first century scholarship. Megan Brandow-Faller, Deborah Coen, Elizabeth Danto, Erwin Dekker, Alys George, Deborah Holmes, Tracie Matysik, Britta McEwen, Lisa Silverman, and others have expanded the contours of Austrian intellectual history, yet they receive no consideration. While this book is not meant to be comprehensive, the substance of it reifies a closed vision by narrowly defining "Austrian" themes and privileging certain intellectual figures and traditions.

Moreover, The Austrian Tradition does not adequately establish the core contention that Austrian history is underappreciated. One could easily argue the opposite: there are few subjects in intellectual history that have enjoyed such a broad readership ever since Schorske's time. If Austrian Dimension decenters Vienna (slightly), it is only to add Prague, another well-excavated intellectual center. It is not entirely clear who the intended audience is, in other words.

These criticisms are not meant to undermine the important contribution Luft makes in Austrian Dimension. The introduction is essential reading for German and Austrian historians. The prose is vivacious, and the book is pitched well for an educated audience or an undergraduate class. As an essay, it is thoughtful and provocative, challenging the reader to reconsider her presuppositions. As a valedictory on a distinguished career, it is a fitting tribute to the fertility of Luft's output and a useful reflection on past historiographical concerns. It will be a work to reckon with for generations of scholars interested in Austrian and German intellectual history.

Nikolaus Hagen et al., eds., *Displaced-Persons-Forschung in Deutschland und Osterreich: Eine Bestandsaufnahme zu Beginn des 21. Jahrhunderts* (Berlin: Frank & Timme, 2022)

Jennifer Popowycz

The edited volume, *Displaced Persons-Forschung in Deutschland und Osterreich: Eine Bestandsaufnahme zu Beginn des 21. Jahrhunderts*, presents the most recent German-language research regarding displaced persons in the post-WWII era. By providing a selection of lectures given at conferences at the Ter Europa-Universität Viadrina in Frankfurt (Oder) and at the University of Innsbruck, the anthology coincides with recent historiographical trends that place DPs in the larger context of flight, statelessness, and general migration movements. By employing a transnational and interdisciplinary approach, the authors in this volume transcend the spatial boundaries of camp life and successfully shed light on lesser-known aspects of displacement, such as communal identity and nation-building projects, the multifaceted roles of international humanitarian aid organizations, and postwar psychological trauma.

The volume is organized into four sections. The contributions in the first section show how the process of self-determination and nation-building in exile were negotiated through disputes and discourse, both internally and externally. Aivar Jürgenson, for instance, provides a fascinating look at the internal disputes within the Estonian diaspora community in Argentina, arguing that images of the homeland and reasons for leaving the native country created fissures within the diaspora community and created group boundaries between "old" and "new" immigrants. Kateryna Kobchenko takes a similar approach by looking at how diverse groups of Ukrainian DPs used statelessness to make and consolidate a new collective national memory. On the other hand, Jana Kasíková looks at the role the media played as mediator between local society and DPs returning home to Czechoslovakia, particularly in areas that served as repatriation centers.

In keeping with the theme of transnationalism, the second section is devoted to international aid organizations. While the administration of displaced persons by Allied occupation authorities and the United Nations has been the subject of postwar displacement historiography since the 1980s, two of the authors in this section highlight little-known facets of the United Nations Relief and Rehabilitation Administration (UNRRA). Stella Maria Frei, for example, sheds light on a group of UNRRA workers who acted as "agents of psychological reconstruction" in an effort to make mental health rehabilitation one of the core tasks of humanitarian agency (206). Wolfgang Piereth, moreover, looks at the UNRRA Training Center in Bad Wiessee—a center that trained displaced persons in the American occupation zone to take over UNRRA administrative tasks. Other authors highlight lesser-known international aid organizations such as the Canadian Jewish Congress and its War Orphans Project (Jim G. Tobias) and the Friends Ambulance Unit in Egypt, Italy, and Austria. (Philipp Lehar). Taken together, these selections provide a more nuanced look at international humanitarian aid in the postwar period and the variety of tasks they were actively engaged in.

Perhaps the most interesting part of the volume is the research conducted on how DPs initially began to process psychological trauma from the war. Stephanie Ligan describes how Polish Jews exiled in the Soviet Union during the war used the DP press as a medium, not just for documenting war and genocide, but as a tool for expressing mental and emotional anguish in the aftermath of the Holocaust. Complementing Ligan's work is a case study on Simon Wiesenthal by René Bienert that documents how Holocaust survivors searched for Nazi criminals using their own means. Unfortunately, this section only includes two lectures. However, the focus on Jewish agency and the processing of psychological postwar trauma effectively opens the door for more work to be done on this research topic.

In an attempt to show the diversity within the category of "displaced persons," three case studies on different camps in Bavaria and Austria complete the volume. Martin Nekola's research on Czechs in Austrian camps after 1948 achieves this goal the most successfully, as it directs attention to a less researched DP group. However, there is a disconnect between the programmatic aims of this section and the individual case studies provided by the other two authors. Evita Wiecki's work on Jewish DPs at the Bavarian monastery of St. Ottillen is, indeed, a case study, but the focus on nation-building efforts prior to the foundation of the state of Israel does not necessarily shed light on the heterogeneous nature of the DP phenomenon and would be better placed in the first section of the volume that emphasizes the development of community identity within DP camps. Similarly, Roland Lory's intriguing inquiry into DPs who were handed over to the Federal Republic of Germany in 1950 makes an important contribution to a topic that is still in its infancy by describing the relationship between homeless foreigners, welfare facilities, and the newly formed West Germany government, but does not contribute to the theme of diversity among DP groups.

Nonetheless, taken together, the selected lectures in *Displaced Persons-Forschung in Deutschland und Österreich* clearly show how DP research is transforming in the twenty-first century and how contemporary research on postwar displacement is moving towards transnational methods that expand the geographical confines beyond Germany and Austria. While some of the stated aims of the anthology are not met, the volume does succeed in exploring lesser-known DP topics such as nation-building projects across a wide range of DP groups, different roles and aims of international humanitarian aid organizations, and the initial processing of postwar psychological trauma. It is an essential read for historians of postwar Europe, as well as scholars interested in migration and nationalism studies.

Anton Pelinka, *Faschismus? Zur Beliebigkeit eines politischen Begriffs* (Vienna: Böhlau, 2022)

Evan Burr Bukey

In this outstanding study, Anton Pelinka, Austria's foremost political scientist, attempts to define an all-embracing understanding of Fascism. In 1945, those nations that had defeated the Axis powers and their allies, including otherwise neutral Spain, proclaimed that Fascist regimes had been utterly destroyed or discredited. With the passage of time, scholars, most notably John Lukacs and Eric Hobsbawm, wondered whether it possible to categorize or define Fascism as a historical phenomenon. Lukacs pointed out, for example, that superficially National Socialism was closely aligned with Mussolini's Italy, but ideologically much more to Stalin's Soviet Union. Similarly, his native Hungary may have been authoritarian, Lukacs argued, but by no means Fascist.

Pelinka's study is much longer and more thorough. He begins by explaining what Fascist regimes had in common: extreme, irrational nationalism; perceived internal enemies; and dictatorial power wielded by messianic individuals, most notably Hitler. Following two introductory chapters, Pelinka proceeds to examine in detail the history of several putative Fascist countries: Italy, Germany, Austria, Japan, and Spain. These lengthy chapters constitute the core of his book.

Readers familiar with the history and nature of Italian Fascism will find little new in Pelinka's otherwise shrewd account. As a war veteran and skilled politician, Mussolini shared the common belief that Italy's victory in the Great War had been "mutilated" and that Prime Minister Vittorio Orlando had failed to achieve the country's objectives at the Paris Peace Conference. In 1919, Mussolini founded the Fascist party, arguing that the "people and nation are one." Fearing the working classes in the north would turn to Communism following the Bolshevik Revolution, the new party attracted numerous middle class and bourgeois elites who accepted Mussolini as "*Duce.*" Because members of a divided multi party government were unable to address serious socioeconomic problems, in 1922 Mussolini was appointed Prime Minister of a coalition government. For the next two years, the Fascists followed constitutional rules and procedures until it became obvious, as it should have been, that Mussolini had assumed dictatorial power. In 1924, the Socialist lawmaker Giacomo Matteoti was kidnapped and murdered by Fascist thugs, for which Mussolini assumed his "historic responsibility," thus enabling him to crush his opponents. And following a failed assassination two years later, the *Duce* declared himself the leader of a totalitarian state.

Mussolini's definition of totalitarianism was vague, coined primarily to justify his monopoly of power. And as Pelinka reminds us, Mussolini never exerted total or absolute power; his regime was limited by the Vatican and the House of Savoy. On the other hand, both the Holy See and the monarchy preferred dealing with autocratic regimes rather than liberal democracies. Here the author stresses that Mussolini's charm and willingness to compromise enabled him to conclude the Lateran Treaties in 1929. The Concordat recognized Vatican City as an independent state with control over Italian education. In return, the Papacy accepted the Kingdom of Italy as the legitimate government of the country.

By 1935, Mussolini had taken steps to overcome the worst aspects of the Great Depression and achieved a measure of domestic stability. He had earned the admiration of such figures as the American ambassador, Winston Churchill, and even the songwriter Cole Porter. But in same year, by invading Abyssinia in a combined arms operation that included the use of poison gas, the *Duce* alienated the Western powers, eventually driving him into the arms of Nazi Germany. It is true that in signing the Munich Pact in 1938 Mussolini regained prestige. But by entering World War II in 1940, he sealed his own fate. Following a series of disastrous military defeats in the Mediterranean, North Africa, and Sicily, in 1943 he was overthrown by the Fascist Grand Council and in 1945 executed by Communist partisans.

In conclusion, Pelinka characterizes Italian Fascism as an improvised, dilettantish regime based on the rule of a single individual: Benito Mussolini. The regime was not as homicidal as that of Nazi Germany, but cruel and brutal nonetheless. Not only did the government take the lives of political opponents and conscripted soldiers, but left Italy in ruins in 1945. Its Achilles heel was vesting power in the hands of a single individual. This was the case of other nations that were either Fascist or regarded as such.

Can one characterize Nazi Germany as Fascist? Pelinka wrestles with the question at considerable length, arguing that the genocidal nature of Hitler's regime can be understood best by discounting theory in favor of consequence. To be sure, Mussolini and Hitler had much in common in that there would have been no Fascist Italy without the *Duce* or Fascist Germany without the *Führer*. The two dictators admired each other, wielded absolute power, and believed in the unity of the nation and the people. But for all his many flaws and shortcomings, Mussolini was not a biological essentialist. In contrast, Hitler's obsession with an imaginary mortal threat posed by "international financial Jewry" took the lives of over six million Jews and other "inferior races" between 1941 and 1945. In short, Hitler, and

Hitler alone, was responsible for the Holocaust.

In recounting Hitler's rise to power and the Nazi regime, Pelinka stresses that National Socialist Germany became a truly totalitarian state, comparable only to Stalin's Russia. Initially, this did not appear to be the case, as Hitler was appointed Chancellor to head a coalition government consisting of right-wing politicians and industrial elites. But, when all is said and done, the failure of the divided, multiparty Weimar Republic to come to grips with the Great Depression, followed by Brüning's deflationary policies, caused millions of Germans to seek an authoritarian leader in order to solve the nation's problems. Henry Ashby Turner once argued that Hitler's seizure of power was hardly inevitable, but, owing to Kurt von Schleicher's ineptitude and Hindenburg senility, that is what happened.

What surprised everyone was the rapidity and ruthlessness with which Hitler consolidated absolute power. The *Reichstag* fire enabled him to outlaw freedom of speech and assembly and other constitutional protections. Within in a month, he and his followers browbeat parliament to pass an Enabling Act, which enjoyed widespread support, not least among the clergy, armed forces, industrialists, and conservative cabinet members. Not until the Röhm Putsch in June 1934 did it became clear that Hitler headed a regime of gangsters. Even so, rearmament and deficit spending combined to restore the economy and eliminate unemployment altogether. In addition, foreign policy success, culminating in the Munich Agreement in 1938, won the support of roughly three-fourths of the German people, most of whom either ignored or applauded Hitler's persecution of the Jews. Pelinka makes no secret of the Führer's charismatic popularity that persisted until Stalingrad and to some extent beyond. But as a native Austrian, the author might have mentioned that both anti-Semitism and admiration of Hitler continued in the Second Republic for decades after 1945.

Pelinka concludes his chapter on Nazi Germany by reiterating his point that Hitler's absolute power and conviction that he knew better than others, including his closest associates, led both to his own destruction and that of the Third Reich. He and Mussolini were infected by what Pelinka calls "a self-defeating virus." However, what made the Führer different or unique was his determination to wipe every Jewish man, woman, child off from the face of the earth. To be sure, he invaded the Soviet Union seeking "living space" for the German people, but his major objective was to eliminate "world Jewry." What is remarkable, in retrospect, is that millions of party members, civilian officials, SS, and members of the armed forces, including not only generals, officers, but also common soldiers, raised no objections. The Holocaust saw non-Germans engaged in spontaneous atrocities, most notably in Croatia,

Poland, and the Baltic states. No one can deny the prevalence of anti-Semitism in Nazi-occupied Europe, but without Hitler's megalomaniacal obsession with the "Jewish Question," the Holocaust would not have occurred. Ultimately, Pelinka concludes, the total destruction of the Third Reich and National Socialist ideology achieved the opposite of their objectives, namely a rebirth of prosperity and freedom in the Federal Republic of Germany.

Is it possible to characterize the Dollfuss-Schuschnigg dictatorship that governed Austria between 1933 and 1938 as Fascist? Or did it constitute the sort of absolutism that prevailed in the Habsburg monarchy following the revolutions of 1848? There can be no doubt that Dollfuss modeled the Christian Corporative state on Mussolini's Italy, not least in his detestation of Marxism, the Enlightenment, and the equality of men and women. But unlike the *Duce*, he and Schuschnigg enjoyed the enthusiastic support of the Roman Catholic Church. And whereas Mussolini and Hitler were revolutionaries, Dollfuss was not. Both he and Schuschnigg looked to that past as means to govern a state that nobody wanted. To be sure, the regime was repressive, for example, in crushing and outlawing the Social Democratic party with what Pelinka calls occasional "dilettantish brutality." Even so, the regime did not persecute Austria's large Jewish population and was relatively tolerant aside from political opponents.

Because the defeated Social Democrats kept a low profile, it was the "illegal" Austrian Nazis who acutely and violently resisted the Christian Corporative regime. Theoretically, Schuschnigg might have restored social and political stability by reaching out to the underground Social Democrats and reinstating parliamentary government. Instead, he sought to accommodate the indigenous Nazis and appease Hitler's government in Berlin. The result was the "Anschluss" in March 1938, an event that was rapturously greeted by a huge majority of the Austrian populace. Could German annexation have been avoided? Most historians concur that given Hitler's belligerency and the intense, turbulent conditions prevailing in Europe at the time, the answer is most likely not. Which, in turn, raises the question as to whether the Dollfuss-Schussing regime can be categorized as Fascist. Pelinka contends it was "half Fascist," depending, he wryly adds, on how one defines Fascism.

Was Imperial Japan's regime Fascist? For obvious reasons, such as distance and relatively little knowledge of Italian and German culture and history, it was not. On the other hand, as many historians have noticed, there were striking similarities in amalgamation and modernization in the mid-nineteenth century. All three countries unified as nation states, established constitutional parliamentary governments, industrialized with remarkable speed, developed well-equipped armies and navies, and sought to strengthen their position and power on the international stage by means of imperial expansion. Considering the global supremacy of the British Empire at the time, these were not unreasonable aims.

During the Great War, Japan participated as an ally of the Western powers and sent diplomats, who joined the victorious powers at the Paris peace conference. Thereafter "the Land of the Rising Sun" was recognized as a Great Power. But rather like postwar war Italians, Japanese elites and policy makers concluded that the country had been denied the spoils of victory, particularly by Great Britain and the United States. From then on there was much talk of "white arrogance." And yet until the advent of the Great Depression, the country operated as a parliamentary democracy not unlike the Weimar Republic. To overcome the disastrous economic and social impact of the slump, a series of authoritarian governments concluded that the dilemma could be overcome by overseas conquest. Here there was a similarity to Italy and Germany, but both Mussolini and Hitler both intended to go to war as early as 1920.

What followed was the conquest of Manchuria in 1931 and, after much domestic turmoil, an attack on the Marco Polo Bridge in 1937 that resulted in a major war to conquer China. After Hitler's invasion of the Soviet Union, Japan joined Italy and Germany in signing the Tripartite Pact that made it one of the Axis powers. Unlike the Grand Alliance of Britain, the United States, and the Soviet Union, however, the Axis powers never coordinated military policy or agreed on common war aims. For Japan, World War II became a brutal stand-alone conflict. In only one respect did Imperial Japan and Nazi Germany share a common belief, in what Pelinka calls "mystical racism," a doctrine that would result in the mass murder of millions resembling those of the Holocaust in Europe.

Even so, there were major differences. Japan was not governed by a single individual, but a group of squabbling generals and admirals who could not decide whether to attack the Soviet Union or seize the natural resources of Southeast Asia. Only after much debate was it decided to "go South" by destroying the US naval base in Pearl Harbor and securing the Philippines. After conquering the Western Pacific, Tokyo hoped to defeat China, become economically independent, and secure an indefensible ring of island bases that would enable the country to negotiate a settlement with the United States. Ironically, it was a war that Tokyo knew it could not win.

Even so, the Japanese came close to achieving their objectives, even after the country's disastrous naval defeat at Midway in 1942. Pelinka contends that it was never really clear who governed the country or directed the war effort, which, in turn, meant that the generals and admirals did not know how or when to call a halt. What the author neglects to mention was the iron resolve of the United States and its allies to demand the unconditional surrender of the Empire of Japan. But who in Tokyo was in a position to accept such terms, even after Hiroshima, Nagasaki, and the declaration of war by the Soviet Union? The answer was provided by the Emperor, who on August 14, 1945, convinced the Suzuki cabinet to surrender.

To what extent was Emperor Hirohito responsible for invading Manchuria, unleashing a war against China, and attacking the United States? Pelinka reveals that Hirohito expressed skepticism, but approved the decisions of the government and armed forces. Rather like fellow monarch and ally Victor Emmanuel III, Hirohito technically might have ended the war much earlier than he did. No one will ever know, although Pelinka contends he was a political weakling. Does that mean that the Emperor was guilty of war crimes? After the Japanese surrender, General MacArthur wisely insisted that Hirohito bore no responsibility for Japanese atrocities. As such, the Emperor became a constitutional monarch, retaining the loyalty of his people while supporting reforms that transformed Japan into a model democracy.

Can Franco's Spain be characterized as a Fascist state? Considering the brutalities of the regime that included violation of censorship punishable by death, thousands of summary executions, clandestine support of Nazi Germany during the Second World War, and the absolute dictatorship of a single individual, most authorities concur that, with some exceptions, Spain was a model Fascist state. Pelinka strongly disagrees. He provides persuasive evidence that, despite state sanctioned atrocities and the *Caudillo*'s ruthless, self-centered cruelty, Spain between 1939 and 1976 was something different, if not unique. For one thing, Spain remained neutral during the Great War. Unlike Italy, Germany, Austria, and Japan, neither Madrid nor the Spanish people felt traumatized by the horrors of the conflict. However, the loss of overseas colonies in Latin America and in the Philippines in the nineteenth century left the country impoverished and deeply divided. The social and political gaps widened during the mid-twentieth century civil war, resulting in bitter divisions following the defeat of the Republican forces in 1939. Having consolidated his military and political power, Franco proceeded to stabilize the country not through reconciliation but rather through repression of real and perceived enemies. His objective was to gain the support of wealthy agricultural elites as well as the Roman Catholic Church in order to institute a monarchial dictatorship he imagined resembled the traditional order. Unlike other Fascist leaders, the *Caudillo* did not aim at a utopian future based on racism and military expansion, but rather the restoration of a glorious past. This became clear in October 1940, when he refused Hitler's proposal for Spain to join the Axis powers as allies in the Second World War.

Vain, colorless, and enjoying limited popular support, Franco never threatened a foreign power that enabled the regime to survive and become relatively tolerant after 1945, not least during the Cold War. But had Franco's Spain been a Fascist state? Pelinka contends that it was not, primarily because the regime changed with the passage of time. Acknowledging the author's clever arguments, this reviewer opposes that view. Between 1939 and 1945, Spain was indeed a prototypical Fascist state.

In his final chapters, Pelinka compares and contrasts the types of Fascist regimes examined in his study. He begins by reminding readers that each and every system claimed to represent the will of the people while forbidding them to disagree, both publicly and privately. They were ruthless dictatorships, relying on cruel and vicious means to imprison or murder dissenters. And yet aside from the Dollfuss-Schuschnigg regime, the Fascist countries and their leaders enjoyed enthusiastic popular support, most notably Nazi Germany. They promised domestic and international security, but in precipitating or participating in the Second World War, the Fascist regimes saw millions lose their lives and in defeat left their countries in ruin, not least Germany, which literally ceased to exist.

After providing additional characteristics of Fascism, such as a secular religion, Pelinka sums up what Fascist or Fascist-like regimes had in common. They were: "totalitarian," though in some countries, such as Italy, more an aspiration than a reality; the dictatorship of a single individual or, in the case of Japan, a handful of military officers; mass movements backing the regime; the militarization of society; internal and external aggressive racism; and above all, genocidal expansion by attacking and waging war on foreign countries in order to enslave or massacre their inhabitants. And yet, Pelinka asks, were these characteristics not also key components of murderous non-Fascist regimes such as Stalin's Russia and Mao's China? Furthermore, as this reviewer noticed in the German Democratic Republic, postwar "anti-Fascist" elites and power holders frequently used the term to conceal or cover up the criminal-genocidal policies pursued by their own countries. Anti-Fascism ("Antifa"), in other words, had much in common with the various forms of Fascism that had existed in the first half of the twentieth century.

Was Fascism a unique historical phenomenon that emerged after World War I, one that in various forms massacred millions of innocent civilians as well as enemy combatants during a second global conflict? Pelinka contends that, in retrospect, Fascism sowed the seeds of its own destruction. There can be no doubt that this was indeed the case. But following Madeleine Albright's book *Fascism: A Warning*, Pelinka reminds us that the recent rise of authoritarian, populist, nationalist movements such as that led by Donald Trump constitute a threat to democracy. To be sure, the former President's attempt to stay in power by inciting an insurrection on January 6, 2021 failed. That the insurgency miscarried can be attributed to the pluralistic American system of checks and balances, features essential to all successful democracies. After all, it was the divisions and weaknesses of democratic governments, most notably the Weimar Republic, that enabled Fascists to seize and wield absolute power in the mid-twentieth century. Looking back, Pelinka proves his point that Fascist regimes had much in common, but also differed in numerous ways. Hitler's Germany was without doubt the most destructive and genocidal, but so, for that matter, is Putin's Russia. Fascism, in other words, has not yet gone extinct.

Anton Pelinka, *Zur Aktualität von Paul F. Lazarsfeld: Einführung in sein Werk* (Aktuelle und klassische Sozial- und KulturwissenschaftlerInnen, Wiesbaden: Springer VS, 2021)

Günter Bischof

Anton Pelinka's introductory text on the principal scholarship of Paul Lazarsfeld, one of the giants of twentieth century sociology and founding figure of modern social studies, is a work of serious intellectual history and very readable. Pelinka, a political scientist, traces Lazarsfeld's most enduring works, *Die Arbeitslosen von Marienthal* (1933) and his paradigmatic election study *The People's Choice* (2nd ed. 1948). Pelinka rightly pays a lot of attention to Lazarsfeld's prospering academic career at Columbia University in New York City. He was one of many Viennese geniuses who were forced to leave Austria in the 1930s, when the Nazis dominated the universities, for lack of opportunities for Jews and socialists.

Marienthal was a small village South of Vienna that lost its only factory in the late 1920s. Marienthal's entire population was unemployed, and thus it offered a laboratory situation to study mass unemployment and its consequences (31-33). Lazarsfeld directed the study along with his team of social scientists, Marie Jahoda and Hans Zeisel. They lived among the people hurting in Marienthal in 1931/32 and introduced the new methodology of "participating observation" (*teilnehmende Beobachtung*) to social science research (40f). Pelinka stresses that Lazarsfeld the social scientist abandoned his Marxist political inclinations, given their empirical findings. The economic crisis of the Great Depression had not produced any revolutionary sentiments in the population but rather made them apathetic and resigned. It turned them into a "tired society" (45ff).

Marienthal was a pioneering study of modern social science research and was only discovered and recognized as such after World War II. It led to the gifted and innovative scholar Lazarsfeld pitching his tent in the United States. A scholarship from the Rockefeller Foundation in 1933/34 allowed him to participate in a project by the Federal Emergency Relief Agency studying unemployment and his consequences in the USA (53). Lazarsfeld returned to Vienna in 1935 for a short time and, given the advent of Dollfuss and Austrofascism, he "extended his visa" (54). In fact, without a firm job offer, he returned to the USA on a non-valid visa. He was lucky to find a job at Newark University and then engaged in radio research at Princeton University.[1] Having studied with Karl and Charlotte Bühler, he began to do market research as applied psychology. Lazarsfeld left his European Marxist roots behind, incorporated the dominant paradigm of behaviorism and began to study American voting behavior. He was not interested into which party voters chose but rather what were the factors that determined people to vote. This increasingly turned him into a sociologist who was interested in the entirety of society.

Columbia University appointed him a professor of sociology in 1939. Together with Robert Merton, he made the Columbia Sociology Department number one in the USA and the world over the next thirty years. Robert Merton was a theorist, and Lazarsfeld trained students in the empirical methods, including math and statistics; their joint seminar became known as the "Columbia Sociology Machine," producing the next generation of sociologists (82-85). In 1940, Lazarsfeld embarked on a vast voter study in Erie County, Ohio. Next to "sample surveys," he again embarked on remarkable methodological innovation with his "panel technique." This meant that voters were interviewed multiple times for the 1940 presidential elections (from May to November) to determine how voters formed their views over time and how opinions of voters hardened towards a decision over time (67). This allowed researchers to determine the influence of campaigns and media on voters. In the end, the study identified five groups of voters: constants, indecision waverers, crystalizers, party waverers, and party changers. Lazarsfeld and his team also studied the importance of "opinion leaders" in a given community (75). Pelinka concludes in Erie County Lazarsfeld and his team analyzed a "society full of contradictions" (78).

Pelinka also elucidates how Lazarsfeld's research on voting behavior contributed mightily to democratic theory. In a lengthy subchapter, Pelinka analyzes major theorists of democracy, from Joseph Schumpeter to Robert Dahl (85-96). Pelinka is also interested in Lazarsfeld's global place as a scholar. Even though he played an important role in locating an "Institute of Advanced Studies" (*Institut für Höhere Studien*) in Vienna in the 1960s, Lazarsfeld was never interested in returning to Vienna. After the political purges by the Austrofascists and the "brain drain" under the Nazis, Vienna was in a "rather desperate intellectual situation" after World War II (96-98). He therefore recommended to the Ford Foundation to start an IHS in Vienna to teach modern social science methods (Pelinka himself is an alumnus of this institution).[2] In the end, Pelinka concludes that Lazarsfeld is situated between the disciplines of sociology, psychology, and political science, having contributed to all of them. The "ex-European" Lazarsfeld is also located between the European and American world. At Columbia, he turned into an American. In Austria, the memory of Lazarsfeld was suppressed after 1945. He was rediscovered in Eastern Europe after 1989.

Endnotes

1. Paul Neurath, "Paul F. Lazarsfeld in Emigration und (teilweiser) Remigration," in *Vertriebene Vernunft II: Emigration und Exil Österreichischer Wissenschaft*, ed. Friedrich Stadler (Vienna: Jugend und Volk, 1988), 360–72 (here 366f); Christian Fleck, "Paul F. Lazarsfelds Weg vom "distinguished foreigner" über den "undesirable alien" zum Professor," in *Soziologie in und aus Wien*, ed. Andreas Balog and Gerald Mozetic (Frankfurt: Peter Lang, 2004), 129–66 (here 148–51).

2. Anton Pelinka, "The Impact of American Scholarship on Austrian Political Science: The Making of a Discipline," in *The Americanization/ Westernization of Austria*, ed. Günter Bischof and Anton Pelinka (CAS 12) (New Brunswick: Transaction, 2004), 226–34.

Günter Bischof and Peter Ruggenthaler, *Österreich und der kalte Krieg: Ein Balanceakt zwischen Ost und West* (Graz/Wien: Leykam, 2022)

Matthew Paul Berg

Readers of this journal will need no convincing of Austria's unique trajectory over the course of the twentieth century, nor of the understated significance of the Second Republic's geopolitical position during the Cold War. Those of us who teach in English-language institutions are well aware that Austrian history (not to mention Austria's place in international politics) is *terra incognita* for most students; Günter Bischof and Peter Ruggenthaler offer this study as a contribution to flagging attention to this field in historical institutes at Austrian universities (18), but with great benefit for us, too. Both scholars are well suited to undertake a contribution such as this. Bischof brings expertise from long and fruitful engagement with both Austrian and US sources, and Ruggenthaler contributes likewise from his work with Austrian and Soviet-era documentation. Each has been at the forefront of scholarship in their respective and overlapping areas over the previous decades. Together they provide readers with a detailed and pleasingly readable monograph. Students new to the theme and experienced researchers alike will find their text, their extensive notes, and the rich bibliographies following each chapter to be valuable resources.

The book is organized chronologically, beginning with reactions to the Anschluss, the positions the Soviets and the Anglo-Americans took towards Austria in relation to the war effort against Germany, and initial planning for the postwar period. Three chapters chart postwar developments into the emergence of Cold War fissures (1945–47), the solidification of the two blocks (1947–53), and the State Treaty that ended four-power occupation and established Austria's position as a fully independent state (1953–55). The authors include two thematic chapters in the first half of the book that expand upon their principal focus. One is an investigation into "soft power" as a form of cultural warfare. Here they discuss Amerika-Haus cultural institutions as access points to the "American way of life" which, together with the promise of economic stimulus provided by the Marshall Plan, suggested a future of comfort and plenty. British and French cultural politics manifested themselves principally in literature and fine arts programs (influence as a substitute for geopolitical hegemony). The Soviets sought to counter a long-standing negative image of Communism with its own brand of cultural politics, but rather less successfully than the other three occupiers; Austrian perceptions, broadly speaking, had been reinforced by Nazi propaganda and the behavior of some Soviet soldiers. The second thematic chapter offers a fascinating synopsis of the role that the four powers' espionage agencies in Austria—particularly in Vienna, where joint occupation offered secret services fertile ground for observation, recruitment, and subterfuge.

The book's second half advances the admixture of chronological and thematic approaches, highlighting Austrian neutrality during the crises in Hungary (1956), Czechoslovakia (1968), and Poland (1980); the Austrian government's role as a mediator and Vienna as a site for mediation during crises; economic and political relations with Soviet satellite states from the 1960s to the late 1980s; the long path towards creation of the Conference on Security and Cooperation in Europe; limits to Austrian economic integration with Europe imposed by the Soviet Union; and the end of the Cold War. The narrative sweep is comprehensive, and it integrates the essential developments one should expect from a diplomatic history survey text.

Diplomacy is fundamentally transactional, and the table at which parties sit is rarely a level one. Bischof and Ruggenthaler trace a developmental arc that begins with Austria deprived of the agency to participate as a fully sovereign and independent state under National Socialism. The Allies' 1943 Moscow Declaration asserted Austria's dual status as first victim of Nazi aggression *and* as co-responsible for Nazi crimes as a constituent part of the Reich (36ff)—a kind of liminal status that left a great many Austrians confused about why they were treated as a defeated enemy, although it was readily apparent that there had been Nazis in their midst. By November 1945, free and fair elections reestablished formal governance in Austria, though it would be four years before elections would restore a semblance of sovereignty in East or West Germany. The country remained under occupation until 1955, and legislation could be subject to veto by unanimous vote of the Allied Control Council (formal occupation ended in both German states in 1949, with foreign troops recast as protectors of sovereignty).

The authors discuss the Austrian federal government's efforts to satisfy four-power demands, including denazification (not without controversy among the Austrian population, yet supported to some degree or other by the political parties) and the Soviet demand for restitution in the form of "German" assets (42–43), even though some portion of those assets were of Austrian provenance, and a subset of those had been "aryanized" after the Anschluss. The Soviets sought to link an Austrian state treaty with a larger German solution, whereas the Anglo-Americans were wary of Soviet subterfuges that could facilitate the westward reach of Moscow's influence. Austrian federal leadership in the People's Party/Socialist coalition sought to exercise its limited agency by promising Soviet authorities it would enact permanent neutrality, which helped pave the way for the *Staatsvertrag* in 1955 (84–8; 103–14).

Full sovereignty gained through this treaty established the basis for Austria's position in Europe until the end of the Cold War and beyond. Bischof and Ruggenthaler note that the Second Republic was clearly Western from the perspectives of cultural heritage and commitment to representative democracy, but these characteristics in no way precluded eager and sincere cultivation of good relations with eastern neighbors. Indeed, the *Staatsvertrag* provided Vienna with the opportunity for a new style of diplomacy within these parameters. Austria committed to abstaining from military or political alliances and demonstrated a readiness to engage in trade and cultural exchange with lands of the capitalist West and the state-socialist East. A transactional strategy grounded in reciprocal stability and growth, rather than zero-sum thinking, drove this diplomacy. The Second Republic and its partners could benefit from cooperative economic relationships and respectful political ties; Austria could increasingly serve as a neutral site for international summits, for formal United Nations and other IGO meetings, and as an honest broker to resolve conflicts outside of Europe. Austria's foreign policy of *active* neutrality required judicious, active engagement with the world, not trepidatious restraint.

Continuity characterized Austrian foreign policy over the first postwar decades of grand coalition, when foreign ministers Gruber, Figl, and Raab (all ÖVP), and then Kreisky (SPÖ) worked with successive chancellors and cabinet colleagues to navigate through the occupation years, achieve the restoration of sovereignty, and cultivate relations with European states on either side of the Cold War divide. The authors show how, upon Kreisky's elevation to chancellor in 1970, Austria's diplomatic strategy expanded to include a focus on international development and heightened focus on northern-southern hemisphere relations; Austrian commitment to new, collaborative European security, cultural and economic exchange, and human rights dialogue; and Austrian interest in integration with western European economies. These features of Austrian foreign affairs persisted after Kreisky left office in 1983. Subsequent Austrian governments, regardless of the coalition makeup, continued to pursue these goals through the end of the Cold War and beyond. Two examples will suffice here. First, Bischof and Ruggenthaler point out that compassion shown to successive waves of Hungarian, Czech, and Polish refugees demonstrated Austria's commitment to human rights without violating its neutrality. This lent the Second Republic a certain understated moral authority in CSCE discussions (the fact that the OSCE has its seat in Vienna lends credence to the assertion). Second, Austrian pursuit of integration into the ECSC/EEC/EU persisted patiently from the 1960s into the 1990s. In the end, it would have to wait until the end of the Cold War, given that the Kremlin long considered this economic arrangement as inherently political (i.e., antagonistic towards state socialism), and thus a violation of Austrian neutrality (228–37). Once Gorbachev formally dropped a long-standing opposition to neutral countries joining the EEC toward the end of 1991, the way opened for Austrian entry into the newly cast European Union by 1995.

"As one of the 'major battlefields' in the Cold War," the authors note at the outset of their study, "Austria has barely received attention in survey accounts in Anglo-American accounts [...]" (17). Where Austrian circumstances are considered in the English-language literature, primary focus lies elsewhere, and Austria tends to receive almost incidental treatment. Bischof and Ruggenthaler do us a great service with this volume, and when the highly anticipated English-language edition appears, they will have addressed the above-noted lacuna definitively. We can be grateful that this original, German-language version offers the most important and accessible diplomacy and international politics-oriented narrative of the subject yet offered. They have established a standard that would be exceedingly difficult to match.

Linda Erker, *Die Universität Wien im Austrofaschismus* (Vienna: V&R unipress, 2021)

Peter Berger

In November 1918, the Habsburg Empire, bled dry in four years of war, disappeared from the maps of Europe. Vienna, once the glamorous center of a multinational Empire, got reduced to the capital of a minuscule state of only six million inhabitants, mostly German-speaking. The new republic's territory, slightly over thirty thousand square miles, covered a portion of the Eastern Alps and the hill-spotted lands along the banks of the Danube between the Bavarian and Slovakian borders. In 1921, a stretch of the Western Hungarian plain was added to it. For a small country, Vienna, with its almost two million residents, seemed oversized, a hydrocephalus in the words of contemporary critics. Military defeat, the breakup of proud Austria-Hungary, and the humiliating Peace Treaty of Saint-Germain (June 1919) were followed by ever more destructive bouts of inflation reducing large sections of the middle class to poverty. The financial and monetary crisis lasted until fall 1922, but it took the Austrians until the late 1920s to reach pre-war levels of economic production and growth. At this time, the threat of the Great Depression was already looming large.

Austrian inflation, so detrimental to the country's social fabric, was, however, a blessing for foreign citizens being able to take advantage of the low domestic price level when expressed in foreign currency. One way of reaping the spoils of a depreciating Austrian Crown was to (temporarily) take up one's residence in Austria, as many young people from Eastern Europe, but also citizens of the USA, chose to do. Most of them came to Vienna to study, and many of these students were Jews. As a result, the University of Vienna, also known by its Latin name of *Alma Mater Rudolphina*, counted a disproportionally high percentage of Jewish scholars – up to a quarter of the total student body – in the years prior to currency stabilization. When these young men and women were singled out as lightning rods for the political frustrations of the numerically strongest student groups—the anti-Semitic, pan-German, and Catholic fraternities—a decade of violent confrontations on university grounds began. Anti-Jewish and anti-Socialist riots reached a peak in the fall of 1932, shortly before Austrian chancellor Engelbert Dollfuss and his governing right-wing coalition abandoned the path of democracy, crushed the Social Democratic opposition by means of brute force, and installed the authoritarian regime referred to by most historians as "Austrofascism." The methods applied by Dollfuss and his successor, Kurt von

Schuschnigg, to force the University of Vienna into step with Austrofascist policies are the principal subject of Linda Erker's book under review here. An extensive introductory chapter deals with the tumultuous period preceding Dollfuss's and Schuschnigg's assault on academic freedom, an assault that may not have happened, says Erker, if Nazi youths had not overstepped their limits by terrorizing their Catholic fellow students in much the same way as they targeted Socialists and Jews. The conclusive section of Erker's study is devoted to the "nazification" of the Alma Mater Rudolphina after March 1938 —and the triumphant return in 1945 into top functions within the educational system of the Second Austrian Republic of many of the men (no women!) who had shaped Austrofascist academic politics.

In Erker's narrative, the stages of the interwar history of the University of Vienna largely correspond with the sequence of political upheavals that shook the Austrian state between 1918 and 1945. The more or less peaceful "Austrian revolution" of 1918 swept away or decisively weakened the old elites of the Habsburg era—aristocracy, military, and the Catholic high clergy—and replaced them with personnel of political parties: Christian Socialists and Greater Germans (*Grossdeutsche*) in the countryside and Social Democrats in Vienna. The Viennese socialists, despite their ambitions at comprehensive social reform, failed to secure a hold on the capital's largest university, where the faculty in its overwhelming majority remained staunchly conservative, anti-Marxist, and anti-Semitic, thus forming a "black" island in the middle of a "red" ocean. A notable exception was professor Julius Tandler, an internationally renowned anatomist who from 1910 to 1934 held one of two anatomy chairs at the University of Vienna. In addition, he was a member of the "red" Viennese city council in the capacity of head of the department of welfare and public health. Tandler was one of Vienna's most visible Social Democratic functionaries, and he was a Jew. This stigmatized him in the eyes of both his fellow faculty and the majority of "Aryan" students of medicine who regularly staged riots during his lectures.

To make sure that no Jewish, socialist or, for that matter, female inroads could be made into the phalanx of "politically acceptable" faculty, professors of the right and extreme right took part in clandestine circles bearing names such as *Bärenhöhle* (bears' cave), *Deutscher Klub* (German Club), or *Deutsche Gemeinschaft* (German Union), to effectively sabotage unwelcome appointments to academic posts.

In 1932 the Austrian government got alarmed by National Socialist successes at the provincial and municipal ballot boxes, events that sped up the end of parliamentary rule in Austria and, in May 1934, led to the emergence of a new anti-democratic constitution. Following Mussolini's advice, chancellor

Dollfuss and his political allies of the ultra-right *Heimwehren* sought to impress domestic Nazi supporters by launching a violent campaign against the Social Democratic party and its Viennese bastion. But the short and bloody war on the Left in February 1934 failed to convince Hitler's Austrian followers of the superior quality of homemade fascism as opposed to its German version. In July of that year, an abortive putsch of Austrian SS men resulted in the killing of Dollfuss in his offices at Vienna's *Ballhausplatz*. As a consequence, the freshly appointed head of government, Kurt von Schuschnigg, ushered in a new stage of Austrofascism, one that was characterized by open confrontation with, rather than appeasement of, the Hitler movement.

In its dealings with institutions of higher learning, and the University of Vienna in particular, the Dollfuss-Schuschnigg administration from 1933 to 1936 resorted to similar means as other dictatorships or semi-dictatorships in interwar Europe, says Erker. Academic curricula were remodeled to contain more of the state's official ideology (in Austria emphasis was on Catholicism, patriotism, and anti-Liberalism). Faculty and the student body were partly "cleansed" of potentially disloyal elements (according to the government, National Socialists, Marxists, and Jews fell into that category). New regulations governing the access to higher studies were to make sure that future graduates would abstain from challenging the existing "Christian-corporatist" order. All this, together with a drastic curtailment of the university's right to disciplinary jurisdiction, effectively undermined academic self-governance and replaced it with state patronage.

Despite occasional redundancies, Erker's treatment of university politics in the years when Austrofascism was strongest is rich in detail and provides valuable insights into the motives and actions of all parties involved: Austria's government and the ministerial bureaucracy; rectors and professors of the University of Vienna (among them many sympathizers with National Socialism); students who supported the regime; and others who, because of their Nazi or sometimes Socialist convictions, were sent to the detention camp of Wöllersdorf in Lower Austria. Elisabeth Stipetić, who had studied philosophy since 1931 and become one of the front women of the illegal National Socialist students' union soon thereafter, was spared Wöllersdorf but got sentenced to a short prison term following a police raid on her home in the fall of 1935. Barred from continuing her studies in Austria until 1938, she moved (without the required official permission) to Germany to complete her doctoral thesis at the University of Munich where the famous zoologist, Karl von Fritsch, acted as her supervisor. In 1942 she gave birth to a child, Werner Herzog, the future movie director and maker of the film *Fitzcarraldo* starring Klaus Kinsky. Erker's occasional excursions into the field of personal history, as in the Stipetić case, prove how correct the great French historian Marc Bloch was when he told his colleagues to follow the example of cannibals. Both historians and human-eaters, Bloch insisted, perform best when they smell human flesh.

Assessing Dollfuss's and Schuschnigg's performance during the uphill battle against National Socialist infiltration of the University of Vienna prior to 1938, Erker identifies some important, if only short-lived, regime victories. In September 1933, the Austrian government banned the *Deutsche Studentenschaft*, a powerful pro-German and Nazi-friendly student association requiring its members to be Aryans, and replaced it with a representative student body called *Hochschülerschaft Österreichs*. In addition, the Ministry of Education created the job of "Austrian student trustee" (*Sachwalter der Hochschülerschaft Österreichs*) with powers to speak and act on behalf of all students nationwide. The Austrian student trustee closely cooperated with local trustees installed at every university in the country, including the University of Vienna. There, a certain Josef Klaus filled the post from November 1933 to January 1934. Decades later, Klaus was to become the first head of a conservative, single-party government in post-World War II Austria.

The greatest challenge confronting the Austrofascists was to neutralize those teachers at the University of Vienna who had expressed, implicitly or explicitly, their support of National Socialism. A first attempt was made early in 1933 when the authoritarian Dollfuss regime required everyone employed by the university to make a pledge of allegiance to the new Austrian state. Speculations abounded that outspoken Nazi-hardliners among the faculty would refuse to take the oath, but to widespread astonishment they all chose to swallow the pill with fingers crossed behind their backs. In the fall of 1933, however, three pro-Nazi members of the Law Faculty, among them the author of a notoriously racist "student charter" and rector of the academic year 1929/30, Wenzel Gleispach, were forced into early retirement. Following the murder of Dollfuss in July 1934, the government exerted further pressure towards academics known for their National Socialist views. Some lost their jobs, notably professors Karl Gottfried Hugelmann (Constitutional Law), Othenio Abel (Paleonthology), and Viktor Christian (Oriental Studies). Some were stripped of their authorization to teach, like former rector Hans Uebersberger, a historian. But others got away scot-free, like the medical scientist Eduard Pernkopf, author of an *Atlas of Human Anatomy* still used today; the historian Heinrich von Srbik (who had earlier been Minister of Education); or the biologist, Fritz Knoll, who headed the University of Vienna as rector from March 1938 to 1943, when Pernkopf replaced him. All in all, the results of Austrofascist academic personnel policies were at best mixed. National Socialist professors who had been purged from the Vienna

University either found refuge in the neighboring German Reich (where they could claim political victim status and sometimes considerably boost their academic careers), or they remained in Austria to be taken under the wings of Vienna's Academy of Sciences, an institution seemingly free of reservations regarding anti-Semitic or anti-democratic feelings of its members. Erker reminds her readers of other dubious aspects of the Austrofascist faculty purges. They were directed, at least in the beginning, as much against teachers with leftist or libertarian leanings as against National Socialists, a fact that resulted in the removal from their posts of men like Julius Tandler (the anatomist), Josef Karl Friedjung (a pediatrician and associate professor), and Heinrich Gomperz (professor of philosophy). And they were presented to the public and most affected persons as motivated by budgetary pressures and not by political considerations. Apart from the obvious dishonesty of such reasoning, it effectively excluded victims of unfair treatment or their descendants from asking for moral and financial compensation from the Austrian state when World War II was over.

In July 1936, Schuschnigg abandoned his uncompromising stance against Nazi-Germany and Hitler's Austrian followers by concluding a pacification treaty with the Third Reich. The turnaround was caused, among other things, by Mussolini's unwillingness (or incapacity) to further unconditionally support Vienna in fending off the German threat. But even with ongoing Italian support, Schuschnigg *cum suis* would probably not have had the stamina to continue their steadfast rejection of Nazism: too strong was their emotional attachment to German culture and the German *Volk*. While the Austrian side in 1936 believed to have extracted from Hitler a cast-in-stone promise to henceforth refrain from interference in Austria's domestic affairs, the opposite was true. The Austro-German agreement, in spite of some minor concessions the Germans made, removed many of the barriers that had effectively checked Nazi propaganda in Austria. Intensified German tourism in Western Austria, desirable as it was from an economic point of view, meant to expose local people to the praise of Hitler sung by German visitors. Permitting the free circulation of German newspapers in Austria worked in the same direction. The appointment of Austrian Nazi sympathizers to ministerial posts, another favor granted by Schuschnigg to the *Führer*, was tantamount to placing Trojan horses at the *Ballhausplatz*. For the University of Vienna, the Austro-German treaty of 1936 meant that no more disciplinary action would be taken against Nazi students, and that amnesty had to be granted to those who were imprisoned or detained because of previous National Socialist activities. Efforts at combating National Socialism at the faculty level stopped, Nazi-friendly professors were no longer in danger of being removed from the faculty—but fifteen of them were offered chairs at universities in the Reich and thus left the *Alma Mater Rudolphina*. Only a handful of teachers and researchers got appointed to chairs in countries other than Germany. Erker cites the examples of medical scientists Otto Porges and Julius Bauer; of Erich Haas, a physicist; and of the mathematician Karl Menger. Being Jewish, they probably quit Vienna to escape the ubiquitous anti-Semitic resentment that Austrofascism had been unable—or rather, unwilling—to curb. The poisoned political climate was also responsible for the murder of professor Moritz Schlick, philosopher and co-founder of the Vienna Circle of Logical Positivism. The Circle's members championed theories considered "Jewish" by many of Schlick's colleagues and students. One of them, Johann Nelböck, shot Schlick dead on the stairs of the university. The victim was a gentile and a native of Germany, but for the student Nelböck he represented "decadent Jewish thought" and thus deserved to be killed. Following the murder, Nelböck was sentenced to a ten-year prison term (but not declared unsound of mind, as Erker seems to believe). He got released on parole shortly after the Nazi takeover in Austria. Schlick's vacant chair was given to an applicant known to be sympathetic towards Austrofascism.

If anti-Semitism reigned supreme in the academic sphere of the 1920s and 1930s, so did "andro-centrism." This is the term Erker employs to denote the refusal of an overwhelmingly male faculty at the University of Vienna (and elsewhere in Austrian higher education) to grant women equal career opportunities. No more than four percent of the teachers and researchers employed by the *Rudolphina* were of the female sex. Non-scientific jobs were less unevenly distributed among men and women: the relation here was 2:1. Given the widespread traditional belief that a woman's proper place was at home and not at the job, the manifest aversion of the Austrofascists against females in paid work does not come as a surprise. And they were certainly not the first and the last to hold such attitudes. When Erker says that under Dollfuss and Schuschnigg, the trend was to offer females fewer career opportunities than before and after Austrofascism, one may ask on what evidence such a statement is based. In the academic year of 1933/34, none of the professors and associate professors of the University of Vienna were women—just like before 1933 and after 1945. Austrofascism thus perpetuated a gender gap, but did not increase it.

What is certainly more shocking in retrospect than the Austrofascists' image of women is how easily they were able to recapture strategic positions in Austrian academe following the seven years of Nazi rule from March 1938 to April 1945. After the Anschluss, the National Socialists quickly fired all faculty known to have been supportive of or actively participating in the

Dollfuss-Schuschnigg regime. Men who, despite their Nazi sympathies and thanks to their political flexibility, had managed to survive in their academic functions prior to 1938 were now running the University of Vienna, the Ministry of Education, and the Academy of Sciences. During the second half of the 1940s, many of them (like the aforementioned Fritz Knoll) managed to sail around the obstacles posed by Austrian anti-National Socialist legislation and, after a brief pause, resumed at least some, if not all, of their wartime functions. It is one of the great merits of Linda Erker's survey to illustrate how smoothly networks of former Austrofascists, ex-National Socialists, and anti-Semites worked to secure an authoritarian, anti-Socialist academic consensus well into the 1950s—while no lobby existed to bring back to Austria and the University of Vienna those men and women, Jewish or gentile, who had been forced into exile by two dictatorships.

List of Authors

Amélie-Jacqueline Apke is a PhD student in Political Science at the University of Salzburg and research fellow at the Salzburg Centre of European Studies.

Matthew Paul Berg is Professor of History at John Carroll University.

Peter Berger is Professor Emeritus of Social and Economic History at WU Vienna University of Economics and Business.

Maria Bertel is Professor of Public Law in the Department of Public Law and Political Science at the University of Graz.

Günter Bischof is the Marshall Plan Chair of History and the Director of Center Austria: The Austrian Marshall Plan Center for European Studies, University of New Orleans.

Andreas Brunner is a founder and Co-Director of the Center QWIEN.

Evan Burr Bukey is Professor Emeritus of History at the University of Arkansas.

Eva Hallama is Principal Investigator at the Österreichische Mediathek at the Vienna Museum of Science and Technology.

Reinhard Heinisch is Professor for Austrian Politics in Comparative European Perspective at the University of Salzburg and Head of the Department of Political Science and Sociology.

Marina Hilber is Assistant Professor in the Department of History and European Ethnology at the University of Innsbruck.

Marc Landry is Assistant Professor of History and Associate Director of Center Austria: The Austrian Marshall Plan Center for European Studies, University of New Orleans.

Katja Maierhofer is the 2022/23 visiting OeAD Doctoral Research Fellow at Center Austria: The Austrian Marshall Plan Center for European Studies, University of New Orleans.

Silke Meyer is Professor of European Ethnology in the Department of History and European Ethnology at the University of Innsbruck.

Andreas Th. Müller is Professor for European Law, International Law, and Human Rights at the University of Basel.

Claus Oberhauser is Professor of History Education at the University College of Teacher Education Tyrol.

Mike Peters is Professor in the Department of Strategic Management, Marketing, and Tourism at the University of Innsbruck.

Eva Pfanzelter is Associate Professor of Contemporary History in the Department of Contemporary History at the University of Innsbruck.

Jennifer Popowycz is the Leventhal Research Fellow at the Jenny Craig Institute for the Study of War and Democracy.

Dirk Rupnow is Professor of History in the Department of Contemporary History and Dean of the Faculty of Philosophy and History at the University of Innsbruck.

Robert Steiger is Associate Professor in the Department of Public Finance at the University of Innsbruck.

Elena Taddei is Associate Professor and Chair of the Department of History and European Ethnology at the University of Innsbruck.

Janek Wasserman is Professor of Modern Central European and German History at the University of Alabama.

Contemporary Austrian Studies

Günter Bischof/Marc Landry, Anton Pelinka/Fritz Plasser/Ferdinand Karlhofer, Editors

Volume 1 (1992)
Austria in the New Europe

Volume 2 (1993)
The Kreisky Era in Austria
Oliver Rathkolb, Guest Editor

Volume 3 (1994)
Austria in the Nineteen Fifties
Rolf Steininger, Guest Editor

Volume 4 (1995)
Austro-Corporatism: Past—Present—Future

Volume 5 (1996)
Austrian Historical Memory & National Identity

Volume 6 (1997)
Women in Austria
Erika Thurner, Guest Editor

Volume 7 (1998)
The Vranitzky Era in Austria
Ferdinand Karlhofer, Guest Editor

Volume 8 (1999)
The Marshall Plan in Austria
Dieter Stiefel, Guest Editor

Volume 9 (2000)
Neutrality in Austria
Ruth Wodak, Guest Editor

Volume 10 (2001)
Austria and the EU
Michael Gehler, Guest Editor

Volume 11 (2002)
The Dollfuss/Schuschnigg Era in Austria: A Reassessment
Alexander Lassner, Guest Editor

Volume 12 (2003)
The Americanization/Westernization of Austria

Volume 13 (2004)
Religion in Austria
Hermann Denz, Guest Editor

Volume 14 (2005)
Austrian Foreign Policy in Historical Perspective
Michael Gehler, Guest Editor

Volume 15 (2006)
Sexuality in Austria
Dagmar Herzog, Guest Editor

Volume 16 (2007)
The Changing Austrian Voter

Volume 17 (2008)
New Perspectives on Austrians and World War II
Barbara Stelzl-Marx, Guest Editor

Volume 18 (2009)
The Schüssel Era in Austria

Volume 19 (2010)
From Empire to Republic: Post-World War I Austria

Volume 20 (2011)
Global Austria: Austria's Place in Europe and the World
Alexander Smith, Guest Editor

Volume 21 (2012)
Austrian Lives
Eva Maltschnig, Guest Editor

Volume 22 (2013)
Austria's International Position after the End of the Cold War

Volume 23 (2014)
1914: Austria-Hungary, the Origins, and the First Year of World War 1
Samuel R. Williamson, Jr., Guest Editor

Volume 24 (2015)
Austrian Federalism in Comparative Perspective

Volume 25 (2016)
Austrian Studies Today

Volume 26 (2017)
Migration in Austria
Dirk Rupnow, Guest Editor

Volume 27 (2018)
Austrian Environmental History
Patrick Kupper, Guest Editor

Volume 28 (2019)
Democracy in Austria
David M. Wineroither, Guest Editor

Volume 29 (2020)
Myths in Austrian History
Christian Karner, Guest Editor

Volume 30 (2021)
Visual Histories of Austria
Martin Kofler, Hans Petschar, Guest Editors

Volume 31 (2022)
The Second Austrian Republic
Eva Pfanzelter, Guest Editor,
Christian Stenico, Associate Editor